and outer journey of this remarkable man, who left us with the gift of the Dances of Universal Peace, and the living grace of a soul who embraced both love and pain in service to God."

–**Llewellyn Vaughan-Lee**, Ph.D., author, *Love is a Fire, the Sufis Mystical Journey Home.*

"The reader of Dr. Neil Douglas-Klotz's sensitively selected and annotated writings of Murshid Samuel Lewis (1896-1971) is taken on the tumultuous spiritual journey of a truly universal being; a voyage propelled throughout his life by the quest for Truth, whether through the teachings of Sufism, Zen Buddhism or any other divinely revealed path. The reader grows with Sufi Sam as he explores with sincerity the inner and outer world, experiences hope and disappointment, and dances through this earthly life with his trademark flashes of spiritual humour and love for all. A collection of writings that will be of particular interest for those westerners who, like Lewis himself, find their path through the teachings of the east."

--**Muneera Haeri,** author of The Chishtis, A Living Light, co-author with Shaykh Fadhlalla Haeri of Sufi Encounters

"Everytime I remember Sam, I end up laughing at myself. That's pretty good work for a dead-rascal-saint."

–**Ram Dass**, author of *Be Here Now* and *Still Here*

"I have no fonder memory of the 60's than the appearance of this strange-looking man, who said things which made me first laugh, then smile, then later pause in a preciation of a spiritual original, a pioneer."

–**Dr. Jacob Needleman**, author of *The New Religions* and *Lost Christianity*

"By being spiritual, Samuel Lewis expanded the range of being human; and by being human he deepened the meaning of being spiritual."

–**Hazrat Pir Moineddin Jablonski**, khalif and successor of Murshid Samuel Lewis

"One of the first exponents of experiential comparative religion."

–**Dr. Andrew Rawlinson**, author of *The Book of Enlightened Masters: Western Teachers in Eastern Traditions*

"The Dances of Universal Peace came to stay, and so does the indelible memory of their pioneer, veteran in the art of carrying the experience of the meditation on the Divine attributes right into the body."

–**Hazrat Pir Vilayat Inayat Khan**, founder of the Sufi Order Inayati

Gardens of Vision and Initiation
The Life Journey of Samuel L. Lewis

An Autobiography
Selected from His Letters, Papers,
Diaries, and Recordings

GARDENS OF VISION AND INITIATION

The Life Journey of Samuel L. Lewis

*An Autobiography
Selected from His Letters, Papers,
Diaries, and Recordings*

Neil Douglas-Klotz

GARDENS OF VISION AND INITIATION

EIAL Books
Abwoon Network
https://www.abwoon.org

Cover photo and photos on pages 96, 333 and 338 are copyright 1971, 2020 Mansur Johnson. www.mansurjohnson.com Used with permission. All rights reserved.

Cover and interior design by Hauke Jelaluddin Sturm, www.designconsort.de

A royalty from this book goes to the SUFI Ruhaniat International, Inc. to support its project continuing to archive, proofread, correct and distribute the writings and audio of Murshid Samuel L. Lewis online.

Content

VI. Journeys Toward the Rising Sun   203

VII. *Homecoming*   265

Foreword

I came into the life of Samuel Lewis in his last, and perhaps best years, from the spring of 1968 until his death in early 1971. He was the first adult to recognize my true nature, and within a few months he became my formal spiritual teacher, and my guide in the creation of a new style of sacred song. For the ensuing fifty years he has been a reliable inner voice of guidance. I thought I knew the man. But after reading through his writings as presented in *Gardens of Vision and Initiation*, I realize that I had known only part of the man. Immersion in seven decades of his thought and action as presented herein, along with the commentary by its editor, has revealed a whole person I am newly glad to meet.

In those last few years, Murshid Sam (as he is familiarly called) had become a dedicated and benevolent transmitter of spiritual wisdom to an increasing number of followers. What has interested me most is how the seemingly endless sufferings of a wretched and humiliating childhood could be so transformed into the labors and joys of sacred completion. Early in his teens, his despair became interspersed with holy visions, feelings of direct communication with forces beyond his personal self. These visitations deepened as he matured and, in his twenties, led him to Pir-o-Murshid Inayat Khan, the harbinger of Sufism in the West. Inayat Khan, Samuel Lewis's first and most influential teacher, immediately recognized both his inner and outer being, and tasked him with ensuring and furthering the Sufi Message in America. As I read through the progression of these letters and spiritual writings I began to understand how Lewis's habitual, confrontational boasting, his obsession with overcoming the pain of early humiliations and rejections, were dissolved, transcended, and molded into a realized, radiant human being.

Early on Samuel Lewis had chosen poetry as a concentration. He knew he didn't have the ability to carry forward the musical part of Inayat Khan's commission, but trusted that someday, in some form, the music would appear. When I first came to Sufi gatherings I was warmed by Murshid's attempts to fashion impromptu musical rounds out of simple mantric chants. When I asked to try my hand at this, he loudly replied, "Sure, go ahead." There soon came into being a kind of music no one had ever heard—polyphonic, heart-filling mandalas of sacred sound, intimate and cosmic at once. We all were amazed, but not Murshid. He'd had to be patient for fifty years, and when he recognized an opportunity to fulfill that aspect of Inayat Khan's commission, he simply said yes. In a 1970 letter to a friend in Pakistan, dictated to his secretary in my presence, he reported the arrival of "a new type of Qawal," an "evolution of western music." As soon as he finished dictating the letter, he ceremoniously initiated me as his disciple "for the time being," a phrase that both surprised and confused me, but I accepted it.

The legacy of Samuel Lewis has taken many forms, each with its esoteric and exoteric aspects, including healing, sustainable agriculture, spiritual commentary, social action, dance, and music. A musical core of our group became The Sufi Choir, which flourished, became many choirs and, along with a large repertoire of songs and chants created for dance and other spiritual practices, took its place in the panoply of Sufi transmission in the Western world. This music also brought an infusion of deep joy and high praise into my own life of composing, writing, and teaching. Several years after Samuel Lewis died, I became a disciple of North Indian raga master Pandit Pran Nath, binding myself into the deep tradition of Inayat Khan himself, and fulfilling my Murshid's prophecy, "for the time being." He had similar prescience into the lives of many of his followers.

American Sufism comprises a many-faceted esoteric school that sends its graduates forward into the world, each on his or her own terms. I am one of the dozens and dozens of teachers who have internalized the Inayati wisdom lineage into our own lives, and into every corner of our thought, work, love and teaching. Murshid Sam's vision of universality was realized first through himself, then through his immediate disciples, then through theirs, and so on into the vitality of the whole of humanity. Refined spirit braided with worldly action—such is the realization of Sam Lewis's vision. Transmission of this realization was the purpose of his life.

Despite the highly unusual experiences of his life story, Samuel Lewis longed to be recognized as a common man, the idiosyncratic guy upstairs, the colorful next-door neighbor who turns grocery shopping into a joyous adventure. And thanks to this volume's great rainbow of words, that is how I now see him: a common man of uncommon consequence.

A particular distinction of this book is how its editor, Neil Douglas-Klotz, through discerning selection and savvy commentary, traces and contextualizes Samuel Lewis's writings so the narrative of this miraculous metamorphosis becomes palpable. Perhaps, as you read through these pages you can feel something of your own life turning toward the light.

— W. A. Mathieu

Introduction

Writers, academics, journalists, spiritual leaders and his own students have applied an expansive array of labels to Samuel L. Lewis. Since his passing in 1971, he's been known as a Sufi murshid, a Zen master, an environmentalist, a peace activist, a missionary to the Hippie generation, the founder of the Dances of Universal Peace, the first exponent of "experiential comparative religion" and the co-founder of a Christian mystical order.

This eclectic list, bewildering as it might seem, nevertheless belies the complexity and adventure of Lewis's eventful life, which bridged two centuries. His own life story, as he tells it in the remembrances presented here, sees him meeting with and learning from many of the remarkable mystics, sages, philosophers, artists, therapists and activists of the 20th century.

Born in 1896 into a rigid and abusive Victorian era family, Lewis gradually overcame a natural shyness and inhibition. He lived a nomadic existence as an adult, finding himself at the center of many of the early 20th century's major developments.

Lewis's life extended into the free-thinking, psychedelic era of the late 1960s in California, where he finally found a community that offered him the acceptance and love for which he had been searching his whole life. As his story unfolds, we hear his views on domestic political turmoil in the USA following the Great Depression as well as American diplomatic relations abroad. Throughout it all, his own spiritual quest interweaves with a mission to bring sustainable organic gardening principles to faraway lands before they could be taken over by the influence of Western corporate agriculture.

As Lewis describes his life, we come to understand how he was led from visionary experiences to inner initiations. He tells how these initiations led him to outer initiatives ranging from social activism and environmental awareness to cultural change through the arts and sciences.

Today, Samuel Lewis is probably best known as the originator of the Dances of Universal Peace. The Dances are a form of spiritual folk dance that, at least potentially, can carry an experience with multiple spiritual traditions into minds, hearts and bodies through music and movement. Over the past half-century, these Dances have grown, expanded and spread around the world. Lewis also created walking meditations, developed prior to and along with the Dances, which have since been applied in therapeutic and educational settings.

Drawn from his voluminous letters, diaries, other writings and recordings, *Gardens of Vision and Initiation* allows us to hear Samuel Lewis's story in his own words, the authentic voice of a spiritual pioneer.

Gardens of Vision and Initiation

More than forty years ago, I began this project with the goal of gathering a unique individual's autobiography from fragments of diaries, papers, articles and unpublished books. The resulting book, entitled *Sufi Vision and Initiation: Meetings with Remarkable Beings,* appeared in 1986. As described below, in light of new research on Lewis's life, I have expanded and re-edited that book almost completely and changed its title to *Gardens of Vision and Initiation.*

The book's new title reflects Lewis's tendency to cross boundaries and defy categories, including being pigeon-holed as a *Sufi.* When confronted with the question of whether to legally organize his teaching, in a recording from April 1968 he says, "Divine truth does not belong to any organization…. As I'm working with my colleagues in other faiths, this will demonstrate this. We're not going to be called 'Sufis' to distinguish ourselves from somebody else."

This book's title also reflects Lewis's general attitudes toward spirituality and religion. In the mid-1960s he wrote a university class paper entitled "Vision and Ritual in Sufism." In that paper he relates some of his own inner experiences and maintains that, while vision can live without ritual, the opposite is not true. Rituals can help to embody a vision and communicate it to others, as Lewis attempted to do with his dances and walking meditations. But unless rituals open a door to actual spiritual experience, they become little more than institutionalized mental-emotional habits, which tend to keep people docile and willing to accept some leader or organization's control of their lives.

According to Lewis's primary Sufi teacher, Hazrat Inayat Khan, one needs to test a vision or psychological insight through direct action in the world. Inayat Khan called this the real *initiation*—"taking a step in an unknown direction," rather than a ceremony identified by the same name.

For Samuel Lewis, initiations led to initiatives that took many forms. Some involved social action. Others helped to bridge the gap between intellectuals and mystics. By his own account, high on his list were the challenges of feeding the world's hungry and creating viable, enduring sympathy among the world's diverse cultures. Toward the end of his life, he worked tirelessly to make spiritual teachings more accessible and experientially real to greater numbers of people.

4

For Samuel Lewis, initiation also led to meetings with remarkable beings —not only human beings, but also plants, animals, soils, rocks, and trees. As Lewis notes, real meetings are mergings. They change the parties involved while at the same time empowering them to become more fully themselves.

Finally as mentioned, plants, horticulture and sustainable agriculture played a central role in Lewis's work, to which his letters and diaries testify. He tended to see his own mission in terms of gardening. Near the end of his life, he said:

> When you plant a single seed, spiritually, you are feeding the whole of humanity. When you put up the smallest place of devotion, you are building the most magnificent temple of God. When you do the smallest thing, you are doing the greatest thing. But when you build an "awe" around it, and it lures people or makes them intoxicated, then you are not doing it (recording, June 1970, Lama Foundation, New Mexico).

A More Than "Spiritual" Life

From the beginning of this project, I became increasingly convinced that to extract the "spiritual" elements from a life that included many other dimensions offered only a limited picture. The depth of both joy and suffering that Samuel Lewis experienced in his life can be felt throughout his writing. He would not have wanted "another guru book" or a foray into hagiography.

About one of the Sufi teachers he met in Pakistan, Lewis comments, "He was the most perfect ordinary human being I ever met." This was Lewis's ideal, a trait he emulated: to get one's hands dirty, whether that meant collecting trash, cleaning out sewers or planting flowers by the side of the road.

Toward the end of his life, he told a group:

> I reached a point where it was possible to sit down with people and by breathing with them, by looking at their eyes, or holding their hands, to feel not only their obvious pain but to feel the pain beyond that pain. And then do something about it. And I am very glad, because if you've got any awe about me, I'd go mad. I've made mistakes. I've dropped dishes in the kitchen. I've burned the rice.... And so I've asked God not to be perfect, to function with all my faults (recording, June 1970, Lama Foundation, New Mexico).

Samuel Lewis warns throughout his writings that whenever a mystic's students place that person on a pedestal, the inner progress of the idolizers stops in its tracks. Though we may experience new insights by seeing through another's eyes, in the end we must live our own lives. Samuel Lewis, the being of love and light revealed in the 1970s film *Sunseed*[1] and in the early Dances, is surpassed only by the being he is now. One should not hope to surpass him or any other human ideal. One *can* hope to surpass oneself.

Lewis was undoubtedly a natural psychic, as even his early writing shows. But extraordinary abilities and sensitivities can prove a curse as well as a blessing. A major part of the story presented here relates the ways Lewis dealt with the liabilities of his childhood and pulled his life together. He did this by integrating a tremendous capacity for spiritual vision with practical life skills in service to ecology and activism.

In addition, new research into Lewis's life shows that even his best-known accomplishment—the creation of the Dances of Universal Peace—arose in part from efforts to heal personal wounds from his family history. It's long been assumed that his inspiration for the Dances came while he was guiding his young hippie students during the 1960s in San Francisco. In fact, he had begun working with a vision of the Dances at least a decade earlier. Likewise, creation of his walking meditations also began much earlier, with the initial goal of transforming childhood education in an Islamic country, Pakistan.

Filling in the Gaps

Several major gaps in the original *Vision* book are addressed in this new one. In the first book, information about Lewis's life from about 1927 through 1954, and from 1962 to 1966 was very sparse. I took several "archive journeys" in the intervening years that addressed these time spans:

- In 1998, my research in the archives of the Sufi Movement in the Hague, Netherlands unearthed a large number of Samuel Lewis's papers, well provenanced and dated. The story of how these materials ended up there appears in Section II of this book. Some of these writings were new discoveries. Those that duplicated what we already had allowed me to date everything more accurately.
- I did similar searches online and found archives of Meher Baba and of Sufi Barkat Ali, who were important figures in Lewis's journey, although for very different reasons. Also very helpful was the wonderful online archive of one of Lewis's friends and colleagues, Shamcher Bryn Beorse, maintained by his student, the author Carol Sill.
- Additional archival research has been done by those investigating the actual history of Hazrat Inayat Khan himself, in distinction from the substantial myth-making that occurred later.[2]

---

1 See www.sunseed.org
2 Particularly useful has been the lengthy introduction with notes by historian Hendrik J. Horn to his 2010 translation, *Recollections of Inayat Khan and Western Sufism by Theo van Hoorn*. Leiden, Netherlands: Foleor Publishing. This material confirmed and helped clarify findings from my research in the archives of the Sufi Movement.

- In 2008, I was able to visit the archives of Murshida Vera Corda in Northern California, which yielded a very important late manuscript by Samuel Lewis on channeling, a portion of which appears in Section VII.
- The diligence of later archivists and the generosity of the Sufi Ruhaniat International also brought another development: the digital scanning and archiving of most of the letters and papers of Samuel Lewis. This enabled electronic searches that, had they been available during the *Sufi Vision* project, might have cut years off its completion.
- Similarly, the advent of the internet itself made it possible to date many of the internal references in Lewis's papers and so the papers themselves.
- Filling out the 1962 to 1966 portion of Samuel Lewis's life, I was aided by the discovery of the remarkable, voluminous correspondence between Lewis and his first Sufi *khalifa*, Saadia Khawar Khan in Pakistan. We had only a few of these letters previously. Among other things, this correspondence revealed Lewis's goal of returning to Pakistan to pursue his work with ecology and walking meditation and how important this initiative was to him.
- Mansur Johnson's wonderful book *Murshid* (2006) has addressed the important period between 1966-1971. It offers a rich context for a more complete selection of Murshid Lewis's letters from this period. The book also provides a moving, personal description of what day-to-day life with Murshid S.A.M. (short for his Sufi name, Sufi Ahmed Murad) was really like—including the pain and struggle.

The Organization of This Book

Section I, *Call to the Quest*, begins with Lewis's own dedication to his unpublished book *The Lotus and the Universe*. Chapters from that book provide a running thread throughout this one. Except for glimpses that surface in his letters, Lewis refers to few specifics about his early life. All of his writing about this time appears in Section I, along with reflections by his closest living relative as well as his close friend, Vera Corda. Then we find Lewis's reminiscence about a "life before this life." Finally, he provides a short three-act scenario that describes the prelude to and first meeting with the "teacher of his heart," the Sufi Hazrat Inayat Khan.

Section II, *Journey Into Sufism*, continues from this point, with Lewis recalling his time with Hazrat Inayat Khan. We learn about the first American Sufi *khankah*, and Lewis's role in it, from his student and friend Vera Corda. Next, this section offers Samuel Lewis's account of his life-changing 1925 spiritual retreat followed by his report of an equally pivotal series of interviews the following year with Hazrat Inayat Khan. The section ends with some historical notes about the tortuous development of Hazrat Inayat Khan's Sufi transmission following his passing in 1927.

Section III, *Journey into Zen*, describes Samuel Lewis's experiences with Zen Buddhism and how they unfolded in parallel with his Sufi path. The main chapter includes a large portion of his "Zen-ish" autobiographical paper "Dharma Transmission." The section ends with an article Lewis wrote for *The Western Buddhist* in 1959, entitled provocatively "How to be a Buddhist? How to be a Buddha!"

Section IV, *Crisis and Change: Journeys into Spiritual Activism*, describes and demonstrates Lewis's work and concerns during the twenty years following the Great Depression. Those two decades saw him living a sometimes nomadic and sometimes homeless existence. Although we do not have much direct autobiographical material from this period, the proper dating of Lewis's work, life and movements, including his activity as a whistleblower, provide a clear context for his writing on domestic and international social issues. Articles from this timespan included the following, which are excerpted here: "The Social Directions," "The Spiritual Attitude and Class War," and "The Book of Peace."

During the same twenty years we also find Samuel Lewis exploring how to change culture through the arts, particularly dance, as well as through understanding the latest discoveries of science. Finally, Section IV ends with the tragic circumstances that led to the dissolution of the Sufi *khankah* in Fairfax, California, which had been Lewis's home on and off for more than two decades. As this era ends, we find him pursuing further education in horticulture and agriculture and preparing for travel abroad, prompted by both his spiritual and ecological interests.

Section V, *Journey Toward the Setting Sun*, selects from Samuel Lewis's writing about his 1956 trip to Japan, Hong Kong, Thailand, Bangladesh, India and Pakistan. Here he begins a "diary" approach to his correspondence, as if he knew in advance that this would be the trip of a lifetime. In fact, after little but rejection in the USA, Lewis receives confirmation and acceptance throughout this journey. After he returns, Lewis begins psychotherapy with Dr. Blanche Baker, and we see how his inner therapeutic journey led him to more meaningful relationships and conscious acceptance of his sexuality. All of this comes together in letters from 1958 in which he expresses his desire for a deeper interchange with people: "To bring nations of the world together by eating, praying and dancing."

Section VI, *Journey Toward the Rising Sun*, sees Lewis head east once again, on a trip to Egypt, Pakistan and India that lasted from 1960 to 1962. During these two years, Lewis continues to pursue his ecological interests and meets additional spiritual teachers, including some who provided guidance through the end of his life. He also finds further acceptance and deep community. He begins to take Sufi students (*mureeds*) in Pakistan, where he plans to return for perhaps the remainder of his years. This section sees his story unfold in many unexpected twists and turns, foreshadowing the final decade of his life.

Section VII, *Homecoming*, describes how Samuel Lewis continued to provide guidance to his main student and spiritual representative in Pakistan. He also began to meet young people in San Francisco who needed and wanted a different kind of guidance, a program of (as Lewis put it) "joy without drugs." Toward the end, we find Samuel Lewis with a foot in both worlds—Sufi Pakistan and Hippie San Francisco—and we are left with the sense that he was living in the inner and outer garden for which he always longed.

Peace and blessings,
Dr. Neil Douglas-Klotz
Fife, Scotland
April 2020

I.

CALL TO THE QUEST

Samuel L. Lewis at age 31 (1927)

Dedication and Introduction

Book Excerpt from
The Lotus and the Universe (1963)

Dedicated to the living memory of President Sarvepali Radhakrishnan and Mataji Krishnabai of India; Sheikhs Abusalem Amria and Muhammad Desoughi of Cairo, Egypt; Pir-0-Murshids Sufi Barkat Ali and Dewal Shereef of Pakistan, and Roshi Sogen Asahina of Engakuji, Kamakura, Japan.

Dedicated in Love, Peace and Devotion to Those with whom I am, world without end ...

Dedicated in Love, Peace and Devotion, to Those before whom I am not, world without end ...

by Samuel L. Lewis of San Francisco, California, also known as Sufi Ahmed Murad Chisti

Beloved Ones of God:

This work is an effort to bring people of goodwill closer together in understanding, especially those of the Asian continent together with those of other continents. It has been stimulated in response to a number of books about the Orient, often written by those who have little acquaintance with the knowledge or peoples used as subject matter.

Others besides scientists know that a single swallow does not make a summer. Yet today one is led to believe that while a scientist may require two hundred trials before coming to any conclusion, many non-scientists take only a single event to reach two hundred conclusions. This reveals egocentricity.

We are besieged by multitudes of books in which the word *Zen* appears in the title without authorization. The Anti-Defamation League of Jewish People has done a splendid job in preventing such occurrences within its realm. The Oriental, not being a dualist, faces this world as it is. True, there are some excellent books being written by the real Zen masters, but their readership is small when contrasted with that of the total of current literature.

Arthur Koestler, in his book *The Lotus and the Robot*, seems to have moral integrity, but without an understanding of esotericism and mysticism. This much cannot be said of all the writers. The term "Dharma Bums[3]" is particularly offensive; one does not know how offensive it is. Much misunderstanding also results from emotional prejudices that are based on lack of real historical background, as is the case of reactions to the Prophet Muhammad and the religion of Islam. We do not believe that before God there is any East or West, North or South.

The people to whom this work is dedicated are all living in this year, though originally one of the names appearing in the opening page was that of the late Swami Ramdas of Anandashram, South India. His recent death [in July 1963] has been felt by more people in India and elsewhere than our cultural and spiritual leaders realize yet.

The idea of a mystic writing on mysticism is not new. In some lands—though not in the United States—only scientists whose knowledge is operational (that is, based on direct experience) are permitted or expected to tell of their experiences.

There is no reason why the same policy may not be acceptable in more bizarre endeavors.

—Samuel L. Lewis
Sufi Ahmed Murad Chisti
Rev. He Kwang, Zen-Shi

---

3   The title of a 1958 novel by "Beat Generation" American author Jack Kerouac, in which the main character (based on Kerouac himself) discovers Zen Buddhism.

Origin Stories

Editor's Note

The story of Samuel L. Lewis's early life, as well as that of his family, remains obscure, some of it by design, the rest due to the reticence of people of his time to discuss matters considered "unpleasant." According to Mary Lou Foster, his surviving cousin, broken homes were the rule, not the exception, in Samuel Lewis's family tree: divorce, bigamy, sadism, hate, insanity were all part of it.

"He would have had to have been a saint to come out of the hate that his environment consisted of, with so much love for so many people, and to be able to instill love in other people," Foster related in an interview with Wali Ali Meyer in 1976.

The bare facts are these: Samuel Leonard Lewis was born October 18, 1896 at 2:20 a.m. in San Francisco. His father Jacob was a Vice President of the Levi Strauss Company. His mother was Harriet Rosenthal. According to Foster, a family story was that she was related to the Rothschilds, of international banking fame. Another family story was that her mother's first husband, a man by the name of Krause, invented the copper rivet in Levi's jeans and became fabulously wealthy therefrom. Neither story turns out to be true.

By all accounts, Samuel's childhood was not a happy one. His parents literally did not speak to each other for 25 years and used their two sons, Samuel and his younger brother Elliot, as intermediaries, according to Foster. She tells the following story of visiting the family in 1946:

"Even for a simple thing like 'Would you please pass the cream'—it was communicated between the sons from one parent

Jacob Lewis

15

to another, and depending upon what space the sons were in, one might ask his mother or ask the other son. It was like his (the father's) son and her (the mother's) son."

This family dynamic led to an intense enmity between the brothers, which was only resolved just before the passing of both (Elliot died in March, 1970, 10 months before Samuel.) Since Samuel was the firstborn, his father had high hopes of his going into business, or if not that, of at least going into orthodox religion. When it became apparent that his interests were more universal, his father was very disappointed. Part of the disappointment may have also been due to the fact that Elliot did not develop into a businessman either, according to Foster. He lived at home his whole life and frittered away his family's money gambling and as a "sportsman."

Foster said that she did not really get to know Samuel until after Elliot's passing, because of the lies that had been told about him by his brother. Having inherited the family home upon Elliot's passing, Foster said that she cleaned out various pictures of Samuel and other relatives that had been defaced and mutilated. According to both Foster and Samuel, it was his brother who turned his mother against him after his father's death.

Samuel had been reconciled with his father just before the latter's death in 1954. His father had agreed to send him back to school in 1949 (Samuel was then 53) and on his deathbed had given him his gold watch. According to Foster this incident, as well as the fact that Jacob tried to disinherit his wife (something illegal in California), touched off a bitter, ugly court battle over the terms of the will, which saw Samuel's mother disowning him in court.

Originally, Samuel had been his "mother's son," said Foster. The fractious atmosphere between his father and mother might have been due to his father's suspicion that Samuel Lewis had been conceived out of wedlock. True or not, Samuel maintained that neither his mother nor father ever forgave him for that.

His mother denied that Samuel was the product of an affair, according to Murshida Vera Corda, who met Samuel in 1937 and remained a student and friend throughout her life. She recalls one interchange with his mother as follows:

> You'd have to hear Fuchsia (Harriet) on the piano to believe it. She had the strength of three men, and all of it came out on those keys. It was tremendous power in those little hands, and this little bird-like alive, vital person would bang away and stop in the middle and say, 'Vera, come here. Did you know my son is named Samuel. Do you know why? You know, they said he was born out of wedlock, but don't you believe it. He was born a prophet, and he came in the spiritual body first.'

In body type, Samuel was originally much more like his mother: delicate bone structure, thin, short (he was about 5'2, she about 4'8"). His brother Elliot was built more like his father: strong masculine features, heavy bone structure. As Samuel describes it, his body and constitution began to change as a result of his Sufi spiritual practices as well as by working as a gardener and laborer in Golden Gate Park. The reader will find only hints of Samuel's family history in his writings. From a family systems point of view, this is not surprising, considering the abusive communication and treatment he received as he was growing up.

As far as we know, there is only one person to whom Samuel Lewis definitely told his whole family history. That person was the late Dr. Blanche Baker, a psychiatrist to whom Samuel went for therapy in 1958 to help clear the emotional effects of his childhood and the development of what he called a "left-handed masochism." Samuel later recounted that he told Dr. Baker he would give her $200 unless she agreed, after hearing his history, that his was the worst story she had ever heard. If that was the case, he would ask that the therapy be free. "I got it free," he said. [See more on his work with Blanche Baker at the end of Section V.]

A student of psychology might ask: did Samuel Lewis become involved in spiritual matters so early in life because of his family situation or in spite of it? A student of Eastern mysticism might ask questions about "karmic cause and effect."

As we see in the first selection below, Samuel Lewis found one of his own answers in a remembrance of a "life before life." He remarked that his soul had chosen to come in early and to be misunderstood in order to prepare the way for the coming generation that would begin to signal a "New Age." He could understand the "generation gap" first hand, because he had lived it from birth.

The best answer to both the family psychology and karma questions above might be another question, this time from Lewis quoting his Zen teacher Nyogen Senzaki: "Is the Zen monk bound by the law of causation or is he outside of causation? Answer: The Zen monk is *one* with the law of causation."

To either ignore or overemphasize one's "unpleasant" history does not allow for the full humanity of an individual—a microcosm reflecting a world of many voices slowly learning cooperation and wholeness.

Intimations of Immortality from Juvenile Reminiscences

Autobiographical Paper

(Editor's note: This paper is undated. References to dancing could imply that it was written before Samuel Lewis studied with Ruth St Denis in Los Angeles in the early 1930s.)

I do not believe there ever was a time in which I did not believe in a former life, but this by no means indicates that I necessarily believed in reincarnation (multi-fold appearance on this plane) or that I was uncreated, lasting from eternity. The child-mind does not philosophize, but it may remember well. Although it is generally claimed that we do not remember the earliest incidents in life, there have been remarkable cases of people who recalled their weaning period.

The child memory seems to be closely connected with the picture memory, or shall we say imagination? In certain forms of hypnotic trances, Dr. Charles Richet[4] has demonstrated pre-existence and even, apparently, reincarnation. While the Theosophists have enthusiastically endorsed his experiments as valid, they overlook two points:

- The interval reported between incarnations is very, very short, and entirely out of harmony with the length of time H. P. Blavatsky[5] gave, even as the minimum period.
- There is no place in his system for *karma*.

Now the acceptance of reincarnation without *karma* is like the building of a house without foundation; at the same time we may build several forms of house on a given foundation. The objection to the above might be met by the Sufi explanation of such souls, now in the body, repeating the life story of some soul they met in a higher world.

Now as to actual memories. Until I was fifteen I distinctly remember having been in a kind of wood. It was gloomy there, being like a perpetual four o'clock in the afternoon, lacking the bright light of the sun, but not being in

---

4   Charles Richet (1850-1935), a French psychologist and hypnotist who became interested in spiritualist phenomena.

5   Russian occultist and co-founder of the Theosophical Society in 1875.

darkness. This, I feel, is the condition of the soul, and the afternoon of the soul continues until about the age of seven when the sun of the soul sets, and we are enshrouded in darkness (until the "New Birth."[6])

As a positive proof of this: when my great-grandmother, who first told me of God, would mention God to me, I always saw a great sky of white or light—no sun in it, and no figure or being or anything anthropomorphic or in form. The human-like God, or the veiled God or mist, or God in symbol came later, particularly after Sunday school studies.

Returning to the wood. There were three of us closely associated. We had been exiled, my chum and his sweetheart and I. We had been leaders of a great group of reformers of some kind, destined to free humanity, but passing through the realm of the Usurper, we had been deprived of our power and I had lost all my wealth and my wife (or sweetheart) besides.

These two souls with me, I feel, were Maurice and Minnie [relation unknown-ed.]. In my last visions of this wood (which continued as mentioned before, until I was about 15) I remember a few souls having gathered around us, and a sign that we would again be leaders in a great movement and recover our position, power, wealth and I my soulmate sometime, somehow.

On one side of this wood there was an open space, but it was also gloomy there and entirely bare and flat, almost like a dry mud flat. Both the flat and the wood extended a long distance back to a land of greater light, memory of which gradually disappeared, but which I must have remembered until I was about 12. However, it was from this land that souls came and they were not permitted to return that way. All the traffic was in one direction, and I should call it downward in the same sense as if all traffic had to go to the South Pole, which is at the bottom of the earth.

It is interesting to note that this South Pole is actually the South Pole of the mystics (or nadir or *sifat*) and the opposite movement has been called the northern movement.

Before we had been exiled into the world of gloom, we had been given some choices. Some of these choices were actually repeated to me during my youth. One of them was the choice between truth and suffering on one hand, and pleasure and plenty on the other. When the Usurper offered me this choice, it seems that at first our entire band deserted us, won by stealth or trickery, and only Maurice, Minnie and I, it would appear, held out, although later a few discovered the treachery of the Usurper. This group continued growing until "birth." I believe that, from the ages of three to fifteen, I went through a great deal of suffering over this memory, which I am now mentioning for the first time. The fact that I was to be separated from my wife-to-be, whoever she is, is further explained by some of the details below.

---

6   Presumably some form of spiritual enlightenment or re-birth.

19

The land where the Usurper overthrew our power was, I would say, a sort of 2 or 3 p.m. in the afternoon of the soul, where it was warm and bright and there were meadows. There was much playing and feasting and dancing. I had evidently been a great dreamer and idealist, for I would not join in the games, and it was in this way that my band left me, drawn by pleasure.

This is rather interesting, for when I was in my late teens, I was in the socialist movement and had a fair amount of influence among the young folks. Then I lost my power through the machinations of a young man who introduced dancing and dancers and used this means to overthrow me. This same youth also caused Maurice a great deal of trouble then and afterwards, playing a part in this world as the Usurper did in the former world. Later, H. Spencer Lewis and also one other person played similarly in the lives of Maurice and myself.

It seems that in the former world, I had therefore taken an aversion to dancing, and this played a part in this life. At the same time, I have always loved to watch good dancing, and sometimes I feel that I shall marry a dancer. I do not know God's Will in this matter at all, but it is not necessary to know.

Before entering the world of the Usurper, we had been in a much brighter world, memory of which only remained in early childhood, as with Wordsworth, but I am sure many more children have this experience than is commonly believed.

This "land of light" was where souls receive their instructions before birth. I was at the top of this class (later, I was invariably at the top of my classes in school), but the idea of school is somewhat a misnomer. We learned directly out of the light with our breath, and this breath came in not only through the nostrils, but through every pore of the body. This learning was the same as food. We lived on it, and learning, living, eating and breathing were all one and the same process.

In that land, there was no idea of parentage, but of brother and sister, and perhaps sweetheart and even husband and wife. We travelled in bands, but I do not remember much and that not very clearly. However, I shall relate a few memories, all of which can be explained by doctrines given in *The Phenomenon of the Soul* and *The Soul, Whence and Whither* [both writings by Hazrat Inayat Khan].

Sister: In that land, I had both a brother and sister. For many years after coming to this plane, I continued to dream of a sister younger than myself, but older than my brother. This continued until I was about 12. I had already met the girl who was adopted the following year, fulfilling the conditions. Also most of the dreams, if not all, materialized in the following years.

In the "land of play," as I call it, the girl was about one and a half years and my brother three years younger than I, but there were no parents. In this world, the periods were considerably shortened.

English Language: I was evidently born with a knowledge of the English language, for as soon as my mother repeated the alphabet, I repeated it and was reading before I was three. I read history at four and completed the Old Testament at six. Now as regards reincarnation, there is this peculiarity: I have always felt that if I lived on earth before, that I was a Jew, and yet every memory I might have brought has been with England or the English language.

For instance, when I was 13, I had to write a story in English class and wrote in detail the first half of "The Lady of the Lake,"[7] which I had never read. The teacher thought I had copied it, although I never heard of it and knew nothing of Scott. This could be explained that I met him on a higher plane, where I also most likely met at least one Sufi poet on the downward course to earth.

Messiah: I always believed in the coming of the Messiah, and for a long time felt that I would meet him, and that the great work for which I had been a leader (on the earlier planes) was connected with him. I often rehearsed conversations with the Messiah, and later, after I was 18, with a Master. But when I awoke to the realization, it was almost impossible to reconcile the dreams and musings with the objective reality. In fact, this has been the wonder of my life.

Morals: Closely associated with the last (no doubt) is the reason why I did not indulge in dancing, sex, smoking, etc. I had evidently been given very complete instructions on these points before incarnation. I have never received any guidance on such matters from my parents.

There were also some other intimations which came during childhood.

Choice: I was several times given a choice as to whether I should have my worst sufferings early in life or later. I chose to have them earlier. Now, while this choice was given to me in this life, part of it—that my wife was to remain unknown to me and not revealed until after certain events—belongs to the group of memories, rather than intimations.

Philosophy: When I was 15, it came very definitely—suddenly at first, but often repeated—that I would be a philosopher. At the time I had but the vaguest idea as to what this word meant, and a few years later I actually scorned studying the subject. This was an initial form of spiritual experience, in some way connected with the *djinn* [mental or artistic genius] period of development through which youth goes. I already knew at the time that I was to pass through my adolescence without meeting my sweetheart—very painful—and that my career would be tragical for some time. This made that year particularly hard, and it was not until I was 18 that I recovered from that

---

7   One of the many King Arthur stories, and also a narrative poem by Sir Walter Scott (1810).

mood, only to fall in time (from the material point of view, at least) into a worse condition.

This was the last intimation, I believe, when I began my spiritual studies at 18. At 18, for entirely different material reasons, but certainly connected with spirituality, I began with Theosophy and *Morals and Dogma of Masonry*[8] and comparative theology. Already at 13 I knew about spiritism and psychic research, and evidently earlier about magic and alchemy.

---

8 Connected with Scottish Freemasonry, compiled by Albert Pike and first published in 1871.

In Quest of the Super-Miraculous

Autobiographical Paper

(Editor's note: This paper is undated, but the title suggests that it was written in response to P. D. Ouspensky's book In Search of the Miraculous, *published in 1949. The world's fair Lewis refers to was the Panama-Pacific International Exposition, held in the Marina district of San Francisco, for which a temporary version of the current Palace of Fine Arts was constructed.)*

Scene I. The World's Fair, San Francisco, 1915.
Youth comes to the Palace of Education. "Lord, I know nothing, show me." He places his hands on his forehead, moving each in the opposite direction as if to empty his mind and walks in. He walks in as if a Socrates and asks and asks and asks.

Then he meets the Theosophists. "All religions are right. They differ on the outside when taken exoterically, they agree on the inside if taken esoterically. All religions are from God. There are seven planes of existence, the lower ones experienced in life after life, the higher ones only by sages and the illumined."

The youth is satisfied. He thinks he has found The Way.

Scene II. November 1919. This way has proven only intellectual.
He is on Sutter Street in San Francisco, looking at a display of books. He is unaware, but soon he is upstairs facing a little dark haired lady. She is Jewish.

"You can explain the Kabbalah?"

"Yes, and all religions."

"What is Sufism?"

"Sufism is the essence of all religions. It has been brought to the West by Hazrat Inayat Khan."

Scene III. June 1923.
It is night. It is morning. Hazrat Inayat Khan is coming. The youth is in a hurry. The train draws closer. Inayat Khan sticks his head through the smoke

23

stack. Youth jumps out of his body. Inayat Khan jumps into his heart. Youth jumps into his heart. The two hearts rush and blend and become the Infinite Whole.

Scene IV. The next day.

It is noon, the summer solstice. Youth enters the Clift Hotel. He is summoned to see Pir-o-Murshid Inayat Khan. There is nobody there, only a tremendous light.

"Come, don't be afraid."

Youth walks on and sees a man and experiences joy.

The Quest of the Super-Miraculous becomes real.

II.

JOURNEY INTO SUFISM

Pir-o-Murshid Hazrat Inayat Khan

Pir-o-Murshid Hazrat Inayat Khan

Book excerpt from
The Lotus and the Universe (1963)

Late in 1919, I found myself very suddenly standing before a lady in an office loft in San Francisco. The lady was Murshida Rabia A. Martin, a qualified Sufi teacher and senior disciple of one Inayat Khan, whom I was blessed to meet later on. The term murshid means director or teacher. Rabia was the name of a great woman saint of Iraq, whose tomb has been visited by many people for over a thousand years.

Earlier studies and researches had brought the writer to the conclusion that common interpretations of religion were either incomplete or incorrect. There must be some deeper meanings in them. Murshida Martin then took me on three journeys:

    a. The mysticism of the Old Testament,

    b. The esoteric study of comparative religion, and

    c. the Sufic discipline.

But though disciplined, she encouraged investigations into the mysticisms of all faiths and was a good friend of Dr. M. T. Kirby (my early Buddhist teacher), just as her teacher the Pir-o-Murshid later became a good friend of Nyogen Senzaki.

Among the Sufis, *ishk* (love), *ilm* (wisdom) and *shahud* (direct experience) are what count. As has been said, "Sufism consists of experiences and not premises" (Al-Ghazali). Historically, Sufis came later than other schools of mysticism, and both historically and esoterically, they can be traced to *and* through Muhammad. But as Professor Titus Burckhardt has pointed out, one does not learn mysticism or esotericism except through direct experience.

It is not my place here to write a biography. The family of the Pir-o-Murshid has continued to see that his books are published, and perennially there are shorter or longer sketches of his life and personality.

Hazrat Inayat Khan was born in Baroda state in India and came from a family of musicians. This family was also long associated with Sufis. Largely through the art of music, the mystics of Islam and Hinduism had mingled and intermingled, each making impressions on the other. The first autobiog-

Rabia Ana Martin

raphy of Hazrat Inayat Khan appeared in his own "Confessions of a Sufi Teacher" [contained in volume 12 of *The Sufi Message of Hazrat Inayat Khan*].

He came to America in 1911 and gave the *bayat* (pledge of initiation) to Mrs. Ada Martin, who immediately became a Murshida with the sobriquet of "Rabia." He entrusted her with a considerable body of teaching[9] which was not, however, put to general usage, for after establishing himself in London, he began to systematize his work along other lines.

In his early days, the teachings were based on two interconnected methods. One has to do with *zikr* (remembrance) and involves a long series of disciplines and practices called *ryazat,* all of them having for their purpose the remembrance of God at all times, in all places, under all circumstances. Perhaps in some form or other all the Sufi and dervish orders utilize it.

The other method dealt with self-effacement, called *fana.* This has three distinct grades or stages: *fana-fi-sheikh, fana-fi-rassul, fana-fi-lillah.* In *fana-fi-sheikh,* one practices self-effacement by holding the ideal of the living teacher before oneself and practicing whatever has been imparted. It can go on indefinitely. At the same time, the experiences of Sufism carry one through what are called states (of consciousness) and stages (of evolution) or "stations."

Fana-fi-rassul means effacement in the human ideal. To most or all Sufis, this is Muhammad, but even "Muhammad" takes on various meanings, until one reaches the interpretations offered by lbn al Arabi and Abd al-Karim al-Jili (in his book *Universal Man*). And *fana-fi-lillah* means effacement in the universal, or beyond name-and-form, or the direct experience of God.

---

9   Samuel Lewis is referring here to the practices contained in the "Book of Instructions for Murshid," which Hazrat Inayat Khan entrusted to Rabia Martin. A copy of the book was found in Lewis's archives. This book demonstrates the sources of Inayat Khan's own training in the Sufi path and includes the ritual body prayer of *salat* in Arabic as well as traditional Arabic *kalamas* (invocations).

All of these were and are living experiences of which there are many examples and exponents, but there is a strange chasm between those who have experienced and the intellectuals who are busy translating or interpreting.

Pir-o-Murshid was first given *bayat* in the Chishti School, which bases spiritual development on music. Its chief center is at Ajmir, India, where the celebrated Moineddin Chishti is interred. But by the time he left India, Inayat Khan had received the training in what may be called "Four School Sufism," which is to say, in the Chishti, Qadri, Suhrawardi and Naqshibandi Schools. The Sufism that was presented to the West was basically a synthesis of these.

Hazrat Inayat Khan went to Europe at the invitation of composers such as Debussy and Scriabin, and for some time he carried on the dual career of musician and spiritual teacher. During World War I, his headquarters were in London. Afterwards they were transferred to Geneva, Switzerland, with much of his time spent between there and Suresnes, near Paris. He visited the United States in 1923 and 1926, returned to Europe, and from there travelled to India where he died in February 1927.

The meeting with this man was a wonder. It was preceded by certain types of dreams and visions that our Western culture must someday learn to re-evaluate and explain. Then occurred a more cosmic experience of *union,* which seems to be common to certain types of mystics. But when I entered the room to meet him in 1923, there was no man there, only a great body of light.

Hazrat Inayat Khan was not the first person authorized to present Sufism in English, but he seems to have been the first to do something effectively. The famous Sir Richard Burton had been appointed as a Murshid, and some Muslims expected him to become a missionary. But certainly common religion of any sort did not appeal to him.

Hazrat Inayat Khan taught us that religion has three stages: faith, love and knowledge. So long as religion remains bound to faith and proceeds no further, it can be caught in the web of egocentricity. We have plenty of literature concerning love and plenty of literature that has arisen because of love. The lesson to be learned here is to extract love from time and link it to eternity. And when we become aware of this eternity, we begin to have the real knowledge (called *marifat).*

The other aspect of Sufism besides that of Cosmic Monism *(tawhid, ahadiat)* is that of the acceptance of a spiritual hierarchy. This has not only been presented by J.P. Brown in his *The Dervishes,* but also by E.W Lane, who was a pioneer orientalist. As the intellectuals took over the teaching of orientalia, this aspect of Sufism has been ignored. And yet it is this aspect of Sufism that both unites all the orders and separates them from the generality of Muslims. There is plenty of material in Sufic literature regarding the saints. Even in this age, books are being published concerning men who have lived in the twentieth century.

Here we come to another great division between the real Sufis and what has been called "Islamic philosophy," stemming mostly from Europeans. Practically all Sufis regard either Hazrat Ali or Abdul Qadir Jilani of Baghdad as the greatest of saints. True, Muhammad lbn Arabi either declared he might be the "seal of the saints" or his commentators have said so. But throughout the length and breadth of the Islamic world, these two—Hazrat Ali and Abdul Qadir Jilani—stand out. Not only is this so in popular opinion, but also in occult experiences.

The general teachings given by Hazrat Inayat Khan were first mentioned in an early work of his called "A Sufi Message of Spiritual Liberty" [contained in volume five of *The Sufi Message of Hazrat Inayat Khan*]. All of his instruction was a detailed expansion of what appears in this work. It covers in outline many facets of mysticism and spiritual development. But, of course, it is at best a sort of laboratory manual; it is not even a cookbook.

In 1925, I had a complete breakdown, went into the wilderness and there experienced a number of visions and states of consciousness quite common to Sufis.

The writer's experiences of 1925 were explained by Pir-o-Murshid when he visited Los Angeles in 1926, and a number of confidences were given, largely drawn therefrom[10]. His death the following year saw the disintegration of the Sufi Movement and the efforts of personalities who had not gone through the higher mystical states to take over leadership. In this they failed, though at this writing (1963) his son Vilayat Inayat Khan is making a valiant effort to restore the Movement.

My own journey in *fana-fi-sheikh* began on February 5, 1930, exactly three years after Inayat Khan's death, when the Pir-o-Murshid appeared to me and helped me "from the other side"[11] to write commentaries on his esoteric works, that is, his lessons for mureeds (initiated disciples). This was a provision in the constitution of the Sufi order.

It is also an illustration of love. We love one another insofar as we are part of one another, or blended with one another. Indeed, love cannot have a definition. Defined love is incomplete love, it is love's shadow. We *become* the other, or as Jesus Christ said, "I am the Vine and ye are the branches thereof." This is the relation of the teacher to the disciples—ever, always.

No doubt during the coming years, there may be more complete biographies of Hazrat Inayat Khan. But his followers must learn that there are many mystics, many Sufi teachers, and that not all mystics are Sufis and not all who call themselves "Sufis" or "*dervishes*" are mystics. We must learn, all of us, that "in God, we live and move and have our being" (Acts 17:28).

---

10 Contained in the "Six Interviews" chapter later in this section.
11 See "Experiences of Fana" at the end of Section IV.

The First American Sufi Khankah: Kaaba Allah

Editor's Note

As Samuel Lewis describes in the following excerpts, many of his early spiritual experiences with the Sufis centered around Kaaba Allah, a retreat center (called by Sufis a *khankah*), consisting of two houses located in Fairfax, California. The two houses were nestled up against Mount Tamalpais near what later became the Marin Municipal Water District preserve.

Behind the two houses, up the hill, was a large outcropping of rock that was dedicated by Hazrat Inayat Khan as "Pir Dahan" (the Voice of the Prophet). He and others felt that this spot had a special vibration and significance, as described by Samuel Lewis later in this section. The area surrounding this rock was also the site of Lewis's 1925 retreat and visionary experiences, which are detailed next in this section.

As we shall see, Kaaba Allah ended in controversy and unhappiness in 1949. During happier times, the Fairfax *khankah* was an oasis for many young people who came there to pray, work and share meals, according to Vera Corda. She described some of the scenes there from the mid- to late 1930s:

> In those days of great poverty in the Depression, you could go there, as many times we did, without food all day. Samuel would never see that you got something to eat first. First, he would take you on a hike, pick an herb here and there to give you, and talk to you. And soon you ended up on the rock (Pir Dahan) and sat down with him. Then he would transcend you out of the flesh totally and into the spiritual body. You would have marvellous experiences with him, some spoken, some in meditation, some merely holding his hand and watching the sunset from the rock. You would come down totally filled. You would not feel hungry, weak or depleted. You would feel a fulfilment of all of your bodies— spiritual, mental and physical—complete harmony. Then you entered for your evening meal, and you weren't even thinking about physical food.
>
> Murshida Martin was extremely generous. Those of us who did not have the money were never kept away from Kaaba Allah. When you were

assigned to your room, you found on the inside of the door your assignment for the weekend. Samuel made these assignments and somehow he had it planned for you to use your energies in a way that you would gain something in the spiritual body, no matter what. You might be working on the rock pile, digging up bamboo, planting fences, digging the earth.

There was a great work going on at Kaaba Allah. At one time, we were levelling the ground where the clotheslines were, which was the only flat area on the grounds. This was a great place where we could do our dancing and games. We played lots of games with the younger children. Samuel's games were always in a circle, big group things that pulled everybody in. If you went down there, you got hauled into it and had a great old time. We took down the clotheslines, which made the old ladies who lived at Kaaba Allah roar, so that we had an even bigger area of hard-packed dirt. Bare feet felt great in it.

On Sunday morning, all the young people would gather together with Samuel and we would visit a church of his choice in Fairfax: Methodist, Baptist, Pentecostal, Catholic, Quaker, Jewish. We visited every church in the area. We were taught that a Sufi enters any house of God and behaves as that denomination behaves. One honors God in that manner. And we learned, by experiencing these different congregations, the love of God expressed in so many different manners. But always behind it, at the heart of it, was one truth, one message.

You were prepared ahead of time. Samuel would tell us how to behave before we entered. He would say, 'These are the manners, your manners of worship. They have nothing to do with your talking to God. When you talk to God, you speak one language, remember that.' When we came back, Samuel would give us the heart of that message in that religion's own texts. Then he would also quote Hazrat Inayat Khan so that you would see that this was also the same message, in a different age, in different words, through a different teacher.

You ate supper and left on the Sunday night train. It was usually beginning to get dark when we would sit down to supper. Everyone had packed before this, and following supper you went back to the meeting room and we walked single file up to the chapel. There we had the last of prayers—short prayers and mostly the zikr again was sung. You left after the zikr in silence. Everybody kissed everybody, said goodbye, but it wasn't in language, it was in gesture. Usually the three oldest disciples, the three old ladies, always stood together in the doorway and said goodbye as we went down to go back to the city.

The Retreat of March 1925

Excerpt from the Papers of Samuel Lewis

(Editor's note: Written sometime after his 1961-62 trip to India and Pakistan, mentioned below, and around the time of the beginning of the Dances of Universal Peace in 1968, also alluded to below.)

Toward the One, the perfection of love, harmony and beauty, the only being. United with all the illuminated souls who form the embodiment of the Master, the Spirit of Guidance.

In the name of Allah, the Merciful and Compassionate, and in the name of all the Messengers and Prophets and all the Sufis-in-Chain, beginning with Muhammad, the Seal of the Messengers.

On March 10, 1925, Samuel L. Lewis[12] of San Francisco left his family home and the city of his birth to go to Kaaba Allah, a Sufi retreat near Fairfax, Ca. He had been in pain for years. Doctors had done nothing for him except to apply medicines and charge accordingly. There was not an organ in his body properly operating. He had been forced into debt by wealthy parents who demanded accounting of every cent he earned, while indulging his brother Elliot in any and all enterprises, honest or questionable, provided they bring in financial returns. In any event his father apologized on his deathbed [1954], and Sam is in excellent financial circumstances for a retired man, due to a combination of his own efforts and the receipt of family inheritances long overdue.

By a series of circumstances not easily explained, Samuel had met Murshida Martin, a Sufi teacher, in September 1919, and six weeks later encountered one Reverend M. T. Kirby. Kirby's spiritual name was Sogaku Shaku. He had been a disciple of Shaku Soyen, who brought the real Zen *dharma* transmission to this country, first in 1893 and then in 1906. Dr. Kirby and Murshida Martin became friends, and Sam studied both Zen and Sufism without conflict. In 1923, he introduced Nyogen Senzaki, another disciple

---

12 This is one of a number of writings in which Samuel Lewis refers to himself in the third person, the rationale being that, by avoiding the pronoun *I*, one did not reinforce the reality of the ego.

of Shaku Soyen, to Pir-o-Murshid Inayat Khan, and they both initiated each other, so to speak. Thus, when Sam went into seclusion, he had already had some training both in Sufic practices and meditative Zen.

He was too weak to carry books with him, so he only brought copies of the works of the Sufi poet Hafiz, a notebook and food. He was put on a special diet by Rabia Martin, one based on teachings and directives of Hazrat Inayat Khan. This was the basic *khilvat,* or seclusion, diet, very much akin to that used by Sufis in seclusion all over the world.

It was with difficulty that he mounted the steps above Forrest Avenue in Fairfax. He fell down when he reached Kaaba Allah, 133 Hillside Drive. This was the last time he ever fell down in his life, and much has happened since 1925.

The first few days, he was too tired for anything but meditation and Sufic practices. But he was able to read a little. On the third day, he completed the reading of Hafiz as the sun was setting. The rays of the sun fell on the book, and as he finished the last page two doves suddenly appeared, circling his head, cooing.

That night, as he was doing his spiritual practices, he felt a presence, and he was sure it was Khwajah Khidr[13]. There are many legends of Khwajah Khidr. Even some Western occultists have accepted the reality—of the *legends.* When it comes to *events,* that is something different. If you believe in legends you are "saved," but if you propose that your belief is based on actual experience, that is a sure sign you are a pretender and damned.

There was a recurrence of this appearance of Khwajah Khidr on the following night and on the next also. He offered poetry or music. Sam chose poetry. On the third night of the appearance, there was a long argument: why was the poetry chosen and not the music? Years later, the music did come, and it is coming, and with it the dance, but these are different stories. After the third night, Sam began writing incessantly.

At the end of ten days, all the health and vigor were restored, and Sam prepared an initiatory ceremony for noon, March 21, the equinoxial hour. It must be said here that Murshida Martin had been a teacher in occultism, especially what is called "Martinism[14]" before she became a Sufi Murshida, and

---

13 A "guardian angel" figure, also identified as the "green man of the desert," who appears to those in need to offer wisdom. Most Quranic commentators identify him as the mysterious figure who challenges the prophet Musa (Moses) in Qur'an 18:65-82.

14 One of several forms of Christian esotericism that emphasize the fall of the first human being and its possible return, sometimes called "reintegration," a form of illumination. Various orders with this name developed through the years from the time of its founder Martinez de Pasqually in the 18th century. Presumably the one with which Rabia Martin (no relation) was affiliated was connected with the 19th century occultist Gerard Encausse (aka Papus), since Samuel Lewis mentions Papus in some of his writings.

she transmitted some of this knowledge to her early disciples. One prepared a ceremony with concentration, and in turn Shiva, Buddha, Zoroaster, Moses and Jesus appeared. Then Muhammad appeared, but double (on the left and right) and on horseback. All the others came singly. Then the six Messengers of God, so to speak, formed a circle and danced and became one, and as they danced, the Prophet Elijah appeared and bestowed a robe.

This is the Robe, not a Lloyd Douglas fiction. The same robe was bestowed in vision by Khwajah Moineddin Chishti at Ajmir, India in 1956 and by Amir Khusrau at Nizam-ud-din Auliya in New Delhi in 1962. And when Ahmed Murad, as he was then called, returned to Pakistan after that, he was given this robe, actually. He has it in his possession now. It is functional. It has been recognized by Sufis who are Sufis.

The disciple was supposed to remain in seclusion 10 days with an additional day before and after. But owing to his exaltation, Sam kept quiet for 14 days until he met Murshida Martin and reported to her. He told no one else until 1926 when he again met Pir-o-Murshid Hazrat Inayat Khan at the Beverly Hills Hotel in Los Angeles. The above was the subject for the first interview. Murshid asked him to write this up and keep it as a record, and it was also the basis for the five interviews that followed.

Visionary Reports

Editor's Note

Over the years Samuel Lewis kept a scrapbook that included not only his writings from his 1925 retreat, but also newspaper clippings and photos from his trips to the Middle and Far East, some of which are included in Sections V and VI of this book.

In a letter to Rabia Martin reproduced below, Samuel Lewis mentions the "Rab," a figure he identified with Fabre D'Olivet, a 19th century French Kabbalist and author of *The Hebraic Language Restored* (1815, first English edition 1921). D'Olivet's mystical translation of the Genesis creation story from biblical Hebrew was re-worked by another of Rabia Martin's early Sufi mureeds, Shabaz Best, a colleague of Lewis.[15] In his long, dense text, D'Olivet offers one of the earliest accounts published in the West concerning the mystical meanings of the various Hebrew letters and roots, along with a comparison with the alphabets of other ancient Semitic languages (Syriac Aramaic, Samaritan and Arabic). I found D'Olivet's book in Samuel Lewis's library in 1976. It heavily influenced Lewis's interpretations of Genesis as the account of a mystical journey, as well as his interpretation of various sacred phrases in Arabic.[16]

Regarding Samuel Lewis's visions of the various prophets, reported in this section: By natural predilection, family history and/or training, Samuel Lewis undoubtedly possessed prodigious psychic powers, however defined. He also regarded the experiences mentioned as a form of *fana-fi-rassul* (mentioned in his article on Hazrat Inayat Khan above). An insider's view of these phenomena might regard the Sufi experiences of *fana*—deep effacement in a particular being—as similar to psychic channeling. There are, however, significant differences, which Samuel Lewis articulated in a paper written later in life, a portion of which is included in Section VII. For one thing, in *fana*, the personal ego is not entirely absent, but rather "to the side" and "in service," while still being present. This makes a difference, particularly because

---

15 Best, Shabaz Britten (1964). *Genesis Revised: The Drama of Creation*. Farnham, England: Sufi Publishing Company.

16 Following the lead of Samuel Lewis, D'Olivet's book has been very helpful to me in my writings on the Aramaic words of Jesus. I have never found its essence contradicted by study of the languages of the ancient Semitic texts mentioned.

one then can bring such experiences into action in one's own life. "By their fruits you will know them," as Lewis was fond of quoting from the Gospels.

As Samuel Lewis notes in his account of "Six interviews with Hazrat Inayat Khan" below, Rabia Martin reported to Inayat Khan a visionary experience of him soon after their first meeting. Inayat Khan's subsequent letters to her convey that such experiences are not due to her own psychic prowess but to the effectiveness of the Sufi "chain" of transmission. Since *fana* has to do with personal effacement, it is incompatible with ego enhancement:

> I never want you to have the feelings that generally those who have the spiritual craze may have of seeing wonderful sights and having magical powers.... I want you to find out the God in the usual things that you are experiencing by your five senses. I am guiding you towards the path of love and wisdom and am glad to know that you are following the same direction. May you advance, day by day and not only become like my self but become my self. Which "self"? My internal self and external self. I wish you to remain at last nothing but love and light. (Letter from Inayat Khan to Rabia Martin, 19 June 1911).

As we shall see, Rabia Martin's difficulty following her teacher's instructions and advice had many unintended consequences.

Writings from the 1925 Retreat

Excerpts from
a Scrapbook of Samuel Lewis

Allegory I
At night, Friday-Saturday, March 13-14.

First Impression:
A certain Great King had a very beautiful daughter whom he wished to marry to one of the kings of the earth. So he summoned a herald with a message he was to carry. The herald visited the court of this king, who was so glad to receive an envoy from the Great King that he ordered a banquet prepared in his honor. Then he loaded the herald with presents and built a statue in his honor and sent him away. But the message he heard not.

Second Impression:
A certain Great King had many daughters. And they were exceedingly fair and of marriageable age. Wishing to marry them to the kings of earth, he summoned a herald, telling him that whosoever married one of his daughters would have a dowry of whatsoever they desired. So the herald visited the court of one of the kings who was so glad to receive an envoy from the Great King, that he rejoiced and ordered a great banquet and prepared a holiday for all his people in honor of the envoy. Then he loaded the herald with presents and built a statue in his honor and sent him away. But the message was heard not.

Then the Great King sent him to another king with a like result. So the Great King sent in his stead other messengers from time to time. And some of the messengers were stoned, and some were tortured and driven away by the people. And some kings were so honored at receiving a messenger that they warred with one another as to who was entitled to the greatest honor for having received the greatest envoy.

But few were those who first listened to the herald and his message and then went to the Great King. And they that went found his daughters so exceedingly fair that they gave up their kingdoms and dwelt at the court of the Great King, where sorrow came to them no more.

Allegory II

Night of March 15:

A man once founded a large business with many branches and departments, and every now and then he sent one of his sons to visit one of these branches or departments. And each son would do his work faithfully, rewarding the competent, encouraging the backward and bringing peace and harmony wherever he went.

Time passed and the sons were no more. Then the business did not prosper. Each department or branch thought itself most important and would not cooperate with the other branches. The sales department listened not to the production department, and the purchasing department listened not to the accounting department nor would the Chicago branch cooperate with the San Francisco branch.

Now one of these sons had a son, and when this son saw how affairs were going, he visited each one. And he found that the departments and branches still revered the memory of his father and uncles, but had forgotten their admonitions and considered that the brother that had visited them was superior to the other brothers. Then this one said: "They were brothers, my father and my uncles, and all wanted to carry out the wishes of my grandsire. Listen and see if their instructions were not the same." But they would not, even though the business was not prospering. And though the new head of the firm tried hard, so bitter was the opposition and so hard were his struggles that he died.

And when he died, all saw how good he was, and that since conditions were bad, they might take his advice though he had gone. And this they did, and the business prospered exceedingly thereafter. And him whom they ignored in life, they honored in death .

(Must this be with thee, O Pir-o-Murshid?)

Hafiz

Written 3/16/25 at 1:30 p.m.

Hafiz: What a joy to utter the name! What a thrill in the heart. I have never had a vision of him and hardly read a line of his poetry, yet picture him and what do I see? Smiles! One big smile, bearing joy to all who greet him. He is like sunshine, bringing comfort and courage. In my days of darkness he was with me, guiding me, encouraging me, showing me the way, always smiling, always cheerful. When I look at the beautiful trees and pleasant meadows of sunny California, I picture him in his rose garden at Shiraz and feel that, had he not been born where and when he was, this country with its lovely scenery and beautiful weather would have brought inspiration to his heart, and ode upon ode would have resulted.

Hafiz is always young. Not a boy or youth, but in early manhood.

He has the spirit and enthusiasm of the child and youth with the wisdom of experience.

Initiation
"Peace on Earth, Good Will Towards Men"
March 21, 1925, 9:00 a.m.

My dearest Murshida,

Here in your wonderful room I sit, awaiting the hour of noon, when the signs of the cross shall be made in the heavens, and the sun pass over the equator. This lovely room with its spiritual atmosphere—here where I have sat in meditation, morning, noon and night for the last 12 days, an atmosphere of calm and peace. Once when I fled here when someone came to the grounds, my strength and courage were not only renewed, but doubled like that of the giant Antaeus in the story of Hercules. At night, if there was any fear, fear itself grew afraid when I neared the threshold and stronger and stronger I became in body, heart and soul. There seems to be a sign over the door: "Abandon all *fear* ye who enter here."

Yet not one hour have I been alone. God said—and it is noted in the diary—that an angel with a flaming sword stood outside, and only those who could see could pass. So the birds remained and other creatures and humans never disturbed me. "You have nothing to fear but yourself." And God has been with me. Even now I was not to start writing until the hour of nine, and when a voice from the silence said "Begin," I thought I lacked at least five minutes. But I found the hour had passed by two minutes. Time and again have I known the time.

And not only this, but in the matter of food, fuel, matches, and so forth, my doubts proved false. I thought I did not have enough wood and went out Thursday and brought some in. And how vain! My original stock of wood will last several days more if I should stay. And the same applies to food and matches.

I have brought with me every word I have written in diary, articles, poems and essays to lay them this morning on the altar of the One alone who is creator. Step by step have I risen, to find myself in him. Every prophecy or hint in the diary has been realized. The Creator offered me poetry or music. I chose poetry, and while these may not be works of art, therein there is a promise and there is an inspiration. I have felt at times like a mosque, with my head as a dome reflecting the light from underneath.

I have felt as a circle with a point inside. Facing the south, the point is God; Hafiz in front of me; Pir-o-Murshid to the left, the Rab to the right, and you behind me. And each one of you always took the same post. When the Murshid and Rab came together, they were on either side. And it seemed that Pir-o-Murshid stood on the left, nearest my heart. When the inspiration came from God, it came through my heart, but when Pir-o-Murshid was there, he seemed to be whispering in my left ear. His nearness to my heart brought love. You seemed to be behind or even in me, my very backbone, giving strength and courage. Hafiz was in my forehead, holding the mirror there that the light from within might be reflected without. And the Rab on the right side seemed to be guiding my hand, even using it himself.

Murshida, I have been shown by the Grace of God, as you can see and read, the possibility of being "a light unto the Gentiles and a glory unto thy people Israel." My words first seem like a baby trying to speak, and day by day the inspiration increased until suddenly I saw "The Art of Creation." And if I have not gone more deeply into the truth, it is because I myself have asked God to guide me slowly and make my steps sure.

Last night, it seemed as though Christ himself were with me, giving me the instructions he gave to His disciples when sending them forth and repeating ever and anon, "Be wise as serpents and harmless as doves." So long as I remain true to God, I feel I can reflect his light and help to spread the Message, to go to Los Angeles or anywhere. "The Lord is my shepherd, whom should I fear?" I am ready to teach the New Testament and explain much of the Old with God's help and under your direction.

I can see now the relation between Moses, Fabre D'Olivet, Murshid and the Tarot in regards to creation. *Bereshith bara Elohim hashamayim wahaaretz:* "In the First Principle God Created the Self sameness of the Heavens and the Selfsameness of the Earth."[17] And what is meant by *reshith* or "principle"? This is what Fabre D'Olivet calls "Providence" and Pir-o-Murshid "Love." And the "Heavens"—this is what F.D. calls "Will" and Pir-o-Murshid "Harmony." This is the action of vibrations, energy. And "Earth"? This is what F.D. calls "Destiny," but Pir-o-Murshid calls "Beauty." The principles correspond identically and can be proven scientifically.

And the more I have pondered, the more I found that the Prophet Muhammad himself was expressing the greatest principles of science in words: that God is Love and Beauty and so forth. I am beginning to see further into the great declarations of Judaism and Islam, to see behind the philosophy of Plato and Pythagoras in ways I could hardly dream of. When I first came here I placed Pir-o-Murshid 's picture over Fabre D'Olivet's and said the Rab looked pleased. And that has seemed to be the key to all thereafter.

Not long after you left for your trip around the world, I broke the rosary and meditated without it. The night after I determined to go to Los Angeles and go into *purdah* (seclusion) beforehand. I looked and it was fixed. Many times I wanted to fix it, but could hardly bear to look at it. And whether it

---

17 A quote from Fabre D'Olivet's book, referenced in the previous chapter.

was fixed by my mother or an Unseen Hand, I care not. But it was a sign, and from that night until now I have been growing, growing in a way to give you comfort. I trust I have not failed, that I shall be pure in heart and remember God. Knowing the Law, how much greater my sin, if I obey not.

"Truth is now on earth." Truth has always been on earth despite deluders who say that it has been kept from humanity except at certain ages and in secret ways. "When the disciple is ready, the Master appears," God has always looked after his children. The mysteries have never been lost and never will be lost, but their outward form may change. Today one joining the Church of Universal Service is really being initiated into the Lesser Mysteries.

My future—that is in God's hands. It is now four and one-half years since I began studying with you and five and one-half since we met. I have always wished to carry on the work of the Rab, and it may be so. I have also desired to continue the true American philosophy of Emerson and Whitman, to serve the Jews and Americans first in humanity, then others. Now I leave all these things to God, yet feeling that if I keep my covenant with God, my wishes will come true. The gift of poetry is entirely from God. I have never cared for poetry, but I feel more and more the spirit of the Sufis, and I almost can say, "with God's help and Hafiz," I may succeed.

You will note in my diary about my name. I feel I have realized my name: *Samuel-Shemuel*: "In the name of the Lord." Even "the word or the voice of the Lord." *Leonard*: "Leon" is a lion, "ard" from *arduus,* (Lat.), valiant. Valiant as a lion.

Initiation comes from the Latin and means "a beginning." Beginning of what? Beginning to live and express oneself. Everyday have I read much from the Gayan [poetic writing of Hazrat Inayat Khan] and step-by-step realized it. I feel I am ready to begin, Murshida. I feel I can say "God bless you" to others as you have said it to me.

My meditations have been like the cleaning of machinery at night so the factory will produce more during the day. I have needed little sleep. My brain has been as a servant, working at certain hours, not allowed to work at other times and often getting tired while working. Much of what I have written may hardly be legible, but the inspiration was so great at times, my hand flew and the writing may have suffered. I have not read my diary or articles over except to make two small changes in poems.

Needless to say, I shall enjoy Pesach (Passover) and Easter this year. I have lived Pesach and Easter. God has blessed me with the finest weather. From the moment I entered and the rain stopped, I felt God in the air. If you read any of this or say anything to the mureeds (Khalifa excepted), tell them that the door is open. I have not had many visions or phenomena, but the greatest of phenomena has been the opening of the door of my heart, and I have felt like Walt Whitman, without a grain of conceit: "I am so full of good things I never knew I contained so much goodness." For I have found I contain God and all Goodness is in God.

Soon I enter into my last meditation before the sun crosses the equator. I again thank you with all my heart and soul and mind for your benefits and blessing and to God above be all honor and glory forever. Amen.

Faithfully and sincerely,

Your mureed and disciple in Israel,

Samuel

(Editor's note: Thereafter followed the initiatory ceremony and experience described in "The 1925 Retreat," earlier in this section. Most of the diaries which Samuel Lewis refers to were destroyed by a fire in 1949. All the papers in this section were found in his "Scrapbook," including the next, a letter to his aunt, immediately following the retreat when he moved to Los Angeles.)

Letter

March 31, 1925

My dear Aunt[18]:

I have slept well these last two nights and am feeling pretty good, but last evening I almost broke down. I keep on learning so many bad if not terrible things about my brother, that I can hardly understand where he could have gotten such wickedness into his system. While I was pondering on these things and listening to the radio, some club took charge of the program (KFI, Los Angeles) and began putting on sentimental songs about "mother." That was just about the last thing to put pep in me, so I had to go to my room.

Well, I have learned one lesson, and that is: if I feel very good or very bad, try to write poetry. I tried, and although I did not succeed very well, got the following in blank verse:

A PRAYER FOR MY FATHER!

God give him strength to fight, though hard the fray.

God give him the courage to bear the battle's blows.

Guide him in these hours of darkness and despair.

Show him the light, and Lord, please lift the veil

That he may see a step or two ahead.

O Lord, I pray Thee lighten his burdens a little,

---

18 This was Mildred Rosedale, the mother of Mary Lou Foster, with whom Samuel Lewis maintained friendly relations over the years. The negative reference to Lewis's mother, combined with the sympathetic one to his father, seems to signal a change in Lewis's relations to both.

A little that, though stormy be the way,
Though terrors seem to encompass him about,
Disperse the clouds, and let a ray of sunshine
Pierce the gloom. O God, may the end be now in sight,
An end to these torments and these tortures.
Though time be needed, let the time approach
When he may have peace and rest, though years pass by
Before he leaves his mortal frame and enters
Into a world where sorrows abide not.
O God, give me strength to aid my father.
May my next years bring happiness to his heart.
Make me a source of pride and joy to him,
And may the future show the way
That he may see in me a son of his,
And I see and treat him as my father.
O God, give him hope, and may thy mercy
And thy grace rest upon him even as I write.
May he have that faith which leads to peace,
That faith in Thee, remover of all pain
And sorrow, source of all that's good.
O God, help my father, I repeat again,
Give him strength and courage, from this day forth.
Amen

This may not be good poetry, but I always put down what comes. Sometimes I have had very good inspirations, and at other times not very good. Prayers, so far, have come in the same rhythm as this.

I shall be in town Sunday to attend the final symphony concert. I presume Hertz[19] will play in the Hollywood Bowl this summer, and if so, I expect to attend regularly.

We had quite a rain up here, but this morning it is very nice.

Well Auntie, I must to work. I trust you are feeling better now, but it certainly is a Hell we are going through.

With love, I remain,

Your nephew, Samuel

---

19 Alfred Herz, who conducted the Los Angeles Philharmonic regularly at the Hollywood Bowl around that time.

Surviving building of the former Sufi khankah in Fairfax
photograph: Neil Douglas-Klotz.

Six Interviews
with Hazrat Inayat Khan

Excerpt from Papers

(Editor's note: As Samuel Lewis mentions, the initial reports of his six meetings with Hazrat Inayat Khan in 1926 were either lost in a fire in 1949 or discarded by functionaries of the Sufi Movement in Europe who took over the organization after Hazrat Inayat Khan's passing. Between 1967 and 1971, he compiled several different drafts of these meetings, expanding upon different topics in the history of Western Sufism. The following is mostly taken from the earliest available manuscript, with additional explanations from later drafts.)

772 Clementina St.
San Francisco, Calif.
26th March 1967

Beloved Ones of God:

It is fitting on this Christian Day of Resurrection to start a record—a rather poor one after 40 years—of "Six Conversations with Inayat Khan." These meetings were never sought by the writer, and the very fact that they were requested by the Pir-o-Murshid earned for the writer the ill-will of the then-secretary, a pattern that has been repeated many times.

Recently, a Vietnamese Buddhist master, coming to this city, sought this person before all others. One awoke this morning with the appearance of Lord Issa (Jesus) who said, *"This is Very Significant."* So feeling the blessings of heaven, one will proceed, realizing all the way–without humility–that time and age have dimmed the records.

One does not remember any longer the exact six meetings in order. One's records were destroyed in a fire in 1949 immediately after some of these records were forcibly seized by a person pretending to be a Sufi, having a following who call themselves "Sufis," but who do not attempt to practice *La Ilaha El Il Allah* (There is no Reality but God, the Only Being).

First Interview

The meetings were held in the Beverly Hills Hotel in the year 1926. The first one was the most significant to the reporter. In the year 1925, one had come to the end of one's tether and had gone into the wilderness to die, he thought. Instead, he was completely resurrected and learned, for the first time, the principle of death and resurrection, of which this day is significant. Briefly, there were encounters with Khwajah Khidr at the beginning, and with the chain of prophets at the end with Lord Muhammad appearing in double capacity, the other messengers singly, and one was vested with a special robe. The whole history of the first *khilvat* of the writer was told to Pir-o-Mur-shid. All records are gone. Three times was it submitted to various descend-ants of Hazrat Inayat Khan in Europe and discarded. The failure of the Mes-sage of God in Europe, and to some extent in America, has been due to too much "Message" and no God, and in the end to personality emphasis. Pir-o-Murshid said, "Heart speaks to heart and soul to soul." This is for those whose ears and inner beings are opening, or opened.

Pir-o-Murshid listened and told me to write. But in the next meeting, something happened, and it will stand as a testimonial, an unfortunate testimonial against those who worship the teacher and discard the teaching, a habit that is universal and only brings misfortune. La Ilaha El Il Allah.

Second Interview

As I entered the room for the second interview, Pir-o-Murshid stood up and motioned to me, took my hands in the spiritual manner and said, "I initiate you for the sixth time in the Sufi order." Later when I looked up Hazrat Inayat Khan's early records, I found he had initiated me as "Sufi." One dare not take that appellation, and it was only years later, receiving such initiation openly from Pir-o-Murshid Sufi Barkat Ali that one could use it. This appellation was also confirmed by Pir Dewal Shereef, President of the Board of Directors, Islamabad University. It has been accepted in Asia by many pirs, many schools.

Practically everything of this second interview, and much of the later interviews, was rejected by presumably good people, and this substantiated what Hazrat Inayat Khan said to me at the time as well as what actually happened later.

I was at the time a rather frightened young man but had another "veil-lifting experience" (in the home of Roderick White on Garden Street in Santa Barbara), which indicated potential–or more than potential, assurance–of the spiritual advancement of this person. What followed during this interview so shocked everyone when I later told them, that its contents and those of the following interviews were rejected, excepting by Mr. Paul Reps who was stationed outside the door during all but the last interview, when he was inside.

Before we sat down, Inayat Khan said to me, "Samuel, I am going to ask you a favor. I want to speak to you as man to man. I am not Murshid; you are not *mureed*. We are just men. If we cannot act as men, it will not help me. Can you act to me as man to man? If so, let us shake hands and then we can sit down and talk as man to man." We did so and sat down.

"How many loyal mureeds do you think I have?" he asked.

"Oh, I guess about 100."

"I wish I had 100. But how many do you think, at the least, loyal mureeds I have?"

"Well," I said, "I don't believe it, but just to give an answer, I would say 20."

"I wish I had 20! I wish I had 10!"

Then he arose in full majesty and yelled at me out loud, "I wish I had 10!" Then he lifted his right hand, and using the index finger of his left hand, pointed to the middle of it and yelled, "I wish I had five loyal mureeds. Samuel, can you believe it, I have not as many loyal mureeds as I have fingers on one hand?"

By that time, the chair in which I had been sitting toppled over like in a Hollywood movie, and I was sitting on the floor, totally amazed. But, by this action and by his loud speech, I received the full magnetism of his *baraka* or blessing, and I believe I still have it. He then told me the story of his search for one honest man whom he could trust. It was only after years that he found one Mr. E. de Cruzat Zanetti[20] to whom, he said, he gave all trust, no compromise. He told me, and repeated later in the course of further interviews, that in case of any difficulty I should write to him.

This was never believed. Neither the disciples of the East (Europe) or the West (America) accepted it. Then he began telling me some things that were also told to Pir-o-Murshid Hasan Nizami on his (Hazrat Inayat Khan's) deathbed. These fall into two classes, the first on succession, the second on the Sufi order.

He began telling me that he wished me to defend Murshida Martin of San Francisco, who had been my original teacher (1919-1923) and in another vein after that. I was to stand by her and protect her, but see to it that she never defended herself. He went over that again and again. He said he expected trouble, and that I was to write to Mr. Zanetti in Geneva about what he told me.

---

20 Executive Supervisor of the Sufi Movement in Geneva from 1923. Born in Cuba, he had academic degrees and worked for the American Embassy in Madrid. In one of his last speeches in Suresnes, before leaving for India, Inayat Khan said, "The coming of Mr. Zanetti into the Sufi Movement has released me from many responsibilities connected with the working of the administrative part of the Movement, for which I am most thankful."

Murshida Martin was then under attack by several people. She had had the *fana-fi-rassul* with Muhammad soon after she met Hazrat Inayat Khan. She had had a long training in European occultism and in comparative religion. But during the years I knew her, although she was a Murshida, I know of only one or two experiences on her part in *fana-fi-rassul* and one in *fana-fi-lillah*. This was much more than others experienced. (I was not initiated into *fana-fi-sheikh* until 1930 when Hazrat Inayat began to appear to me "from the other side"). I was told, over and over again:

A. Pir-o-Murshid Inayat Khan intended that Murshida Martin be his successor.
B. She was never to defend herself on any occasion and positively never in public.
C. She was to divest herself of all right to handle funds.

This was the history. The aftermath was terrible. The first thing that happened after the death of Hazrat Inayat Khan was my removal from the board of trustees[21], which handled the funds. Never after that until the disassembling of the *khankah* (in Fairfax) that Pir-o-Murshid blessed was I ever permitted to say a word about finances.

The funds were handled by a Board of Mureeds with the Murshida, but with the advice and consent of her family, and never was any undertaking done without the family. When this person refused to countenance private deals in which her family benefited, he was never forgiven, ever.

It must have been this spirit that was felt in Europe, where the vast majority of disciples refused to accept Murshida Martin as successor to Pir-o-Murshid Inayat Khan. But they surely felt the *nafs* [ego]. It is to one's great regret that Murshida Martin always insisted on defending her *nafs* in public, and this led to her downfall. True, when she visited Pir-o-Murshid Hasan Nizami in New Delhi, he proclaimed her as successor to Hazrat Inayat Khan. There were deliberations and newspaper notices, and she was accepted—or at least respected—in the undivided India. But none of this had the slightest effect in Europe.

Still, if we have to see life from the standpoint of another as well as of ourselves, the outlook is that there is nothing that can be called exactly right or exactly wrong. Later on in life—much later than the above events—when an outsider came along and insisted that Rabia give up public self-defence and control over funds, she did so without a whimper. She could not do that at the dying request of her own Pir-o-Murshid, but for an outsider she did that. Her death was a tragedy.

---

21 of Rabia Martin's organization, which was independent of the two European Sufi Movements.

Third Interview

This had to do with the papers for the disciples. There were several rules and constitutions in the short career of Pir-o-Murshid Hazrat Inayat Khan. At that time, he had papers called "Gathekas" for nonmureeds, some of them later published in *The Unity of Religious Ideals*, "Gathas" for the first three years and "Githas" for the next three years. He gave me some instructions about them. There were further instructions at other meetings.

The Sufi Movement had been envisioned as covering twelve grades, but the last degrees were for teachers only. Only if there was a "full graduation," the person became either a "Khalif" or its equivalent, but that was outside the immediate instructions.

Pir-o-Murshid told me how he wanted these things handled. He made me *esoteric* but not *exoteric* leader in Los Angeles. That is to say, my authority was limited to the teaching of disciples, the training of applicants and their first *bayat* (initiation). There was little in this meeting that did not extend to others elsewhere.

Fourth Interview

The Sufi Movement was to be divided into three sections, and this also appears in the literature called *The Sufi Message*. There was to be: a) the *Sufi order* for mureeds and spiritual instruction, which was the heart and soul, and without which there can be no Sufism whatever; b) the *Universal Worship*—a ritual including scriptures of all faiths, which was connected with the Universel temple and which became organically active but socially ineffective; c) the *Brotherhood*, which was to be the intellectual side of the teaching to bridge the gap between mysticism and universal culture.

According to the teachings of Sufi mysticism—and this has nothing to do with anything from India—there are developments in the sciences of breath that enable the adept to see into the future, to ascertain the purposes of life, and that can be used by an enlightened teacher to direct the progress of disciples toward the accomplishment of those purposes for which they were born. Hazrat Inayat Khan felt—and no doubt he was right—that this person was essentially an intellectual, and he directed him toward the integration of the mystical and the intellectual.

He went into exact details and told me to work with Miss Sakina Furnee[22] in Suresnes, France, but if anything happened to her, I was to take over the

---

22 Devoted Dutch *mureed* of Inayat Khan who served as his secretary from 1921 and head of the "Brotherhood" work from 1922. She learned shorthand in order to be able to transcribe Inayat Khan's lectures accurately and a great many of his works were preserved due to her. He changed her Sufi name to Nekbakht shortly before leaving for India, and it is under the name "Nekbakht Stichting" that she founded what became the archives of Hazrat Inayat Khan in Suresnes, France in 1950.

Brotherhood work. She did retire on Pir-o-Murshid's death. This appointment was never recognized in Europe and has been de-emphasized in America.

It is very difficult, although times are changing, to present in the Western world a picture based on mystical attainment which transcends all religious separatism. Still one has gone on trying to bridge the gap between mysticism and general culture, and the last few weeks show, that if one persists for forty years, he will surely succeed.

But this success comes when there is no practical, working Sufi Movement. Now one has reached a complexity, because the young—to whom one was not originally sent—accept his spiritual prowess. And at the same time there is increasing acceptance of this person all over the world as one bridging the gap between the intellectual and mystical worlds. If Sufi Ahmed Murad Chishti has any rights as *khalif* or murshid, these came from pirs outside the Sufi order of Hazrat Inayat Khan.

One would prefer to work in and with one of the various constitutions laid down by Hazrat Inayat Khan. Long after he had left the world, he asked that the disciples, particularly in Europe, either restore the constitutions—any one of them—that he had given, or have a visible constitution that could be seen by others. Instead there have been nothing but unsubstantiated ego-claims, as if there were no Universal God.

It is notable after all these years that the instructions Pir-o-Murshid gave are coming to pass. Pir-o-Murshid said, "Neither can I be broken nor God, but the one who would break me, he is broken." Shortly after the death of Hazrat Inayat Khan in 1927, the writer encountered the late Ali Kulli Khan[23] of the Bahai Movement and asked him what would be the difference between seven hundred conflicting religious sects and seven hundred conflicting universal brotherhoods. The question was not answered, and today we see the rise of an ever-larger number of verbal universal brotherhoods, mutually exclusive.

But Hazrat Inayat Khan, contrary to both his legal successors and to disciples, proclaimed that universal brotherhood would form of itself. And he also told his former disciple Mr. Paul Reps that there were far more people who were not his disciples who were closer to the "Message of God" than the so-called "Sufis." The well-known Paul Reps, who will again be mentioned, will probably confirm this and especially confirm that the New Age young people are going to bring real brotherhood.

None of the legal entities, either the Sufi Movement or other entities, can ever bring universal brotherhood.

---

23 An early translator of Mirza Muhammad (Gulpaygani), a Bahai scholar who helped spread the faith in the United States.

Fifth Interview

This had to do with the science of commentaries. Originally, this had been part of the general teachings. There was an esoteric constitution (there were several), which distinctly called for commentaries. Each person to become a "Khalif" was supposed to write a commentary on the "Gathas," the first three years' instructions, and each Murshid on the "Githas," the next three years' instructions. While this was explicit in the esoteric constitution, years later when I saw a copy the section had been removed.

[from 1970 draft:] One read later in records that have since been suppressed, that the Gathas and esoteric papers belonged to and belong to the Sufi order and not the Sufi Movement. The Sufi Movement was organized to facilitate the outer workings for the Sufi order, a matter that has been investigated further by Pir Vilayat Khan, who received full recognition from the Chishti Order in India. This validates any claim he may make, regardless of the actions and attitudes of any legal entity calling or mis-calling itself "Sufi" or anything else.

The descent of *baraka* and similar operations (which are found in the mystical processes of perhaps all faiths) continue to go on. God, so to speak, does not consult any legal group as to whom God may bless or manifest to. There is no *bayat* to any legal entity. There may be a *bayat* to a representative of the Sufi order—Sufi order not Sufi Movement—or to teachers of the seen or unseen, who do not consult with legal entities as to who is worthy or unworthy. [End of section of 1970 draft.]

Sixth Interview

Pir-o-Murshid asked me to study all his constitutions, all his records and submit findings to Mr. Zanetti in Geneva. This was not an easy task. The records were scattered. Murshida Martin had a "Book of Murshids," which she put away for safety, and at her death nobody was able to find it. But at her death, one found a lot of scattered miscellany in strange places. These covered the complete *ryazat* (spiritual practice) of Hazrat Inayat Khan.

This last was the most important of all the meetings. Pir-OMurshid went over everything with patience. I have since found several attempts on his part for a constitution. One was based on prowess in *zikr*, never completed. Another on advancement in *hal* (mystical states) and *makam* (stations). Another on different bases. Many of the principles are found in volume ten of *The Sufi Message*, now published. For practical purposes this volume includes everything needed for a Sufi school in any and all parts of the world.

However, there are now many efforts on the part of those who have some prowess in *hal* and *makam* to come together, realizing the unity of all knowledge, the passing of the importance of national boundaries, and the coming of a movement toward the brotherhood of man.

This has been written rather hurriedly in face of a number of dramas and climaxes surrounding the writer, and it is hoped that at some leisure time, or in *khilvat* if possible, one can submit a more sober report. At this writing, Pir Zade Vilayat Khan seems to have assented to his father's wishes about this person being a leader in "esoteric Sufism."

There are many means by which problems can be solved. The tragedy is a school of Sufis discarding one after another the esoteric sciences that could be used to settle problems, and resorting to ego-reasons, or rather just ego, then justified, instead of to Allah.

The rise of a new generation, not to say culture, that wishes divine experience directly, and not personalities and personalisms, means *inshallah* that the Truth *(hikmat)* will manifest despite all the arguments, unsubstantiated statements and claims of all persons. This includes those of the writer himself, who is not without faults. But in a law court, an eyewitness is permitted the box, not on his private merits or demerits but on whether he has been witness to events causing litigation.

Around 1946, the writer entered into *fana-fi-rassul.* Although this came from Muhammad, the *khatim al mursaleen* ["guarantee" of the chain of Messengers], it was followed almost immediately by a similar experience with Jesus (Issa). And on this day, it was the appearance of Lord Jesus that has prompted the report at this time.

With all love and blessings to whomsoever reads this and to whomsoever has access thereunto.

Faithfully,

Sufi Ahmed Murad Chishti Samuel L. Lewis

Baraka (Blessing):
Direct Experience at
the Rock Pir Dahan

Autobiographical Paper

(Editor's note: Found in Samuel Lewis's archives, most likely written after 1949, when one of the two houses at the Sufi khankah burned down. The second house and the meditation spot named Pir Dahan survived. I regularly meditated at Pir Dahan during the time this book was originally being produced, in the early 1980s.)

In the spring of 1926 Sufi Inayat Khan visited the properties at Fairfax, California, and named a certain rock *Pir Dahan* (the Voice of the Prophet), and the house of meditation *Kaaba Allah* (this house is no longer in existence). I was in Los Angeles at the time, but the man who brought Inayat Khan to Fairfax is the same Saladin Paul Reps who has recently visited Hasan Nizami in India.

The psychic and mystical events and the *baraka* experienced by myself (and a few others) in the building of Kaaba Allah would resemble a fairy tale. I did find some parallels in Eflaki's *Lives of the Adepts*[24] and in Palladius' *Lives of the Solitaries*[25], which I shall refer to in another paper.

1. *Elsie Norwood,* now living 65 Ramsdell St., San Francisco. Shortly after the demise of Sufi Inayat Khan in 1927, Mrs. Norwood, who has been a clairvoyant and disciple in both Sufism and Vedanta, claims she saw on the rock Pir Dahan, all the great prophets of all ages greeting Sufi Inayat Khan, and the Buddha was the greatest in maintenance of the pure spiritual state. She had this vision steadily over a long period.

   I wrote this experience in poetic form and presented it to the Rev. Ishida, Zen monk and tea-master, who was then a guest of Nyogen Senzaki, the Zen master in San Francisco, and he was so pleased he gave me a tea-ceremony in honor thereof.

---

24 Shemsuddin Eflaki, who collected stories of Jelaluddin Rumi and his descendants and published "Acts of the Adepts" in 1353.

25 A collection of stories about the early "Desert Fathers and Mothers" of Egypt by Palladius of Galatia in the early 5th century CE.

Several years later, when I was in difficulty and went to see Mrs. Norwood, there was with her a clairvoyant from Stockton, California. This lady asked me to come the next day, at noon, when she looked at the rock and told me what she said was my spiritual future. The chief difference was that she saw Jesus Christ as the leader, as against Buddha in Mrs. Norwood's report.

2. *Nyogen Senzaki.* Zen monk and, to me, Master; friend of Watts and Spiegelberg. A friend of many year's standing. Visited Fairfax one year to commemorate Sufi Inayat Khan's passing, went to the rock and immediately entered *samadhi*. He reported it had the highest vibration of any place he had known in America.

3. *Sabin Orgler,* Jewish mystic, visited the rock in 1932. Same general experience as Mrs. Norwood and the psychic, except that he saw Moses in place of Buddha and Christ, as above. All saw "angels ascending and descending."

4. *Vera Zahn* (later known as Vera Corda), San Francisco. Disciple in Sufism with some psychic faculties. Always felt the vibrations and had various experiences there.

5. *Theodore Reindollar,* long resident of Marin County. Visited Tlemcen [Algeria] during the war as my representative. Returned to Fairfax in 1947 and claims rock is in full possession of *baraka*. A disciple of Sidi Adah in Tlemcen, where he has been staying.

6. *Samuel L. Lewis.* Some of my reports in writing and poetry, some very exact prophecies (some not so much). In September 1940, one night at 10:30, went to rock to offer prayer and sacrifice (of sleep, etc.) to pray for the safeguarding of the city of London. Placed myself before the tabernacle, which had been built at my direction to "house" the *baraka* ("*shekinah*" theory). Heard a voice from Heaven: "Go back, go to sleep and forget everything. If you can absolutely relax and sleep, London will be saved. London is saved." That week the Germans suffered their first terrific losses in bombing flights.

—Samuel L. Lewis

The Early Days
of Sufism in America

Editor's Note

The period of time following the passing of Hazrat Inayat Khan in 1927 was fraught with confusion and dissension for the people who wanted to continue his work. Most of the controversy centered around two points: who his spiritual "successor" was (or would be) and how the organization would be run. These two issues—successorship and organization—seem to have plagued most of the known Sufi orders around the world during the 1200-1300 years that the eternal wisdom has been known as "Sufism."

Hazrat Inayat Khan himself was very clear that the "Sufi order," an esoteric school, was separate from any legal organization (as Samuel Lewis repeats in "Six Interviews"). For instance, in an address to his advanced students in Suresnes, France on 17 June 1924, Inayat Khan says:

> Esotericism must be considered something beyond conception. That is, that which is within conception cannot be esotericism, it is exotericism. Often I am asked by the workers of the Sufi order, "If anyone asks us 'What is Sufism?' what shall we answer? What are its tenets? What are its principles? What are its dogmas? Its doctrines?" We may give the objects of the Movement, the thoughts of the Sufis, the ideas from our publications; but that is not the answer. If Sufism was tangible, then it would not be Sufism.
>
> All different ideas that you receive from your Initiator, they are your Initiator's ideas, they are not Sufism. You may give them to another because it is something that you have benefited by yourself as Sufism. Yet, for you to understand for yourself, you must know that Sufism is beyond all ideas. Therefore if it came to argue on this point with those belonging to the occult, mystical, esoteric schools of different denominations on the point of the difference between their own philosophy and Sufism, you will find yourself at a loss if you will discuss on comparative doctrines, dogmas, or principles.
>
> Sufism does not stand for any doctrines, dogmas, or principles, calling them its own. The Sufi says, "Wisdom does not belong to me alone or

my sect. It cannot be labeled with the word *Sufi*. Wisdom belongs to the human race, wisdom belongs to God. I, as any other being, desire to understand better every day more and more. And it is my pleasure and privilege to share what I consider good and beautiful with my fellow men."

Never in the history of the world has Sufism been made a sect which wanted to make many of the same sect. It has never been nor will it ever be. It is an esoteric school of long traditions. It remains as such. Yes, it happens that the Message born of this School is destined to reach far and wide. That gives us a different task, of spreading the Message, which stands apart from the Sufi order, which is an esoteric school. It has been our honor that the seekers came to us in all ages. We did not seek them. And this dignity we must always maintain.

Research I conducted in the Sufi Movement archives in the Haag, Netherlands in 1998, revealed the following facts:

When Hazrat Inayat Khan left for India in late 1926, he left a letter to be opened in the event he did not return. According to these archives, after Inayat Khan's passing the person to whom he entrusted the letter, one of his Murshidas, Sharifa Goodenough, burned it. She never revealed whether she had opened it or read the contents. Several years of controversy followed in the Sufi Movement organization in Europe. One group felt that Inayat Khan's brother Maheboob Khan was best suited to take over as his successor and elected him as such in 1930. Another group felt that since Inayat's wishes were not clear, no one should be designated the successor, and the group should continue without one, with the organization run by committee.

As we have seen from Samuel Lewis's "Six Interviews" report, he and Rabia Martin believed that Inayat Khan had left her as his successor. However, the Europeans did not consider her claim a credible one. In Europe, the Sufi Movement split into two different organizations and remained so until after World War II. In America, Rabia Martin formed her own organization, which also had branches in Brazil and Australia. The Brazilian branch, under Shabaz Best, preserved many of Samuel Lewis's writings from the 1930s that feature in Section IV. Best's widow sent them to the Sufi Movement archives after WWII, where I found them in the Hague.

The issue of a "true" spiritual successor may be a chimera or perhaps a language problem. One essential principle of Sufism, as Samuel Lewis was fond of quoting from the 12th century Persian Al-Ghazali, is that it is based on "experiences, not premises." Many seeds are sown by a teacher; which actually grow into living plants can only be known by the passage of time.

Two of Inayat Khan's mureeds who have provided some additional perspectives on this early period of Sufism in the West are Paul Reps, who co-authored the book *Zen Flesh, Zen Bones* with Nyogen Senzaki, and Shamcher

57

Bryn Beorse, a solar engineer and alternative economist, author of many books on these topics as well as spirituality (for instance, see www.shamcher.org).

Paul Reps offered his understanding:

> Inayat Khan was the most remarkable man I ever met. It was as if one's soul were speaking all the time. When we would ask him something, he would say "Call me Inayat," because he was completely humble and completely at peace, relaxed and concentrated at the same time. His eyes looked right through your forehead all the time when he talked to you. And yet, he was completely at ease and said nothing for himself. He was always letting you do the talking and drawing you out. But he was certainly practicing what we might now call "Sufism," the mind on the breath or however you want to interpret it.
>
> This presence, with this great gentility and kinglike bearing simply overcame those who had never seen anything like it. They were very much impressed and extremely touched by his sympathy for them and felt, "Here, at last, is the one person who understands me thoroughly." And feeling that way, with such love, they began to feel, "Now I am really right." And the contact and the message dug so deep into their system that they felt, "I am really right, but all the other people may be wrong." And so all of these various appointees and representatives of Sufism in different countries began to have that kind of feeling. They began to get at odds with each other.
>
> Inayat Khan felt very deeply, "I must put God first. I must turn to the Only Being, because these Westerners are not doing this and this is what they need." That's what he expressed and this is what is called his "Message." But his Message was his Being, the way he felt about it. It might have been the greatest Message ever. It might have been the Message for the times. It was certainly a most beautiful expression, which then people began, strangely enough, to quarrel over. Unlike other teachers, the teaching was humble instead of assertive. However, he had all of these initiates that he gave various ranks to, and they fought so much that, upon leaving for India, he said that if he came back again to the Western world, he wouldn't have anything to do with these ranks. You see, because it was misused.
>
> I think he realized his life was short. I asked him once, "Murshid, why do you organize?" He said, "To reach more people." He was searching for ways to reach people. Now we have a guru on every street corner, but it's easy for them to reach people because people—young people— will come to them.

Shamcher Beorse gave his version of events in an interview before he died in 1979:

> In Suresnes after Inayat's passing, four of his former disciples came and said that "I" was appointed leader, because Inayat had spoken to them in such terms and said, "You are a great sovereign, you will do so and so…" And so they expanded on that in their own consciousness to the fact that they were the one leader. And of course all of them were equally wrong.
>
> The idea that one person is the successor, or personifies a teacher, is always wrong. No spiritual teacher ever had a successor, or can have one. When disciples feel they are fulfilling the mission given to them by their teacher, then they feel a successor. In that sense, every teacher has had successors, plural. Some of these successors may be, from the eternal point of view, even greater than the teacher, who knows? But they are not the same as the teacher. They don't represent him in all spheres and in all senses. But if anyone claims to be the One Successor, then that person repudiates a great number of disciples, perhaps in some cases everybody but themselves.
>
> Sam is a genuine mystic, as good as they come and as good as they have ever come. Personally I see no difference, at least not a lot, between for instance, Hidayat (Hazrat Inayat Khan's youngest son) or Jesus Christ or Sam or Inayat Khan or Vilayat Khan, when it comes to spirituality and some of you young people. Some people get onto the stage as the Great Messenger, but a lot of people are just as great messengers without being on the stage as that.
>
> The aim of the Sufi, of course, is to see that greatness in every person, and the relative greatness of the dogs and the cats and the cattle and the elephants. The same with the Sufis abroad. Sam seems to have fallen in with them and to be a reborn great Sufi. I walk around and see some great and some I think are not so great. Then something comes up in my mind quickly about their difficulties and their problems and I go away half smiling and half weeping.

III.

JOURNEY INTO ZEN

Nyogen Senzaki

He-Kwang's Zen

Editor's Note

"Lord Buddha was not interested in reincarnation, he was interested in deliverance, in moksha, in raising us above suffering. And he gave certain theories, not that they were necessarily metaphysically correct, but so they could bring us into this universe of love and joy and ultimately peace. And if anybody says that Christ didn't teach the same thing, well, they are crazy. He taught exactly the same thing" (audio recording of Samuel Lewis, February 29, 1968).

Samuel Lewis pursued a simultaneous study of Sufism and Zen from 1919 until his death in 1971. The first three chapters in this section are taken from his unpublished book *The Lotus and the Universe*, written in 1963 to counter Arthur Koestler's *The Lotus and the Robot* (1960). At the time, few people in the West who had actually undergone Zen disciplines had published books on Buddhism or Zen. This situation has happily changed over the intervening years.

With regard to Samuel Lewis's Zen teachers, the talks of both Nyogen Senzaki[26] and Sokei-an Sasaki[27] have been published, the latter by the diligent work of the First Zen Institute (www.firstzen.org) in New York City, which Lewis mentions in one of the pieces below.

In the early 1960s, however, Lewis felt that he needed to, in the strongest terms, counterpose his own experiences against Koestler's opinions in *The Lotus and the Robot*. Essentially, Koestler was trying to make the case that all mystics are either phonies or charlatans, and that Western science and secular culture could provide all the answers we need today. In *The Lotus and the Robot* Koestler states:

> Taken at face value and considered in itself, Zen is at best an existential hoax, at worst a web of solemn absurdities. But within the frame-

---

26 From Senzaki, recommended are *Like a Dream, Like a Fantasy* (2005) and *Eloquent Silence* (2008), Somerville, MA: Wisdom Publications.

27 From Sasaki: *Original Nature* (2010) and *Three-Hundred Mile Tiger* (2013). Also highly recommended is the collection of his autobiographical writings, which are teachings in themselves: *Holding the Lotus to the Rock* (2003), all are from The First Zen Institute of America in New York.

work of Japanese society, this cult of the absurd, of ritual leg-pulls and nose-tweaks, made beautiful sense. It was, and to a limited extent still is, a form of psychotherapy for a self-conscious, shame-ridden society, a technique of undoing the strings that tied it into knots.

Mankind is facing its most deadly predicament since it climbed down from the trees; but one is reluctantly brought to the conclusion that neither Yoga, Zen nor any other Asian form of mysticism has any significant advice to offer.

Samuel Lewis, the Rev. He Kwang, began the penultimate chapter in this section, "Dharma Transmission," in 1966. Here in a very different style, he shows his Zen as he talks about its history in America.

In the final selection, "How to be a Buddhist? How to be a Buddha," a journal article written for *The Western Buddhist*, Samuel Lewis de-constructs and re-configures traditional Buddhist terms according to the experience of a mystic.

In Search of Satori

Book Excerpt from
The Lotus and the Universe

Zen for the West by Professor Sohaku Ogata[28].

We begin here with a reference to a book, not with a quotation. A quotation may seldom help us to attain *satori,* that is to say, enlightenment or *samadhi.* A book may not be of much use either, but if we must have books, this is an excellent one.

The following incident is true. A gentleman built a beautiful garden in Santa Barbara. It attracted much attention and many people (including the writer) came long distances to see it. It was called a Japanese garden, or occasionally (whenever the late Mr. Hearst had an outburst) an "oriental" garden. A Japanese ambassador who came to Los Angeles decided to visit the place. The owner proudly conducted him around.

"What do you think about it?" he asked.

"Wonderful, wonderful," replied the ambassador, "We have nothing like this in Japan."

This well applies to much of the material paraded as Zen before the American public in books, lecture courses and even in some university studies.

Among the minor speakers at the Columbia World Exposition in Chicago in 1893 was Master Shaku Soyen[29]. He gave the first presentation of Zen Buddhism to America, and for a long time Zen meant nothing but meditation and meditation-practices, not lectures, not doctrines of any kind.

Shaku Soyen received a cordial welcome in San Francisco and was invited to return in 1906. At that time he brought with him two monks of his Rinzai School, Daisetz Suzuki and Nyogen Senzaki. Both of them were linguists and scholars, though the former became famous therefor and the latter hid his light under bushels.

The Rinzai (Chinese Lin-chi) School was brought to Kamakura centuries ago by Master Eisai (also famous for his contributions to tea ceremony

---

28 Published by Dial Press, now a division of Random House in 1959. Still available online.

29 1860-1919. Usually cited as Soyen Shaku, as the "surname" in Japan is traditionally placed first.

and art). It is a school of rigor that especially appealed to the nobility and Samurai, the warrior caste. It still flourishes, though far outnumbered in membership and strength by the Soto School, which is more democratic and milder (or more compassionate). But both are meditation schools. Both speak about *dharma* and Buddhism, and meditation is the means, not necessarily the end.

Shaku Soyen published his now little-known *Sermons of a Buddhist Abbot.*[30] If he had only had the "foresight" to have used the word, nay the magic word, *Zen* in the title, it might now be a bestseller. Instead, it is not even on the required reading lists of many institutions purporting to give instructions in Buddhism or Zen.

Another early influence toward imparting Zen to the West was the famous lady writer L. Adams Beck (Elizabeth Barrington)[31]. Although her later books were devoted to Buddhism and Zen, her outlook always seems to have been cosmic and beyond sectarianism. It was she who first arranged to bring the Reverend M. T. Kirby (Sogaku Shaku) to America to give the first public lectures on Zen after those of his Master (or Roshi) Shaku Soyen.

Kirby was a monk by nature, and psychologists could no doubt have a field day studying him. He was a scion of a fairly prosperous English family, but from early youth was inclined toward monkery. He joined a Roman Catholic order, but it proved too "worldly" for him (so he said). He thereafter went to Japan, with the example of Lafcadio Hearn[32] before him, became converted and studied under the great Master.

Like most Westerners and like nearly all university graduates, he had a terrible time trying to control his ego and his mind. Scholars either do not understand that the mind can be in a state of rest or they do not want it. It is like wishing to have your cake and eat it, too. Monks in zendos have been divided into (a) "rice-bags," who have come to escape the turmoil of life and have a place to stay, (b) "sutra reciters," whose delight is in the intellect, and (c) those with a real insight into *dharma*.

Kirby had already gone through the "rice-bag" stage, but controlling his mind was almost too much. Some Rinzai monks *seem* to be tinged with sadism. That is on the outside, for the Rinzai students recite the Four Vows

---

30 Later reprinted as *Zen for Americans*, but now widely available online under its original title.

31 Born in Ireland in 1862, died in Japan 1931. Author of many beautiful novels dealing with occult or spiritual experiences. In the Buddhist realm, particularly recommended are the novel *The Garden of Vision* and her biography of the Buddha, originally published as *The Splendour of Asia*.

32 1850-1904, Greek author of collections of Japanese legends. Emigrated to Ireland, the USA and finally Japan, where he settled.

of the *Bodhisattva*, and there is no absolute differentiation between oneself and another. Teachers really take it upon themselves to see that all devotees advance in the *dharma*, and it is no child's game. Only when the pupil succeeds may the teacher rest. So processes of discipline are taken very seriously.

Kirby had been raised in comfort. Suffering and tribulation were hardly known to him. He was trying to rise above difficulties he had never had to face. How could he go through the Buddha-experience if pain, poverty and disease were so foreign?

But instead of finding peace in the zendo, our brother was finding everything else. The master seemed to have become more and more impatient, more and more angry, more and more apt to administer "thirty blows"... actually.

After one severe thrashing, Kirby could stand it no more. He fled down the hill, threw his arms around a tree and sobbed in utter despair. In that instant, *it* happened—the *satori* experience, the reality.

I was a very young man when Kirby told me his story. In those days, we in California pictured Tibet as the land of the masters and the Himalayas as particularly holy. There was no distinction between magic and wonder-working and spiritual development. If you could perform phenomena, you must be especially advanced, it was thought.

At the same time, the Japanese had come here and introduced their Pure Land Buddhism. It was nothing like the folk-mythology concerning Tibet. It did not even resemble the early teachings that were originally recorded in the Pali language. So Kirby had to face an enormous task. But he was so successful that after a while he received a promotion and went to the Hawaiian Islands. He planted at least the seeds of the *dharma* there, and there has been a continuum of instruction in English.

Kirby could speak Japanese. At the time, Japan and Great Britain were allied. There were open conversations in his presence, and he warned me and others over and over again that the Japanese intended to occupy the Hawaiian Islands someday. Who believed him?

Buddhism teaches peace, Buddha teaches joy. The selfless religion opens only to a universal outlook, and here was the Reverend M. T. Kirby involved in Japanese imperialistic politics. He could not give up the *dharma* with which he was thoroughly imbued. So he left first Hawaii and then Japan and went to Ceylon where he became a Theravadin monk and may best be known as the teacher of Dr. Malalasekera[33].

On December 8, 1941, after Pearl Harbor, the British Secret Service took Kirby into protective custody. I vowed then and there that whenever anybody

---

33 Gunapala Malalsekera, 1899-1973, Sri Lankan academic and diplomat.

told me that my country, the United States, was in danger, I would go to the authorities. My friends, this leads to no satisfaction. The story of M. T. Kirby was repeated in part in the life of Nicol Smith (author of *Burma Road)* and Robert Clifton (Phra Sumangalo) and others. Before one can inform or warn his country, he should remember the old Greek story about the boy who cried "Wolf!"' This has been the attitude toward Americans who have had unusual entrees into exotic societies (unless, of course, they be journalists— then we believe anything!)

Kirby left two heritages, which might be called Theravada and Zen Buddhism. Theravada teachings flourish in Southeast Asia and rely on Pali texts. Sometime after Kirby left San Francisco, one Dr. Thompson arrived bringing the whole Tripitaka, the canon of Southern or Hinayana Buddhism. He also introduced the Siamese cat[34]. The scriptures have to date been put safely away, and there has been little serious study of the historical Buddha in our country, unless it be in universities. The Siamese cat has made Dr. Thompson famous forever.

Kirby introduced me to Beatrice Lane, who later became Mrs. Daisetz Suzuki. This brought me into contact with that marvellous literature of Mahayana, which takes one years to scan, many more to study. I believe that she, more than anyone else, inspired her husband in the work that has occupied much of his life.

The next introduction was Dr. Kenneth Saunders. He started out as a Christian missionary and became a deep student of Buddhist and other Oriental art. He gave grand lectures on Angkor Wat and Borubodor, and it was from him I learned about the "Lotus Gospel." He wrote at some length, my dear Koestler, on the Lotus in art, religion and symbology.

I first met the late Nyogen Senzaki early in 1920. Like Dr. Kirby, he had been a student-disciple of that wonderful Shaku Soyen. He occasionally attended meetings at the Hongwanji Temple on Pine Street where Kirby officiated. When that monk departed, he urged me to become friendly with his brother, a friendship that continued until the latter's death in 1957.

At that time, Senzaki-san had two quite different careers. He served as cook and valet and did any work, no matter how menial, to maintain his livelihood. On the other hand, he was a respected linguist and translator, well-versed in languages and literature, and a specialist on the German poet-philosopher Goethe. As a servant, he acted humbly toward everybody; as a scholar, people acted humbly toward him.

Kirby and Senzaki established "Mentorgarten." It was a sort of open forum

---

34 Joseph C. Thompson, 1874-1943, medical officer in the US Navy, for which he spied in Japan. Later became interested in psychoanalysis, moved to San Francisco and began to breed Siamese cats in a cattery he dubbed Mau Tien, "Cat Heaven."

for Asian subjects, though we did celebrate Japanese folk festivals and Mahayana religious holidays. There was no special emphasis on Zen, but we did have silences, especially at the end of meetings. Anyone who had been to Asia or could contribute from studies of Asian scriptures or direct investigation was welcome. Only one thing was forbidden, and that *absolutely*—speculation.

In our search and spiritual ventures, one of the most interesting of all persons contacted was Robert Stuart Clifton. He came to San Francisco around 1928, then began officiating at the Hongwanji Temple on Pine Street, the same place where I had met Kirby, Senzaki and Daisetz Suzuki.

Phra Sumangalo (R. Clifton)

Two aspects of Buddhism are presented by Hongwanji. It continues the Pure Land teachings, especially as formulated by Saint Shinran Shonin. This is called *tariki* in Japan, meaning salvation through other than self. But it is based on the "vow of Samantabhadra," which represents the *Bodhisattva* in an exceedingly high and profound form seeking to save all humanity from misery at any cost. The Pure Land methods are far more widespread than our literature or so-called study courses indicate, and neither on Pine Street nor in the Orient did I find the total separation of methodologies that one does in Christianity or even in Hinduism. Both in America and in Japan, Hongwanji promulgates the universal and Pure Land teachings together. And nowhere are there any statistics put forward to prove that any one Way is better than any other Way.

All Buddhism involves compassion: compassion and salvation are not separate. The whole career of Robert Clifton exemplified this. During his lifetime, he had crossed both the United States and the Pacific Ocean many times. He had been to Japan for Pure Land instruction. In New York, he met Sokei-an Sasaki and became convinced of Zen. He later became a novitiate at the Soto Temple in Tsurumi, between Yokohama and Tokyo. His spiritual realization gave him a universal outlook. Later in life, he also passed through the Theravadin discipline (for which he became known) and Tibetan (kept rather secret). He became known as Phra Sumangalo, a leading personality in the whole Buddhist world.

Partly through his efforts, as well as through the cooperation of others, there is now a World Buddhist Fellowship. Buddhists have accomplished what other religions have not: an organization including all sects and interpretations of their faith, a mutual recognition. It is regrettable that our State Department and press never took this man seriously. We are spending millions of dollars today in efforts, and they are not always successful, to obtain an equilibrium of status in Southeast Asia which was ours if we had listened to him. His name will go into history, if not into the press. The *Encyclopedia of Buddhism* will contain objective articles and historical data that our universities will later seek while the public remains ignorant of the true facts of a true Asia.

Did Phra Sumangalo find the "Great Peace?" He did exemplify love and compassion and has been recognized in many lands, by many people. Is this not enough for a "Lotus-man"?

Zen is Meditation

Book Excerpt from
The Lotus and the Universe

"Friends in dharma, be satisfied with your own heads. Do not put any false heads above your own. Then, minute after minute, watch your steps closely. These are my last words to you."
-Nyogen Senzaki in "The Iron Flute"

One can hardly repress tears. Twice have I seen this noble man melt: once on a celebration of Shaku Soyen's birthday and again on a celebration of the birthday of my first spiritual teacher, the Sufi Pir-o-Murshid Inayat Khan. With all his development, all his problems, all his sufferings, even being a *Bodhisattva* did not mean to lose his humanity, ever.

Friends, there is nothing in an emancipated soul that compels him to drop his humanity. The Sufi, the Yogi, the *Bodhisattva* may spend much effort in watching his footsteps closely. This is beyond the ken of the metaphysician, of the "false head." Zen is operational. It is based on discipline, practice, experience.

Zen for the West by Professor Sohaku Ogata has been mentioned. Sokei-an and Ruth Fuller Sasaki have contributed much. We now have excellent zendos. Indeed, we even have the Chinese coming out and instructing us in wisdom. We need no more false heads. "Kill the Buddha"—never. Kill the Mara[35]—yes.

The biography of Nyogen Senzaki is being written by others, whether piecemeal or complete, I do not know. The simple servant I met in 1920 has become a legendary figure. The great doctor of philosophy remains unknown. The Buddha-*dharma* claims there is no abiding ego. *Sensei* (teacher) used to say, "There is no such person as Nyogen Senzaki."

In 1926, he suddenly dropped all his learning and began to speak in pidgin English. He denied everything else and held us, for a time, strictly to meditation with nothing else but a word or two from Shaku Soyen, and tea. The Bible may teach "Naked came I out of my mother's womb and naked I shall return thither; the Lord gave, and the Lord hath taken away" (Job 1:21).

---

35 The demon that tried to seduce Gautama Buddha.

This is good Judaism, or Christianity—at funeral services. It is good wisdom always. Read the Gospel of St. Thomas and you may not be able to distinguish between that Jesus and a Zen master. It does not matter.

Yes, Senzaki-san gave me *koans,* and gave the others around me koans, too. It is not necessary to discuss them. The aim of the koan is *prajna.* This is translated as "wisdom" and loses its significance thereby. It may be called the operation of the One Mind. Read the "Sutra of the Sixth Patriarch" and try to prove it—to yourself.

One of the early visitors to the zendo in San Francisco was the Reverend Ishida, a Soto Zen tea-master. This was my first contact with a teacher of this school, and it was noticeable that he seemed more concerned with compassion *(karuna)* than with any other discipline or morality. He performed a tea ceremony and gave us the impressions intended by *The Book of Tea* by Okakura Kakuzo. The "Great Peace" is beyond the distinctions of Taoism, Buddhism or any other spiritual pattern.

The *Bodhisattva* is patterned after one of the great archetypes that we find in art, in folklore and in ritual, and Master Ishida was, to me, an incarnation of Samantabhadra, the *Bodhisattva* of Compassion. His tea ceremony had the same import as a pure Christ (if not Christian) communion.

Some Americans have accepted the tradition that the Dalai Lama is an incarnation of the *Bodhisattva* of Mercy, Avalokitesvara. Avalokitesvara (Kwan Yin, Kwannon) represents Mercy; Samantabhadra, Compassion; Manjusri, Wisdom; Maitreya, the "future Buddha" and so forth. And then there is Fudo...ah Fudo!

Fudo is Jesus driving the moneylenders from the temple. Fudo is Jesus castigating the scribes and Pharisees. Fudo is Jeremiah standing before the king. Fudo is Bodhidharma refusing to praise the emperor. Fudo is the wise guide who does not confuse sentimentality with love.

Roshi Furukawa of Engaku-ji, Kamakura, was the very embodiment of Fudo. Many only knew him as a severe mentor, and yet because of him, disciples experienced *satori.* What good is all the negativity, guised as mercy, if it does not lead to deliverance from sorrow? When the pupil fails, the *karma* of the failure is on the teacher. Buddhism does not recognize ego-personality, and people are in error if they presume any self-teacher is whipping any self-pupil because of failure. The self-centered person cannot comprehend the ways of *Bodhisattva.*

And yet when I was privileged to visit Roshi Furukawa's temple at Kamakura in 1956, my friend Kiichi Okuda and I were received with open arms and treated as a school boy treats his best pals after a long absence. There was nothing but love and joy.

The zendo in San Francisco also hosted the Chinese Master, the Venerable Tai Hsu. He was the chief teacher of the Chinese Lin-chi School, which corresponds to the Japanese Rinzai. Much milder than the Reverend Furuka-wa, he was just as adamant on one point: that speculation has no place in Buddhist teachings. Here he failed; he did not impress America, which has, alas, only too often accepted both speculation and personality as the doors to what is called "Buddhism." Tai Hsu and Senzaki-san used to communicate by writing. Our Japanese mentor told us he did not understand Mandarin, but could easily read the classics. One day the two Buddhists were invited to the house of Mrs. Leila Havens in Piedmont (near Oakland, California). By some mistake, they took the Claremont Avenue train and got off at the Piedmont Avenue crossing in Oakland. Nobody was there to meet them.

Senzaki-san told us that after a while he became very nervous and walked back and forth in a fidgety manner. Master Tai Hsu looked at him and said, "Isn't this a wonderful day? Look at all the trees in bloom and see the beautiful flowers. How we can enjoy ourselves here!" Our Japanese friend at once apologized. Just then a car that had been sent to look for them turned up and they were quickly escorted to their destination.

The event resulted in a marked change in Senzaki-san's behavior and attitude. He himself henceforth showed less of Fudo and more of Samantabhadra.

Tai Hsu's later career was very tragic. In his organization, the *buddha*, the *dharma* and the *sangha* were not so properly united that the wise or illuminated person controlled the destiny of Buddhism. The tradition that a holy man must not touch money has often resulted in funds being misused on both a large and small scale. The successes of all Tai Hsu's campaigns were frittered away. But he did influence Dwight Goddard, who gave us *The Buddhist Bible* and tried to present the whole of the *dharma* to the American public.

In 1923, the Zen Nyogen Senzaki met the Sufi Pir-o-Murshid Inayat Khan in the home of Murshida Rabia Ada Martin in San Francisco. The two men sat down at a table, looked into each other's eyes and both immediately entered into that *samadhi* that so many lecturers tell us about but do not experience themselves. The details have been written in Senzaki's memories. They corroborate Emerson and dismay dualists.

After that, the Zen master considered himself to be a disciple in Sufism and the Sufi teacher, in turn, regarded himself as a devotee in Zen Buddhism. In the Hadith, the Prophet Muhammad said, "Seek wisdom even as far as China," but the path of the Muslim seeking such wisdom is not always easy, either.

Senzaki-san showed himself to be a universal person in other respects. His favorite quotations were not from Buddhist texts. One was John Tauler's, "The eye with which I see God is the same eye with which God sees me." Another was from Abdul Baha: "People of the world, you are as branches of the tree and leaves of the branch." He did not only quote them, he lived them.

Shortly after the zendo was moved to Los Angeles, I was in severe difficulties, and when publicly attacked, a former friend who was functioning as a Buddhist teacher turned on me. At that time, I had to visit Los Angeles, and when I entered the zendo, was amazed to hear *sensei* (teacher) excoriate this pseudo-Buddhist in no uncertain terms. It was almost in the language of a Henry Miller. In a short time, the *karma* this man had set into operation overtook him and he disappeared.

At another time, two women I knew were going around Los Angeles spreading vicious gossip about a Vedanta swami. True, all swamis are not masters or saints, and not even every Vedanta monk has reached a high state. But I found that this particular swami was totally incapable of any sort of vice or tort or misdemeanour. That sort of evil did not appear capable of having a foothold in him.

A personal vindication of the swami resulted in these women trying to spread the same gossip about me, and they immediately followed it up by visiting our Zen friend. As soon as they came to the zendo steps, he walked out and greeted them: "Get out or I call the police!" This was rather a shocker to those who had never heard of Fudo.

"But Mr. Senzaki, you do not know what we have come for!"

"Get out or I'll call the police!"

"But Mr. Senzaki, we wish to join the temple and study with you."

In those days, our friend had a battered old hat which he often wore. He took it from the shelf and walked down the front steps.

"Where are you going?"

"To call the police!"

I never heard from or of these women again, and there was no more personal gossip about either this person or the swami.

Not that Senzaki-san always admired the swamis, either. He called on another one who gave a sermon on how to "Be Equal-Minded In Pleasure and Pain." Our Japanese friend said he enjoyed the talk so much, he would like to have an interview. This was granted.

There was a vase on a table in the waiting room, and just as the door opened for the interview, the monk got up in an awkward manner and knocked the vase over.

"You clumsy fool," cried the swami, "that vase cost me $200!"

"Oh," said Senzaki, taking out his wallet, "I'm very sorry."

To the amazement of the Indian, he showed the wallet that contained hundreds of dollars (at that time), calmly peeled off the amount requested, gave it to the swami with a flourish and a bow and departing said, "Thank you very much. Now I know the meaning of being imperturbable in pleasure and pain. Thank you very much."

These and many other anecdotes prove that a Zen monk seldom, if ever, behaves like a Zen monk of the lecture hall or necessarily like the questionable translations of Chinese tales of centuries ago. My friend Paul Reps became interested in Senzaki-san shortly after the Japanese went to Los Angeles and helped in the publication of *Zen Flesh, Zen Bones, A Hundred Zen Stories* and other works, which are particularly Zen-ish, not based on speculative enigmas.

Sensei introduced the koan teaching. This does not mean—or prevent—a witty saying: "In Zen there are no miracles." Once there is a spiritual attachment, neither time nor space nor conditioned existence *(samsara)* can interfere. Someday one may speak as plainly of occult experiences as of physical ones. I hope someday this will be permitted and welcomed.

Here one can only relate our last conversation with Senzaki-san in 1957. I had returned from Japan the long way, and entering the zendo, remarked: "When Sam Lewis and Sogen Asahina met, were there one, two or no persons in the room?"

"Have some tea," he replied.

Further conversation was unnecessary. Both of us knew a phase had been completed. The koan—nay the koans—had been solved. If anyone asks, what did Nyogen Senzaki give me, the answer is: *buddhahridaya* (Buddha heart).

Seek and ye shall find.

Learning Zen from Zen Teachers

Book Excerpt from
The Lotus and the Universe

The Cat's Yawn—title of Sokei-an Sasaki's work.

Some may slander or argue against Zen.
They are playing with fire, trying to burn the heavens in vain.
A true student of Zen should take their words as sweet dew-drops.
And that sweetness will also be forgotten when he enters into the realm of
non-thinking.
—from "Shodoka[36]," translation by Nyogen Senzaki

Friends, *Bodhisattvas*:

It is very hard to write those experiences that take one deep into the recesses of personality, or beyond personality. The emotions that accompany or follow meetings with those more advanced in the spiritual realm vary, and one has to express them in terms that cannot convey these variations.

Sokei-an Sasaki was not a swami Ramdas or Sufi whose love vibrations permeate the atmosphere. Nor did he show power or beauty or repose. He was in one sense the most ordinary person one could meet and in another sense the most complete. If his followers seem slightly fanatical or devoted, this has been because of the *dharma* transmission left by him, and no one who has fallen under his influence has ever been the same afterwards.

My first visit to him in New York took place in September 1930. I was then in part a guest of the Roerich Museum, which was the center of many activities. Among them were groups dedicated to Tibetan-Mongolian Buddhism and to the Theravadin teachings (Maha Bodhi Society). It was there that I was first told about Sokei-an, a Zen monk living in New York.

The Roerich Museum tried the impossible: egocentric Buddhism. There was no *sangha* (community of devotees) in the usual sense, and soon the individuals were in conflict. Some of this story is too well-known to discuss here. But one of the final efforts of Professor Roerich was to establish a cancer

---

36 Chinese Zen discourse dated to the 8th century CE, usually attributed to Yongija Xuanjue.

research center in the Himalayas, where people seemed to be unusually free from this disease. Unfortunately, even now there has been no proper world survey to ascertain why people in some places do not develop this disease; in other words, there is no etiology (study of causes), yet we still seek cures.

Sokei-an had then only recently opened his zendo. His teacher was another disciple of the oft-mentioned master Shaku Soyen. He had learned to amalgamate the verbal and the super-verbal, the intellectual and the *prajna*. Fortunately, his teachings have been preserved in "The Cat's Yawn."[37] To me, this is the same as the "lion's roar" of the Buddha, the "wind-bell" of the San Francisco zendo (Soto School) or the "thundering silence."

I remember having attended nine lecture-meetings of Sokei-an, and after each talk he permitted just six questions. He never dodged, he never equivocated, he went straight to the point, and I know of no occasion on which anybody ever went away confused or dissatisfied. This has been confirmed by several of his early disciples. Besides these, I was fortunate to have had a number of private interviews and meditations.

In common with all Zen monks, Sokei-an considered speculation as most dangerous. There is a great gap between the devotees of the First Zen Institute on Waverly Place in New York and the respectable who have attended Professor Suzuki's lectures. At the Institute, they learn and practice Zen; on University Heights, the chemistry of the orange-peel is so alluring that they have no idea of the juice that quenches thirst and gives life.

Following the Rinzai pattern, Sokei-an used koans and, indeed, paid more attention to them than did his "Uncle" Nyogen Senzaki. Buddha had taught that all humanity had the enlightenment and perfect wisdom but did not know it. The koan is one method by which we may realize we are truly "sons-of-God." Discussion only hampers.

Sokei-an explained and discussed *dharma*. The word *dharma* (philologically connected with the word *form*) may be interpreted to mean "law, essence, universal harmony, thingness," even *Tao*. It is human beings who have divided the *dharma*: the "legal" (Sanskrit, *astika*) schools now being known as Hindu, and the "illegal" (Sanskrit, *nastika*) include Buddhism. But each teaches *dharma*, whether as *sanatana dharma* (eternal way or perennial philosophy), *arya dharma* (noble truth, etc.) or *saddharma* (perfect wisdom). In Sokei-an they were all blended—there was just *dharma*. It is to the nonconformists that one leaves discussions about *Zen*, whatever *they* mean.

Between lectures and answers to questions, there was revealed a profound knowledge of the *dharma*, including the wisdom of the Upanishads, the cosmic Indian psychology (no European has touched more than the sur-

---

37 The title of the journal formerly issued by the First Zen Institute in New York City. Back issues appear at www.firstzen.org

face of what this Japanese monk knew), the basic philosophies of Mahayana and a lot more. One learned to transcend the time and space and even to "see" into the future.

My friends, do not seek such faculties. It will bring only misunderstanding and enemies. You will be misunderstood. Find your true nature first and then, if you will, look a little.

In 1945, I returned to New York, full of anticipation, to learn that on the day of my arrival Sokei-an Sasaki had entered into *parinirvana*[38]. It was the saddest period of my life. Since then it has been impossible to experience such sorrow. Devotees on Waverly Place, New York and Waverly Place, San Francisco will understand.

In 1956, while travelling with Kiichi Okuda in Japan, we visited Mrs. Ruth Fuller Sasaki the first thing upon our arrival in Kyoto. "What did Sokei-an teach you?" she asked. "I cannot tell," I replied. "There was nothing secret, it is simply that one cannot quantitatively tell." No, friends, there is nothing secret.

Suzukis may come and Salingers go, but friends, if you are near New York City, you should visit the First Zen Institute. Occasional visits show the remarkable development in *dharma* of those who are curious or sincere and who do not determine their spiritual future by leaning on anybody else.

There was at one time an artist named Sabro Hasegawa living in San Francisco who had rooms in the then-prospering American Academy of Asian Studies. I told him that Nyogen Senzaki had taught me seven forms of laughter. He said, "Come here sometime, when nobody is around, and I'll show you the *eighth form of laughter.*" It turned out so, and by the *prajna*— that universal impersonal communion-communication—this aspect of the *dharma* was awakened.

The laughter was also part of the entry to Japan. While metaphysicians lecture about synchronicity, it is interesting that on the day of this person's arrival in Japan, the first Sesshu exhibition opened. Sesshu was one of the greatest—if not the greatest—of Japanese Zen artists. Sabro had lectured interminably on him, and yet it was my fortune to be at the opening of this show, and to enjoy it to the full.

Someday it may be possible to write an "advice to diplomats," but this is useless in a world that proclaims Christianity and confines "love" not so much to sex as to a very narrow portion even of sex—so that instead of love (in a true sense) being much vaster than sex, sex (in any sense) has come to be much greater than the "love" proclaimed by the media. Exit love, exit life, and there can only be physical and mental debilitation.

---

38 "Nirvana-beyond," or "after-death." Usually used to refer to someone who achieves nirvana in his/her lifetime.

When Kiichi Okuda and I visited Master Furukawa at Engakuji (described in the last chapter), we were sent to his successor, Roshi Sogen Asahina. This master signaled for us to sit in meditation and immediately: the "lotus experience"—no longer any Kiichi Okuda or Sogen Asahina or Sam Lewis and yet the reality of "I am the vine and ye are the branches thereof."

After it ended, Roshi spoke to us about God and Christ. There is no time between "here and eternity," and the Zen experience is *sudden*, but it is not a sudden philosophy that is presented. In mathematics, one jumps from the numbers to the infinite—suddenly—and the same in the spiritual experience.

Then we were taken through the compound behind the Engakuji monastery and saw scenes described in L. Adams Beck's writings. And the fact that I knew about Roshi Shaku Soyen was enough to have me honored and taken to the tomb of his teacher. When there is no ego-self, there are no walls, no barriers. This is true the world over.

As we left the monastery, I said to Okuda-san, "This was an omen." Though just arrived in Japan, the doors had already been opened. And it was so, for over the next month and a half, we penetrated places not usually open to either tourists or Japanese. But as Edna St. Vincent Millay has beautifully put it: "The world stands out on every side/ No wider than the heart is wide."[39]

Just where does Zen begin and where does it end? Later on, Mrs. Sasaki sent us to Phillip Karl Eidman, then staying in Kyoto, a living *Bodhisattva* if I have ever met one. He explained the relation of the different schools and sects to one another. I am only hoping that he is selected, if he has not been already, to instruct Americans about Buddhism.

The Nishi Hongwanji Temple at Kyoto, where Professor Eidman resided in 1956, contains one of the most beautiful gardens I have ever seen and some of the most exemplary art work. There also was a form of sudden-*prajna* experience. When the self ceases as a discrete being, the whole universe may be opened before us. This was a teaching of Lord Buddha. This is inherent in the actual *dharma*. True, Buddhism is based on the experiences of life, and perhaps pure religion in every form is experience—from very simple, emotional types to union-with-the-All wherein oneself is not.

I remember on the first day in Japan, stopping at Tsurumi at the great Sojiji Zen Temple where Okuda-san asked me, "How do you feel?"

"I feel very strange," I replied.

"Well, you are in a strange country."

"But that is not why I feel strange. I feel strange because I do not feel strange. I feel I have come home. I know these trees, this landscape, the

---

39 (1892-1950), American poet, playwright, early feminist activist. The lines are from her poem "Renascence."

surroundings. I know the people, the ceremonies, the robes. The only thing I do not know is the language."

When we later visited Sojiji, we met the Roshi, who immediately gave instructions in Zen. Instructions? The "pagoda-communication" or communion is not a dualism between one and another. Theosophists, who affirm that there are seven planes of existence, are liable to treat them like a chessboard of the "Alice-Through-the-Looking-Glass" experience. Neither are they like the Hanging Gardens of ancient Babylon, which symbolized them. Each phase transcends the previous one, and the six lower planes belong to the wheel-of-life (not necessarily the wheels ordinarily depicted). The finite in consciousness does not grasp the infinite any more than school arithmetic grasps the infinite of multiple integration.

It was my privilege in Japan to be introduced to the Kegon, Kobo Daishi Shingon and Shingi Shingon teachings; to have visited the Royal Cemetery and, ultimately, the Imperial Grounds and Imperial Botanical Gardens, the outer semblances of inner union. When a biography or autobiography is written, the details may be supplied.

We have set up too many barriers, or rather we have permitted exotics to set up too many barriers before us, to enter into proper communication with Asians. The Viet Nam complex is only one phase of it.

Dharma Transmission

Excerpt from Paper

(Editor's note: This paper was written after 1963, since it refers to the death of Robert Clifton, aka Phra Sumangalo, which occurred in that year.)

Grandpa Roshi

Grandpa Roshi (the Venerable Shaku Soyen) returned to San Francisco in 1906. On his first trip to the U.S. in 1893 (to the Columbia Exposition in Chicago to speak at the World Congress of Faiths), he had met a Mrs. Russell of San Francisco. She had invited him to return and stay at her home in a sort of village near the city called Oceanside. It has long since disappeared along with her home, so it is impossible to make a pilgrimage to the first Zen shrine in America.

***

Grandpa Roshi brought two of his sons: Daisetz and Nyogen. To Daisetz he said, "You are my skin, my flesh, my bones." To Nyogen he said, "You are my marrow, my heart." Then he returned to Japan. From Daisetz, we get Zen philosophy, not to be confused with what is called "Zenism." From Nyogen we have the *dharma* transmission, no relation to Zenism.

***

Great-grandpa Roshi lies buried in a grotto at Kamakura, Japan. Grandpa Roshi had two daughters. One of them, L. Adams Beck, has described this grotto in her *The Garden of Vision*. The other, Beatrice Lane, married her brother-in-dharma, Daisetz. She wrote, she collaborated and she left the world. Her husband became famous.

***

Three ladies have had the *dharma* transmission in this line: L. Adams Beck, Beatrice Lane and Ruth Fuller Sasaki. This has nothing to do with Zenism.

***

The Reverend M. T. Kirby had been a Roman Catholic monk. He did not obtain enlightenment. He went to Japan and studied under Grandpa Roshi. He became enlightened and received the name of Sagaku Shaku.

He Kwang met Kirby the first month of 1920. At that time, there were no laws by Zenists about the behavior of Zen monks. Sagaku Shaku told the story of his enlightenment. He told it plainly, openly and like a child—or a scientist.

Sagaku Shaku gave instructions in Pali Scriptures and in Zen meditation. He told about the historical Buddha. He did not see any Buddhism apart from Buddha. He did not see any Buddha apart from Buddhism. There were no rules in those days by scholars or metaphysicians. Only that which was connected with Buddha Sakya Muni was Buddhism, but Buddhism was connected with both Lord Buddha and Amida, the Infinite Light.

Sagaku Shaku was so successful he was promoted. He went to the Hawaiian Islands and deposited the *dharma* with the Reverend Ernest Hunt. In San Francisco, he turned things over to his brother-in-*dharma*, Nyogen Senzaki.

***

Nyogen Senzaki was a homeless monk. He worked as a menial. He had been a professor. He knew many languages and much literature. He regarded this learning as a jockey regards extra weight in a race. This was before the days of Zenism.

***

We had the "Mentorgarten." It was an open forum. Anybody who had been to Asia could speak. We sat around the fire and listened. We had short meditations. If there was no speaker, we had longer meditations. Everything was informal. Any knowledge was accepted. Only one thing was barred—speculation. Speculation was the one evil. We had many great Buddhists come and go. They all said the same thing: speculation was the one evil. This was before the days of Zenism.

***

The Prophet Muhammad said, "I am an ordinary man like you." Nyogen always acted as if he were an ordinary man like others. He had greater scholastic learning than most of us and hid it; he had greater wit than most of us and did not hide that.

The Mentorgarten was a place of learning, of entertainment, comradery and meditations. We meditated according to the teachings of Shaku Soyen.

***

Shaku Soyen had written *Sermons of a Buddhist Abbot*. We did not study it. We did not reverence Shaku Soyen. Nyogen treated him as if he had been his father. Nyogen was an orphan and his early history reminded us of King Arthur. We regarded him as a sort of spiritual King Arthur. His meditative prowess was his sword.

***

Nyogen did not tell us much about himself or much about Shaku Soyen, excepting on rare occasions. He had us become acquainted with his atmosphere.

***

In 1926, the twenty-year probation put on Nyogen by Shaku Soyen ended. The first zendo was opened. No more entertainment, excepting on special holidays. No more discussion excepting on special holidays. We learned to meditate. We jumped from 15-minute periods to half an hour to an hour, sometimes two hours. We had theoretical breaks every 15 minutes.

At first 15 minutes seemed like an aeon; after a while, 15 minutes seemed like a breath.

***

We did not waste any time trying postures. We kept the back straight. We learned the Zen breathing. We then went out to battle with our egos. After a while one of us attained enlightenment and was named "Zoso". As soon as this happened, we were sure Nyogen had the *dharma* transmission.

***

After Nyogen went to Los Angeles, this one said to Zoso, "Nyogen is not a homeless monk, Nyogen is a master, he is more than a master, he has the *dharma* transmission." "Of course." We vowed to silence until one of us was left. Zoso is gone, Nyogen is gone, and when Nyogen was gone it was discovered—or rather uncovered—that he was the *dharma*-master of the age.

Zoso and this one did not take our disciplines from Zenists. Our speech was our speech, silence our silence.

Nyogen was of the Rinzai School and used harsh methods. The Reverend Gido Ishida was of the Soto School and used soft methods. We did not learn anything about the differences of schools, we only studied the methods toward enlightenment. Ishida seemed all heart, Nyogen seemed little heart, but this was our illusion.

***

One meets a teacher, perhaps on common ground. The teacher accepts. Then generations pass. The pupils of the pupils of that teacher reject. Whether they teach that the ego is real or unreal, they reject. Their teacher is always a special case. Then the children of the enlightened keep the world in more darkness than the children of the dark.

Nyogen used to say, "There is no such person as *Nyogen Senzaki*." Now that we have the Zenists, there are persons, there are people and there are differences.

***

If Gido Ishida offered "the taste of honey," soon the pot of honey came and transformed Nyogen Senzaki. This man, both exceedingly fair and exceedingly stern, was transformed in a moment and never returned to his Fudo pattern.

***

Master Tai Hsu could change an atmosphere and an audience. He did not have to preach joy. He did not have to say a single word about "enlightenment." He took all the weight of the zendo.

***

Master Tai Hsu behaved like some of us thought a master should behave. We always went away lightened and happy. Meditation became a joy, not a chore.

***

Not long after Master Tai Hsu departed, Roshi Furukawa came from Engakuji Temple in Kamakura. Too late. You cannot bring Fudo back after Samantabhadra has taken over.

***

It is folly to think in dualistic terms. Roshi Furukawa appeared as Fudo in San Francisco. Years later, when myself as Kiichi Okuda and my appearance as He Kwang came to the temple in Kamakura, we were turned away by the attendant: "Roshi was very aged, Roshi was in retirement, Roshi would see nobody." We sent him our cards.

We could hear footsteps running rapidly down the hill. Roshi welcomed us with joy and the light-heartedness of a child. We were not master and pupils, we were not even *sangha*-members. We were boys on a picnic.

The first meeting with Roshi Furukawa was to experience the hard sternness of the traditional Rinzai monk. The last meeting was to experience "unless you be as little children, yours is not the kingdom of heaven." Let it remain that way.

***

Professor Perlham Nahl used to come occasionally to Mentorgarten. He had been an art teacher at the University of California where one had studied drawing with him. A friendship has been established.

Professor Nahl went to Japan to study and returned a convert to Zen Buddhism. He introduced the principle of immediacy. He practiced the One Mind. He illustrated the teaching both in his own work and by introducing both Chinese and Japanese instructors. He became responsible for bringing Professor Obata to Berkeley. The doors were opened.

When the doors were opened, there was a great increase of interest in the Orient. Professor Nahl introduced the real and hidden values in the Zero and in the Infinite. One still remembers them.

***

In 1915, Professor Cassius Keyser of the Mathematics Department of Columbia University came to Berkeley to lecture on fourth dimensional and non-Euclidean geometries and on hyperspace. He introduced us into what

84

he later called, "The Pastures of Wonder." The more one studied Keyser, the more one learned about zero and infinity and hyperspace and non-Euclidean geometry and psychology and everything else. Among his pupils was the late Count Alfred Korzybski.

One could discuss the zero and infinity and trans-space of Keyser with Professor Nahl and the relation of these projections with actual *satori* and *samadhi* experiences. There were no social bars, there were no institutional bars.

Some mathematicians threw out their own George Cantor for presuming the infinite might be real. We had no ecclesiasts then to throw out social peasants who found the infinite to be real.

***

Years later one gave a public lecture on "Infinity and Space in Mathematics, Art and Spiritual Awakening." An elderly lady arose: "Where did you learn this?" It was Miss Katherine Ball, long-time art teacher in San Francisco and specialist in Korean and Buddhist Art.

"I have taught thousands of people, and I think three understood me," she said. "You are one of them."

One learned much about oriental art from her. This was one form of *dharma* transmission.

***

Hierarchical Zen stands out as the greatest contribution from Uncle Nyogen. He told us the stories of Mahakasyapa and Ananda. Ananda was the cousin and friend of Lord Buddha but never received the enlightenment during the Tathagata's span of life. And when he tried to get the "secret" from Mahakasyapa, the latter turned on him and cried, "Ananda!" Then he was enlightened.

***

Tathagata Sakya Muni never presented any "Buddhism." He came to restore *arya dharma*. All he discussed was *arya dharma* (noble truth or essence). For our purposes it is not different from *sanatana dharma* (eternal way), which Aldous Huxley has loosely interpreted as "Perennial Philosophy." It also inspired Nietzsche and other great savants of the West.

***

We are taught that if we become enlightened, we could write sutras ourselves. But nobody expects others to accept that! Yet Sagaku Shaku introduced us into "The Sutra of the Sixth Patriarch." This poor beggar chap Hui Neng was not very welcome among the elite. The story of the transmission of *dharma*, robe and bowl has become an idyll. But let any beggar monk come into our respectable places, and the whole thing would be repeated.

***

85

It is very unconvincing that any eternal God of justice should stop revelation at any particular point in time or with any particular people.

***

The Bible says that the risen Jesus gave so many instructions that not all the books in the world could contain them. Muhammad said: "Quran was revealed in seven dialects and each has an inner and outer meaning." Human institutions will have none of that. So there is a great gap between "Buddhism" and *dharma* transmission. The Christian people do not accept that Jesus gave all those teachings. The Muslims do not accept that Quran has so many meanings. And the speculators, taking over the vocabulary, do not relish *dharma* transmission.

***

Jesus started out with the Beatitudes. The great Brihadaranyaka Upanishad explains the importance and immensity of *ananda* (bliss). People say "The Garden of Eden." He Kwang says "The Gan of Bliss." Why should the word *gan*[40] be translated (as "garden" or "paradise") and the word *eden* not be translated? The Upanishads emphasize the Universal Bliss that is found in all beings from the grade of humankind (or *manas*) up through infinity. It is *ananda* that separates humanity from the animals.

***

He Kwang offers the Ananda story as a koan. So many people write books on koans who have never been under the koan discipline. Uncle Nyogen gave the *ananda*-story and the *ananda*-koan. Now everybody is unhappy. We say, "The kingdom of heaven is within you." Jesus said, "The kingdom of heaven is at hand." When people go on the path of *dharma* transmission, this will be a very valuable koan.

***

In the days when the teachings of Lord Buddha were regarded as the basis of Buddhism, we used to say:
May all peoples be peaceful,
May all peoples be blissful, May all peoples be happy.
So He Kwang invites everybody to the Ananda-koan.

Roshi (Sokei-an Sasaki)

This is a most difficult task. Unless one understands that we have at least three bodies as Indian wisdom teaches; unless one comprehends the potentiali-

---

40 The Hebrew words *gan eden* are what appear in the Genesis 2 account of creation.

86

ties of the three *kaya*[41] beyond such limitations, it is impossible to explain Roshi.

The First Zen Institute of America in New York stemmed from him. There is an active movement in *dharma* and *dharma* transmission extending from him, but while we persist in the valleys of individuation we cannot understand a person who broke all the laws of culture and tradition without breaking any of them.

Uncle Nyogen was asked, "Is the Zen monk bound by causation or is he outside of causation?" Uncle taught, "The Zen monk is one with the law of causation." Unless you can understand and appreciate, you cannot grasp the incarnation of the "Cat's Yawn" known as Sokei-an Sasaki.

***

1930 was like any other year of importance in spiritual history. One came to the Roerich Museum in New York City to study the *dharma* in art-form. Nicholas Roerich gave us the *dharma* transmission in painting. It has been done before. Kenneth Saunders had explained the *dharma* transmission in sculpture and architecture. We did not need the verbal-transmission. Thus one entered the zendo of that remarkably ordinary man. When Bodhidharma faced the Emperor of China and told him there was nothing sacred in the entire universe, he might have also said that everything in the entire universe was sacred—for this was the teaching of Avatamsaka (Kegon) transmission.

Roshi Sokei-an Sasaki was one of the most approachable men ever encountered. Not until one met Swami Ranganathananda Maharaj of the Ramakrishna Order years later did one meet someone so approachable, so simple and utterly profound that words are but the shadows of conveyance.

One heard nine lectures, but had innumerable personal and impersonal sessions.

***

Each lecture was followed by six questions, this being the upper limit. If you were an intellectual, you received philosophy. But if you had the *dharma*-eye, you *saw*. One of his lectures was on "*dharma* eye." This makes a reality of *samma-dhrishti* ("right views"), the first principle of Lord Buddha's "eightfold Path."

When you received this spiritual *darshan* (interview), you received. When you were taken beyond *maya*, you entered the realm of the Immeasurable.

Once Roshi was asked if he could see into the future. He answered, "It is too terrible." *Dharma* transmission is not intellectual, it does not stop at *manas* (mind). It includes *vijnana*, *ananda* and *prajna*, which intellectuals do not understand.

---

41 Mahayana Buddhism proposes three *kaya*, or "bodies," of the Buddha—*nirmanakaya* ("transformation body"), *sambhogakaya* ("enjoyment body") and *dharmakaya* ("dharma body").

Indian languages have no terms for *electricity* and *magnetic* and *turbine*. Indians do not object to adopting our terms for these. English has no equivalent for *vijnana, ananda, prajna* and *samadhi*, and so we grasp any words— appropriate or inappropriate—and become confused. The end is likely as not psychedelism or trance-mediumship, which have no relation to these things.

***

Roshi opened these eyes to the whole history of the period 1930-1945[42]. Some of these records were miraculously preserved from a fire which destroyed twenty-five year's research and a whole oriental library. Roshi took one into *prajna* without destroying levels between the seemingly finite and the seemingly infinite.

***

The painting of the Buddha's *parinirvana* shows that the artist had the *dharma* transmission. *Naraka, Preta, Tirthaga-yoni, Raksha* and *Asura* are the creatures of darkness. They were welcomed at the Buddha's tomb. These are Sanskrit words. They have no European equivalents unless we accept that there are more things in heaven and earth than are thought of in our philosophies. We do not do that. We call what we do not know "unreal." Roshi explained these terms.

***

In the "grand experience," as illustrated by the Cosmic Wheel, all the above creatures exist, within or without. The world, especially the Western world, has refused to accept what has not been experienced. You cannot experience radioactivity and relativity and quantum mechanics without the experience of the laboratory outside. How does one know what is experienced in the laboratory within if one does not go in?

***

Sagaku Shaku explained the four Stages of meditation by lecturing. Roshi explained the four Stages of meditation by meditation and *dharma* transmission.

We sat comfortably. One is not convinced that special *asanas* (postures) causally produce *samadhi* or *satori*. One is not convinced that anything can causally bring *samadhi* or *satori*.

Uncle Daisetz has given long articles. Roshi brought his presence. "A single day with the Lord is worth a thousand years."

***

After Roshi, the scriptures became open books. To the world, the scriptures

---

42 Both Sokei-an Sasaki and Nyogen Senzaki, as Japanese nationals, were interned in concentration camps by the U.S. government during a portion of World War II, Sasaki on the East coast, Senzaki on the West.

are full of mysteries or contradictions or even falsehoods, but after Roshi they became clear channels of light.

***

Uncle Nyogen used to say that Tathagata said: "I see now that all creatures have perfect enlightenment. But they do not know it, I must go and teach it to them."

Roshi gave the "Cat's Yawn." "Come clothed or unclothed, with a gift or without a gift." Roshi gave the Cat's Yawn.

Maya means the "measurable" not the unreal. How can a sane mind consider the *unreal?* What is unreal? What is real?

***

Since all the scriptures cannot include all the teachings of Jesus, since the Quran teaches that if all the pens were one pen and all the seas ink, they could not present the Revelation of Allah, one does not apologize for providing more details of Roshi.

***

One day a person asked Roshi if one could smoke and still have enlightenment. This was long before tobacco was honored by being accused of occupying the seat of Iblis. At another time, it was alcohol. Indeed, anybody may be accused of occupying the seat of Iblis except the ego itself, which according to real Buddhist teaching is identified with the Evil One.

Roshi said, "That is a good question and it needs consideration. Pardon me." Then he slowly withdrew a cigarette from a package, very slowly got out a lighter, very slowly took three puffs, put the package and lighter back into his pocket and asked, "Will you please remember that question?"

***

Ruth Fuller will go to glory, if she is not already there, by the aid she gave Roshi on all levels, even extending to marriage to protect him.[43]

***

The saddest day of one's life occurred in 1945. One was going to New York again, full of anticipation and glow. One was so happy. On the day one arrived, Roshi took his last breath.

One appeared at the funeral in tears. One seldom weeps; many were in tears. One is almost in tears as one writes. This is not a good condition to be in while writing on *dharma* transmission.

***

Whatever has happened, the Cat's Yawn can still be heard. The First Institute of Zen in New York can still be visited.

---

43 Their marriage ultimately freed him from an American internment camp.

Metta[44]

Physics, biology and psychology are the basic sciences of the West, and all other sciences seem to be related to one or more of them in some way. But there are also sciences that apply to aspects of the universe or of life and one may say these belong to heart. Heart-sciences do not conflict with other sciences but need their own terms, drawn from heart-experiences.

***

In the world of heart it is possible to establish relations of harmony or relations of unity. In the field of harmony there is no one necessarily superior to the other. When two worms copulate they are both male and female. When two hearts copulate there is no male, no female, no superior, no inferior.

***

In our historical career Phra Sumangalo and He Kwang each taught the other, each learned from the other and together they cooperated, working together.

***

Phra Sumangalo taught by the heart without discarding the book. Now we have types of "Buddhism" that discard both heart and book. Belonging to one school (in our sense) he taught at temples of others' schools. He never departed from the teachings about Buddha, and if he did not achieve the full heart-view of Buddha he never neglected the Perfect One, the Fully Enlightened One, the Most Supreme Buddha.

***

When Robert was at Sojiji near Yokohama he reported that the chances of a peasant for enlightenment over a cultured person, in particular over a Ph.D., were 15 to 1. Our anti-Christs who deny and defy that little children will get into the kingdom of heaven before the rest of us are always horrified by such corroboration.

***

Champion is he in every school of inner discipline who can unlearn, who can unburden himself. When those who call themselves Buddhists will do this, that separative faith will be saved. When those who do not call themselves Buddhists will do that, the *dharma* will be transmitted even though in an untraditional manner.

***

The tender-hearted have to receive the blows from all the world. Phra Sumangalo left his blessings to the poor, half-learned peasants of Viet Nam whom we have been ignoring all too long. The hypocrisy of perfumed words only adds to the criminality of unwise acts.

44 Pali language term in Buddhism for the world of heart, or compassion.

How to be a Buddhist?
How to be a Buddha!

Journal Article

(Editor's Note: Written for Roshi Taizen Saito, Sojiji, Tsurumi, Japan. First printed in The Western Buddhist, *Autumn 1959.)*

There are many people in all parts of the world who claim to be Buddhists, and some say there are 500 million followers of this form of *dharma*. Yet although they accept this huge figure, many of them have been speaking in derisive terms of others and one is not always sure as to what they mean by *Buddhism* and *Buddhist*.

Lord Buddha never actually taught "Buddhism." He sought to revive *arya dharma,* which means "noble wisdom" or even "ageless wisdom." He said that all people had perfect enlightenment but did not know about it. He laid down certain fundamental principles but these are fundamentals only insofar as they are expressed in words. They cannot be called absolute. For words are creations of minds at certain stages of cosmic evolution. It may be difficult if not impossible to express in words what belongs to other stages of evolution.

Buddha Sakya Muni tried to express his experiences in current terms. These were memorized by disciples, some of whom, according to the records, did not experience enlightenment. Still, the words were remembered and recorded. Many of these words have been accepted with reverence even by those who would not be called Buddhists or included in the 500 million.

Among these words are *anatta, anicca* and *dukha.* These belong to the Pali language, which was employed as the literary vehicle of the time. *Anatta* means that there is no inherent self in things. *Anicca* means that every thing (not everything) is subject to change and decay. *Dukha* means that pain is an essential ingredient in life. In this, every follower of *dharma* should show compassion and respect to the Theravadins, for they are Buddhists, and they have both respected and preserved fundamental teachings.

We have from the same source the very celebrated Pali formula: *buddhamsaranamgacchami* ... I put my trust in the Buddha. *Dharmamsaranamgacchami* ... I put my trust in the *dharma. Sanghamsaranamgacchami* ... I put my trust in the *sangha.*

Their repetition in some form may qualify what is a Buddhist, as apart from one who may be known as a non-Buddhist.

Here one may ask: If there is no "self," no ego, who is it that says *gacchami*, "I put my trust"? How can this first person personal pronoun be used if there is no self? Who is it and what is it that becomes enlightened?

From a certain point of view, this Pali formula of the "three jewels" constitutes the essence of the *dharma*. Not the essence of Buddha or *sangha*, but of *dharma*. And this acceptance of *dharma*, in this form, constitutes the essence of Buddhism, or the *aryadharma* of Lord Buddha.

Those who accept this formula without realizing Buddhahood may be called Hinayanists or Theravadins, which is to say, followers of the old or traditional teaching. In a sense, they have the *dharma*, but have they the Buddha-jewel and the *sangha*-jewel? Do they really know the "Eightfold Path"?

One must comment on the usual interpretation of the Eightfold Path as offered by the Southern Buddhists:

A. The interpretation is not given from the standpoint of the experience of enlightenment.

B. The whole Tripitaka literature is presented as if it were a supreme revelation offered by a unique personality appearing in the midst of total savagery.

This may be far from the truth. The India of Sakya Muni was of a very high order socially, intellectually and theologically. There was, if anything, too much prosperity, but the easy acquisition of wealth did not bring peace of mind. Much time was given to disputations and one mission of Lord Buddha was to end useless disputations. The very fact of these disputations proves it was not an era of idiots. Buddha did not come to destroy anything but ignorance. Consequently it is a mistake to ignore the Indian culture of the time and of preceding times.

Naturally there have grown up interpretations of the Eightfold Path quite diverse from the experience of enlightenment, and even showing verbal contradictions. The word *samma,* which appears in each of the elements of the Eightfold Path really means "highest" (correlated to our word *summit* or *universal,* not *right).* True Buddhism does not propose any "right" way of life as against any "wrong" way or ways, but a superlative, universal, supreme Way—an all-embracing *anatta* view, terminating in *samma-samadhi* consciousness of totality.

In the Pali literature it would appear that one of the first missions of Buddha Sakya Muni was to elevate humanity to perfection so that all who joined his brotherhood became *arhats,* that is, perfect, enlightened beings. Yet this universal point of view seems to have become lost and while Buddhism spread both as a religion and philosophy, it did not always carry with it this experience of *samadhi,* or *satori* as it is now called.

This led to a break between those who had the experience and those who did not. It was something like a break between those who could write cookbooks and those who could cook. Humanity cannot live off cookbooks. It must have food.

The same diversion may be seen in the interpretation of *sangham saranam gacchami*. Was this sangha—or community—composed of monks only, or did it include lay devotees *(sravakas)* or was it confined to those who experienced enlightenment? Could it not also be that many monks, i.e., *bhikkus* or *bhikshus*, may not have achieved spiritual emancipation and that many lay devotees did?

As the power and authority rested with the monks, theology and institutionalism were fostered. All Buddhists did not achieve enlightenment; many non-Buddhists did.

There is also the formula *namatasa bhagavato arhato samma sambhodasa*, which is translated, "Salutation to the Perfect One, the Wholly Enlightened One, the Most Supreme Buddha." This formula identifies the *arhat*-experience with the Buddha-experience. It does not leave large gaps between one stage and the other. But in Mahayana literature there are such gaps. One may sometimes wonder if, having become freed from one set of recipe-writers, one has not fallen into the hands of another set without finding any real cooks and so obtaining bread.

From another point of view, the *dharma*-tradition is not a *dharma* transmission. That is to say, it cannot be limited to doctrines. The "three jewels" emphasize Buddha, *dharma*, *sangha*. *Satori* also emphasizes Buddha, *dharma*, *sangha*. But this is not a verbal experience, it is not a limiting of truth to words. It signifies the truth of Buddha-enlightenment passing from person to person, and it also means a *sangha* transmission of truth-in-the-while-of-manifestation.

Here we have something more than philosophical truth. We have living truth. Buddha-transmission goes from enlightened person to enlightened person, and this has been from the time of Sakya Muni to now. This is also called transmission of *dharma*.

And what does the experience of enlightenment bring? Not some philosophical explanation of ten kingdoms, which may exist in theory or in actuality, but the conscious realization of them both within one's "self" and in the universe.

Then there is no difference between self and the universe. Then there is no difference between self and self, between self and totality. We are everything we comprehend or apprehend. What we understand is—or becomes—us; separations are in words and illusions.

Thus there is much more in universal Buddhism than in becoming a Buddhist. One becomes *Bosatsu*, the *Bodhisattva* who sees all beings, enlightened and ignorant, with the same compassion. One does not frown upon the multitudes who do not know the *dharma* or who have incomplete notions of *dharma*. One treats all from the standpoint that nothing is true except enlightenment, and yet this enlightenment belongs to all. Thus one is able to help others, though one does not consider one's actions as help-to-others.

In other words, the supreme end of Buddhism is that everyone is a *Bodhisattva* and comes to realize that one has always been a *Bodhisattva* – or Buddha.

IV.
CRISIS
AND CHANGE –
JOURNEYS INTO
SPIRITUAL
ACTIVISM

Samuel L. Lewis and Shamcher Bryn Beorse at the latter's home in Keyport, Washington, 1969. Photo: Mansur Johnson.

Dark Nights and Dancing Lights

Editor's Note

T he Great Depression prompted changes in the life of Samuel Lewis, as it did in the life of the rest of the developed world. Charged by Hazrat Inayat Khan to take a leadership role in the "brotherhood work,"[45] he set about to bring the wisdom of the mystic into the world's economic, social, political and cultural life.

From 1934 to 1935, Lewis worked for the Townsend Plan in San Francisco. In an application for Federal employment in 1942, he described the nature of the work as "political." Francis Townsend was a physician who promoted one of several plans at the time for guaranteeing an income to the elderly. The Townsend Plan advocated that every person over 60 be paid $200 a month. The average monthly income of an American worker at the time was half that. There was to be no means test, which meant that a millionaire would receive the same monthly amount as an indigent person. The only stipulations were that a person needed to be "free from habitual criminality" and needed to spend the money they received within 30 days to help stimulate the economy. Townsend proposed to fund the Plan with a sales tax of two percent on every transaction in the U.S.

Lewis writes that his work for the Plan included "research, extracting from Congressional Record, writing and copying radio speeches...work constantly changing." At the time, the Townsend Plan was tremendously popular, but a Congressional committee deemed that the proposed two percent tax would not be nearly enough to fund it. Nevertheless, its popularity, as well as the popularity of similar plans like that of Upton Sinclair, led Franklin Roosevelt to push the original Social Security Act through Congress in 1935. Townsend objected to Roosevelt's plan because it needed to be funded by workers' contributions rather than directly from the federal budget.

As for "reasons for leaving" the organization, Lewis writes: "Found corruption within—investigated by Congress." A U.S. Congressional investigation in 1936 determined that the organization had raised more than a million dollars, but that much of it had gone to Townsend himself, who had been

---

45 In Hazrat Inayat Khan's last organization, the "brotherhood" meant the work of changing culture through spiritual means, of befriending the whole human family.

taking a monthly salary of $1000 (about $18,000 in today's money). The chief organizer for the Townsend Plan testified that Townsend had told him he would make "handfuls" of money from the scheme. Lewis later wrote:

> The legal set-up of the movement was made public in the hearings—a set-up eminently suitable for the purposes of racketeering. It was revealed that Townsend and Clements [the co-founder of the movement] each had received $79,000 in little over two years[46] from their interlocking corporations. It was disclosed that local units or Townsend Clubs, scattered throughout the United States, having no legal entity, had no control over moneys collected and contributed to National Headquarters and could not demand an accounting.[47]

Townsend himself refused to testify, but Roosevelt commuted his 30-day prison sentence for contempt of Congress, ostensibly because the President did not want a martyr for old-age pensioners on his hands in an election year.

From 1935 to 1938, Lewis collaborated with researcher Luther Whiteman in Los Angeles on various writing projects. In 1936 they co-authored a book entitled *Glory Roads: The Psychological State of California*. The book talks about the "states of mind" of California as reflected in various alternative developments in science, technology, spiritual movements and economic systems, especially those responding to the Depression. The book gives serious attention to experiments in a "reciprocal economy." These experiments included what today are called "clearing credits," "barter credits" or "lets," a system by which goods and services are exchanged using an alternative, non-interest bearing currency cleared through a central office.

The book sharply critiques various utopian movements that pretended to respond to social issues of inequality but instead were being run by demagogues who financially benefitted only themselves. Naturally, a large part of the book is dedicated to the tragic soap opera around the Townsend Plan Movement.

Despite publication by a mainstream publisher, *Glory Roads* did not stay in print very long. Its detailed, semi-journalistic accounts of current events did not have a long shelf-life and were overtaken by subsequent national events. Those events involved President Roosevelt's "Second New Deal," which included the Social Security Act and the Works Progress Administration (WPA), as well as the increasing tensions in Europe due to the rise of Hitler. A short excerpt from the book appears in this section.

---

46 Just over $1.4 million each in today's money.
47 From Lewis, Samuel and Luther Whiteman. (1936). *Glory Roads: The Psychological State of California*. New York: Thomas Y. Crowell Company.

Through Whiteman, Lewis met Shamcher Bryn Beorse, a Norwegian *mureed* of Hazrat Inayat Khan who was later active in the Norwegian underground opposing Hitler. Beorse, quoted in Section II of this book, was a trained engineer and economist who authored several books on alternative economic and solar energy systems. Just after World War II, Beorse helped institute a nationwide "clearing credit" scheme in Norway to help the country rebuild.

In the 1930s, Lewis lived off and on in a utopian community of shacks, known as the Dunes, on the beach in Oceano near San Luis Obispo, California. His companions there included Whiteman, Beorse, the astrologer Gavin Arthur, the poet Hugo Selig, and a loose-knit group of other poets, freethinkers, revolutionaries, wanderers, and bootleggers. Both Beorse and Whiteman later wrote books about this community. In one of his books, Beorse wrote:

> The inhabitants of the dunes are called "Dunites." They are men, and sometimes women, who, for a variety of reasons, have drifted into this dune paradise and become squatters. Some of the dunites are hiding from a wife or a husband or a sheriff. Some are extremely conscientious objectors. Others simply wish to meditate upon the vagaries of the world and the wonders of the spirit. A few, like myself, come to the dunes driven by an irrepressible curiosity and a shortage of rent money....
>
> The Dunes were a place where time stood still. A place with little official interference or insolence. A place which did not confine one within four walls except at night, and not always then. A place which did not imprison our bodies and souls in steel or concrete monsters, directly, as the mean and simple do, or subtly, by the persuasion of custom and alleged economy, as the civilized do.[48]

During the Depression era, many people became homeless. We know that Samuel Lewis also lived off and on in Los Angeles during this time, where he studied with Nyogen Senzaki and also with the dancer-mystic Ruth St. Denis.

St. Denis, together with her bisexual partner Ted Shawn, had founded the Denishawn school for dance in Los Angeles in 1915, following their long joint career touring worldwide, resulting in St Denis' massive popularity. She and Samuel Lewis met in the mid-1930s, when she was around 50 and he was around 45. St. Denis wrote and taught about her own vision of dance as a force for spiritual and cultural renewal. She inspired Lewis's early, unpublished book *Spiritual Dancing* on transforming culture through music and

---

48 Beorse, Shamcher Bryn. *Fairy Tales are True: Silent Reach from the Dunes to the Khumba Mela* (pp. 25-26, 39). Alpha Glyph Publications. Kindle Edition. https://www.fairy-tales.shamcher.com

dance. Based on internal references we can conclude that *Spiritual Dancing* was most likely written in the late 1930s to early 1940s. A selection from that book is included in this section.

Following his time with the Townsend Plan, Lewis worked from 1937-1938 as a researcher, writer and "Engineer 6th class" for the federal Works Progress Administration (WPA) in San Francisco. The WPA was one of the most ambitious of Roosevelt's New Deal programs. It put millions of unskilled and unemployed people to work building roads and other public infrastructure. The goal was to provide work for most unemployed people until the economy recovered. Lewis reports that his WPA work included "field and research writing, explaining housing projects, social rehabilitation, usages of manual labor in engineering projects, road building, landscaping, cement work in connection with the constructions of the Golden Gate Bridge." Although the WPA did not work on the Golden Gate Bridge itself, it did work on the approach roads to it, as well as on the lighting. The bridge opened in 1937.

Lewis's next job, which lasted for most of 1942, was with the U.S. Government Ordnance Office in Oakland, California. He describes his work as "direct cataloging of shipping tickets ... edit checkers reports ... supervise or handle secret statistical reports ... trace missing items." In an application for further employment with the government, he notes cryptically: "Have a number of skills or knowledge, which are to be reported in forms submitted by Army Intelligence to Department of Psychological Warfare, Washington. Am not advertising same, as they are to be used in the war effort, but may combine them with ordnance work."

Receiving citation for unknown work done for U.S. Army Intelligence in World War II.

We know nothing definite about Lewis's work for Army Intelligence during the war, but however it unfolded, he later received a citation for it. In a talk given many years later, he alluded to what today would be called "remote viewing" of troop movements psychically. During this time, he also helped to resettle Jewish refugees in California.

According to his spiritual successor, Murshid Moineddin Jablonski, Samuel Lewis said the following about his spiritual work during the war:

> During World War II, I was taken out of my body every night for weeks on end. I was part of a team headed by Abdul Qadir Jilani. The only rule was that you couldn't look to the right or left to see who your companions were. That wasn't important. You paid attention to your leader. We would travel over the battlefields, eventually arriving at the gas chambers where the Jews and other 'undesirables' were being executed. Our job was to enter the souls of the victims and assist their transition to the next world. This is the work of the Spiritual Hierarchy, and it is no fun.[49]

All of these experiences pushed Samuel Lewis to further explore cultural change in the "seen" world using spiritual principles in the unseen world, as well as through art, education and science.

The writings reproduced in this section are all dated to the period from the 1920s to shortly after World War II. They reflect Lewis's concerns and questions as he seeks for answers based on his inner experiences. Excerpts from two of his papers—"The Social Directions" and "The Spiritual Attitude and Class War," evidence his strong stand against the exploitation of people and the planet by individuals and corporations that amass wealth without considering the welfare of those less fortunate than themselves. He also rails against the "artificial life" that has taken humanity away from nature. In the excerpts from his "Book of Peace," Samuel Lewis considers the place of the mystic in politics as well as the challenges involved in forming an international government.

The excerpt from Lewis's book *Spiritual Dancing* foreshadows by twenty years his creation of the Dances of Universal Peace and the walking meditations he created with the goal of transforming education. Finally, in the excerpts from "Introduction to Spiritual Brotherhood," Lewis looks deeply into human biology to find the mysteries of reality unveiled. This early foray presaged later discoveries in epigenetics and psycho-neurology.

This section closes with another turning point in Samuel Lewis's life—the dissolution of one of his homes, the Kaaba Allah Sufi *khankah* in Fairfax, and the upending of the Sufi organization of Rabia Martin.

---

49 Jablonski, Moineddin. (2016). *Illuminating the Shadow: The Life, Love and Laughter of a 20th century Sufi* edited by Neil Douglas-Klotz. p. 24.

"Glory Roads"

Book Excerpt From
Glory Roads: The Psychological State of California
by Luther Whiteman and Samuel L. Lewis (1936)

From the Introduction:

What is it in California that causes this state to give birth to so much that is new in reform, in science, in religion, and in politics? Has California some source of enchantment by means of which all manner of magical rabbits may be conjured? Is there something in the atmosphere of its deserts, mountains, and sea shore, conducive to the lush growth of cults and cultists, or is California actually a state of mind as much as it is a political subdivision of the American Commonwealth?

California since the days of the Padres has been a land of prophets and profits. Its inhabitants still seek prophets and profits with no sign of abatement. Even more characteristic than its terrestrial upheavals are its emotional explosions. These disturbances give birth to new cults, new messiahs. It has been ever thus….

In these pages we have made an attempt to record only some of the better known Crusades of the depression years, and to picture only some of the more important of recent Messiahs. A dozen minor prophets have been passed over unmentioned. Much that is germane to the subject has been perforce omitted. We have made no attempt to stress the dramatic; we find ourselves in the midst of drama.

From the Concluding Chapter: "Can't it Happen Here?"

A student of political and economic movements in Los Angeles is amazed, not to say appalled, at the tendency of all these movements, major and minor, to adopt programs that, if carried out, would mean mass regimentation. Where regimentation is not advocated outright, the leadership of the movement is probably in the hands of an autocrat who, in the old Grecian sense, might be called a tyrant, appealing as he generally does, often without sincerity, *against* the dominating social class….

The symptoms of fascism first appear in the marginal groups. It is those who are most affected by economic and social maladjustments that are prone to follow Messiahs and accept the promised security of benevolent schemes, schemes that are incompatible with democracy as we know it.

Elect a Congress subservient to this extra-governmental body, led by racketeers and ignorant pseudo-messiahs, and democracy is dead. All that the situation would lack is an alliance of political racketeers with big business and finance as in Germany—and this is not so far distant as one may think, if the Townsend movement keeps its strength. Then let this monstrosity use the Black Legion[50], now blackening the good name of Michigan, as storm troopers, and the *Putsch*[51] is not far distant.

---

50 A militia group and white supremacist organization in the Midwest of the USA during the Great Depression, an offshoot of the Ku Klux Klan. At one point the FBI estimated its membership at 135,000 including public officials such as the mayor of Detroit.

51 German word for a *coup d'etat*.

The Social Directions

Excerpts from Paper for Sufi students (1930s)

Competition and War

You will see yet more conflicts like the late war [World War I] unless very powerful influences move for peace. They must be more powerful and compelling than the forces that make for war. Diplomats and soldiers who think in terms of conflict and national advantage, cannot provide any suitable foundation for a lasting peace.

Whatever be the advantages in the League of Nations, it has ignored the existence of God. At the present time, it is too much based on the idea of self-preservation. God is creation, preservation and assimilation. When the preservative element predominates, destiny holds sway, and when the dynamic power of change attains the upper hand, the will of humanity is paramount. Between the conservative and the radical, there is no room for peace, nor has any place been allowed for God.

The liberal point of view based on compromise is not necessarily the correct one. What is vital is either to bring about a reconciliation between the different groups, to permit the existence of all under the regime of broadest tolerance, or to provide a means of meeting problems with the greatest control over all emotions. This is only possible when the principle of Providence is admitted and recognized, so that the creative energy of God, the divine principle, can attain its proper influence over the hearts and minds of people, and so move out into the objective world.

Capitalism is based on the possession and ownership of tools. There are struggles over these tools—their ownership, possession, use and management—and this leads to war. Competition in itself is war, though no blood be shed. While war may not always be condemned, and while many of the prophets of God have permitted warfare, if not actually engaged in battle, that which magnifies the ego of personalities, communities, nations, or even the idea of institutions, is wrong in the sight of eternity.

Peace and Justice

There can be no pure peace without justice. Cessation of bloodshed followed by the enslavement of peoples may even be worse than war.

Today millions of innocent babies are born into the world only to have to waste their lives in slavery, to pay an immense indemnity for the damage committed in a war waged by their grandparents, who are born to hate and fear children with whom they have had no dealings, and so born that the atmosphere is filled with psychic and mental neuroses, making health impossible and disturbing physical and moral equilibrium also.

God is love, God is kindness, God is mercy. Think of the anguish in God's heart when innocent babies are born to German mothers, or still more innocent children to the Jewish parents in Poland and Romania! With every such delivery Christ is crucified anew, even most by those who claim to be his followers. Yet the world has too often ignored or condoned such occurrences, and now the whole of humanity is suffering from its karma.

For that reason the greatest caution and foresight is required by those on the spiritual path. If one joins the forces working for injustice, one is then more to blame than the ignorant unjust, for to such a one guidance has already been given and one's eyes should warn one.

Law and the Penal System

Who is there who can measure the distance between saint and sinner? Who can perceive the length between goodness and badness? Humanity, in its egotism, has established laws and institutions, claiming superiority to the proclamations of the masters of old. It is true that Christ may have in one or two instances tried to soften the interpretation of laws of Moses, but who has given humanity the permission to substitute its much harder laws, not based on divine principles, but born of its own self-will?

Justice has fled and cannot return until humanity returns to God. Motive is important, act is of lesser consequence. Yet in a world claiming to be Christian to some degree, no teachings have been more ignored than the social proclamations of Jesus. This can no longer be. The dualism between theory and practice has created a chasm in the body politic, the wound of which can no longer be healed.

Not only must the penal system be radically altered, but the prison in time must go. Laws must first be obeyed by those who would enforce them. The greater the social position, the more the authority, the more the advantages in life, the greater the evil and the less the good in the same deed. It is no virtue for the saint to be good, but it is a greater sin if the one who has advantages in life does evil.

All criminals are the result of social weaknesses and personal weaknesses. For the former they may be irresponsible, but for the latter they must be treated as diseased. Today science is pointing out remedies. But the prison tends to place a person amid vicious companions or in solitary confinement with his more vicious thoughts, and gives the devil full sway. Knowledge is not sentimentalism and repentance must precede forgiveness, but to remove legal responsibility from an individual and to deprive him of social freedom does not need to carry a stigma nor to suggest any punishment that does not eradicate the cause of crime.

Every soul on earth came from God and returns to God. If one were utterly wicked the body could not function, and if death did not result, insanity would. There is a Spirit of Guidance within us, and once this is perceived, even the worst among humanity can become rehabilitated. In the eternal life, a day or seventy years is nothing, and life on the earth is the preparatory school for a much greater existence in the hereafter.

Artificial Living

Humanity has moved far from a natural life. Much is spent in the building of solariums, for the purchase of medicine, for visits to physicians and for the maintenance of sanitariums. All this comes from an artificial life, a life that has devitalized the body and corrupted the mind. Surely God created bodies for a purpose and minds for a function, that humanity should know God and see God.

It seems no longer possible to return to nature and to God, but truly, there is no price too great for it. Instead of the verdant fields, the theater is preferred to the picnic, and the auditorium and the salon are appropriated for the dance.

Look at the happiness of the flowers in the meadows, and the sweltering of those in the hothouse! So it is with humanity. Physicians find many causes for disease, but how few admit it is unnatural living! Although their methods have improved in some directions, they are not succeeding in preventing the ailments of the body nor can they end the fatigue of the mind. Those who have not mastered their vehicles, surely they cannot save the world.

O brothers and sisters, in the search for happiness we must be pure and strong! Instead of hating or envying the Japanese it would be well to emulate them in their love for nature and their response to the seasons, as well as their control of emotion. Far better is it to deify flowers and the phenomena of nature than to desecrate the body temple.

The Expansion of Love

If there are angels they must surely be mystified by humanity's use of the term *love*. Why has so much mud been thrown upon it? In times past, humanity regarded love with reverence, even in its baser or more natural aspects.

By love is meaning lovingkindness, benignity, charity of heart, unselfishness, self-surrender. It is a feeling not only between person and person of whatever kind, but also between one person toward many, as a parent toward children and it may also be the collective feeling of many toward one, as of children toward a parent.

Lack of love and humanity has destroyed great civilizations before this era. Only a greater degree of unselfishness will preserve humanity as storms are rising higher and higher. Sympathy, not brute force, is needed. Those who go to church and shoot their hungering fellows plot in heaven the destruction of their communities.

It is not only the radical who endangers the social order but most of all the official who in blindness and selfishness shoots those who petition a redress of grievances. Does God not hear? And especially in America there is danger, for this country was founded upon definite principles. The founders swore before God to make their land one of freedom and enlightenment. Now gross materialism reigns.

Does God not see? And will God not take humanity to account? In refusing to extend privileges and in withdrawing rights, the mighty prepare for their own punishment. Already in heaven they have sown the seeds of destruction of themselves and their institutions.

There have been times when loyalty to a family was necessary, when the honor of the tribe was paramount, when the glory of one's culture stood above all else or when patriotism was considered the highest virtue. It is humanity that divides in this way, it is God who unites, it is love that brings together.

Today humanity faces this situation: the choice of love toward all humanity and peace, or else war and strife. What is thought in the mind shall come to pass. Hatred is murder, and envy is robbery. Jealousy is lust, and miserliness is gluttony. Whatever is sown in the heavens is reaped upon earth.

By walking in love, by showing kindness to each other, surely salvation will come, even in material form. But if we neglect or ignore the welfare of our neighbors, then like a just parent, God will permit our deeds to react upon ourselves.

The Spirit of Unity

In all things there is a spirit of unity. If there were not this basic unity, there would be no things. And yet unity does not depend upon things. Shadows depend upon the existence of light, yet the light is not dependent upon the shadows. Humanity can divide, integrate or alter ideas, but whenever the mind grasps anything, it is because of the unity in it.

Now consider the world and its inhabitants, the spheres of humanity and the realms of animal, vegetable and mineral. Each of these groups has varying grades, yet is considered as a unity. There is some difference in every form, yet the crystal may be a unity for the molecules, the body is a unity of cells, and the state or organization is a unity of bodies. This shows that the spirit of unity is inherent in all things as such.

Growth brings a wider outlook: of the mind in thoughts, of the heart in love and even of the higher emotions and deeper feelings in one's spiritual evolution. It is our horizon that must become enlarged.

The whole world is now becoming as one country. There is now no longer any entirely self-sufficient country. So each must consider the other, even for the purpose of self-benefit and self-interest.

Unity is not uniformity, neither is it democracy or equality. Unity is the spirit of understanding that binds differences. This is true of the atoms in the molecule, of the minerals in the rock, the leaves on a tree and the persons in a household. Who is equal to another? In what is that person equal? Just what is equality?

Neither in material things or material wants are we equal. Each is born at a different time. The needs of the body alter with age, occupation, season and health, as well as with sex and culture. All do not have the same desires, ambitions, or characteristics. Unity is not monotony. It is the harmony among differences.

In all things let us appreciate the good in another. If we must become alike, let it be in emulation, by striving in the spirit and working for common good. God will take care of us. Has not the earth existed long? And have not nations and cultures been in much travail? Yet God has preserved them even in face of great calamity.

All cultures and all religions that continue to exist are here because there is some good in them from God's point of view, regardless of our own opinions. All love the good, the beautiful and the true. There is not one soul not dear to God, not beloved by Christ or Buddha, or by all the saints who have ever come to earth. Jew and gentile, Muslim and *kafir*, Hindu and *mleccha*, Christian and heathen, all are dear to God for it is God's spirit that forms every soul.

And what is unity but the Spirit of God? Unity is God and all division comes from humanity's lack of understanding. As we divide upon earth, so are we divided in heaven.

The Spiritual Attitude and Class War

Excerpts from Paper for Sufi students (early 1930s)

At the present time we have just experienced a very important event in the economic and social crisis [the Great Depression], which may be extending itself before long. No doubt there are very many causes for controversy. The first question that arises is: if class war is a form of war, and if the mystic is against all forms of war, should the mystic labor for peace? No doubt the mystic should labor for peace, but one can question whether peace without righteousness is peace, whether peace without justice is peace.

We have seen that after the Great War the nations of the world came together and, instead of working for peace, each worked for its own satisfaction. As a result, although some countries obtained what they thought they wanted, many countries felt that the treatment they received was unfair and unjustified. They claim today—and there is some basis for their claim—that the evil peace following the war has helped cause all the trouble that is going on today. Instead of advancing toward peace, not only do nations remain at enmity with one another, but within many countries we find a division of classes.

In striving for peace, one cannot come to any rapid conclusion. Besides, the Healing Service has its prayer and its concentration for peace, which are very helpful[52]. But outside of that, there are at least five points of view that the advanced soul may hold.

The View of the Prophet
The first is that of the prophet. In some ways, this view is the most important, yet at first glance it may not seem wholly spiritual, for the prophet tends to be very much on one side. You can examine all the books of the prophets from Moses to Jesus and Muhammad. When it is a question of human rights against property rights, their stand is definite, firm and strong. They see no property rights. This does not mean that they favor a certain social and political order—they simply see no property rights when the same conflict

---

52 The early version of Hazrat Inayat Khan's "Healing Service" known by Samuel Lewis contained the prayer "In unison with the will of God, we will to have peace."

with human rights. This holds equally true for a conflict between humanity and private property as between humanity and socially-owned or communal property. To the prophets, all property regardless of the type of ownership, is the work of humanity, while humanity itself is the work God.

True, God did make humanity "out of the earth"—that is, from *prakriti*, and breathed into it the breath of life—that is, *purusha*. But the human personality is *purusha* and Saum [a prayer of Hazrat Inayat Khan] teaches, "Raise us from the denseness of the earth." If the workers and employers are concerned with the denseness of the earth, they are both wrong, for "the earth is the Lord's and the fullness thereof." But the employers are worse than the workers from the prophetic point of view, for they claim to own everything.

No doubt we find a vast abyss between the popular Christian point of view and that of Jesus. We find an enormous difference between the popular Jewish point of view and that of Moses. And we find some difference between the popular Islamic point of view and that of the Prophet Muhammad. But there is not much difference spiritually and metaphysically between the various great prophets who realized their oneness with God.

And what is their thought? They are not concerned with human institutions, with constitutions—written or traditional, with codes of laws, with so-called rights, with habits, with customs. These are of human making, and they have little to do with God. Little is gained by mere talk about spiritual principles. Read Moses, Micah, Jeremiah, Jesus, Qur'an, and you will always find the cry of humanity and for humanity. For the *nabi*, there is no compromise concerning human exploitation and the miseries caused the poor by the rich. The prophets never have been neutral, they have each sounded their warning cry.

With all the talk of justice and mercy, of divine justice and divine mercy, few pay close attention to the words of the holy ones. If you want to follow the Bible, the sacred books of the Jews and Christians, if you love Qur'an, then from the prophetic point of view one must say that not only are the workers justified, but they are entitled to more than they have demanded. They might even be congratulated upon their forbearance.

According to the laws of Moses, it is doubtful whether the modern corporation could find any justification. Moses was interested in the welfare of people, not in the special form of their institutions. He probably would not care much about machinery, or whether business was conducted on a large scale or on a small scale, being indifferent in this regard. His attitude would be determined by whether poverty was increased or decreased. He would favor any change that would lessen human misery and he would oppose any change that would increase it in the long run. The attitude of the other prophets is very similar to that of Moses.

Coming to the consideration of the "public." From the monistic or non-dual viewpoint, there is no public. If you consider yourself as separate from the workers and as different from the employers, you are setting yourself apart from humanity and are not much better than the animals. When one says, "you are different and I am different," one is making a division. So from the prophetic point of view, there is no public, there are no neutrals. All are concerned, whether they realize it or not.

This point of view appears very radical, and it is very radical. The prophet always views the roots of things and examines their causes. It looks socialistic but is not necessarily so, as the prophets were not opposed to private property. What they opposed was the unilateral enforcement of poverty upon a mass of people. There is no need for that today. If one were to speak from this point of view, it would be to urge stringent regulations upon the great owners of property who have collected so much wealth amidst starvation. The prophet sees the humanity of the multitude, and repeats in thought the words of Christ, "Let him who would be greatest among you be your servant."

You cannot be neutral or compromise when a robber is arrested and tried. No doubt the robber would be willing to compromise and divide his theft, but you would regard that as unjust. From the spiritual point of view as interpreted by the prophet, there also can be no compromise when bodies, hearts and souls are deprived of sustenance, of maintenance, of the full opportunity for living. In such matters the prophet would no more compromise than would the average person compromise in a criminal lawsuit.

The View of the Saint

The point of view of the saint differs from that of the prophet, even with the same realization. The saint is not interested in issues at all, as issues divide people. The saint is interested in humanity, especially in human hearts, and acts almost as if there were no property. He is not a socialist, an individualist or an anarchist. The saint reflects the angelic sphere, where there is no property as we understand it and no good and no evil as we conceive them. In *Djabrut* there are only hearts, and the saint is interested in human hearts.

From the saint's point of view all suffering is wrong, and to cause suffering is wrong. But the saint recognizes the inevitability of human suffering in *samsara*. The saint does not necessarily want to compromise but might see the expediency of it. The prophet will see things from the standpoint of eternity, while the saint is in a certain sense more practical and, wishing to bring peace, will strive in a practical way.

The saint recognizes the cause of strife as *nafs*, the ego, proving it to be in all parties. The saint's attitude is not neutrality so much as spiritual indifference. It does not mean being indifferent to the idea that one or both parties are wrong, or even that they are right. It does not mean having no interest or having interest. The saint is not interested in turmoil but rather in humanity. Like the "Mother of the World," the saint feels human suffering and must do everything to allay it. You cannot explain it by reason, although on the surface, the saint's attitude appears much more reasonable than that of the prophet.

The View of the Master

The master's point of view differs from that of the saint or the prophet. The master also sees the *nafs* in the situation but seeks moral reform. The master dislikes the attacks of groups upon each other, which are based in part upon each hiding their own faults, seeing only the evil in others. The master is more analytical and sees the futility of doing anything until this problem is faced. The master does not come out openly and attack anybody, for that would not help. This is the difference between the spiritual and the lay reformer or moralist.

It may be that the master will ignore the situation altogether and put no thought upon it. Yet this is not indifference. It is based upon the metaphysical principle that if you give no thought to a difficulty, if turmoil is not supported by thought, the turmoil will pass away, and the difficulty will go. According to this view every problem is fed by the thought we place upon it.

The View of the Sage

The sage is more likely to be in the world and even directly involved in the trouble. The sage does not strive like the master to keep thought entirely free. Sages have to face the situation and cannot abolish it by refusing to think about it. Their own egos are involved in it.

The sage concentrates upon peace, righteousness, God, or upon some divine attribute. By steadfastness in that direction the sage helps to bring about some adjustment, first in the unseen and then in the seen world. Sages are not necessarily neutral or indifferent and may take sides because of necessity, yet they keep peace in their hearts, feeling that this will lead toward a better solution. This may or may not be satisfactory as the average person views it. Yet wherever there is a sage, there will be some settlement, and the Sufi who is directly involved often turns out to be the best peacemaker.

The View of the Mystic

There is no one spiritual right way or wrong way. If one asks whether it is possible to combine any of these views, it may be answered that there is yet another possibility. That is the attitude of the mystics, who combine more or less all of these attitudes within their personalities. At the same time their own view may be very different from them all. Instead of observing the suffering as outward phenomena, they may be experiencing it within and will be able to do nothing except to try to clear up their own condition.

Mystics may have a disturbance or pain and may appear to be rather selfish trying to settle their own affairs. Yet there are no affairs that are necessarily their own, for they feel within themselves all cosmic conditions.

The mystic's world within is not separate from the world without, and in consciousness the mystic touches the hearts of many people. In bringing peace to the heart within, the mystic brings peace and justice to the world. For this reason there is a prayer for the Murshid in the Healing Service, the idea being that by the Murshid's peace, the world has peace, and by the Murshid's disturbance, the world is in disturbance, as Hazrat Inayat Khan himself taught[53].

All these matters merit considerable thought and meditation. They show how difficult it is to indicate one right way. Whichever path the holy person takes, those who favor the other methods may criticize one, so one cannot escape the condemnation of the generality. But all five ways are the ways of God, and God's paths ultimately lead to peace.

---

53 The early version of Hazrat Inayat Khan's Healing Ritual that Samuel Lewis knew begins with the Sufi Invocation followed by a five-minute silence. During this silence "we pray for our Murshid(a) and the success of his/her great work." This is followed by another five-minute silence "for the needs of the world."

The Book of Peace

Excerpts from Paper for Sufi Students

The Problem of a "Nation"

The problem of a nation is not so different from the problem of the individual, only on a grand scale. There are two aspects to the personality: the soul, which is an accommodation for Allah to touch the life on the surface and is really nothing but Allah, and that collection of thoughts, ideas, emotions and sensations attached to name and identity. So nationality also has the same two aspects: the accommodation for a group of individuals over a larger or smaller area to act as a unit, and the series of acts, ideas and ideals attached to the government, laws and industry of the same area.

Just as a human being is both *soul* and also called by the name attached to his or her *nafs*, so a nation has a spiritual and a material aspect. Some, seeing all the sins of a nation, particularly the wars caused by nations, believe only in internationalism. They believe that the family of humanity can only come about when all belong to the same nation, the same government, and that such a move would automatically end all wars and other international troubles, making it possible to reduce armaments and remove taxes and other burdens.

No doubt there is much truth in this, but there is another point of view. It has required ages to build the family and clan into the tribe and the tribe into the nation. This was not a rapid or an easy process. Humanity, forgetful of the past and troubled by the present, with an eye to the future, does not always take into account the many difficult stages passed through to build even the type of governments that exist today. With all their faults and shortcomings, when one looks upon the past, there seems to be so much improvement. One can see there something of the evolution of the whole of humanity, slow though that may be.

When one observes the governments of the day and perceives their weaknesses, one wonders how a super-government can be built. For instance, there is moral corruption. This appears mostly in despotic or irresponsible governments. No doubt there are certain resemblances between these two forms. In each there is a great temptation for personal aggrandizement and a lack of the feeling of proper responsibility toward the governed. One sees more morality and honesty in the governments of small nations than in some of the larger nations, because there can be a closer check on the activities of officials in such places, and so a greater sense of responsibility.

Under the circumstances one can question whether there can be found highly qualified persons for an international government with a full sense of responsibility. This raises the questions: what are the moral qualifications, and can they be secured? Certainly not while materialism is the ideal philosophy and wealth the goal of life. An international government so constituted might end wars between nations but could not bring peace between cultures, religions, and social and economic classes and political groups. Soon the whole world would be filled with war and chaos.

From the mental point of view, humanity is not quite ready for the abolition of nationalism either. Outside of the question of language and literature, which is very important, one can question whether there are yet enough high caliber people to manage or direct the affairs of the world in any one department.

When we look at the larger nations, we see the difficulties they have in securing suitable executives and leaders. Few even of the best and most moral leaders—political, social and philosophical—are sufficiently developed to grasp the various aspects of the affairs of their country. So we can see that much is yet needed in education, science, morals and philosophy to rear men and women who will be able to handle such problems.

From the spiritual point of view, such training should include meditation, concentration, and the deepening and widening of the horizon far beyond that of many of the intellectual leaders of the day. By turning to God as a universal ideal, it is possible to rise above all distinctions and differences that divide humanity. Thus the Sufi Message prepares the way for a stable international government, should that be necessary, and at the same time offers the solution for the larger problems of the day, which will steadily grow as the activity of humanity increases.

The Tower of Babel and the Power of Music

Those who are anxious to see an international government established with national governments existing only as divisions of it, are not always aware of the contributions of culture and nationality to civilizations as well as the functions they have served and will serve in organized society. This does not mean that a world super-government is not desirable. It is desirable and will come about when it is possible to have it function properly. Large units of government have some advantages over small units. If nothing else, they broaden the horizon of the citizen.

Many desire an international language, but the language of the heart is one thing and the language of the head is another. The great contributions of poetry and literature stand as monuments for the whole of humanity even when they cannot be translated from one tongue to another. What remains is the spirit of genius, which stands above all languages and yet must express itself in some particular dialect.

The story of the tower of Babel tells of a time when the entire humanity spoke one language and how it arose that people began to speak differently. Now the word *Bab-el* means "gate of God." It is only at God's threshold that one language is spoken, and this is the language of the heart. The true Babel or "threshold of God" is not on the physical plane but on the heart plane. Its universal language is not speech but music.

Music is, has been and will be the only universal language. While many are trying to convert others to learn some artificial language, and while some are educating scholars in various speeches, the whole world today is listening in some form to the music of other cultures, other peoples, other civilizations. And not only listening, but often appreciating it. Musical instruments, radio and phonograph will do more to unite nations than enforced training in the languages of each other, where words and thoughts are poured into the brain, but no feeling enters the heart.

Each nation has still to perfect its music. Those who have nothing to give, though they be masters of earth, will fall. Those who contribute to the art or advance the art, though they be the lowliest slaves, will rise from their estate. Until each nation responds to the music of other nations, what is there to unite them?

No doubt science plays its part in drawing nations together, but only up to a certain point. Science can be the handmaiden of war as well as of peace. Science is rather the product of individual genius than of nations. Of course, science has still a great part to play in the world's history. It serves to unite people regardless of culture or nationality, yet without bringing them closer together in spirit.

In the past religion has brought people closer together, but religion has also divided people and led to war. Obviously, the instruments of war cannot be the tools of peace. Yet there is an aspect of religion and also an aspect of psychology that will bring people together. This is devotion to a common ideal. Teaching concentration and meditation as aspects of education will also help, besides making people more reverential and devout unconsciously.

But for some time it will be music first, and then spiritual philosophy, that will unite peoples. So there is a great deal to be accomplished yet by individual nations. A Sufi may watch national progress and encourage such developments, without considering nations as the absolute of social life.

As humanity broadens its horizons outwardly, it will also turn inward. Likewise nations themselves, faced with the problems of continued existence, will search for ways and means of spiritual and mental protection, as well as intellectual and artistic development. In the end they will find these means of preservation far better and more useful than strong guns and heavy armaments.

Bringing Allah Without Religion

The problem of bringing all the world to the acceptance of a unique Being, *Allah*, which is the Soul and Substance of existence, is one that need not be disturbing. It is one thing to praise Allah and another thing to preach Allah. Many have been preaching without realization. Now the world demands realization, demonstration, experience. Otherwise it will be difficult to combat agnosticism and skepticism.

We must not forget that Allah is the Doer. There will be other roads by which Allah will become known to people. In science it will be the study of consciousness and vibrations that will destroy materialism, even as is being done already. Not only will people become more interested in psychism and occultism, but the more reserved will understand the intuitive faculty. This is more important than psychic or occult faculties.

Another method of bringing people to Allah is through the philosophy of love, harmony and beauty, by constantly raising the ideal. Love that now unites individuals will draw in its train kindness and goodwill, until one person is kind to another, anywhere and everywhere. This is a large undertaking. Although some atheists and materialists also preach and believe in kindness, the fact that they are unaware of the *nafs*-ego makes it difficult for them to maintain this state under all conditions. No doubt, willpower can control the emotions, but what strengthens willpower? It is here that meditation and concentration are necessary.

Through meditation the sympathetic chords of the heart will be aroused to respond to others. This will broaden one's vision and one's horizon. Then, often unbeknown to oneself, one's intuitive faculty will be operating and the rational faculty will be relied upon less. This will eliminate many little differences and disagreements that play so large a part in life and are often, directly or indirectly, the cause of sorrow, pain, turmoil and worldly conflict.

Likewise the growth of harmony will unite groups in the interest of music, art and culture. Every eclectic or international movement in these directions should be encouraged. All such groups will not be established by Sufis, and may not even be founded upon outwardly spiritual bases. Yet we should never think that, because one is not conscious of God, that person may not be the instrument of Providence. If this were not so, humanity would be in a pitiable state. Allah does not wait for our growth but may employ anyone at any time for any purpose.

Especially studies in music will awaken faculties. Studying various kinds of music, even in theory, due regard for the arts of other nations, and a broader exchange between East and West and between both and the peoples of Africa and America—all will help. Until this is accomplished, the variety of temperaments and psychic natures will make it difficult to secure and maintain harmony and equilibrium between one person and another.

Although the average person does not perceive it, the Sufi recognizes God in all sorts of love, in all forms of harmony and in all aspects of beauty. Therefore God can speak to all people in their language. It would be unwise to speak to a believer on love and harmony without ascribing them to God; likewise, it would be just as unwise to refer to a deity in the presence of unbelievers. In their company one might speak of love, harmony, beauty, kindness or any ideal at great length and win their sympathy and admiration. All such attitudes and actions are needed in the cause of God.

Remember it is Allah who is the Actor. This is the chief danger confronting those who are very eager and zealous to spread the "Sufi Message." This work is not some propaganda for a particular idea, creed or way of life. Action and attitude will always carry more weight with the public than speech or thought. It is by example most that one can bring others to an appreciation of the divine ideal.

Ideal Governments

No form of government is ideal, and every form of government can be ideal. Communism does not satisfy the heart and soul as it is practiced today, but the communism of Plato, Pythagoras and Jesus would bring peace, happiness and prosperity. Socialism has not proven successful, but the socialism of Moses would make the world almost a utopia or an Eden. Capitalism ignores all spiritual admonitions, but there is nothing to prevent a capitalistic state from accepting the teachings of Muhammad, thereby making it possible to remove many of the present-day evils without a revolution. Many look upon feudalism with horror, but a state founded upon the principles expounded in the Dharmashastras might preserve a civilized people in splendid conditions for a long time.

To say that communism, socialism, capitalism, or feudalism is most desirable is to say that thought-power is dependent upon skin or outer covering, and happiness upon the shape of the skeleton or structure. Any form may be abused, and they are generally abused, yet each one or combinations of them—or even entirely different types of economic and social orders—might prove successful.

It is easy to conceive of a thinking animal without a skeleton—say a sort of glorified ant—but it is almost impossible to conceive of one without nerves and blood. The life of a nation does not depend so much upon the form of its government, but upon the spirit of the governed and their contentment with respect to the process of governing. Weak, immoral, hypocritical, verbose and emotional leaders either demoralize people or cause disrespect for themselves. Strength and morality must be one in the hands of the monarch.

The greater the authority, the greater the responsibility, both to God and to humanity. Yet what is earthly power? Without spiritual force all the authority in the world will not help a person to govern. The virtuous, vigorous, strong person will be one. It is through concentration and right living that power comes to an individual. This was the secret of many rulers of the past, and it will become a necessary requisite for rulers in the future.

Mystics in Politics

The part mystics should play in politics is not easy to define. Much of what one sees today is self-seeking emotionalism disguised as human welfare. There is no law against having an opinion on philosophical, economic, or social subjects, but it is another matter when called upon to take sides with this or that person, for this emotional condition or that popular fancy. These matters belong to duality; it is not politics, economics and social action that mystics should flee, but they must beware of duality and all that inhibits the expression of God's will.

At the present time, there are such stirring problems that the popular feeling will become more sober. Some may strive to escape their problems by indulgence in pleasure, alcohol, drugs or vice. This is like saying the cure for poison is more poison. It is this attitude that has helped bring on the debacle and will make it worse. So long as humanity is intoxicated with life on the surface and forgets its true nature, it summons evil after evil. It is just like the Greek story of Pandora. When the gods wished to punish humanity they gave her a box containing all possessions, all pain and all pleasure. Seeking the possessions and the pleasure, they received the pain, and their folly caused their affliction.

One always needs sobriety when a problem is at hand. Mystics are not always sober, for the practice of the presence of God is very stimulating to the heart and mind and leads to spiritual intoxication or ecstasy. But when a problem is at hand, one's duty is to serve God rather than to search for God. By serving in humility and modesty one may be serving Allah without being aware of the divine Presence.

It would be wrong for mystics to stand back when they hold the keys to a situation. Yet it would be awkward and even dangerous if they were too forward and presented ideas before the world was ready for them. This shows how important it is to train and develop the intuition. It always helps one to see how closely related are self-perfection and service to God and humanity. No matter how great the inner desire or the outer need, without the sufficient development of the personality, any forward effort for the world would be fruitless.

So in the very first year of Sufi instruction, moral science is presented for the control of the ego and the development of the true personality. This may seem to be an individual problem, and in a certain sense it is so. But there is another point of view. Until the intuitive faculty is restored, and there is greater response to the heart, no efforts, even of geniuses in human flesh, will solve the greater problems of the day or herald the dawn of universal peace.

The unity that is to come must not only be an outer unity of governments, institutions, education and religion. It must not stop even with morals and a greater degree of mystical and occult knowledge. The science of attunement that in the physical world appears in the radio, and in general as the science of radiant energy, must further be developed on the mental plane between people, between thought and thought.

Nor can it stop there. To establish a harmony is one step; to maintain it is another. The mind is like an organ that can produce music, but whose pipes tend to change in pitch. It is the heart, the will whose seat is in the heart, that can correct and control the mind. So until heart is joined to heart in sympathy many may cry, "peace, peace!" but there will be no peace.

What joins hearts? Call it love, sympathy, admiration, attraction—anything. Behind it all is that universal chord that is the heartbeat of Allah, which created the world through love and which will perfect it through love. It is not an easy task to accomplish. It may seem almost impossible, but with Allah all things are possible and in loving surrender and obedience to Allah, even paradise can be regained upon earth.

Light and Morality
The difference between the human view and absolute principle of peace is due to the existence of the human mind. A crystal will cause white light to appear as various colors, and at the same time some of the light is invisible. In the same way the mind of humanity divides morality into those morals it can appreciate, those it cannot, and those it often considers non-existent. Yet

some morals may be as real in their own sphere as infrared and ultraviolet light, which are not perceived directly by the eye.

God's light is one light, and God's moral one moral. So the Sufi recognizes "There is one moral, the love that springs forth from self-denial and blooms in deeds of beneficence."[54] There are not several morals, although one speaks of justice, mercy, kindness, benevolence, love, sympathy, goodness, and charity as separate qualities. These are all rays from the one moral light. Therefore we read in *The Way of Illumination*[55]: "There are many moral principles, just as many drops fall from one fountain, but there is one stream that is the root of all, and that is love. It is love that gives birth to hope, patience, endurance, forgiveness, tolerance, and to all moral principles. All deeds of kindness and benevolence take root in the soil of the loving heart."

From the human point of view, prosperity, ease, justice, charity, welfare, security and cooperation may be considered different from one another and from peace. From God's point of view this is not so. There is light or no light or degrees of light, but you cannot divide light from light or split moral light as the physicist does the sun rays. You can seemingly partition the moral light, you can attempt to emphasize one moral, but it will have no security. It will bring no lasting good.

Scientists have demonstrated that a specific color will cause a specific effect. It will turn in a certain direction and too much of it or lack of it may cause harm. So it is with any particular moral. If one is all devotion and nothing but devotion, there may be no generosity. If there is only generosity, there may be instability in conscientiousness. Each moral by itself is not subsistent. No matter how humanity tries, it will never be able to establish any particular moral everywhere until it recognizes One Moral as basic. And it will never understand that moral until it comes to a comprehension of the fundamental unity behind all things.

As we look back on the Great War, we see that the peace has not only not brought peace, it has brought economic adversity, ill will, suspicion and the spirit of revenge. In other words, it has not brought peace. Today people want to blame everything on the war. The war has been made the scapegoat for crop failures and bank embezzlements, for crime and gross selfishness. It was not the war that caused these things, but that which is at the root of these evils itself caused the Great War and all other wars—the spirit of aggression in humanity.

This spirit cannot be overcome by changing economic conditions or revolutionizing the social order. Stopped in one place, it will crop up elsewhere.

---

54 From the "ten Sufi thoughts" of Hazrat Inayat Khan.
55 One of the books of collected talks, the "*Sufi Message* volumes," of Hazrat Inayat Khan.

The Sufi need not oppose attempts to alter the political face of the world, but neither should the Sufi be misled by them. They will accomplish some things, and the results may be called good or bad. It would be better to call them "natural," for every activity brings in its wake certain results, and those who seem to benefit thereby will call them good. But from a spiritual point of view, they are passing phenomena, not deserving of the qualitative "good" or "unfavorable."

Until this one moral is seen, until the spirit of aggression is checked at its source, and until the heart of humanity begins to function actively, there can be no peace. From the standpoint of the cosmos, poverty is war, cruelty is war, insanity is war, and disease is war. Hatred, revenge, spite, selfish aggrandizement, envy, jealousy—are all war. Until the *nafs*-ego is crushed at its source and the heart of humanity is purified, all one can do is to pray for peace, cooperate for peace, and repeat daily, "In unison with the will of God, we will to have peace."

This is all one can do, but by doing it faithfully and thoroughly, thereby one can do all.

The Dance of Life

Book Excerpts from
Spiritual Dancing (late 1930s – early 1940s)

(Editor's note: At the beginning of this manuscript, Samuel Lewis notes: "The disciple was requested to write commentaries upon his teacher's works, and has completed in manuscript those based upon Art: Yesterday, Today, and Tomorrow. This book deals with Sufi Inayat Khan's views upon the various arts. The separate commentaries have been grouped around Art, Architecture, Music, Drama, and Poetry." Of these, Lewis's dedicated commentaries on drama and poetry remain undiscovered.)

Introduction
The dance is the way of Life, the dance is the sway of Life. What Life gives may be expressed with body, heart and soul to the glory of God and the elevation of humanity, leading therein to ecstasy and self-realization. Verily, this is the sacred dance. Past the portals where Havelock[56] has glanced and recorded, where Isadora[57] has wrongly entered, where the mighty Jinn[58] involved the psychic forces that he could not control, let us venture, pioneering as angels where fools may fear to tread.

When humanity has been terrorized by conflict and faced with the ruin of its civilization, when the power of wealth has dominated justice and the concept of fiction-money has led to utter destruction, when the Holy Spirit has been driven ever further away on its path of ascension and again reached zenith to the undoing of so much near and dear to us—let us, in spite of what occurs before our eyes, invoke that same divine spirit through love and beauty that we may restore order and balance to humanity.

When doctrines divide and "-isms" turn one against another, without speech, without silence, let us demonstrate. Let these demonstrations manifest

---

56 Havelock Ellis, author of *The Dance of Life*, 1923. Ellis, a British physician, social reformer and sexologist, one was of the first to study what is now called transgender expression as well as psychedelic drugs. Samuel Lewis makes several references to this book throughout his writings.
57 Isadora Duncan, 1877-1927.
58 Vatslav Nijinsky, 1889-1950.

everywhere. Not what we think or say but what we do shall avail. May we therefore bear the torch of holiness and make of our bodies temples of sacred worship. Verily, humanity is the noblest work of God.

From the East and from the West we invoke thee, O humanity! The prophets of old spoke with fiery tongues. The flame is never quenched, though eyes be turned aside. Now look with hearts and minds and eyes. On with the dance! The dance itself shall mount through the seraphic flames of Jacob's ladder, leading humanity through sacred initiations from the netherworld even unto Thy courts, O Jehovah! Seek and ye shall find, and in the hour ye think least the Son of humanity shall come and the Daughter of humanity be there.

The Dance Revolution

When we separate the spiritual from the "real," the "practical," and the "beautiful," we build a concept that of itself is not spiritual. Our thought of God is not divinity. It is one of the many thoughts of our mind and is less than we are. Korzybski[59] has pointed out that the word *p-e-n-c-i-l* is not a writing tool, it is a word. The word *G-o-d* is not the divine being, nor is the thought that we hold of the ultimate reality. Spirituality is beyond word and thought.

The Russian revolution abolished old forms. It substituted a new social order and an accepted social philosophy. Because of this, human nature did not change, and psychologically the upheaval was less than what appeared on the surface. To its friends, it introduced a new group of messiahs. To its enemies it meant the substitute of tyrants without ancestry and breeding for those who certainly had ancestry and occasionally had breeding. But the revolution did stimulate art, especially the heterodox and new schools. And it gave encouragement to people to become more interested in all the arts.

Then came a counterstroke. Art had an aim: not beauty, but propaganda. The new order started out to uproot everything ancient. But it had to admit that science is science, and that chemistry and physics do not change because the cabinet falls. (That was before the time of "pure Aryan science.") Those who talk about socialistic biology and capitalistic biology are not very convincing. The demand for great ability and skill became more important than one's private philosophy of art. The popularization of art in Russia stimulated the aesthetic movement. Every talented person was encouraged, though handicraft became a statecraft.

---

59 Alfred Korzybski, founder of the field of "general semantics." His best-known quotation is "The map is not the territory." Lewis often applied Korzybski's principle of requiring a consistent, experiential definition to various terms that are often used without a definite referent—like *truth, democracy, terrorism* and so forth.

The revolution proposed here goes deeper. It does not abrogate skill but would offer encouragement to every type of artist. Even burlesque may remain. It does not say of the ballet that its principles are contrary to physiological mechanics. It does not believe that the study and performance of ancient dances should be detached from art and joined to anthropology. It would utilize all forms and methods and only demand a sincere feeling for beauty.

In and around Hollywood there is at least one teacher[60] whose methods are based upon cardiac mechanics and heart-concentration. Its pupils learn, more or less consciously, to invoke psychic forces. They imbibe philosophy from the dance itself. Their spiritual faculties unfold without anything being said of them. At the same time, they emphasize interpretative rather than program dancing. To them the right interpretive dance offers full scope to the will of the performer and gives her every opportunity for self-expression.

The changes that are taking place today and may take place tomorrow may have their counterparts in the past. When Akbar was Emperor of India he proposed methods that were at once revolutionary and synthetic. What he accomplished in the political and religious arenas is more or less known. What he did with the arts has not been so broadcast. This great eclectic strove to preserve all the earlier culture and traditions that might be used to benefit his empire and its peoples.

His work with the dance is noteworthy. He worked hard to restore the ancient Vedic themes of *apsaras* and *gandharvas*. He encouraged Hindu teachers to come out of hiding and train their pupils openly. He also protected the Islamic schools, too often engaged in bickering with one another when they were not combating "idolatry"—that is to say, Hinduism. He encouraged the introduction of Persian forms and Arabic instruments. Uday Shankar,[61] whom we admire today, is greatly indebted to this marvelous ruler.

Fundamentally, Akbar was a spiritual man and only incidentally an aesthete. He gave his allegiance to his spiritual teachers, Selim Chishti and Mubarak, Sufis of the Moineddin Chishti school. This school specializes in the use of music for spiritual development, employing all three forms—vocal, instrumental and dance. Mubarak's sons held the highest positions at the Mogul court and cooperated loyally with their monarch. All arts were encouraged and wonderful buildings constructed. The work of Akbar was completed in the reign of his grandson, the celebrated Shah Jehan, builder of the Taj Mahal.

---

60 Ruth St. Denis, who together with Ted Shawn founded the Denishawn school of dance in Hollywood in 1915. Some of the school's more famous students include Martha Graham, Doris Humphrey and Charles Weidman.

61 Indian dancer Uday Shankar, who toured the USA and Europe with his troupe in the 1920s and 1930s.

There have been societies in many places designed to preserve the folk arts. The harm done to them by this diabolic war can never be measured. The folk dances have a direct appeal. Their spirit belongs to the people. They illustrate the dance as an index to human character in accordance with Havelock Ellis' famous question "What do you dance?"[62] When civilization and order are restored, as restored they must be, let us remember that humanity does not live by bread alone. Its spirit needs sustenance. The peacemakers should do their utmost to encourage these arts.

Every art in a sense is like an unwritten scripture containing the epitome of a civilization. And our understanding of dances will enable us to understand the people that perform them.

The art and music appreciation courses in public schools have done something to awaken ideals and ideas in the young. We must not stop there. We need to avail ourselves of methods now left to private schools of art. For it is not enough to awaken only the practical or "human" qualities. We must foster genius. Just glance at all the attempted suicides among the young! Ask the psychologists how many more have pondered this fatal step. Maybe we should be thankful that we are now arising beyond the period of crass materialism to a broader outlook.

After all, what does the dance do for us? First and foremost, it inculcates the sense of rhythm and enhances our response to it. This is really a response to life. It makes us more living, which is to say, more spiritual. It brings out the beauty of form and movement and envelops our personalities in the enjoyment of them. It takes us beyond ourselves, bringing an incipient state of non-being, which is really a balm for the soul. Whether one follows classical, romantic, popular, exotic, oriental, occidental, or personal models of dance, we find a modicum of intellectual significance added to it, and so body, mind and heart can unite.

No doubt we can learn from the orient and in return teach Asiatics. If we need anything from India it is the spirit, particularly that spirit that underlies the sacred dances of that country. We have our peculiar physique, traditions, and forms. We need abandon nothing. We want to employ everything we can on the pathway toward God-realization.

---

62 In the *The Dance of Life* (1923), Ellis proposes the ongoing development of the human soul and spirit through music, dance, the arts and morals. From the chapter on dance: "'WHAT do you dance?' When a man belonging to one branch of the great Bantu division of humanity met a member of another, said Livingstone, that was the question he asked. What people danced, that was their tribe, their social customs, their religion.... Dancing, we may see throughout the world, has been so essential, so fundamental, a part of all vital and un-degenerate religion, that, whenever a new religion appears, a religion of the spirit and not merely an anaemic religion of the intellect, we should still have to ask of it the question of the Bantu: 'What do you dance?'"

Dance and Psychic Energy

The dance is an art that reflects life itself; the dance *is* life. We cannot limit it to humanity alone. There are movements in nature such as sub-atomic gyrations, Brownian movements of pollen, the wind among the trees and waves beating on the shore, which our poets would call dances. Besides this, birds and beasts have their art forms, usually employed in courtship. They reveal something of the nature of the performers.

Physical movement alone is sterile, and that which does not involve emotion may be excluded from art. The march may be called a dance. It is a rhythmical, physical movement of the body, usually to the accompaniment of music and having a distinct purpose. The march does not demand grace or beauty. In it *yang* dominates over *yin*.

The goose-step is an extreme example. The goose-step involves a maximum of *yang* to practically the complete exclusion of *yin*. Metaphysically, the goose-step and war are one. The goose-step is a war march, as much or more than any "savage" dance is a war dance. It makes use of force without stint or qualification. It involves destructive psychic as well as physical forces. To abolish war we must abolish warlike movements.

Indeed all bodily movements involve psychic forces which, while operating on the physical plane, are partly magnetic and partly mental. We can say they are mental in origin and biophysical or bio-electromagnetic in operation. This bioelectricity moves along the nervous network and forms an aura around it. When the body moves, this aura is extended in the direction of movement, always ahead of the physical center of gravity.

So we can say there is a physical center of gravity in or near the heart, and a psychic center of gravity determined dynamically by the direction of movement. The former is more or less static, the latter is dynamic even in repose. In repose the psychic field of force may be extended according to the one's condition of thought and the quality of one's breath. Understanding this will help explain several kinds of metapsychical phenomena commonly ascribed to spirit communication.

Use or misuse of psychic energy tends toward stimulation or fatigue. When stimulation is under control, there is ease and joy. It is a part of life to increase that joy, even to the degree of ecstasy. But before the nature of ecstasy can be understood, one must learn the relation of mind to body and of heart to both mind and body. Otherwise, one will experience that debilitating false ecstasy, which is nothing but psychic inebriation.

Heart and the Dance

The mystical traditions associate each emotion more or less with earth, water, fire, air, and their combinations—each with the others and with the "ether." The bloodstream is involved in all emotional surges, and emotions are connected with what we might call the "shadow side" or ego-aspect of heart. As psychic power is raised or lowered in the play and interplay between mind and body, so emotions ebb or flow between the life of the heart on one side and the life of the mind and body on the other. Together mind and body give rise to what Yeats in *A Vision*[63] called "The Mask," which Sufis understand as the *nafs* or "false self."

By *heart* we mean more than the physical organ, but rather the center of all higher feelings. In the heart's development, three factors come to the fore:

a. aesthetics, or the appreciation of beauty;

b. love and will, the aspects of power;

c. intuition, insight, and inspiration, which lead to direct realization, to balance and perfection, to the "Oversoul."[64]

When mind unites with body, psychic power is generated. When heart unites with body, we find increased impressionability and more emotional response, owing to receptivity and fineness. When heart, mind, and body are in communion, then spiritual forces find a proper channel for manifestation. They come into play with doubtful results when "Mask" covers the heart. They add to holiness when the heart, like a great central sun, illuminates mind and body.

When the heart life is developed it brings joy. When the love-will nature is enhanced it also leads to joy, and the union of these aspects produces joy. That is to say, when our sense of love and feeling of beauty commingle we experience joy. Tasting this joy, we love others more, we love life more, and our faculty of appreciation increases. This may be called "spiritual optimism." This optimism must not be confused with the egocentric person who refuses to look upon facts and seeks some escape mechanism, some ethereal airplane, some method of self-hypnosis.

We develop the intuitive faculty through use, self-confidence and trust. All of us receive impressions that are surely not imaginations, for imagination leans upon the past whereas intuition and insight are linked with timelessness and eternity. Imagination is a mental faculty, more or less alert as the will-power is dormant (this is also true of the dream state). But intuition is quite independent of personal experience, though not so independent of will. Reliance upon it often strengthens the will and leads one toward the Universal Will, the source of all power and wisdom.

---

63 Privately published in 1925, *A Vision* is a late occult work written by William Butler Yeats in collaboration with his wife Georgie Hyde-Lees. Yeats published a revised ver
⋅ ⋅ ⋅ ⋅ ⋅ ⋅37. The work explores the relationships between imagination, history and
: and has birthed many other books seeking to decipher Yeats' and Hyde-
plex system of metaphysics.

r-Soul" is an essay published by American Transcendentalist Ralph Waldo
in 1841.

Love does not arise of itself. We need to love another. When there is self-centeredness, there is no love; for it, self-sacrifice is needed. The same faculty, when used to concentrate efforts and motives, and to give a purpose to life and hold us to that purpose, is what we call will-power. Whichever aspect of heart we refer to, when heart dominates mind and body, it can become the channel for spiritual forces. To make this practical, one needs meditation and concentration.

Meditation is an art of controlling all movements of mind and body. When the body is rested and the mind stilled, a pathway opens toward repose and peace. How often the body stands before us as a rebel, difficult to tame and control! And what is this mind but a veritable devil, which forces us in directions we would not take, which brings us bitterness and tribulation. In meditation, one becomes again like a little child. One has no memory, no past, one is ever about to be born. One is ready.

Concentration is an art whereby all forces are centered upon the immediate duty. For this we need the mind and there needs to be control of body by mind. But what controls the mind? At this point, one's feelings come into action. The heart, like a central beacon, pours forth its rays upon the mind, illuminates it and directs the thoughts constructively.

This is the basis of spirituality in dancing, in art, and in all of life. If our deeds were preceded by meditation (or prayer) and concentration, then every act would become spiritual. Every recital, whatever the theme, school, technique or purport, would be an offering before God.

A Spiritual Revival

Can we today perform a sacred dance? If we hold before our heart's eye the vision of divinity, the feeling of divinity, and the spirit of divinity, then divinity we shall become. We can partake of the cup of nectar; we can again turn into Ganymede to pour and quaff the Olympian ambrosia. Nevertheless, we must be willing to embrace the divine Saraswati, goddess of music and art, as well as Kali, the seeming monster. When we find both heaven and hell within and recognize them as but small portions of our being, we can become as gods and move and whirl. We may express all that is, was and will be. The veil of Isis again may be lifted.

How much of this can be imparted to others, it is difficult to say. Certainly a laughing, applauding, self-conscious though appreciative audience will not behold it, though they have keen ears and eyes. Goodwill will bring them nearer to the dancer but not to the One Who is the spirit of the dancer. When we watch in wonder, in silence, in reverence, then the Holy Spirit may manifest to and through the person who is performing before us and can communicate a blessing to us. The term *mystery* connotes silent lips and open eyes. The uninitiated could not partake of the mysteries. This was true yesterday, is true today, and will be true tomorrow.

We look for a universal spiritual-aesthetic revival. The cultivation of ecstasy and attainment of superconsciousness are steps on the way. We are here to complete our humanity, not to avoid it. Therefore we must hold before ourselves the idea of the holiness of humanity and the sacredness of the body. Institutions, themes, forms and ideas are inferior to humanity, for humanity was created by God, and these things made by humanity. As we grow in understanding, consideration and compassion, spiritual art will unfold itself accordingly. The human heart-awakening must come first.

One should express a warning note here. If the dance or any art be cultivated for psychic or magical purposes, the world will not evolve, it will retrogress. On the other hand, if there is the hoped-for spiritual awakening, then all the arts will reach a higher status. Perhaps then the magic, the psychic powers, the unknown forces and faculties, will appear as quite natural. With the coming of the reign of God in the human heart many marvels will be added.

This will lead to contemplation, that most profound of practices. In it one assumes the omniscience and omnipresence of God to begin with and holds it ever before one. In this practice prayer, meditation and concentration unite. There is no distinction of religion or even of personality. The mortal is elevated toward immortality. The resurrection may be experienced without any departure from the body.

"You must be born anew," said the Master Jesus.

"We must be born anew, we shall be born anew!" is the echo of the coming dawn.

The Mysteries in Nature

Book Excerpts from
Introduction to Spiritual Brotherhood

(Editor's note: Lewis wrote the following sections in 1944. He returned to the book and added seven more chapters in 1969.)

Heart Mysteries

Ishk—the divine, all-pervading love—operates as gravitation, adhesion, cohesion and chemical affinity on the material plane. It manifests in and through other chemical and physical forces as well. Whatever, whenever and wherever attraction, attunement and affinity appear, they are due to the all-pervading and omnipresent activity of *ishk*. The rock masses, the formation and behavior of crystals, the settlement of ore veins and many of the phenomena studied by geologists become clear to the mystic who is aware of this presence of *ishk*.

When we pass from physical to chemical activity we also find *ishk*. The great problem before the disciple on the path is to break or control his ego or *nafs*. This *nafs* operates as a blind force that holds the seeming self together. It appears as inertia in the physical world. Love absorbs *nafs* on the path of spiritual unfolding, while the qualities of love remove the outer qualities of *nafs*.

If we refer to our fundamental principle that God alone exists, we can trace through all things this same principle. According to *tasawwuf* [mysticism], Allah or God exists as if in two aspects: one called *zat*, the other *sifat*. This *zat* is the universal, all-pervading essence that is beyond all qualities, characteristics, and descriptions—there is only One. As the One reproduces itself as the many, each aspect of the many is collected around a center, becoming at least momentarily a soul, self, cell, atom, chain-molecule, and so on. These manifest "many's" form units based upon the non-eternal ego or *nafs*. Every *nafs* is subject to change, decay, and death.

The *zat* of God appears as if possessed of many qualities that are collectively known as *sifat*, although actually *zat* has no existence apart from *sifat* and *sifat* none apart from *zat*.

In the physical world the human mind has divided and analyzed the sunlight and other forms of light, perceiving many aspects or forms of phenomena in them. But just as physically light rays and X-rays are strained through gratings, so mentally light rays, qualities and universals are strained, so to speak, by the human mind. This straining or filtering seems to produce many out of one—the one being fundamental, the many being psychological as well as material.

* * *

With regard to the heavens, the *ishk* pours from plane to plane and from person to person, from higher degree to lower. The journey from plane to plane is known as light and from person to person as life or love. The same energy passing through the atomic (or material-forming) structure behaves as heat and gives rise to entropy. In esoteric symbology, the former is ascribed to the sun and the latter to mars. The former includes all degrees of love; the latter includes many radiations of electricity, and radioactivity. In all these things we find a behavior like entropy.

The spiritual teaching is this: that God radiates to all, as in Portia's beautiful words from *The Merchant of Venice*: "The quality of mercy is not strained. It droppeth as the gentle rain from heaven upon the place beneath. It is twice blest. It blesses him that gives and him that takes." The spiritual teachers radiate love because that is their nature. They are giant dynamos of love and, by an inductive attunement, they awaken *ishk* in others. Being awakened, the recipients in their turn awaken others so that souls may become, so to speak, endless strings of interconnected lights.

The groundwork for this is in the heart. Biologically we may trace it through the evolution of the circulatory systems. We can see parallel movements to this in the radiations of the earth, and we can study them in radioactivity, phosphorescence, the electrical sciences in general and electro-chemistry in particular. Through all these things, we find a sort of "Toward Democracy"[65] movement—a tendency to equate and correlate— and underneath, a growth.

Breath Mysteries

If only the heart-mystery existed, although evolution could occur, forms could not persist as such. The tendency of heat, for instance, is to increase size, and the tendency of light is often to produce chemical activity. These things, therefore, stand opposed to inertia. Inertia is not life, it is associated with *nafs*, that tendency of things to remain things. The philosophy of inertia is materialism. The physics of inertia has come to a dead end with the rapid discoveries of radioactivity, relativity and the quantum unit.

---

65 *Towards Democracy* was a book written by English socialist poet and philosopher Edward Carpenter in 1905. Carpenter was also an early activist for the rights of homosexuals.

The question then arises: is there anything in bodies that maintains them, despite heat and its companions, and which is real, living and not of the nature of inertia—that is to say, not inert? There is such a thing, which in its highest sense we can call *breath*. We must distinguish this breath from the simple oxygen-organic processes that are an aspect or result of breathing and not breathing in itself.

The late Sir Jagadish Bose[66], inheriting the tremendous knowledge of his ancestors, applied it in the scientific field and made numerous discoveries. He found analogues to human and animal processes in the vegetable and mineral worlds. Not only do plants experience fatigue, but we find stresses, strains and even psychological moods in metals.

Now the mystic would explain it this way: not only do beings breathe, but things also breathe. The movement of the tides, ascribed to the moon, are also an effect of the earth's breathing. The earth as a whole breathes and its breath affects the whole mineral kingdom. What is it that keeps the rock masses as units, the mountains as mountains and the continents in their place? These are living things, though in calling them "living" one may have to dissociate from the traditional view of what constitutes living forms.

The ancients had two views of these things. One group, which may be found wherever there was polytheism, ascribed the rhythms of the world to planetary influences or to the same forces that are centered in particular planets (for instance, the Chaldaic and Sabaean traditions). The other schools— and their influences upon our civilization have been much greater—ascribed these rhythms to what we know as the elements, usually rendered as earth, water, air, fire and ether.

The Greeks do not seem to have complete teachings about the elements, but the Hindus do, and a traditional elemental outlook has been preserved in certain Asiatic regions to this day. According to this view, not four but five elements appear on each plane: earth, air, fire, water and ether. Ether, however, is the quintessence, the source of the other four, as well as the connecting nexus with the next higher plane of the universe, or between the earth and the heavens.

Spirit enters into matter according to the degree of evolution of a material form, and the elements arrange themselves in the order of earth, water, fire, air and ether. So in the lowest stage of the mineral kingdom, we find the greatest proportion of the earth element, and the ether appears only in humanity. But when we make an analysis of those atomic substances that form the body of earth and those that form the body of a human being, they all seem to fall into natural groups aligned with earth, water, fire, air or combinations thereof. This is especially true of those elements that appear in organ-

---

66 Indian biologist, physicist and polymath, 1858-1937.

ic bodies. We also find a material aspect of the etheric element that manifests in the inert chemical elements and is least apparent in the very active ones, for instance, fluorine and oxygen.

The Greeks believed that the universe was created from fire; we cannot say they were entirely in error. We have already pointed out the tremendous part the sun plays in all matters connected with earth. But if there is any physical atom that is the prime constituent of all the atoms, it is hydrogen. The breath of hydrogen is that of the *tejas tattva* [Sanskrit] or fire-motive, the color of which is red. This appears in the study of the flame-spectra of this element, its psychological behavior and other characteristics.

Oxygen has the color blue, and its breath is that of the air element. Carbon has the colors yellow and black, and its breath is that of the earth element. Nitrogen has the color green and has the water element but also, because of its inertness, is a vehicle for ether. The reason is this: the inert elements and the ether as such are not fit vehicles for living substances, which must evolve to a state of proper attunement. Yet there must be a check on unabated activity, such as appears in oxygen. A detailed study shows that people who absorb too much oxygen become very egotistical—*nafs* is aggrandized and spirituality reduced to a minimum.

At the same time, it is also true that gases breathe the air element (*vayu tattva*), liquids the water element (*apas tattva*), solids the earth element (*prithivi tattva*) and conductors of electricity and radioactive elements the fire or *tejas tattva* (also called *agni tattva*). All things in the universe vibrate, and it is this vibrating that is the essence of their breathing.

To continue the study of water: the individual personalities of oxygen and hydrogen disappear in the molecule of water, which does not externally reveal its ancestry. Water has some very unusual characteristics. As a liquid derived from two gases, its vibratory number is the mathematical result of that of its ancestors, but its behavior is connected with that new number and not with theirs. The *apas tattva* is more than the chemical H_2O; it is the very sea. The ocean dissolves some gaseous elements, in accordance with its breath. It breathes, the breath is its livingness, and it passes this breath and life to whatsoever is within its bosom.

Each drop of rain has breathed in some air, some gases. That makes it a living water. Even the springs that have dissolved gases have more life in them than those that are salty. Rain and aerated waters are most healthful and contain the best materials for blood salts.

Those who look for God and spirituality in nature need not look in vain. There are three witnesses on earth: water and breath and blood. The study and commentaries thereon are endless, but the very search gives life.

Blood Mysteries

The breath is, of course, a channel for plants and animals. But the breath of the human beings is more refined and carries vibrations that are undertones from the hidden spheres of the unseen world. Not only does the breath of a person indicate one's evolution, it also tells of one's immediate condition. The breath is the connecting link between the above and the below, between the below and the above.

Under initiate or Yoga training, one finds it easier to dominate those vegetable and animal aspects of life and so to transmute qualities, forces and even atoms. When the water and breath and blood become harmonized, the breath also becomes the channel for the Holy Spirit. Then the organism assimilates an increasing degree of *akasha* into the organism (*prakriti*) and into the faculties or *siddhis* (associated with the heavens or *purusha*).

The blood contains the fire element, which is more obvious after it is purified at the lungs. This blood becomes, at least momentarily, an ocean of life. The lower animals live in the ocean and assimilate water into their bodies but use the ocean itself more or less as their blood stream. The study of evolution shows the gradual growth of the circulatory system—a growth in power, assimilation, function and character. The study of a human being's blood is the study of what one is, was and may become.

The blood receives the vibrations from the highest spheres, indicating one's evolution. Evidence of this evolution is in a person's love life—taken in its broadest sense.

In the lesser human being, this love—the reflection of *ishk*—operates through *prakriti* and reaches its expression instinctively. In the greater human being, this love becomes increasingly the direct channel of *ishk* operating through the *purusha* until, through the awakening of consciousness, the soul comes to its full realization.

This growth is not a matter of will or a matter of thought. So many claim to love others but do not themselves give power, energy, vitality and inspiration to others. These are the signs of love. *Ishk*, operating even through the instincts and passions and giving an intoxicating impetus to another person, is of more value than a multitude of philosophical claims or subjective wishes that do not extend life and blessings.

For the end of love is in blessing and culminates in that state that enables a person, through love for others, to inspire them in their turn to increase the sway of love and blessing. This is the baptism of the Holy Spirit.

Endings and a New Beginning

Editor's Note

Samuel Lewis also lived at Kaaba Allah in Fairfax intermittently between 1928 to 1942. In the job application mentioned at the beginning of this section, he described the work he did while living there as "writing, translating, lecturing, teaching. Also caretaking, landscaping. Mostly piece-work. Generally made $75-100 per month....Machines and equipment used: typewriter, mimeograph, garden tools."

This simple description belies the amount of inner spiritual work, as well as esoteric writing, that Lewis did during these fourteen years. While Rabia Martin travelled to her various Sufi centers in the USA, Brazil and Australia, Lewis offered classes for mureeds at Kaaba Allah, probably on the weekends. He produced some of his deepest esoteric papers during this time, including "201 Suras on Breath," and "Githekas on Self Protection," both of which were also used in other centers of Rabia Martin. Copies have been found in the archives of fellow mureeds from Brazil (Shabaz Best) and Hartford, Connecticut (Sundar Giffin).

As Lewis reports in the following paper, "Experiences of Fana," he began to receive "direct mental transmissions," not only from Inayat Khan after his passing, but also from other prophets. These experiences were along the path of *fana-fi-rassul* that he reported in the first chapter of Section II of this book. He also wrote some of his most important mystical poetry during this time, including "The Day of the Lord Cometh," written in 1938 just after Hitler had annexed the Sudetenland region of what is now the Czech Republic. He also wrote "What Christ, What Peace?" in 1942 in the voice of Jesus Christ. Both poems are included in the published book *The Jerusalem Trilogy* (1975, Prophecy Pressworks).

From 1926-1944, Lewis had attempted to protect and defend his first Sufi teacher Rabia Martin according to Hazrat Inayat Khan's directions (detailed in the "Six Interviews" chapter in Section II). His great devotion for her shines out from much of his early poetry, including "A Psalm of Prophecy" (1927):

> Shout it from the hill tops!
> Proclaim it on the mountains!
> Re-echo it in the Valleys!

> For a woman will rise, a woman will rise and go forth,
> Forth from her native city
> to bear the Message of God to all lands.
> A woman is to bear it that all may hear.
>
>   ...
>
> Here cometh the daughter of Zion, the Israelites;
> Out of the West doth she come,
> For in these days will the sun rise in the West
> and all men seeing believe.

Yet just before her death from cancer in 1947, Rabia Martin turned over both the Sufi properties and her organization to Meher Baba, a guru from India whom she had become convinced was the "avatar" of the age. Martin had never met Baba in person, but was persuaded of his importance by several socialite friends, including Norina Matchabelli and Elizabeth Patterson. Martin demanded that all of her mureeds either accept Baba or ask her to release them from the pledge of *bayat* (initiation). She began then to teach from writings of Meher Baba. Shortly afterwards, she fell ill due to cancer.

Khalif Samuel Lewis then began to channel Meher Baba in order to help Murshida Martin. For instance, in the latter entries of his "Book of Cosmic Prophecy," Lewis channels the voice of Baba and makes specific recommendations for the property in South Carolina being prepared by Baba's students for a center called "The Abode for One and All":

> On this 13th day of July 1945, do I, Meher Baba, the Avatar, incarnate for this age, take over, so to speak, this esoteric diary and Book of Cosmic Prophesy, to utilize it to the full for the purposes for which it was originally intended, to integrate it consciously and completely with those works personal and impersonal which have come through the mind of this vessel. To coordinate it and them with my own writings and with all those inspirations that have come to and through men and women who are conscious of My Presence and My Being on one or more planes from the lowest to the highest....
>
> Myrtle Beach [in South Carolina] has been carefully selected. Islam teaches that the sacred place would be where the swift waters and the salt and the bitter waters met. On the blessing and merits of these waters I shall speak more when I come but I have asked that the lakes be kept free from human emanations and vibrations. If you touch these waters before I have done so with my living presence it may require much rain and drainage to purify them psychically. But of these matters I shall speak more especially with My Living Presence.

Before her death, Rabia Martin appointed Mrs. Ivy Duce as a Murshida and her successor to carry out the transfer of her organization and spiritual community to Baba. Duce then visited Meher Baba in India, who felt that he had been empowered to "re-orient" Sufism. He duly renamed the organization "Sufism Reoriented."

During this time, Samuel Lewis decided to try to work with Meher Baba within the organization. He gave a short talk in 1948 on the first anniversary of Rabia Martin's passing in which he said:

> Though we be few in numbers, though we are but slightly awakened, though our souls be but raising their heads from lethargy, the years will show that this, our first celebration under the Sufi order and Movement as it shall be constituted, is also the first in significance, and we should remember this more during the coming year.
>
> And let our real celebration not be now, but during the coming months, when without our Murshid, without our Murshida, we shall work and strive as though they were here in the flesh, remembering that time and space cannot overcome the things of the spirit, and that "Whenever two or three are gathered in my name, there am I."

According to Samuel's close friend Vera Corda, however, many mureeds like herself were outraged that Rabia Martin had turned the organization over to a total stranger and chosen as successor someone who had never lived or worked at Kaaba Allah. She and others chose to resign. The root of the issue, she felt, was that Rabia Martin began to rely on Samuel Lewis for his visionary and channeling capacity instead of developing her own. Then Martin began to doubt Lewis and had no way to confirm or deny his messages from her own experience.

This interpretation is confirmed by a report from one of Martin's other mureeds, Don Stevens, in the Meher Baba archives.[67] Describing an interview with Rabia Martin just before her passing, Stevens wrote:

> She then did something completely out of character and began a story at the time of Inayat Khan's departure in 1927 for India and his instructions to Murshida Martin on the manner she should employ to reach him in case of any emergency. This was to use Samuel Lewis, who, Inayat Khan told Murshida Martin, was quite able to transmit and receive messages psychically. Then Inayat Khan died. This last instruction Murshida Martin had presumably not forgotten. Soon, however, she had the impression that the replies received by Samuel from Inayat

---

67 meherbabatravels.com

Khan, always seemed oddly slanted to Samuel's own tastes, desires, and good.

In addition, as Samuel Lewis reported in his "Six Interviews with Hazrat Inayat Khan," he and Rabia Martin also fell out over her use of the Sufi organization to financially benefit her family. In light of his experience with the Townsend Movement, he was unlikely to remain silent when the same type of dishonesty appeared in his spiritual organization. His objections led to him being removed from her Sufi organization's board of trustees.

In 1946, while working at the Baba community in South Carolina, Samuel Lewis had more visionary experiences of Hazrat Inayat Khan (detailed at the end of this section) during which he felt that the Pir-o-Murshid turned him over to Jesus and Muhammad for further guidance.

A fire in 1949 destroyed one of the two houses of Kaaba Allah in Fairfax, including many of Samuel Lewis's esoteric papers. This event served as one of the last straws. Lewis had already become known as a troublemaker in the Baba Sufi organization and was subsequently blamed for the fire.

Lewis moved elsewhere in Marin County and, with financial support from his father, began attending City College of San Francisco. In 1951, he took an associate degree in horticulture and agriculture. Following his father's death in 1954, Lewis received a legacy that opened the possibility for him to travel to the East and Mideast to meet spiritual teachers and to spread information about organic agriculture.

In Section V, he describes these trips, which became the defining experiences of his already eventful life.

Experiences of Fana
(Effacement)

Excerpt from Paper for a University Class

There is always the question in Sufism as to how far individuals perform and how far they are subject to grace. The theory, as it appears in *Kashf al-Mahjub* of Al Hujwiri and other books, is that one's station *(makam)* is the result of one's effort, but one's state *(hal)* is the result of divine grace.

Fana-fi-sheikh: In February 1930, I went into seclusion to commemorate the third anniversary of Hazrat Inayat Khan's passing. He appeared to me in quite physical form and began communicating in what we might call a telepathic fashion. In 1926, when I had called on Hazrat Inayat Khan at the Beverly Hills Hotel to report on the 1925 retreat, he sent for me constantly, and there were six interviews [See "Six Interviews" chapter in Section II]. One of these concerned the science of commentary. Indeed, just before his death in February 1927, he sent a letter of praise and approval for the first efforts. But after he appeared in 1930, it seems that the major portion of these commentaries were nothing but direct mental transmissions from the teacher.

From that point on until 1945, one felt an increasing awareness of the Pir. This did not often produce any emotional effects, which are quite common. The records were in two forms: the commentaries and the diaries. Most of the diaries were destroyed in a fire on the night of December 31, 1949. These included a tremendous number of auguries, which the public would call "prophecies." Some of these foretellings were prophetic, and these were in a book that was saved from the fire. They make Nostradamus and Blake look like amateurs, but they are nothing, absolutely nothing compared to the sayings of the great saints, Christian and Islamic.

Fana-fi-rassul: There is a tradition that the Prophet Muhammad lost a certain tooth, and there is one school of Sufis in North Africa where the initiation ceremony consists of knocking out that tooth.

I was living in semi-seclusion in the woods of South Carolina in 1946, and every day Hazrat Inayat Khan would appear. One day while brushing my teeth, a tooth fell out, the very one missing in the Prophet's mouth. Hazrat Inayat Khan appeared and laughed and laughed. The next day Rassul Muhammad appeared. During the following period, both Jesus Christ and Muhammad appeared intermittently. I have seen Jesus in so many guises. True or false, he has never appeared to me looking like Galahad, but in human form exactly as Khalil Gibran pictured him. But seldom has he appeared in human form and the last times as the Spirit of Guidance.

Once one has contacted the Messengers of God, one will never confuse them. They are at the same time both the incarnation or humanization of the spirit of the universe, yet different from each other. Therefore the Arabs (or Muhammad) have given them special names. And before the Christians object to this, Jesus is known as *Ruh Allah,* or "The Spirit of God."

In my own particular life, the expressions have come out in poetry and occasionally in music and dance. But if one gives Buddha any name it is "The Voice of the Silence."

A great elevation is often accompanied by a great rejection. For after the appearance of these Messengers came the "dark night of the soul." During this period, Swami Ramdas appeared to me at work and predicted he would see me in 52 weeks. When I told people who had known him, I received the usual derision, but in exactly 52 weeks he came.

V.

Journeys Toward the Setting Sun

*In Japan 1956. Next to Samuel Lewis is James Kinoshita
of The Friends of the World.*

Pilgrimages

Editor's Note

The dictionary defines a pilgrimage as "a long, weary journey, as to a shrine." However, the Latin roots of the word carry the meaning of "traveling or wandering through open spaces or fields."

In 1956, at age 60, Samuel Lewis approached his first pilgrimage at a time of life when other people were thinking about retiring. His life to that point seemed to be several lives, most of them unsettled, unresolved and disconnected. The drama of his birth family continued, his interests in changing culture persisted, as did his intense study and practice as simultaneously a Sufi and Zen student.

His journeys to Asia and the Middle East introduced him to new gardens large enough to allow him to integrate all of his work—spiritual and intellectual, scientific, cultural, humanitarian and psychological. That he was able to accomplish so much in the following ten years is staggering. Meeting the great saints and sages of the East catalyzed his practical work on land reform, desert agriculture, seed exchange and drought-resistant crops. The confirmations he received from outside allowed him to begin to process his life's unresolved emotional questions. In the following letters we see humor and self-parody mixed with deadly serious warnings about coming political problems in Vietnam and Afghanistan as well as ecological troubles in the rest of the world.

How much Samuel Lewis affected the course of history during this time is unknown. Many of his political predictions turned out to be true. Much of his advice on "foreign aid and foreign understanding" has now gained popularity through the works of the late E.F. Schumacher (*Small is Beautiful*) and other writers concerned with sustainability, world hunger and environmentalism.

What seemed to make the most difference to Samuel Lewis was that he had personally contacted, on their own ground, more Asians than almost any other American in history. This ranged from a Hindu street sweeper to the President of India. As he was fond of saying, this was "not-news" in a society where the media, then as now, is oriented toward sensationalism and celebrity personalities.

Yet this person-to-person approach might have made more difference —and might still be make more difference—than all the speeches and expressions of high-handed *noblesse oblige* that the USA has offered to the rest of the world.

"You Must Go to Japan"

Book excerpt from
The Lotus and the Universe (1963)

Oriental philosophies are not learned from books. If they were, our professors could explain the Upanishads easily and clearly. All of Asia, whatever be its religion or philosophy, proclaims the spiritual teacher, the guide, the one who has become liberated.

Years ago (1953) my friend and spiritual brother, Paul Reps (Saladin) said to me, "You ought to meet Swami Ramdas."

"Who is Swami Ramdas?"

"I don't know."

"Then why do you think I should meet him?"

"Because he has what you need."

"What is that?"

"Love and laughter. That's all he teaches—love and laughter."

Surprisingly, within three days, two other people said exactly the same thing. At that time, they did not even know each other. It remained an enigma, and then one day it was an enigma no longer. At that time I was working as a gardener in San Francisco. One day, the heavens suddenly opened up and the guru Swami Ramdas appeared . He gave me his blessing and a prediction that he would appear in person in exactly one year. This was presented to others, including some well-known professors. Alas, there are none harder to convince of the reality of mystical and occult experiences than those who lecture on them—and are often well paid, too.

Exactly 52 weeks after the above happened, Swami Ramdas did arrive in San Francisco with an entourage. He spoke several times and his speeches and the expected debates are recorded in the book *Ramdas Speaks,* a series covering the Guru's world travels.

Swami Ramdas and his entourage accepted this person at once. The bond was made. Several years passed by. My father died and I received a legacy. Poor all my life, I did not know what to do when Paul Reps reappeared and said:

"You should go to the Orient. They are waiting for you."

"Why?"

"You must go to Japan and teach them Zen, and to India and teach them true Yoga and to Islam and preach Sufism."

My friends, this is exactly what has happened and is happening. This is not an autobiography, although one may come sometime. The day has not arrived when the mystic may speak on mysticism and the occultist on occultism out of his own experiences and out of the experiences of those whom he has contacted—exactly as in the sciences. The day has not yet come, but some day, *inshallah* (God willing)....

"Marinite Tours Orient: Leaves As A Gardener, Comes Back a Dervish"

Newspaper Article from the
San Rafael Independent Journal, May 13, 1957

Sam Lewis, 60-year-old Mill Valley bachelor, was a gardener for the state highway department a little over a year ago.

Now, back from a tour of the Orient, he is a member of the mystical *dervish* orders of Chishti and Naqshibandi.

The tale told by this wandering Marinite approaches the fantastic at times.

Lewis says that his father did not believe in college and as a result took him out of school and made him go to work.

"However, when I was 52," Lewis adds, "my father evidently changed his viewpoint and although it meant dropping a regular job, I went to San Francisco City College, taking courses in horticulture and chemistry. I took a degree in 1951."

After working as a gardener for the state until 1956, he received a sizeable inheritance from his father's estate, which immediately sent him flying to the orient.

"My interest in that part of the world stemmed from my studies in oriental philosophy and religion," he explains, adding that when he reached Japan, he immediately made contact with one James Kinoshita, described by Lewis as secretary to "Friends of the World," an organization designed to promote world peace through the international exchange of trees and seeds.

"Actually," says Lewis, "this man Kinoshita is a front man for the emperor himself, who is quite a horticulturist."

After traveling to Hong Kong and Bangkok, Lewis flew to East Pakistan, then visited the Indian cities of Delhi, Bombay and Madras, where he conferred with horticulturists and scientists in several fields.

"In India and Japan," Lewis declared cryptically, "those who do not make religion a profession are religious and vice versa."

Lewis avers that he is the first American ever admitted to the *dervish* orders, contending this was done as a result of his intense study of the orient together with his religious experience. The Chishti order, he explains, is one using music, while the Naqshibandi can be described as "one having symbolic significance."

When he left India, Lewis flew to London to visit the famed Kew Botanical Gardens prior to his return to Mill Valley.

And now, this horticulturist and *dervish* from India is again devoting part of his time to gardening, while he also prepares to lecture on his experiences.

May 1958:"Mill Valley, California, horticulturist enthusiast Samuel L. Lewis, right, last Thursday presented to Los Angeles City Recreation and Park Commission a supply of Gingko tree seeds from Japan for planting at municipal parks and play grounds. Lewis made the presentation as a member of "The Friends of the World," an organization that seeks to promote world peace through the exchange of trees and seeds" (Los Angeles City Recreation and Parks Department photo and release)

Japan, 1956

Excerpts from Letter-Diaries

May 15 Tokyo Station Hotel

The journey over was a surprising one. No illness but indisposition for the first week, due in part to the pressure and parties before leaving. List of passengers with addresses given. Some may become good friends. To my amazement and in contradiction of past enemies, I became a sort of leader in both entertainment and serious matters. Did some poetry writing, too, but mostly canasta.

Good old [Kiichi] Okuda-san met me at the pier. The customs, etc., was not difficult but exciting. Did not feel as if I was in a strange country at all. Other than the language and a certain percentage of old type clothing, everything seemed familiar. The trees interested me, mostly plane and ginkgo, with pines in the parks. The azaleas are in bloom. Flower arrangements everywhere. Some planting on the highway.... Bought first map of Tokyo and marked out place for Friends of the World.

May 16 Tokyo Station Hotel

O Sabro-san [to Sabro Hasegawa, see Section III]:

Today I begin my plan of writing a letter and using the carbon for my diary. I arrived in Yokohama yesterday morning and was met by my good friend Kiichi Okuda. He was manager of Daibutsu in San Francisco's Chinatown and in partnership with Shibata. We are always good friends. I hope someday that American students who are interested in Zen will come to know what "good friendship" means. Emerson said, "He is my friend in whose company I can think aloud."

But in the friendship of Zen there is generally one thought between two persons and also sometimes one silence between two persons. While many people were guessing at my reasons for coming to Japan, and some had a slight appreciation of my lesser reason, Okuda-san knows my deepest reason.

It has been raining very hard. On our way to Tokyo we stopped at the Soto-Zen temple and it seemed almost like home. I cannot explain it. I did not feel as if I were in a strange country. But between the rain and the fact that hundreds of children were visiting the place, we went on.

There was an exhibition of Sesshu at the Museum in Ueno Park—of originals. Only the heart can speak of such things, and the heart prefers a kind of silence, interrupted by oh's and ah's. There were hundreds of children there, and they were delighted that an American should enjoy their fine things.

Why does one feel happy with such things and not with European art? The inner being has a sense of space as well as of form and may regard the two as aspects of a oneness-of-nature. The line does not tell everything any more than the senses tell everything. The space was living and full, just as we know now that there are all kinds of sound and light vibrations which we pick up only by instruments. But there is also an instrument within us that may pick up these things in a better fashion.

It stopped raining at sundown and tomorrow we hope to go to Kamakura. We must be back, because I have been invited several times to dinner. I have met my old friend Kaoru Nakashima who used to be vice-consul in San Francisco. It was a wonderful meeting. He learned that Okuda-san and I have the same secret, and neither of us looks much different than fifteen years ago, while Nakashimasan has aged, just as most people do. Okuda-san is now past seventy but does not act or look as if he were even close to sixty. There are some "secrets" in Zen that seem to belong to the essence of life and even the body may relate them.

May 17
O Sabro-san:

Today the weather has cleared and we spent much time at Kamakura. We climbed inside the Daibutsu and also visited the Hachiman[68] shrine. We were very fortunate to witness a wedding ceremony there and hear the flute music first-hand, which we both enjoyed.

But most of the time was spent at Engakuji monastery. This has been the place of my dreams for longer than a generation. My true journey has some aspects which, when I tried to explain them to Mary Tabushi, she said, "One does not speak of such things." I answered, "That is correct, one does not speak of such things, and that is why there are all sorts of wild dreams and rumors going around." But there is no such thing as a coin with one face.

The first thing we were told on entering Engakuji was that the old Roshi Furukawa was still alive but in retirement. We sent notice of our presence to him and in a few moments, to our surprise and delight, we were ushered into his rooms and served tea. It was a grand meeting of old friends. The old Roshi is now way into his eighties but full of life and fire. Although he has retired, he

---

68 A divine figure honored in both Buddhism and Shintoism, associated with war-craft, archery and agriculture, sometimes called the divine protector of Japan and its imperial family. His symbolic animal is the dove.

still has plenty of vigor, though no doubt he could depart at will. He showed us much of the grounds himself, and then introduced us to his successor, Sogen Asahina. Sogen is a very vigorous, muscular-looking man but also has what I would call "the eye of the *dharma*." We were served ceremonial tea by the attendant. I took three sips to each cup and hoped this was correct.

We learned from him that Ruth Sasaki is in Kyoto, and we may see her before many days. He gave me his book on Zen and was very happy when I identified the pictures of Prof. Suzuki and my very dear friend, Robert Clifton, who is now in Thailand. He has asked me to edit the English portion of this work, which I may do later. We seemed to understand each other, speech or no speech.

After tea, he continued to show us the part of the grounds open to the public and then asked his attendant to take us to the part of the grounds not open to the public. We were led to the tomb of the teacher of Shaku Soyen and also to the tomb of Baku Zenshi (if I remember his name correctly) who founded the first temple there. The attendant seemed to be excellently informed on both Rinzai and Soto Zen. He gave us minute details in the lives of the monks, some of whom we saw working around. I was charmed by the trees and vegetation there.

May 18

Morning and afternoon were spent in outer affairs. Some time spent trying to locate held-luggage, then more time in arranging trip to Kyoto.

Late in the afternoon things began to happen. My baggage was located, things all in good order. Dried figs and perhaps part of chocolate to be sent to Roshi Furukawa. One jar coffee and copy of Netsuke book for Kaoru. Rest of books to go to Itako with rest of food. Also some fertilizer.

Balance of fertilizer given as gift to Friends of the World. We got in touch with James Otoichi Kinoshita, chairman of the board who came over with some literature. It was obvious that he, and his organization, are not only working along the horticultural lines I had planned but also more or less along the same spiritual lines. The result was a long and profitable conference. He said he would arrange meetings with the proper agricultural scientists. This was enhanced when he brought up the subject of rapid growth trees for fuel and swamp drainage. I told him of *E.globulus* and he may arrange for me to meet representatives in New Zealand and Australia.

May 23 Tokyo

My dear Harry (Nelson)[69]:

On the third day here I went to Kamakura and was "taken behind the

---

69 Harry Nelson was Samuel Lewis' main horticulture teacher at City College of San Francisco.

scenes." This gave me the opportunity to witness natural park scenery that was here used as a backdrop to the landscaping. Ginkgo trees are prominent all over and at Kamakura also I saw one of the old and historic trees, which was huge. Of course, there are lots of cherries, plane trees and conifers. *Cryptomeria* more in temple grounds than in parks....

In the evening I was guest at tea given by some VIPs, chief of which was Baron Nakashima, who seems to have played an important part in his country's history and development. While most of the discussion was around Buddhism and semantics, it was all done by leaders of The Friends of the World and will, I understand, lead to invitations to parks, gardens, etc.

When you consider that I have taken up here just one-third of one day's accomplishments, you may get an idea of how much is experienced.

May 24 Kyoto

Here I am in a Japanese inn, Seikuro Ryokan, dressed in a kimono, typing. We arrived last night and my first night sleeping on the floor was *sleeping*.

I had ordered a Japanese breakfast with coffee. Not being sure whether I had ordered a Japanese or American breakfast, they brought both. The slogan "eat a larger breakfast" ran into almost gargantuan dimensions.

We located Ruth Sasaki by phone last night and had very little difficulty in finding her. Ruth jumped right in and asked me some pointed questions. I told her that when Sokei-an Sasaki had in my presence said, "Yes, I see the future of the world, but I will not tell you about it," I caught the whole thing and foresaw World War II and the downfall of Hitler even before his rise. I told her you could find evidences of that in my poetry, and in one notebook saved for many years, but I never told before that I got this in a single glimpse from Sokei-an. I then told her of the immediate cosmic communications I got from him. As I had told her about Furukawa over the phone and then how I brought Sokei-an and Senzaki together, there were no more doors.

KO (Kiichi Okuda) places Ruth Sasaki in the same class as Abbot Asahina—among the realized souls. I see no reason to change such a stand. We did, it is true, go over some semi-mundane matters so I could visit the N.Y. headquarters in a more intelligent manner. There is now a Roshi there. We both accepted our visit to RS as a pilgrimage to a living *Bosatsu* and of the first order.

We then went downtown and bought two sightseeing tickets. Having an hour to spare, we then taxied to the Sanjusangen-do temple. This contains the Hall of the Thousand Buddhas, which is an actuality and not a symbolic term. It is incomparable. The figures are all of the same size and of the same materials but with different *mudras* [symbolic gestures] and details. I do not know if it were possible for a single one to have been made by anybody without some enlightenment, and the huge number made examination impossible. Besides, they are in rows and I do not know how to examine or judge those in the rear. However, there are so many in the front rows that you get dizzy. Unless, of course, you practice some meditation or spiritual concentration.

On the tour, we were then taken to the grounds of the Imperial Palace, very grand with all sorts of trees, and taken to all sorts of places which made it difficult for the photographers. "You must not take here, you should not here, here it does not matter and here you must take and we will not go on until you do." It was all very difficult for them. Fortunately, I have no camera. Add to that where you must and must not walk, and the fact that we were permitted to walk where the school children were not and it becomes complex.

One thing is illegal, and that is to stand in front of the throne. This is not only discourtesy to the emperor, it is also discourtesy to the hundreds of sightseers who also want to look at it.

We got home tired and very hungry and supper was slow coming. Then it came: first tea, then a sort of custard with a soupy base which had to be eaten warm—some fish in it. Then the heaven-human-earth dishes with fish (raw) on the "heaven" side with onions, a kind of anchovy with some kind of bark or vegetable product on the "human" dish, and pickled vegetables on the "earth" dish. Arrangements, size and shapes according to symbols.[70]

It is now the morning of the 25th. Got up at 5:30 to type and be ready to go to Nara as early as possible.

May 25

We took the 9:15 to Nara and arrived before 10. We went to the Shoso-in Treasure House containing almost the oldest art works outside of Horyu-ji. Almost cried before the Buddha there and chanted. The skill and inward calm of the artists was terrific.

We then went to the Daibutsu [great hall of the Buddha], which is the largest wooden building in the world. The Buddha was stupendous and we saw the guardians and attendant Bodhisattvas flanked by many children. Before leaving, Okuda-san explained that I was interested in Kegon[71]. This had been said before and brought most friendly greetings, but here we were invited to climb up and around the Buddha. We saw the details, where there had been gold inlay and the wonderful carvings in pictures and Chinese characters, some of which survived fire and what-not

---

70 Heaven (*Tian*) and earth (*Di*) are the two poles of the "Three Realms" in Chinese cosmology, with the humanity (*Ren*) occupying the middle. The first "movement" from non-separation to separation creates heaven, the procreative principle, and earth, the receptive principle, with humanity in between harmonizing them, at least ideally.

71 The Japanese transmission of the Huayan or "Flower Garland" school of Mahayana Buddhism, based on the Avatamsaka Sutra, which is full of mystical imagery, such as "in each dust mote of these worlds are countless worlds and Buddha...."

through the ages. This Daibutsu was originally financed by the Emperor and in some sense continues to be imperial property, although now part of the national treasure.

The monk said that Kegon was Buddhism par excellence and not sectarianism. That came later. We were united in a spirit of devotion. We were then taken through a courtyard (restricted) and saw the Bo Tree which was brought in, I believe, from Ceylon. It does not grow so tall and massive here as in India, but still is a large tree.

We were then introduced to Kainu Kemitsukasa, secretary-general of the Kegon Order and abbot of this temple-monastery. All the beauty of the day, the seeing of the oldest treasures, the Daibutsu and the people have gone to my head. Now my introductory work for Japan is to all extent and purposes closed and my real work may begin.

May 28

After Horyuji, it did not seem possible to have another banner day, but yesterday was something again, for we are sure we have met a *Bosatsu*. Philip Eidman is an invalid, confined to a wheelchair and with twisted fingers. Yet his knowledge of Buddhism seems second to none. He has *karuna* as well and perhaps better than wisdom, and he has plenty of intellect. Eidman gave us some knowledge of the weaknesses and strength of present day Buddhism.

Zen is in a deplorable state due to the legal anarchy concerning ownership and operation of the monasteries. It is neither congregational nor episcopalian but has resulted in either "abbotism," the head monk controlling all without recourse, or the "museum attendants" holding the property and letting the monks get along as best as they can.

I told Eidman that so far I had seen two types of temples: the wealthy and the collectionists. At Nishi Hongwanji, which is wealthy, they have one collection box per temple. At the Kwannon temples and Horyuji you are reminded every moment to contribute. Kwannon temples cut across sects and everybody seems to accept Kwannon. But instead of divinity helping humanity, the poor are giving and giving and with the number of statues abounding and the temples, the collection must be something, only it is not collected. It is just piled up, and I wonder what would happen if a typhoon came along and blew all that paper money around.

Buddhism is also divided between the intellectuals and the devotees, and there are several self-imposed philosophers who know all the book-Buddhism, but who are utterly lacking in compassion and humanity. Eidman has met many real awakened saints in Japanese country districts and in Burma. He is confident that their inner power will be strong enough to overthrow the self-imposers and the dilettante politicians who are making a cause of Buddhism.

May 29

The work with Kinoshita covers many facets, and we prepare to work together closely. The idea of an international tree-andseed exchange and of building up the greenhouse, nursery, etc. at City College goes ahead. I mailed a cut-out from one of the papers on rose growing in Japan. I also took out a membership for Harry Nelson (City College) in The Friends of the World. This will enable Harry and JK to correspond and cooperate while I am off in other lands keeping separate contact with each. We settled visits to other experimental farms and gardens and actual visits to gardens on June 1 and 2. Then, after I go to Itako and spend some time writing, to return to Tokyo and meet VIPs who are interested in the same subject.

May 30 Sojiji, Tsurumi

So far cost has been somewhat above even the highest estimation while the results far overbalance that, being beyond the wildest dreams and fulfilling down to the letter what Paul Reps and Hugo Selig predicted.

After our experiences at Engakuji, Daikokuji, Nishi Hongwanji Tokyo, Nishi Hongwanji Kyoto and especially Nara, we could not expect any more climaxes, but one came just the same. If I cannot pay Okuda-san in money as I hoped, he is the living witness to experiences that we share together marvellously. This has led to the conclusion to start studying Japanese.

We were hosted by the Senior Monk Thizen Saito and offered tea at least three times and given cakes for souvenirs. We were taken all around with changes from shoes to sandals to stocking feet, which I do not mind at all, in fact enjoy. He explained to us the position of Amida and Buddha in Soto, which is exactly the same as that of Allah and Muhammad in most of Sufism—this down to details.

We talked about the need of English-speaking masters of meditation going to the States. The monk in San Francisco does not know much English and, ironically, he has been more successful in attracting Americans than Japanese. I have been asked to write at least one paper, to come and speak and even to live. The paper came to me inspirationally on the spot: "How To Be A Buddhist?—How To Be A Buddha!" This I may write at Itako for I have a full program the rest of the week. But at night the inspirations continued for my poem "The Ascent of Mt. Fuji."

I am not fooled by weaknesses or mistakes, but I do not let them cloud the vast areas of agreement. The whole nation must be lifted out of a miasma. Industrialization, followed by militarism and then defeat are three terrific shocks to these people.

Japan 1956 (holding placard is Kiichi Okuda).

June 8-9: Itako

I am living in a village, northwest of Tokyo, which is the home of my friend Kiichi Okuda, Japanese style. Not far away from my ryokan[72] was the Rinzai Zen temple, and we stayed so long that KO became hungry, but I was so interested I did not think about eating. Some of the original trees of this temple are still standing. They have preserved the actual trees which were admired by Basho long ago. This, to me, is one of the great wonders of Japan.

Although the Bible teaches that "God does not dwell in temples built by human hands," here I realized it more than at any other place. These people simply would not cut down any imposing tree to build any house of worship. Not only that, but they give trees—not people—memorials. They put all the human memorials on a huge tablet and let it go at that.

Tomorrow morning I shall be catapulted into a series of events which will climax my visit socially and scientifically, as it has already been climaxed spiritually. The receipt of the letter from J. Kinoshita, outlining the program for the coming week ends all of my past rejection forever. To be guest of a peer of the realm and later on to be invited to the Imperial Gardens, an honor restricted to high diplomats, climaxing a number of honors, makes this diary look like a fairy-book.

---

72 A traditional Japanese inn, usually with bedding on a futon on the tatami-matted floor, serving breakfast and dinner. Existing since the 8th century CE.

What Inayat Khan proposed to me in 1923 is coming true and coming true rapidly.

June 10-14

Yesterday we went to the Kitori shrine, which is northwest from here (Itako). I notice that whenever there is an old or majestic tree someone starts a shrine. The word *kami,* often translated "god," seems to be rather "nature spirit," and more related to the Grecian ideas than anything of the Indo-Germanic peoples....

I had to continue something of my program of reading, singing and telling stories and games to children. When I became tired, we went to the iris show with the intention of voting and were begged to do so upon entering. We had no particular basis upon which to vote, but I selected one with a unique (to me) color combination.

Unfortunately, at this date (6/14) I have heard neither from Hong Kong or Thailand, and if I do not hear soon will go to Thailand Embassy for advice. This becomes important because Baron Nakashima wants me to call on the P.M. of Thailand with his ideas, also Radhakrishnan[73], to whom I must write.

We discussed, all rather mélanged, Buddhism, Friends of the World and Universal Love. My later discussions with the Baron [Nakashima] show an anti-Christian feeling, and I have proposed that instead of his Buddhist-Confucian front he work with all the Indonesian nations. So far as Christianity is concerned, I defend Christ, but see no room for any "God" that excludes trees, flowers, mountains, atoms and light. It is not Christianity that is to be feared, but ignorance that goes by the name of enlightenment.

June 15

I have seen Kwannon staring out of the eyes of millions of women. I see all the longing, hope, sadness and futility, deep passion and compassion, and these smothered by a strange combination of total exploitation and masterful spirituality, which does not seem to belong to this world.

The conversations with leaders have been at the highest level with requests to carry messages to other countries, or with introductions. Hongwanji and Zen, Kegon and Nichiren have treated me as a friend. I have been invited into homes, slept in ryokan, eaten their foods, enjoyed their baths and been here only a month.

The highest talks have everywhere centered around Universal Love, of a quality and type and degree one would hardly expect. The hearts of all lovers beat in unison, but the world, while saying it, does not know it – yet.

---

73 At the time Sarvepalli Radhakrishnan (1888-1975) was the Vice President of India. He served as India's second President from 1962-1967).

June 27 Tokugawa Biological Foundation

The basic purpose of this laboratory is to study from both the scientific and economical points of view the adaptation of the algae Chlorella for food. Ford Foundation put up $300,000 in 1954 and the Japanese government an equal amount....

I called attention to the work being done on microbiology and its value in plant feeding and questioned the use of inorganic fertilizers. They have come to the same conclusion: even for algae, the inorganics are "dead" and are really forcing rather than feeding. They have come to the conclusion from their experiments that plants need many of the trace elements that have been shunned alike by the medical profession and the larger producers of fertilizers (inorganic).

Chlorella has the tremendous advantage of being a relatively cheap nitrogenous food, which is also replete with vitamins and trace elements. If added to unpolished rice it should be a perfect meal. Besides, there would be and could be no objection to it in India excepting taste. I ate some with Tendon (shrimp and rice) immediately afterwards, and with vegetable curry rice today, and to me, they made harmonious tasting meals. The taste is somewhat like seaweed, which I happen to like.

Hong Kong and Thailand, 1956

Excerpts from Letter-Diaries

July 1 Hong Kong

When I went to the Embassy of X in Japan, more to test where I really stood after being so well received by the Japanese, I presented the following:

- Introduction of trees for swamp drainage and for arid areas.
- Introduction of economically valuable cacti in desert regions.
- Introduction of fertilizers that will not leech out with rains and which will cooperate with micro-organisms (this may invoke enmity of certain large businesses and goodwill of others).
- Methods of getting fresh water from the ocean at low-cost.
- Introduction of algae as a source of low-cost proteins with natural minerals and vitamins, obviating the need of medicinal expenses to supplement foods.
- Respectful visits to shrines and holy places of any and all faiths.

First, I was refused audience on the ground that I was too important (a new one for me). Then, after 1½ hours, I was asked to terminate the interview and meet the ambassador.

I represent the reality, not realism. I represent views based on actual historical and cultural knowledge against superficialities. I represent direct observation, as insolence, against indirect methods.

The rise of Buddhism, Confucianism, etc. will not be reported. The ways these will be used against the U.S. will be bypassed. The possible alliance of [Gamal Abdul] Nasser and [Jawaharlal] Nehru with these forces will cause both the U.S. and Russia to retreat. And our confounded trust in super-power with the superficial claims to religious beliefs will cause us to be distrusted even by some of the most anti-communist groups in the world.

I have been to more places where the supreme teaching was love and compassion. And this "love" has nothing whatsoever to do with the four letter word covering the behavior of cats (and their human counterparts) in the daily press. I can only repeat my warnings: in the orient, one reporter is worth four communist agents. And what is more, the U.S. pays for the reporters and thus saves China and Russia money.

Of course, the actual teachings of Christ could counterbalance all this. But not even Schweitzer and certainly not Stanley Jones—a thousand times less Billy Graham and a million times less the playboy from Orange County.

I am well prepared to meet any Indian or neutralist in debate, but know this is difficult. I shall carry Whitman and Emerson and Jefferson, and above all Bobby Burns's "A man's a man for a' that."

July 3

Dr. Leung Tit San belongs in the same class with the Buddhist abbots met in Japan. We were together for two and a half hours, and it was nothing but a symphony of close harmony. It was another glorious occasion where I found myself in complete accord with an oriental on oriental matters, where in some instances occidentals have refused to accord, or have given downright different interpretations of oriental "wisdom."

The Human Body: We proposed two points that are entirely out of accord with present day Western teachings. (A) The human body and human personality is essentially a cosmos. (B) There is something more fundamental than even blood, which he says roughly speaking means "air" or "breath" and yet is not either. I found absolutely nothing that was essentially different from Kabbalah and the highest aspects of Sufism and Hindu teachings, which things have seldom if ever been given to the Western world.

The immediate conclusion is that the human body reflects everything in the universe. He says that the bladder is more important than the heart. His further explanation threw, for me, more light upon the *chakra* in the gonadal region than anything I have gained from Indian or *tantric* writing. It is both cosmic and down-to-earth and none of the hyperbolic psychic stuff thrown out to the West by the pseudoenlightened. I could follow his nerve tracings and believe he could knock all the neurologists over.

Chinese Wisdom: Truth is universal. It was mutual recognition that brought Taoism, Buddhism and Confucianism together. They are still together on Mt. Omei-Shan, which he assures me is the repository of the greatest living wisdom. By this he means the greatest living sages, illuminated men. It is also a region of great beauty and if it be possible I should go there some day.

American Medical Association: He is utterly uncompromising on this point. To me there is no such thing as "medical logic," just a huge trial-and-error society with a monopoly on drugs and practices.

I called his attention to "Gestalt Psychology," and to the crazy pattern that in America if you don't accept Gestalt you may be regarded with suspicion, but if you want to apply "Gestalt" to physiology, you are ruined. The AMA simply won't let it.

Breath: It is about time to take a lot of fake mystery away and put out the true mystery there. The relationships between breath, consciousness, time-and-space functioning, etc. have been sealed off. In order to understand Chinese medicine, as well as all herbologies stemming from ancient wisdom, it is necessary to change our entire concept of space.

Can we prove that space is not living? We have a glorified vacuum, or void-psychology of space, which has only a negative satisfaction. European science, up to and including Paracelsus was based on the existence of vital forces in bodies—human, animal and plant. Christianity has done incalculable harm by making use of words like *pneuma* and *psyche* and clothing them with entirely different meanings than that of the Greeks. *Pneuma* (as used in the Greek New Testament and elsewhere) in particular seems to come very close to the Chinese conception of fundamental-wind (or air). And thus Galen and Hippocrates may have some contents not too far from Chinese science.

July 11 Bangkok

Here I am in the land of the "free" or Thai. I arrived after a comedy of errors, but somehow or other located the house of Princess Poon Diskul. She was not at home but presiding over a big Buddhist meeting. The Vice-President greeted me and to my surprise, I learned that my very dear friend Robert Clifton—now Bhikku Sumangalo—was in a house nearby (monastery). We met and spent 2 hours together and then I was directed to my friend K. Patel. Mail on both sides had not come through.

Patel seems to know everybody in Southeast Asia and could be of greatest assistance to the United States. Actually all power is in the hands of the monks. I met the Chief Abbot through him and found that he is the Chief Abbot's chief lay assistant. So I can meet anybody in Burma or Thailand.

Yesterday I was with Princess Poon about 2½ hours. We spent a good deal of time at the National Museum. I regret to say that both there and while with the Senior Monk of the Chief Abbot, while they both extended all kindness, they walked too fast for me. Now I am one of these guys who is a rabbit at climbing mountains but a snail in art galleries. This is confusing, and I don't blame anybody, but that is the way it is.

Now, for the record I am going to give you the nasty news. All Buddhists and pseudo-Buddhists theoretically believe in karma—that we reap what we sow. Then they make many, many exceptions. That puts the stock of certain schools of Asian studies in the U.S. pretty much below zero. When I mentioned my own criticism of certain Buddhist intellectuals while in the U.S., I was all but thrown out on my ear, only to hear these same people criticized in Japan. When I told Princess Poon I had done this she all but embraced me.

Religion and devotion are not elaborate forms of metaphysics without beginning and without end. The devotion of the heart, the expression of calm compassion, the extension of love, the actual growth of wisdom that is reflected in one's daily deeds—these matter. I have met so many leaders now, wise men, realized people, and they all tend toward universality and the experience of cosmic illumination. Some are engrossed in deep translations and interpretations and some in aesthetic movements. But there is no real difference.

There is a coming together of hearts which neither politicians nor Roerichs can understand. My host, K. Patel, understands and he is one of the leaders. Neither materialistic Russia nor materialistic America will dominate the world. But the United States has to make some changes, and I hope you will, at least, see my point of view: if the United States wishes to further either capitalism or democracy in the orient, she must stop supporting Christian missionary movements. It is that simple.

July 13

Today I went to Mahatato Temple where people come from long distances to practice *dhyana* (meditation). It is a *samadhi-dhyana*—I don't care what the books say.

Bhikkus (monks) seem either to smile or scowl, and my bet is that the smiling ones are the realized ones. I saw a boy go into *samadhidhyana*, and the monk first explained why and how the boy was strong and I tested it. I also realized more fully the source of my own strength. There is more attention to breath than text-books suppose.

July 14

The next visit was one of the high points of my life. It was to the Annamese[74] Temple which is called War Samanamboriharn. I was told that these people have no use for Americans and one would be unwelcome. I experienced no such difficulty.

In the first place, on entering, I pointed to a scroll on the wall (rough outline painting) and said, "That is Tamo." It was correct. I saw an altar which was very elaborate. Again the Omito figure dominated with a comparatively small Buddha. But there were many kinds of Buddhas, including the Burmese type.

I was told that the Abbot, Bao-rung, was an illuminated soul. I must say that he looked very much like Roshi Asahina in Japan. In fact, the whole resemblance was remarkable. Later, he looked over to me and this confirmed it in so far as one can judge outwardly. The chief difference is that Bao-rung gives up all his time to help humanity and to heal people. He seems to understand the nervous system, and prods the vital spots with an instrument that seems pointed, but did not puncture any tissues. It was like a sort of chiropractic on finer bodies, or based on the physiology of the traditional Chinese system.

---

74 The dominant ethnic group among the Vietnamese.

Pakistan (Bangladesh), 1956

Excerpts from Letter-Diaries

(Editor's note: The selections from letter-diaries for Dacca are supplemented with material from The Lotus and the Universe, *Chapter 15, "In Search of Sufis." After a bloody nine-month war with Pakistan in 1971, East Pakistan attained independence and became Bangladesh.)*

July 20 Dacca

I got off to Dacca bright and early and all bound with red tape and arrived to find that my host friend had just left Dacca for Chittagong. I was left a message that led me to the Shah Bagh Hotel. Hardly had I signed the blotter when I found myself talking to a University of California student from Berkeley who knew the first reference I gave him and also knew Muin Khan, who had invited me here in the first place.

I completed a letter to Vilayat (son of my first teacher in Sufism) and went out on what is to me one of the most remarkable of all my adventures so far (and they are crowding in on me thick and fast). Through a chance meeting in the hotel lobby, I met one after another the family of my friend Muin Khan. This included Sophia Kamal who is the leading poetess of East Pakistan. Her husband asked me if I wanted anything, and I said I would like to meet Sufis. In half an hour I was in a courtyard filled with men of all sorts and I was about to sit down when the gentleman next to me demanded:

"Who is your Murshid?"

"Pir-o-Murshid Sufi Inayat Khan."

"Just a moment..."

He turned away from me quite abruptly, stood up and said, "Brothers, there has just arrived in our midst a man from whose speech I judge is an American. He is a disciple of the late Pir-o-Murshid Hazrat Inayat Khan whose works you know I am now translating into Bengali. I think we should meet this American brother."

Maulana Abdul Ghaffour was the Chishti Pir-o-Murshid in Dacca. He had been a professional athlete, a champion football player, adept at other games and had been manager of a stadium in Calcutta prior to partition. He had been suspected of being mixed up in politics and had to flee, leaving members of his family behind. Here again one was struck with the very "un-saint like" behavior of the Murshid. When I came into the courtyard he was show-ing one of his disciples how to fly-cast, what flies to use and when. Perhaps there was something in it vaguely resembling *Zen and the Art of Archery*[75]. Hazrat Inayat Khan's invocation "Toward the One ..." is equally Sufic and Zen.

I asked the Maulana a very deep question and he came up with appropri-ately deep answers. He gave me my new *ryazat*, or spiritual practice, and pre-dicted my future for a limited period. I shall not go into details, but despite the deprecations of some of the followers of Hazrat Inayat Khan in Europe and America, he more than confirmed what Murshid said to me in 1923 and 1926, and added to them. I no longer have any choice. It is the same as fore-told at birth—either world fame or ignominy, no middle path here.

I read my "Sand and Glass." a tribute to the Prophet Muhammad on his birthday two years ago. This has come quickly on my first day. All the things of my life are clearing. I am with friends of Murshid and even before I knew it had the spiritual directions for my next stages.

Everything I have felt or thought or said has been confirmed, and this by an illuminated soul. It was foretold I would get guidance, but this has come with suddenness and swiftness. I cannot turn back. The work that God has given me will, *inshallah*, be fulfilled.

(further entry on the 20th July:)

One thing I cannot overestimate is the kindness and hospitality already received. It is the finest yet. I met the Japanese as if we loved each other, but I meet these people as if we were part of one family, very close indeed.

July 24
The visit to Dacca is like an elongated comic opera. Each day the Sufis give me a big feast, then the Vedantists give me a larger one....

When you meet real saints, real qawwalis, real sages and real Sufis and feel that marvellous spirit, you can ask for no more. But neither can you sur-render to less.

I was strongly challenged last night but reached this agreement: either Islam or universal religion. Either Islam proves its superiority, or it must join with other religions as one of several ways. It will not bow down to other reli-gions, but it must either take its place alongside of them or prove its prowess. It does not prove its prowess by argument and force, still less by rage and anger.

---

75 (1948). By German philosophy professor Eugen Herrigel, about his experiences with *Kyudo,* Japanese archery.

I admitted it was possible for sages of other faiths to reach the higher stages and perhaps even the highest. But I had to add I have not yet myself met any non-Muslim superior to my own teacher, and I have met the greatest in Buddhism and Christianity. The real test will be with the Hindus. If they have love and insight, I shall have to admit it.

Therefore I am not against Nehru as some people are. I speak here of his philosophy. My stand on Kashmir is that if we surrender to God, this will straighten out the problem. But the Muslims are going to lose Kashmir, because they have made the *thought* about Kashmir a partner to the *thought* about God, and sometimes they think more about Kashmir. This is not Islam and can only have the same results as happened in other lands. Seek wealth, property and empire and you will lose both them and God. Seek Allah and you may gain wealth, property and empire. At least this is my stand now.

July 27
Last night I went to an Islamic wedding. The place was packed. The scene stepped right out of the Bible and offered what our Christian mission-ary friends have seldom displayed. Perhaps it would not be fair to say I was overfed. Guests were limited to one helping, then the servants, then the poor relations, then the poor from near and far until all the food was gone. I un-derstand that about 700 persons partook thereof.

Not only did we not see the bride, but the groom proved to be quite an unimportant person, a sort of manikin on display. All the people came to see the Sufi teachers. I sat between the Chishti and Qadri pir-o-murshids, so it happened I was not only greeted more than the groom, but even more than the respective fathers-in-law, who bore the brunt of the proceedings.

I must now state once and for all that this nonsense in San Francisco about there being no Sufis or that they are unimportant must stop. Pir Maula-na is the most perfect *ordinary* man I have ever heard about, but his father was extraordinary (about that later). Through the Pir I have met leader after leader here—civil, military, professional, educational. There is hardly an im-portant man in East Pakistan that I have not met.

I did not have a chance to rest when my friends took me to the tomb of Pir Shah Ali. *Dervishes* came to East Bengal around 856 A.H. and began con-verting the peasants and established the first mosque in a wooded country. A century later the Pir came and really established Islam, this long before the Mogul conquest.

My name has been changed from A. Murad to Ahmed Murad by Pir Maulana. My initials will be S.A.M., which stands both for Sufi Ahmed Mu-rad and also for SAM, my usual name, short for Samuel.

July 29

There was a grand send-off dinner. I was feted and had the most loving embrace from a large number of men, some saintly, many officials and intellectuals, but all loving. I was advised to visit the tomb of Pir Maulana's father Dadajan in Calcutta. He is reputed to have been *Qutb* or head of the Spiritual Hierarchy recognized by all the *dervish* orders and is popularly known as "the Murshid." The symbol of Atlas holding the world on his shoulders gives a faint idea of the *Qutb*, who feels the responsibility for all the sorrows of the world. In other words, he is also *Bodhisattva*, but in another terminology.

The departure from Dacca was most notable. I was accompanied by the army chief Brigadier Ghulam Muhammad Khan, his aide Captain Muhammad Sadiq, Ansar Nasri of Radio Pakistan, Abdul Wahab who was translating Inayat Khan's works and who brought many associates, a delegation from Dacca University and the whole income tax department.

I also found fellow Sufis on the plane. I came directly to Mr. Haidar's house in Calcutta. After a short supper, we went to the Murshid's shrine and I started to chant *zikr*, but soon the Murshid was using my body to chant through. He then told me that I need not wait to go to Ajmir. He confirmed the "flute music" that plays through me and said that I was to use this gift immediately. Also, he gave me the blessing of the crescent and star at the top of my forehead, above where Murshid Inayat Khan had made his sign. He said he would guide my footsteps in India, certainly until I went to Delhi and visited the dargahs (Sufi tombs).

Now I have been nominated as a candidate for the Waliyat. My directions with regard to the disciples of Pir-o-Murshid Inayat Khan are simple: I am to be the Shams-i-Tabriz and Vilayat the Maulana Rumi.

The whole trip has been stupendous but the Pir Maulana said it will be more so. "Food for India" and "Water for Pakistan" still stand out. There is much to be done, but I must take one thing at a time.

Pir Maulana says, "This breath is the one that counts." At the same time, there is an all-abiding, all-pervading Divine Breath.

India, 1956

Excerpts from Letter-Diaries

July 29 Calcutta

I have just returned from Dakshineswar, the temple compound famous for its association with Ramakrishna, Vivekananda and the Tagores.

I am not to be taken as an authority. I can only see according to my own light and training. I differed somewhat from the Hindus on the subject of awe. I differ from them very, very strongly upon returning from the temple. I entered the place with more interest in architecture than in religion or sculpture. I left with the same feeling. There is a distinct flavor of the buildings which is akin to frozen music.

I admit that I have a tremendous respect for Ramakrishna, Vivekananda and the Tagores. The Swami Maharaj of Dacca (of the Ramakrishna Order) who gave me an introduction is a saint, there is no doubt about that in my mind. But there is an almost impassable gulf between Indian scriptures and Indian worship, only part of which is bridged by the architecture.

There are several temples in the compound, and I liked better than those the meditative place under the banyan trees. Saints build up atmospheres, and ignorant people have enough *savoir faire* to know they can benefit by breathing in those places. There is a possibility that someday I shall write on "real saints, real sages, real shrines." I stand between those who deny their existence and those who clothe them with awe, imagination, fantasy and hyperbole.

August 1 New Delhi

The diary is getting full. I spent two days in Calcutta, chiefly in the company of disciples of Maulana Ghaffour. In addition to twice visiting the shrine of Pir Maulana's father, we also went to the tomb of a Syed saint and I felt the atmosphere very strongly. I then sought some healing power to help my friends.

Ansar Nasri had given me an introduction to Hussein Nizami (son of the late Pir Hasan Nizami of Delhi), which I had showed to many people and had somehow misplaced. So upon arriving in Delhi, I hailed a taxi to take me to Hussein, only to discover this. By a fluke the taxi stopped right in front of Pir-o-Murshid Inayat Khan's tomb. Went in and cried copiously.

Then I met Hussein, who is a fine, spiritual young man, and had a long talk about Sufi publications in English and an international Sufi alliance. To-gether we visited the tomb of Nizam-ud-din Auliya and Princess Jahanara. Once again one was greatly impressed and chanted zikr.

August 5

I am in a land made famous by Kipling. My actual life is much more like that of an actual strange character of some of his stories. I want here to restrict the communication to horticultural notes. My host here in India, Ra-jenda Singh Parmar, has risen in the world since we last parted company and has told me that he can introduce me to almost everybody in horticulture and farming....

East Pakistan is having a famine. There is plenty of meat to eat, so I did not starve and was actually given a feast every night. The land is rather bar-ren, and I have written to Washington on the need to have more people from the South come and advise. The country has had only three products: rice, jute and tea, the last of which you can't eat. I came out boldly for diversified crops. I also learned more of the failure of chemical fertilizers and the need for organics.

August 19

After having a most satisfactory meeting with representatives of the Arya and Brahma Samajes, I reached an impasse with the leader of Sanatana Dhar-ma in Simla. My point was that equality in size of statues of Kali and Krishna and equality of ceremonials did not result in the same spiritual elevation. Finding he could not satisfy me, he sent me to one Swami Baskrananda.

I called on the swami the next day, after finding he was head of a Parlia-ment of Religions in India. Their methods are very straightforward. If you went to a nuclear physics colloquium, you would have to present a paper or some evidence of your laboratory research. In a similar way at these par-liaments, you must have had some religious experiences to be permitted to speak. Otherwise you would be ruled out; opinions and documentaries re-garded as wasting time and also showing lack of consideration for others.

I felt very distinctly that the swami wanted me to attend such colloquia at some future time and also to present his ideas abroad. We then went into the discussion of the day before, and on the whole he was getting the best of me. I then asked for a recess and chanted my "Flute of Krishna." He never said a word but sat and stared me straight in the face with an expression almost of amazement. To him I had proved my point.

Stopped at the Anandamayee Ashram. I had been told of the place twice. I went in and most immediately felt an elevating atmosphere, the nature of which is hard to explain and which I intend to write up in their magazine. I

170

told someone there my criticism of the magazine. It was short: Mother says, "I want to be honey." The disciples say, "I want to taste honey." I told her that was the destruction of the work of every divine personality in the history of the world. But as I have received a blessing at least 10,000 times that of Dakshineswar, I have been asked to write that, too.

August 24 Delhi

Returned to Delhi and saw Hussein Nizami as soon as possible. He gave me a book that I have asked him to send to the Pakistani consulate in San Francisco. This book has the picture of Rabia Martin in it, and I am going to have it translated from Urdu to English as it contains some material about Murshid. I am to have a special photo taken at Murshid's tomb.

I have gone to the Jama Masjid, which looks better in photos than fact, the opposite of the one in Calcutta. But when I was shown the hair of the Prophet, I broke into a loud cry. It was a cry neither of joy nor sorrow but like that of a *madzub*.

August 29

At night I went to the Tara Singh[76] testimony. It was remarkable. The meeting was opened by a descendant of Nizam-ud-din Auliya. Hussein told me that Guru Nanak (the founding Sikh teacher) was originally a Sufi. There were other Muslims also, one speaking passionately for the Kashmiris. He did not think much of the politico-religious state. There were also several Indians. One of the main speakers was the Sikh in opposition to Tara. When it was nearly over Nehru came in, and he was the only one who did not speak like a politician. In the end Tara and Punditji (Nehru) went out together, and the next day news came of a political alliance. It is hard to tell what it means: Sikhs accusing each other of not wanting to line up with Hindus and pro- and con-communalism—quite confusing to a foreigner.

Later visited Hussein and we visited the tomb of Humayun, which impressed me very much. Next we circumambulated the grave of Dara Shikoh[77] with "Ya Allah" seven times and then repeated "Allah Hu" 21 times. Then visited the ruins of the *khankah* of Nizam-ud-din Auliya. Wish to meditate

---

76 1885-1967, Tara Singh was a Sikh religious and political leader who led the demand for a Sikh majority state in Punjab, India. Nehru maintained that India was a secular country, and that the creation of a state based on religion violated this. Singh began a hunger strike in 1961 at the Golden Temple, but later ended it when he compromised with Nehru. A *linguistic* division of Punjab did occur in 1967, with Hindi-speaking areas redesignated as part of the state of Haryana.

77 1615-1659, eldest son of Shah Jahan and brother of Princess Jahanara Begun. Dara was broad-minded with regard to religion and inclined to mysticism and philosophy, but lost a war of succession with his younger brother Muhiuddin, later Aurangzeb.

where he did, to spread out a carpet and also give spiritual help to humanity therefrom. This should be possible on my next visit.

That evening at dinner I was introduced as an American Sufi.

"What does Sufism mean?" someone asked.

"God alone exists."

"That is the same as Vedanta."

September 17 Nasik

I went out for a walk early and ran into a real swami. Then in the evening I thought I would speak to a stranger in the hotel. I had just written some poetry, which I hope to be able to present to the Nizam of Hyderabad—at least I can hope—and pushed it in front of the stranger. He proved to be a Chishti Sufi. You see, the unconscious, when God-guided, is more successful than anything.

Every 12 years there is a great pilgrimage to Nasik where Rama is supposed to have stayed 11 months. People go there and bathe in the river. Yesterday was the climax and the crowds were in tremendous multitudes.

We got to the river and I baptized myself. There were all kinds of ceremonials going on, and I can say the sideshows out-distanced the circus. After a lot of walking, which I enjoyed, we visited the "fruit swami." He began immediately to talk about God and self in ways I think one ought to talk about God and self.

A Mrs. Kabali makes it her business to collect funds to give to him and this is used to distribute fruit to the people. Another lady was distributing bread free. She gave to multitudes sitting quietly against a wall. But a crowd began to follow her and make demands. She called the whole thing off. In this you see the best and worst in India. There is an extreme lack of human consideration, with an intense devotion. Evidently the fruit swami has his own disciplinary methods. But he impressed me both inwardly and outwardly and gave me spiritual instruction, by which I do not necessarily mean intellectual dissertations.

He explained to me the two methods of spiritual training, called the "monkey method" and the "cat method." In the monkey method, the baby holds onto the mother, and wherever the mother goes the mother carries the baby. In the cat method, the cat picks up the kitten and teaches it to walk. So the cat tries to make its offspring an adult as soon as it can, and the monkey tries to keep its offspring an infant as long as it can.

So you have two types of spiritual training: those who lean on the teacher to do everything and those who teach their disciples how to become adults. He told me I was on the cat path, that Ramdas would take care of me, and that he had nothing more to tell me. In the end, I chanted for him and he has invited me to Brindaban.

Brindaban is one place where Krishna lived just as Nasik is one place where Rama lived. I accept these places much more than I do Benares, which has become a pilgrimage center built up largely by priestcraft, I think. The Ganges was not originally the "sacred" river it became. What makes a river sacred?

September 19 Hyderabad

I see that I am going to be very busy. It is evident that my ideas of flooding this country with farm literature is having a fine response. It is all the more important because Indian magazines and also stores lean heavily toward Russia. Russia is well able to give them cyclotrons and tractors but not simple machines that can go out into the fields. It is impossible to take any but the lightest two-man equipment into the paddy fields.

Another thing was brought up. There are many pharmaceutical factories, and after they take the vitamins and hormones out of livers, etc., the leftover animal matter contains a good deal of nitrogen. They do not seem to know how to powder or dry it. It cannot be applied directly, for it not only acidifies the soil, it partly sterilizes it, and the labor to put it down deep is too costly.

Hyderabad, India, 1956: At home of M. Fayazuddin Nizami Chishti (second from right). Next to Samuel Lewis is Usman Solehani, Minister of Parliament.

173

India 1956: To left of Lewis is Fayazuddin Chishti; at far right is Neelam Nizami, the young esoteric head, son of Hussein Nizami.

They know nothing about Milorganite[78], sewer sludge transformation, etc. here in Hyderabad, and there is certainly a cry for nitrogen fertilizers. I'll try to follow this up.

October 1 Pondicherry

It is indeed a strange experience to find oneself in a realized Shangri-La or Shambhala—to find in fact what has appeared in books or legends. Talbot Mundy's Shambhala or Hilton's ShangriLa may have excited many. The Roerichs wrote long tales of fancy and fantasy and considered the "truth" of them more important than the facts of life. One stands constantly between the surrealists who vainly consider themselves realists (and in no case will examine the world as it is), and those metaphysical people who are only interested in hyperboles which they also call "truth."

The Sri Aurobindo Ashram belongs in all three classes—it is fact, yet it is full of fancies. Most of the people here want to be realists with regard to their own accomplishments and skeptics or downright scoffers with regard to those of others. The worship is directed to Sri Aurobindo and the Mother, which obviates a good deal of prejudice, sectarianism and nonsense, but

---

78 An organic biosolids fertilizer produced from sewer sludge by the Milwaukee Metropolitan Sewerage District and still sold throughout the USA.

equally veils the Cosmic God so that it becomes a sort of backstage hand who obeys orders. This is a terrible indictment of what is undoubtedly one of the most serious and also marvellous places in the world.

This place seems to be organized much like the human body is organized, with its cells, systems, organs in one grand whole. I think this has always been the "ideal" society and one finds it in Swedenborg[79] also. I myself lean very much toward the same view. My objection is that the integration, while sometimes real and valid, is also accompanied by views that it is an extension of Hindu spirituality and rather offhand attitudes are taken toward other faiths.

I have not seen all of this place. I recognize transformations in human nature here. Men like Billy Graham and Glen Clark would be compelled to bypass this place. Yet for all that, I do not see any Universal God here who created all humanity, sinners and virtuous alike, and who controls the destinies of the universe, not under any rules and regulations of anybody.

In a sense, it is a shame to say this. One is very well treated. The place is being constantly visited by pilgrims, many from India, and some from all parts of the world. Nehru and Prasad have recognized it. There is no idolatry and little of superstition. Yet it does retain some Indian customs and, alas, a lot of Indian chauvinism masquerading as integrated spirituality. And also despite its literature and word-usage, very, very little *yoga*.

The Mother is a sort of saint, and to me her *darshan* seems effective. She has a kind of real motherly love, the magnetism of which is too strong to be a mere affectation.

October 6 Kanhangad

This is written at Anandashram, Kanhangad, which is some miles below Mangalore on the South Indian-Arabian sea coast.

I am with Swami Ramdas, who is my guru. He is the embodiment of love. It rather surprised the people here that I came as a disciple, not as a visiting tourist. The events that I experience have little to do with the news. You can be sure that when there are large strikes and boycotts in the U.S., the press will exaggerate the Muslim-Indian outbreaks, and when there is a great internal language problem, the Indian press will be full of disturbances over "integration" in the U.S. The American weeklies we get here will over-exaggerate trivialities and water down real troubles. There is a gradually awakening social consciousness, and many are becoming "just like us"

We have 5:30 a.m. singing, then 15 minutes meditation until 6. At 10:30 we have another meeting, and there are no more spiritual gatherings until 7. From 7 on there are music, instructions, meditations and conversations until

---

79 Emanuel Swedenborg (1688-1772), Swedish Christian mystical theologian.

not later than 9:30. Lights out at 10. This is fine for me. In the afternoon one can see "Papa," i.e., Swami Ramdas. He is an all-embracing love who uses love first, foremost and always without discarding intellect.

October 14 Bombay

The week at Kanhangad was very different. Swami Ramdas is a real guru and gives spiritual unfoldment through music, meditation and love. Very little intellectuality. My plan is to come to India next by Bombay and then I could visit him at either *ashram* and conduct my researches accordingly.

Papa Ramdas
& Mother Krishnabai:
The Real Yogi Meets
the Real Commissar

Book excerpt from
The Lotus and the Universe (1963)

Q. *What have you to say about communism?*
Ramdas: Communism without violence is true religion.

The life in the body of Papa Ramdas[80] is no more. His physical work in this incarnation has been completed. Many will be mourning his departure, and many more will rejoice that he manifested the love-life (*ananda*) that he preached. There is a relation between guru and chela, between master and disciple (and also between pir and *mureed* in Sufism) that is based on the principles already enunciated and not on the persistence of ego-individualism where this ego-individualism cannot be.

Brother Arthur [Koestler], to write books is one thing. To meet a real person is something else. To find a Yogi facing, if not a commissar, then a strongly-organized communist movement is something else. But we of the West are so sure that "God" is on our side that we cannot always appreciate a God who has no sides, no limitations. Swami Ramdas was never a student of semantics in our sense. He did not stop where Mary Pickford did in her book *Why Not Try God?* In a true scientific and yet noble spirit, he sought and even after finding continued to seek as if the living God were a mine of ceaseless treasure, a fountain of truly living waters. That God is the Reality, the Life, the Love, the Bliss is neither new nor original. Papa Ramdas was not the first, nor will he be the last of such a stream.

The Scriptures say: "Prove all things; hold fast to that which is good" (1 Thess. 5:21). But instead of trying to prove, religion has often become dogmatic, asserting and assuming. Churches opposed the scientific evolution of the 19th century, both the doctrine of evolution and the manifest evolution

---

80 Swami Papa Ramdas died 25 July 1963

of the sciences. They have as well ignored the spiritual evolution of the day.

The lover of God is the lover of humanity. He does not have to hide in forsaken caves and monasteries. Jesus has told us, "Let your light shine before men." This can be a reality even here, even now and not just a symbol.

Go down the Malabar coast and not far from the town of Kasaragod, there is a little railway station called Kanhangad. A taxi or a man may be sent to take you to Anandashram, the "Abode of Bliss." It is like stepping into a Marie Corelli novel: someone will shortly appear and whatever has been your thought or wish will be provided. This is due to the living grace operating through Krishnabai, the Mataji or Mother, about whom we shall write later.

Like all conformations, Anandashram has been subject to change. Its early history is recorded in the writings of Swami Ramdas and in the records that have been scrupulously maintained. The divine grace that it proclaims manifests in all its operations.

Anandashram is Sanskrit for *Gan Eden*, which we translate as "Garden of Eden." Both mean, the "Abode of Bliss." All religions proclaim the primordial and the ultimate bliss; some insist that bliss and everyday life are not separate. This is the teaching of scriptures, unfortunately not the teaching of people, for people proclaim (they do not teach) what they themselves have not experienced. Bliss is operational. God can be and is known.

Swami Ramdas, whom many of us called "Papa," was what he preached. His writings and his personality alike were vibrant. He has given us his life down to little details. He has been both a man of the world and a *sadhu* (recluse). He has known both society and solitude; pain and pleasure have been his wont and his limitations. He lived in God, for God, with God.

One need not write at length about Swami Ramdas. One can obtain his books. He explained his Yoga as being *bhakti* in the beginning, then *jnana* and finally *bhakti* again. These words have no exact equivalents in English and are made more confusing because so much literature is offered from and by those who are neither *jnanis* nor *bhaktis*. *Jnana* is said to be the path-of-wisdom and *bhakti* the path-of-love-and-devotion. The terms are not exact. Even the most sober—and incidentally the greatest—of *jnana* yogis, Sri Shankaracharya, has given us beautiful love poetry.

Yet to this writer, Papa was the finest of the *mantra* yogis. He affirmed the name, he taught the name, he used the name, he manifested the name. Someday, it is hoped, the Christian world will look beyond "Hallowed be Thy Name" to the name (or word) that Jesus used. Sometime, it is hoped, the people of the synagogue will turn from *shemy rabbo* (the "name of the lord") to the word (or name) Moses used.

Practical people may wonder whether this has any meaning in the everyday life. We hear all over both from Zen-ists and others who seek emancipation that truth and everyday life cannot be separated, that *nirvana* and *samsara* are identifiable. Some people are sure that God must be against the communists; others are equally sure God must be against others. But is God *against*? Even the most bigoted Muslims must sooner or later recognize that Allah has permitted non-believers to discover and to invent improvements to the conditions on earth.

Papa Ramdas and Mother Krishnabai. Inscription gives their principal practice, the mantra Om Sri Ram Jai Ram Jai Jai Ram

The communists in the province of Travancore-Cochin in India have plenty of votes. India has abolished caste somewhat like we abolished alcohol consumption in the U.S. (though ultimately caste cannot persist in India nor segregation anywhere.)

There are many Brahmans in Travancore-Cochin, and there are many Brahmans who have had trouble with their parents or in-laws or the government there, just as in the United States. So among these well-born are plenty of crusaders who, through humanitarian zeal or through frustration or dissatisfaction, have become leaders in "working class movements." And in India, as elsewhere, this consists mostly of hating those in power. Personal observations indicate that politicians in Travancore-Cochin are more concerned with hating each other than in promoting justice.

Elections in Travancore-Cochin are hard-fought and close. The Congress Party wanted Papa's support. Logically, this seemed obvious. But God-conscious people, and even *vijnanavadis*, do not see the distinctions that analysts and dualists make. All of God's children have stomachs.

Papa loves everybody. From one point of view, I am a Muslim being a Sufi; from another point of view one could call me a Buddhist, for the whole life has been commingled with the intellectual and spiritual pursuit of the *Buddhadharma*. With Papa, I was his child, and in the last visit my closest companion was an Englishman who had the same sort of background and foreground.

If Papa had met Friedrich Engels, they would have probably gotten along fine. Actually at Anandashram, Papa concentrated on feeding the poor and not on treatises on the subject.

Anandashram lies at the foot of a mountain. There are some hillocks on the grounds, and the barn has been located on the summit of one of these. The barn is kept scrupulously clean and the washings gravitated into a surrounding foss [canal]. All available animal droppings are also thrown into the foss along with vegetable wastes. In other words, it is an organic gardening farm.

Springs have been found at two points where geological formations indicated they should be, and so a complete irrigation system has been provided. There is absolute regulation of water supply with the addition of the manure run-off, so together they are used to fertilize the soil. This is in accord with current practices in greenhouses: better a constant supply of weak fertilizers than periodical feedings. All this in a district where there is ample rainfall.

A sort of three-story farm has been established. Coconut palms are the foundation plants and the giants. There are two programs which operate under them, and these go on simultaneously:

A.) There is the continuous harvesting of protein crops. Besides the coconut, one finds cashews, peanuts and other legumes. It is also hoped that pecans and avocados may be added someday. And, of course, there is a perpetual supply of milk and usage of milk products.

B.) There is proper spacing so that smaller trees like papaya, cashew and banana can grow to full size. Below them are herbaceous foods including vegetables and legumes. Some leguminous plants are plowed under to provide further nitrogenous manure.

I did not see any rice growing at the Ashram nor did I make inquiries. Rice, milk and milk products are the basic foods served. There is also an endless supply of delicious "Brahma Coffee," which is supplied from a neighboring region. One can have all one wants—at breakfast, at least. No one starves and there are always guests—visiting *sadhus* and the poor of the surrounding region.

The economy has helped bring about an unplanned prosperity. There has been a slow increment in the purchase of land. This means the settlement of more farmers, who are selected for skill. The latest group included many Muslims. There was a vast diversity of class, religion and aptitude among the newcomers, and this in turn redounded to the good of the community.

Here we find poverty is faced, not by dialectic, not by ethereal planning, but by substantial effort. While the Congress and Communist Party people stood glaring at each other, the expanding Ashram has been caring for more and more of the poor of the region.

Theologians may dispute as to whether Jesus said, "The kingdom of heaven is within you" or "The kingdom of heaven is among you." The newly-recovered Gospel of St. Thomas gives both versions. Anandashram manifests both versions.

The *ashram* also has a hospital and clinic; attention is now being paid to having a suitable staff at all times. The "garden" is dominated by a kind of cotton bush that functions horticulturally like an ornamental rose. It supplies bolls continuously and keeps one person busy full-time through the year attending them, harvesting, spinning and weaving.

The real Yogi has met the real Commissar—and without hatred, without malice, without fear. Truly, God alone is great (*Allaho Akbar*)!

Mother Krishnabai

Papa has declared himself to be a little child, and he was remarkably childlike, only without ceasing to be a sage, a philosopher, a seer, a saint and a mystic. And like a little child, he was most fortunate to have had a loving mother in the person of Krishnabai.

Howard Williams, who coined the title "The Mother of Us All," calls Mother Krishnabai a living miracle. Her heart and being comprehend everything and everyone. She has assumed responsibility for the operations of the Ashram at all levels.

The Ashram is farm and hospital, hotel and retreat. She supervises every facet, down to the slightest detail, and she does this naturally. In the dining hall, in the kitchen, in the offices, in the chancel, in Papa's rooms, she flits like a stream of light. The guests are holy devotees, God-seekers—so received, so treated. The guests are her little children, needing food, needing comfort, needing solace and so treated. The poor of the neighbourhood are her charges, everyone needs love and protection. Mother Krishnabai is the servant of the servants and yet ...

The first meeting with Mataji Krishnabai came in San Francisco. There one learned again that *karma* yoga does not consist of lectures. In San Francisco, Mataji helped prepare a dinner for Swami Ramdas and one could observe her manners. It was like preparing for the communion service. Later I saw her both supervise in the kitchen at Anandashram and prepare the meals. She is the heart-blood of the *sangha* which brings all the vitality and takes away all the poisons.

India, Pakistan, 1956

Excerpts from Letter-Diaries

October 22-25 Ajmir

My coming to Ajmir was nothing but a series of miracles. Before I had put my baggage down, my room was invaded by Chisthi Sufis. How they found out about me, I don't know. I was with them constantly for two days and am now officially Ahmed Murad Chisti.

The impetus to study Indian music reached its height here. I have heard nothing like the Sufi qawwalis. They make Chaliapin and Marian Anderson look like amateurs. It is beyond belief what happens to the human voice actually in love with an actual God (as Murshid taught).

I spent many hours at the dargah of Khwajah Moineddin Chishti, the most celebrated Islamic shrine this side of Iran. There are a number of ceremonies that take place around the dargah. One has to kiss the steps, the cloth, the railing. Here I was given a strange blessing in vision, with two types of tassels put around me, and later a robe and shirt with the instruction that I was henceforth to represent Chishti Sufism in all non-Islamic lands. This was confirmed by Syed Faruk, my Hadim (guide), before I could report it verbally. I had an inner initiation from Moineddin Chishti and an outer initiation from Syed Faruq Hussein Chishti. Similar things happened in vision and outer form.

I also saw what I had seen in pre-vision: great iron pots that were used to feed the poor. There are many beggars around, too many in fact, but no starvation, and there has been little starvation in India, only malnutrition.

I saw many tombs and places of saints. I was taken up on a holy mountain, not an advertised "Mt. Abu" but one which you have to get "Masonic permission" to visit. That spiritual masonry which got me "in" at Hyderabad overwhelmed. I visited the shrine of Pir Wali Bakhtiar Kaki twice, the successor to Khwajah Sahib Moineddin Chishti.

The first meditation, I heard all around me: "What do you want? What do you want?" I answered: "Divine Guidance." "Go, you have it." The next time, I received a supernal instruction in the love and compassion side of Islam with a stern warning for the Pakistanis, who are 90% politics, 10% religion, and that religion in turn 90% smokescreen.

This visit, which was to have been the supreme goal of my trip, justified itself, and I left Ajmir feeling wonderful—excepting for too much food. Each group there seemed intent on showing that they could give me a bigger feast than the next. I learned a little of the connection between these Chishtis and the Nizami-Chishtis of Delhi.

With this combined backing of all the official Chishtis of India (five branches) and the U.S. government, there will be no repetition of the former nonsense in San Francisco with the "Professors Oxford." We are bringing peoples and countries together. Far from my greatest expectations, I have been in a series of whirls since reaching Japan.

October 25

After all the feasting given me in Ajmir, I became ill from dysentery upon leaving. I arrived in New Delhi, got the same rooms as previously and was about to collapse, being quite weak. But Pir-o-Murshid Inayat Khan appeared and said I should go to the Egyptian Embassy. So I went. There was virtually no one there, but there was one gentleman.

"What do you want?" he asked.

Out of me came, "I am interested in Moineddin Ibn Arabi and Islamic art before the Turkish conquest."

His jaw dropped. "How did you find me? I am the world's greatest authority on those two subjects! This is the first time that I have ever left Egypt and have just arrived here—and you found me." I told him how, and we became excellent friends. It was Dr. Muhammad Kemal Hussein. I came back from the embassy healed.

I visited Murshid's tomb as if for the last time. He told me he was everywhere, and as he had already manifested elsewhere, it was not necessary to pay spatial obeisance.

October 28 Lahore

The entrance into West Pakistan bears some resemblance to that into East Pakistan: hotel reservations not received. While this was being straightened out, I was able to contact the Ahmadiyyas.

Ahmadiyyas differ from Sunni Muslims on:

A. Death, etc. of Jesus (having about the same view as Roerich);

B. Selection of a reformer;

C. Modernization of customs;

D. Liberal versus rigid interpretation of Quran.

Yet I find rigidity here and suspicion of each other among Muslims who are divided also into Sunni, Shia and Ismaili. I shall try to follow this up. I am as yet unsatisfied with the way they write their books, using whitewash instead of ink.

November 4 Rawalpindi

Went to dinner on November 3 to meet a lot of VIPs. Spoke a few moments, and when I said I would introduce Sufism to Harvard was given an ovation, followed by questions and discussion with a few. One young man wants to introduce me to a saint.

I have since spoken on the influence of the Prophet on human destiny and on November 6 at the Forestry Experimental Station on "Forests I Have Dwelt in and Visited." Well-attended and met some fine scientists. I am awaiting tree lists from both the conservationist and director of the Forestry Station at this writing.

November 6 Abbottabad

I came to Lahore and was treated royally by the staff of the *Civil and Military Gazette,* the paper Kipling once worked for. I also made friends with the chief of security police and later with the public prosecutor (Boy—you'd better!). Then my geography got weak. In India, I had to use a railroad, highway and airlines map to get any idea of where and how I was to go. Here I have a railway map only and it is partial: little villages and big cities get the same consideration.

Abbottabad is not on the rail map and is much larger than many places that are. I am somewhere between Kashmir and the Indus Valley. The hill people are Pathans, where men are men and the hunting season is all year around. I saw the Rock Edicts of Asoka. Many centuries ago, he forbade the killing of birds, so the Pathans did not kill birds, only "mad dogs and Englishmen that went out in the noon-day sun." Now it is very quiet, especially the Pathans. The "civilized" Urdu people are busy doing nothing but having sit-down strikes to yell at Englishmen and favoring Egypt, and most of them do not know where England or Egypt are, much less the Suez Canal, and anything is better than working hard....

The Forestry Dept. has done a lot of work on medicinal trees and shrubs, which is out of my line, and a little—too little from my point of view—on mycology. The above leaves a lot of room to follow up. They have worked out an ecological map based on acacias for Western Pakistan. I once worked out the same thing for oaks in South Carolina.

November 12 Rawalpindi

I have before me *Great Men of India,* edited by L. Rushbrook Williams. The article on Aurangzeb is by Elizabeth D'Oyley, and on page 184 I found the prayer which I have searched for for years, having lost my copy:

"Less wise than Akbar his great-grandfather, he (Aurangzeb) could not see that no power on earth can make men think alike, and that God is to be reached by many ways. Wrote Abul-Fazl, friend of Akbar:

O God, in every temple I see people that see thee,
and in every language I hear spoken, people praise thee.
Polytheism and Islam feel after thee.
Each religion says, "Thou art one, without equal."
If it be a mosque, people murmur the holy prayer;
and if it be a Christian Church, people ring the bell from love of thee.
Sometimes I frequent the Christian cloister, sometimes the mosque.
But it is thou whom I seek from temple to temple.
The elect have no dealings with heresy or with orthodoxy;
for neither of them stand behind the screen of thy truth.
Heresy to the heretic, and religion to the orthodox.
But the dust of the rose-petal belongs to the heart of the perfume-seller."

November 18 Lahore

A tonga-wallah took me to a wrong shop, and there I learned that the brother of the owner was in Brooklyn seeking to start a Sufi order. Returning later, a merchant hailed me and explained that I could not buy anything more as God had put a limit on my purchases. I told him my name was Murad, meaning I was under grace and therefore different from a *mureed*, who was under the guidance of a spiritual teacher. A man standing nearby overheard me and identified himself as a *mureed*. As a result of that "chance" meeting, I have been to the assemblage of Naqshibandi Sufis, witnessed their ceremonials, took part in their zikr and was given a cap and beads. We also had a long conversation, as several of them spoke good English, and at least two had been to the U.S.

The *khalifa* in charge was very handsome with beautiful eyes showing love and spiritual light. After the experience of the meeting, I told one of the mureeds that I had never seen a man more like Jesus Christ than their *khalifa*. "You should meet our Murshid" was his reply. As he lives near Rawalpindi I hope to meet him. I had to bless them all and embraced nearly all the older men (an experience which left me "high" for two days afterwards.) Everybody was happy and they chanted loudly and joyfully "Allahu" as I was leaving. There is a great possibility that I shall become a recognized saint, a joke to the Western world and a very serious matter here.

November 23 Multan

It is gratifying to learn that I am fully accepted here as a Sufi, both by the actual Sufis and the professors of Sufi philosophy.

I have been with the chief engineer at the town hall here and learned about the problems of flies, soil fertilization, etc. They are doing compost work here, and I could come back and do a big job. We shall learn more when I get through the ropes at Karachi. But success is now beginning to tire me. I feel as if I have done enough, and more than enough. I will now go to the biggest people in the U.S. without compunction. I have learned not to be afraid of anybody.

These things were foretold again and again by Murshid. But I never was successful in communicating what Murshid told me, excepting to five people, four of whom, thank God, are still alive. One of them, in turn, added to Murshid's predictions and these have also come true. It is now done. The question will be what it means.

December 3 Karachi

There is the moral side of Sufism and the esoteric side. The one you learn by following the precepts and practices of others; the second, though you are given directions, you must perform for yourself. The moral emphasis is much greater than in Hinduism; the esoteric certainly less than in *tantra*. But Sufis never give long discourses on the wonders of wisdom. Discourses on the wonders of wisdom are only veils over truth. They often do not even awaken the intuitive qualities in us.

I am satisfied today with what I have accomplished. The immediate result is a bigger outlook before me. Sometimes I shudder at it.

December 3

I am winding up, I hope, my Asiatic tour. It has been somewhat more successful than my brightest hopes. The only disturbing factor is that either my mail has not gone through or I have failed utterly to convince my S.F. pals of what is being accomplished. That some mail has gone through is assured, but that mail has stopped is also evident because invariably my reservations do not go through.

I have entirely changed my point of view. I have converted myself to my own philosophy. This was one of integration, having an all-over view. It is very hard to understand, but once understood it goes over. Humanity is one. This knocks out with one blow all the dualistic views of those Pakistanis and Israelis and Chinese and Muscovites. What is a *class*? The Negroes contend there is only one race, the human race. If "race," is untrue, how much more untrue is the artificial "class"?

In practice, in S.E. Asia, if you are a great landlord or capitalist and pay lip-service to Marx and tribute to Mao, you are a "worker," and if you are a peasant and do not like forced collectives, you are a fascist enemy of the "working classes." Just take the stories of Alice by Lewis Carroll, treat them as realities, and you get some idea of Asia.

December 5

It is with some difficulty that I pen my closing words on leaving Pakistan and the continent of Asia. The recent events of my life and the future plans, such as they have been made, seem to stem from the instructions and advice of Pir-o-Murshid Ghaffour. The events that led me to the brethren in Dacca and the subsequent events seem all part of a sort of drama, an act of which is closing. As a man, and as an American, I have my personal ideas as to India and Pakistan . But as a servant of God and one who may be on the path of *Ansar* and *Abdal* and even *Wali*[81], I am supposed to help Pakistan.

December 17 London

Despite "Joy to the World," despite *nirvana*, despite Islam, there is almost universal gloom here, and I am running around calling myself "Puck of Pukhtunistan" and laughing. Jon says I look younger than 12 years ago, which may be true. I am Alice at the finish of the two books, finding all those great characters to be mere pawns or cards.

---

81 Levels in a Sufi spiritual hierarchy. See glossary entry for "Abdal."

The Journey Continues Within

Editor's Note

In 1952 Samuel Lewis met Gavin Arthur, the grandson of the American President Chester Arthur, who became a longtime friend.[82] Arthur, an astrologer and bisexual sexologist, later authored *The Circle of Sex* (1962), which looks at the varieties of sexual expression viewed as a circular orientation of the twelve zodiacal signs, rather than in a linear way as sexologist Alfred Kinsey had begun to do in 1948. Kinsey's work was already controversial, as was that of William Masters and Virginia Johnson, who began research into the human sexual response in 1957. Arthur's was even more so. One needs to remember that Western countries only began to decriminalize homosexual behavior in the mid- to late-1950s, and it is still illegal in many parts of the world.

Arthur introduced Lewis to Dr. Blanche Baker, with whom Lewis began to work in 1958 to heal trauma from his birth family. Baker was one of the first psychologists in the USA to put her career on the line by opposing the position of the American Psychiatric Association at the time that homosexuality was an abnormality or illness. She had been influenced by the "client-centered therapy" of Dr. Carl Rogers, who maintained that the most important factor in psychological healing was the atmosphere of "unconditional positive regard" held by the therapist for the client.

According to Gavin Arthur:

> He had this fearful inferiority complex, which she cured. I believe she really did, because after Sam got through with her course of psychoanalysis, he emerged as a very, very different person. He no longer had a chip on his shoulder all the time. And because he had devoted all his time to seclusion, when he felt that the world hated him, he was drawn into his shell. He made good use of the loneliness by becoming a tremendous scholar.
>
> [Dr. Baker] had a most remarkable gift for a psychoanalyst and also

---

82 Despite having lived in the "Dunes" community near San Luis Obispo at the same time, the two did not meet during that period, according to Gavin Arthur.

she could hypnotize. She would hypnotize her patients, and they would not only remember the birth trauma, she could hypnotize people into memories of former lives. And I think she helped Sam to orient himself and to find out why he had been born into this unattractive body and unattractive nature, where he mostly antagonized people. So if you know why you have handicaps on account of past life experience you can very often get rid of those complexes.

Every man needs a Diotima, like Socrates had in that priestess of the Eleusinian mysteries. If you want to be a philosopher, you have to have a woman like that. And Sam didn't have any woman like that until he met Blanche. I think this was the turning point—meeting a woman that he could talk to, absolutely in depth, as he would to a man.

In the following section, Samuel Lewis describes what he received from Blanche Baker. Just before beginning to consult her, he embarked on folk dancing as a passion. As he later described, dancing then became a "form of communion and communication." During this time, Lewis embarked on deep, emotional—albeit seemingly Platonic—relationships with several women and men in and around the folk dance scene in the San Francisco Bay area. The psychic Ramona Carillo, whom he met in about 1950, describes their early meetings:

He really had me sort of quite entranced with all the mystical developments that he had already acquired at his age. Then from time to time I saw Sam. Every time he would write something he would come over and bring me a package of poems and chat. And then very often, when he would go abroad, he would come back and invite me to have dinner or meet him someplace. One time we went to Chinatown and had a lovely Chinese dinner, and another time we went to I believe it was Mannings or someplace like that.

Lewis maintained a relationship with Carillo on and off until his death. Included below is an excerpt from his long 1950 poem, "Cantos Ramona," dedicated to her.

Lewis also maintained a long correspondence with another of his dance partners, Leonora Ponti, to whom he wrote frequently during his 1960-1962 trip to the East. Some of his letters to her during this period are also included below.

Before he left on that journey, Lewis describes how he came to fulfill various needs for personal relationship through the dance, and then finally became disenchanted with anything except a deeper aspect of it. As he speaks of folk dance fulfilling for him a "father instinct" and a "husband instinct," the influence of his therapy with Dr. Baker becomes clear. In a 1958 letter to Ponti, he describes a vision of this future, which would only become a reality ten years later:

> To bring nations of the world together by eating, praying and dancing is a program. I have other facets to my program: to help feed multitudes. I am working all the time at it. It has placed me under both strain and joy.

Shortly after this, in 1960, he embarked on his longer, second trip abroad, this time to Egypt, Pakistan and India.

Therapy with Dr. Blanche Baker

Selection from recordings and letters

October 2, 1968

(Describing his therapy on audio for a group of his Sufi students:)

I went to Dr. Blanche Baker, a psychiatrist, and I said to her, "I'll give you $200 unless my case is the worst case you ever had. And if it is, I'm going to ask you to treat me free, but first I have to prove that it's the worst case you ever had." I got it free.

I had trouble with my eyes earlier in life due to physical injuries. Dr. Baker, who was part psychiatrist, and part drugless physician, retrogressed me right to birth for the purpose of healing this. I found I was a seven-month baby—premature. Astrologically, this is funny, because I'm a mercury-type, in a hurry.

At one point in my life, I became totally and absolutely pessimistic to the point that I was a sort of left-handed masochist. I began expecting pain. My life readings have all been consistent. During one of them I finally began to see my whole karma, the justices in the injustice. If you take a single life, there's always injustice, but if you take a whole series, it all balances out. This has given me a much greater capacity for pain than almost anybody I meet. If I have a sort of composure, it isn't a real composure, it's a composure of having gone through such a tremendous quantity of pain, so that other things don't, by comparison, bother me. Perhaps, in the end, that's wisdom.

When we had a group therapy at Dr. Baker's and when it was my turn, I said, "My problem is that I don't feel pain. I don't know whether that's a problem or not, but things that used to scare me have been scared out of me, and I don't think that's good at all. If you were to look at my body, half the time you'd find cuts and scars—I don't feel them." I asked them in this group therapy what was wrong, that I didn't feel pain and I didn't have fear and I wasn't comfortable about it. Maybe it's a compensation or an overbalance, not a mastery. Most of them thought it was a compensation, but they didn't have any clear answer. It is not necessarily good, because pain is a warning. When you don't get it, you don't get warned.

December 31, 1960

[To Gavin Arthur from Cairo, Egypt:]

The death of Blanche has not made me wish to return to San Francisco. I shall probably return. It will be a different return or no return—that is, if it be not a different return, it will be no return at all. Life teaches me, it does not teach everybody. I see the same mistakes made. I have never asked to avoid mistakes, but I have said that if I repeat the same mistakes I ought to be punished.

Dr. Baker and I worked out my two basically detrimental karmic patterns. One was a pattern that was "inherited"—the pattern of the dominating woman, which was in my Neptune square Moon. After that I saw it was imperative not to have an older women dominate me. Of course there were not many older women. My mother is in a sad state. I was going to write to Gladys Phelps, whose birthday it is, and decided against it. Her mother did the same thing to me, returning nothing but evil for good[83].

The other woman who tried to destroy me did everything humanly possible and accused me on top of that. Someday you will come upon her name. She had a position of influence and she smashed my peace élan, caused me to lose my job and home and accused me of all kinds of villainy. Then a strange thing happened—my mother who wanted to get rid of me—also refused to join her. They worked independently against me, and at the climactic moment fought each other just long enough to enable me to escape. I got out of the clutches of that woman but not from my mother.

---

83 According to Murshida Vera Corda, in the 1930s Samuel Lewis and Gladys Phelps, the daughter of the librarian at Rabia Martin's San Francisco Sufi center, "had a love life that went on for many years. They were very close. They had a great love and attunement between them, although she married a pharmacist. But he had known her before that marriage. And all through those years he was a guardian, mentor and father to her three children by her first tragic marriage."

Cantos Ramona

From "Cantos Ramona"

(for Ramona Carillo, March 30, 1950)

Canto V

Echo is the shadow of sound,
Shadow is the echo of light,
Now that I have found
You, it is to let you know
That all I write is but an echo,
An echo in the night.

Canto VI

The warm delight of flesh is nothing
Before that grand exhilaration
Which the dance devises; everything
Disappears before the compelling elation,
When the consciousness is magnified.
Space and the self move side-by-side,
Rhythm speeds the spiral gyration
Which takes the dancer into the beyond
Where the lover is lost, but love is found.

"Eating, Praying and Dancing is a Program…"

From Letters To Leonora Ponti

January 29, 1958

The motifs from the past and the present combine love, joy and common ideals, one of which is the brotherhood of people through the arts. I cannot overemphasize this point and equally I cannot explain why it should be such a dominant theme in life.

My attitude toward Gracie[84] is not that of man toward a woman, not of a person toward another person, but as *life*, a part of oneself to another. The same is true concerning Leonard.[85] Sometimes I call this "fourth-dimensional" love, but sometimes it is also like no-dimensional love. It has nothing to do with other kinds of friendships. But it is contagious, self-explicit and even spontaneous. You are either in or out, and there are no halfway houses.

My trip to the orient is beginning to affect me psychologically like Darwin's "Voyage of the Beagle" affected him. It took years for him to get it out. The difference is that he withdrew from society, and I have not. But in going into the dance world, there was one motive: changing from an introvert life to an extrovert.

There was another, born of Havelock Ellis[86] which he called "the dance of the soul," which Leonard and Madelynne[87] understand, and again you either have it or haven't it.

At the moment, every time I come to town is a drain on time, energy and even money. I want to dance to discipline my body and to let it feel the same sort of sympathy the heart can feel—for people or other lands. This comes out of the older International Institute tradition. It is a dominant in my life.

I believe the mutual understanding of the dance is one of the ways to destroy world tensions. But mere pleasure, Leonora, becomes now a burden—it

---

84 Grace Perryman, a friend from the International Institute in San Francisco.
85 Leonard Austin, another friend from the International Institute, who also attended folk dance clubs.
86 See footnotes on Ellis in Section IV "Spiritual Dancing."
87 Leonard and Madelynne Green, teachers at one of the San Francisco area folk dance clubs Lewis attended.

steals from me what I want most. I wish you could understand this. I have something I cannot say until I write it out on paper, and in one sense, all the above and everything else is a pain to me, preventing me from accomplishing that which is closest to my heart.

April 5, 1958

My contact with Peter and Margaret have promoted my "father-complex." It seems to be going ahead great guns. Then you may ask why don't I bring these people into F.D. [folk dance]. Yes, into F.D., yes. But not into a place where I feel there is no constructive policy and the same type of background as in the "Fun Club."[88] I went to the "Fun Club," because Frank Dillard is very close to me, and there are a few people whom I might yet "father." But don't think I go in for fun-fun. As such, I get little enjoyment....

Why I dance and what I dance can, in a sense, not be explained at all. If they can be, they would be very definitely in the terms of Havelock Ellis's *The Dance of Life*. I must assume that you have not read it. I did not get the full import of that work excepting through experiences, many of them not common. And when experiences have been "common," I think I may have a special personal evaluation of them.

Dancing is to me both a form of communion and communication. Recent creations, not born from suffering, travail, trial and joy have little in them to interest me. I am getting out of earlier difficulties by developing innate faculties in myself, such as the father-instinct and husband-instinct. These are very real.

And this brings me down to the last point, the husband-complex. I have been turned down again and again and again. And never despaired. My life is that of a billiken[89] that is always knocked down to bounce back up. I took on the whole University of California recently and won my point. Of course I found plenty of allies who were in the same boat and needed a champion.

I lived for years under a "Beauty and the Beast" complex. I always felt intuitively that if any woman anywhere gave me a symbolic or psychic kiss, it would bring great changes in my character and career and outlook. Well, Leonora, it has happened.

I have been attracted to certain women here and there, and mostly to my own trouble later. I have followed the roles of a Lochinvar[90] and other storybook characters. It did no good. So then I became more like Vanderdecken,

---

88 Another of the many San Francisco area folk dance clubs during that time.

89 Merriam-Webster: "a squat smiling comic figure used as a mascot."

90 A character from the Sir Walter Scott novel *Marmion*. Lochinvar is a young knight who loves a woman forcibly engaged to be married to another. On her wedding day, he asks her first for a dance, then sweeps her off her feet and rides away with her.

the captain of the Flying Dutchman[91], who only had a chance every so many years. But when he met his Senta, it relieved him from the curse. Only with me it was "Beauty and the Beast," and no curse. And a real beauty has given me the "kiss"—it is true it has been at long distance, but it is true. And I feel both very sure and reassured that it is so. Time and tide separate us, but not in the heart.

This bodes quite a change in life. It will not take me out of the dancing field, it will alter it. All the dreams and schemes I have discussed with Leonard Austin are on the way to realization. To bring nations of the world together by eating, praying and dancing is a program. I have other facets to my program, to help feed multitudes. I am working all the time at it. It has placed me under both strain and joy.

I want to dance more than ever, but dances of release, dances of rejoicing after turmoil, and not mere Pollyanna-ish, superficial movements, created in recent times and palmed off as "folk dances." They are not a part of my psyche or my life.

---

91 A legendary ghost ship doomed to sail forever and never make port. It appears in several literary and artistic creations, most particularly the opera of the same name by Richard Wagner, in which the love story of Vanderdecken and Senta takes place.

Sex and Gender

Editor's Note

Throughout his life, Samuel Lewis repeatedly reflected on his own sexual life. In one of his letters, he described his own ideal as "polygamy with the same woman." A short selection of his writing on sex and gender from the 1930s and 1950s appears here.

In the first, "Sex and Work," he reflects on the human needs for sexual expression and deep relationships and the way that these needs increasingly conflict with the Western emphasis on work and economic production. This is one of many previously unknown writings of Samuel L. Lewis discovered in the Sufi Movement archives in the Hague, Netherlands in 1998. It was labeled: "From the archives of Shabaz Best of Rio de Janeiro, sent to him in the early 1930s and believed to have been prepared by Samuel Lewis (Khalif) for study classes at Kaaba Allah."

Twenty years later in the 1950s, most likely while in therapy with Dr. Baker, we find Lewis writing reflections on gender in the selection below entitled "The Different Types of Human Beings." He proposes that "genius" tendencies in sexual and gender expression, those that did not easily fit into previous, fixed cultural norms, were increasingly coming into existence. He argues for both education and changed laws to allow people with seemingly unusual gender and sexual expressions to live comfortably in society.

In his personal correspondence, Lewis often labeled himself a "genius" type, a term that he associated with two of his inspirations in this field, Havelock Ellis and Edith Ellis, bisexuals who were pioneers in what would now be called transgender psychology. Other gay, lesbian and/or bisexual writers whom Samuel Lewis frequently mentioned or quoted, in addition to Gavin Arthur, included Edward Carpenter, Ted Shawn, and Edna St. Vincent Millay.

Samuel Lewis with Gavin Arthur
(from the film "Sunseed")

Sex and Work

*From "On the Control and
Sublimation of the Vital Force" (1930s)*

Sex in the human being is a sign of divine presence just as much as eye or even heart is a sign of the divine presence. God has made humanity after the divine image and given collective humanity (*adam*) all the attributes and powers in existence. An individual man or woman may or may not have all these attributes, but the seeds to infinite bliss and unending possibility lie in their hearts.

***

[Sexual] inhibition is likely to produce very one-sided individuals whose sternness does not confine itself to social or personal matters. It may result in lack of fineness, kindness of heart, human consideration, appreciation of beauty and all expressions of joy. There is a tremendous difference between continence, that is to say, willing self-control for the sake of an ideal, and inhibition, restraint for its own sake. Beauty is a fundamental in life. When it is absent, something is missing in life.

The opposite state of affairs, continual search for self-expression for its own sake and not for any higher purpose, results in loss of strength and self-respect. If it does not appear evident at the time, it does later, and if it does not result in physical weakness, it certainly harms one mentally. Throwing off restraint opens the way to psychic leakage.

Every act of the body uses up some of its magnetism. When the physical magnetism of youth is wilfully wasted, nothing can take its place. When with it some of the mental and moral magnetism are consumed, one is already beginning to lead a death-in-life.

***

It is necessary that human beings should mate, it is not fundamental that they should be clerks, assembly line workers or unskilled laborers. We must not be bound mentally by the social forms we see around us nor by the industrial organizations or prevalent institutions. These come and go. It is a pity that many reverence institutions, many others put their faith in change, but few are looking for a truly humanitarian salvation.

199

Specialization concentrates mental effort and leaves much of the brain unused. There are deep longings for self-expression and for peace and joy in the heart. When balked, they manifest as increased sexual desire. Now it is not wrong and it is sometimes imperative that human beings find expression through physical embrace. This physical act, the skill of a trained hand, the efforts of a concentrating mind or a simulated imagination bring most of the happiness in life, because they are all forms of life expressing itself. When the pathways are blocked for either man or woman, be sure there is danger ahead.

Shorter hours of work will give more time for companionship. Constant companionship substitutes a slower process of exchange of psychic energy than the faster revolutionary embrace. Men and women will have ample opportunity to adjust themselves or to part company. There will be occasions for romance, which should stimulate the finer qualities in both. The encouragement of music, arts and crafts and kindred endeavors will be very helpful toward attuning people for marriage.

Instead of the road to marriage being swift and the door to divorce slow, the road to marriage would be slow and the door to divorce swift. This of itself would provide for fewer divorces and happier marriages.

The "Different Types of Human Beings"

From "Intimate Relationships" (1950s)

The advance of civilization, or evolution, seems to have drawn into the world more and more people who can be known as "geniuses." The genius is a true type, falling into several definite classifications according to temperaments and outlook, but all more or less "in the clouds."

Their glandular structure and functions are not the same as those of the human type, and there seem to be definite processes wherein the hormones created in the sexual glands manifest elsewhere and lead to the accentuation of characteristics. The result is that the genius is not always so faithful to his corporeal partner, in some respects reverting to the condition of early youth.

The subject of sublimation has not been given consideration. But it was a genius, Havelock Ellis, himself married to another genius, Edith Ellis, and in love with still another genius, Olive Schreiner, who dared to study many aspects of sex relationships and complications considered too "awful" by the world in his time[92]. He himself did not feel strongly any pelvic urge although he never lost the attraction for the opposite sex, or at least one or two members of it.

It would seem that the body of the genius is in many respects finer than the purely "human" body and of course much more so than the animal body. The light striking the earth plane careens and is reflected back towards its course. The psychic and mental faculties are much more refined, but all of them do not develop; some abort, others are accentuated.

So the genius seems unbalanced and he is unbalanced from the strictly "human" view. But it is only an "unbalanced" person who can work day and night, whether in the laboratory or studio, to turn out something which the world will delight in, while condemning the author thereof.

---

92 Havelock Ellis (1859-1939) wrote the first medical textbook in English on homosexuality. He also published works on the great variety of sexual practices as well as on transgender psychology. Edith Ellis nee Lees 1861-1916, was a women's rights activist and openly lesbian. She and Havelock lived in what they called an "open marriage," which was a central subject in her autobiography. Olive Schreiner, 1855-1920, was a South African author, anti-war campaigner and feminist who met Havelock Ellis in London in 1884.

Artists and actors in particular seem unstable in their marital relationships. If they knew better, they would not always live in the same house, or if in the same house, not always in the same room. Their attraction is usually longer and deeper if not indulged in too much. It is like rare food and wine, which the gourmet delights in, but does not ever overindulge in, in order to maintain his delight.

Too often the very proximity of the other sex, whatever be the motives and factors, leads to a kind of revulsion that terminates in homosexuality. This subject is rather complex, from the healthy aspect found in young children who play with their own, to the "wolf-and-lamb" of the gutter. But without regarding homosexuality as abnormal and unusual (and it may be neither), we can say that the genius types can only remain in each other's company as their love is great. Besides they love solitude and when they do not have it, they tend to turn away from their mates.

As the world has not given room for relaxation, solitude and peace, and as everyone is more or less agitated, we can see most of all in Hollywood, where so many geniuses have congregated, a sort of "dance of life" in which the tendency is to change partners.

Perhaps if one were to look directly into the world of the geniuses, one would see the same things. One does see it in adolescents, and the genius is not so different from the adolescent except, perhaps, in the one or two fields in which they have specialized.

The answer to this situation can only come in providing a complete, all around education for the genius-type and for all human beings, or for the correction of our laws to make it easier for them to live in this world. Such changes would on the one hand diminish suicides and perhaps murders, but on the other hand might disturb the equilibrium in other groups.

So what is needed most is a recognition of different types of human beings, a serious study of some of the traditional metaphysics and psychology of India, and nowhere more than in that country itself by the inhabitants thereof.

VI.
JOURNEYS TOWARD THE RISING SUN

*Samuel Lewis, wearing robe of investiture as a Sufi Murshid
given by Pir Barkat Ali of Pakistan in 1962.
For the photo Lewis exhibits the Sufi practice of tawajjeh,
or sharing magnetism through the glance.*

Egypt, Fall 1960

Excerpts from Letters-Diaries

August 27 Onboard, Mediterranean Sea

Dear Leonora,

I have not kept a diary. In crossing the Pacific, my stomach was bad and my head good. In crossing the Atlantic, my stomach was good and my head bad. Still I prefer the latter. We ran into hurricanes and billows until we neared the Azores. After that, things calmed down, head got better and I have been feeling fine since.

I found that many of the officers seem to like folk music. One man specializes in Polish dances and on American things that we use in square dancing. Purchased a small transistor from Japan just before I left New York. Got it at an inside price. Around the Azores, we began picking up Portuguese stations and more and more of them, and then Moorish stations. We had a near collision last night, and the whistles woke me up just in time. For we were passing Gibraltar, and I thought the whistles were signalling that. I found nearly everybody was up to see the lights on either side.

Have written a few other letters, but again don't know where I shall post them. We do not land until Beirut, which means a quick trip, but after that… I get off at Alexandria.

September 8 Cairo

I am now in Cairo, and I find things totally different from most reports. The first thing I ran into is that, for all practical purposes, the United States has gone "underground" and is doing very well indeed.

The countryside, coming down from Alexandria, looked far more prosperous and energetic than anything I have seen in India or Paki stan, or for that matter, Mexico. It may be that I have come during the "bright" season. The Nile impressed me far more than the Indus or Ganges—all of these are different from the rivers of the "Far East," where many people live on boats and fish or trade therefrom.

I am both going slow and yet not losing time, trying to fall in with the local rhythm. As Monday was Labor Day, I could do nothing with Americans and called at Al-Azhar, the famous Egyptian University. I may be going there again.

My main Egyptian host is now in the United States, but I shall be a guest of the Government Agricultural Department on Saturday. Another host is also away, and I shall wait until he returns. He is head of one of the banks and also the Chamber of Commerce here. Make no mistake about it, this country is not "neutralist" economically. It is definitely ahead of any Asian nation except Japan. I shall not compare it to Israel, which was heavily subsidized from abroad.

One of the outstanding features is the willingness and the policy to "begin at the beginning:" Our old homestead idea of "40 acres and a mule," slightly modified, is the basic feature here. The U.S. is helping this become established, both in the older lands already cultivated and in new lands being opened up. The water research is going ahead full speed. Americans are working with Egyptians at their level and pace. There is no published material; it is all done slowly and quietly.

The banking and business sections indicate a nation quite bourgeois in outlook, but with strong doses of humanism and humanitarianism. After all, there is plenty of land. American engineers are undertaking hydrological surveys and on a grand scale. This land used to be rich, and water is underground at many places. It has strange physical and chemical properties that are being studied. This will lead to indications as to what crops may be sown. There are, fortunately for me, many University of California graduates in high places in both American groups and in the UAR government itself.

In other words, here is a land running on essentially capitalistic bases, modified by monetary power, and the enormous tracts of lands that have become deserts. On the other hand, the people are more strictly Muslim in a certain sense than elsewhere, and this keeps them from following the United States with its strange mixture of Christianity and libertinism, which become confused in the eyes of foreigners.

Recognition of folly in the past, such as cutting down trees, is quite evident. The planting of eucalyptus trees, which I tried to "sell" in India, is operative here on exactly the basis I wished to see: fast growing trees, giving firewood and enabling the farmer to return dung to the soil.

September 10

I have not been in Egypt one week and my troubles have begun. No, not that kind. Things happen so fast that there is not enough time to record it in my diary or it is too hot—and then more things happen.

There are, however, two passwords. The first password is *"assalaam aleikhum"* which means *"pax vobiscum"* in Arabic. By means of it, I got a courtesy visa and entered this country as a VIP. All they looked at was my radio and typewriter (and to think what I might have done with Luckies and Chesterfields!).

September 20

The subject is the problem of the Nile. Now I am not so vain as to presume I can offer a "solution" to a large problem. I came to a conclusion, which may have merits and demerits, but have been terrifically stimulated by two books borrowed from the American Library near here. The first is *Out of the Earth* by Louis Bromfield. The second is *Theory and Dynamics of Grassland Agriculture*. Both these works emphasize the need of restoration of organic matter to the soil.

Turning to the Nile, I have been opposed to the Aswan Dam for many reasons. One is that the cost is too much for the nation, and the same money, used in salt water conversion plants and in a more complete hydrological survey including chemical analyses of soils and water, would be more effective.

In one respect, the Nile resembles the Indus. India and Pakistan have just signed an agreement with regard to the waters. On the other hand, it resembles the Colorado, where a number of states have entered into a pact almost like an international agreement. But there is no such pact concerning the Nile. And it is always possible that Ethiopia may indulge in engineering projects like Colorado, carrying water over a watershed into another region where feasible, to open up large tracts. Ethiopia is a land of extreme contrasts between wet and dry regions, and she may do something about it.

In the southern part of Sudan, there is a region called the *Sudd*. It is filled with papyrus plants, often called worthless. Sudan also has vast deserts, though there is some rain in parts. Presumably these deserts, like those of Egypt, have a high pH. It came to mind that it might—just might—be possible to dredge the region, making channels and taking the muck and organic matter and putting it on the land. Simple grinders might do the work (or there may be other methods) and this would benefit both the river and the land.

Today I visited the Vegetable Experimental Station and took up the soil problem briefly. They told me that manure was plentiful and cheap. Granted, but the pH of manure is certainly higher than that of most leaf molds. And with a high pH in the soil already, this is only a partial corrective. Next Sunday, I am scheduled to go to the Soils Department and will report to you what I find out there.

September 18

Many factors are working for me here. The two outstanding are my interest in Islam and my being a life member of the University of California Alumni Association. The third element in my position is the type of integral thinking I indulge in.

Today's venture was my second to Al-Azhar. They understand pretty well the situation in the United States, and I told them that I was in no hurry for

207

a plan of action. I took a note over to Al-Azhar Mosque, but the attendant speaks English and welcomed me. This made me feel very happy.

There are actually two mosques, one being a grand courtyard, surrounded by alcoves. There were many classes in these alcoves; so far as I could see, they have co-education with the boys and girls, not particularly different than in our country. The inner mosque is, I presume, the famous one. There were a few classes going on, entirely of older people. As I belong to the Chishti tariqa, they told me some of their objections. I admit ceremonially and outwardly there is "saint worship," but inwardly there is something else, and there are only two ways to convey that "something else." One is by a visit and the other is by disciplinary instruction.

The tone here is of high intellectual approach, and I am thoroughly in favour of it. I am not looking for saints. I am not looking for noble moral outlooks in others that are not reflected in my own life. So far as I can see, President Nasser did work out a grand revolution in so many directions that we in America, who have never bothered to study Egypt, may never really discover it.

My "undiplomatic" ways of life constantly open new doors for me, and I am seeing all kinds of things, but mostly in the technical fields to date. Tomorrow I shall try to find an Egyptian versed in both modern science and Sufism. So I am having a grand time, despite my grumps.

October 2

Two weeks ago I was told I would be in for a grand surprise and met one M. M. Billah, who is a leading scientist here and a member of the Shadhili Order. It was love at first sight, and has been ever since.

Actually it is very difficult to delineate between "orthodoxy" and "Sufism" in the lives, not of the poor, ignorant and superstitious, but in the lives of the most educated and enlightened people here. Yesterday, Mr. Billah said he that he would like me to accompany him on the birthday of the original Syed Hussein, the Prophet's grandson. His tomb is here in a mosque that I have visited. There will be a gathering of *dervishes* from all over the Near East. And praise to Allah, our birthdays fall on the same date. I am looking forward to this occasion like a child to a great party.

Last week I visited most of the historic mosques. It is difficult to write much at the first visit, because some of them are architectural monuments, some quite artistic and others must be distinguished by their inner atmosphere of (what to me is) sanctity. I have heard some chanting almost up to the level I heard in Ajmir. I called my companion's attention to the difference between the singing of the devotee and that heard on the radio. He had not noticed it before. Sometimes I wish I had a tape recorder with me, but one must not interfere with the connection between the devotee and Allah.

October 15

I have been going around in deep waters, and what happens is that I generally get in deeper and deeper water about everything. I am scheduled to meet the head of the Pan-Arab League and I can turn over to him the research I did in Cleveland, Ohio. I have been going around trying to find out whether the food supply may or may not be augmented by algae research and will write that below. Then my friend Mr. Kinoshita (of The Friends of the World) in Tokyo wrote that he is going to send soy and garlic seeds here. After I mail this I go to the Vegetable Experimental Station, only now with a long list of stuff....

October 19

Yesterday was my birthday, but here it was the birthday of Hussein, the grandson of Prophet Muhammad, who is said to have obtained the divine wisdom and to have died a martyr. Although the people are not Shias, the day was a holy holiday, and the night time was the climax of a festival that began Monday.

The same is true of the Arabs as with all other Asian peoples I have met: it is very difficult to delineate between Islam and Sufism until you get deeper into what is called *tariq* [the esoteric school]. The first nonsense that has to be cleared away is that there are not many Sufis or persons interested in Sufism and that they are a lot of fanatics and superstitious humbugs who are lazy or worse. My immediate introduction has been through Muhammad Murtaz Billah. I do not know whether he was converted to Sufism or not, but if so it was by his wife. And who is his wife? She is a top graduate, who is now training for her Ph.D. by doing research on ice cream.

The Khan el Khalili is a bazaar district near Al-Azhar. It is full of narrow streets and lanes and has many small mosques and still more khankahs where Sufis meet. One needs a guide at night unless one has a compass. Last night was something like a mixture of Chinese New Year and a summer fair at the same time. Tremendous crowds surged down alleys, lanes and what not. Progress was made difficult by boys using a sort of football formation to surge forward, endangering the blind. There was considerable lack of human consideration.

There were many women in the more open places, but the narrow spots had only men. There are women *dervishes* who meet separately, I found, but so far only the Chishtis have had the men and women do *zikrs* together.

It took us quite a while to find the Shadhili *khankah*. Each group meets separately in the same building. My friend's sheikh is no more, but two or three khalifs led the ceremonies. There was some reading of Qur'an and chanting, then the *zikrs*, singing the name of Allah, which I could join.

The first thing noticeable was that these *zikr* groups perform functions like both antiphonal and choir singing in the Christian churches (but to me with a rather purer sound). Later on, there were melodious songs—beautiful arias, not just chants—in which others, including the younger men, repeated a phrase of *zikr* as a sort of rhythm-background. Then we held hands and performed *zikr* standing close together and later on in a sort of jump movement with some swinging their heads. This was heightened in speed and loudness for a while and touched the depths of my being. Then they varied the *zikr* phrasing. I notice all Sufi schools do this somewhat, passing from the intelligible to the semi-intelligible or non-intelligible intellectually. On this point, Alan Watts has been entirely correct.

I find when one says *Elah* instead of *Allah,* it is much easier to sing and feel. I noticed also that these men tended to pronounce the name of God, i.e., Allah, as I have been wont to do. I have been corrected in parts of India, but stubbornly refused to withdraw. Whatever impetus I have had for my pronunciation, it accorded with the Shadhili chanting and must have made me more welcome.

The ceremony was long and involved. After it, we had some discussion, food, more discussion and finally tea. The one thing I objected to was the insistence that I must learn Arabic. And so far as Sufism is concerned, the "mantric" modification of words makes the argument seem weaker than ever.

On the other hand, in conversation with those who speak English, I find surprisingly great agreement. Orthodoxy is needed for the beginners. It is best to be trained in some form of ceremony, law and custom, but that is introduction only. The men explained "spiritual liberty" exactly the same as my first Pir-o-Murshid Inayat Khan did, and they had the same attitude toward religion and religions. The educated ones were far from dogmatic and were all universal. There was agreement that Muhammad was the "seal of the prophets," which meant recognition of all prophets and their teachings. This was far from the Arabism of some of them.

Around 10 o'clock we went to the Syed Hussein Mosque, where three groups of *dervishes* were holding forth, but the place was too crowded. Then we visited some other *khankahs* where the groups were completing their sessions. Most of these were "wild," but the largest one seemed to be made of intellectuals, who were sober and far more numerous. The Rufais were more ecstatic than the Shadhilis, but some of the latter were also very wild. I did not meet the Naqshibandis. The first and most obvious impression is the fact that there are many thousands of Sufis here.

I find that not only do the *zikr* sessions take the place of hymn and other singing, but there is undoubtedly a lot of blowing off of steam and even transmutation of sexual and lower faculties. This is obvious when one sees so many hundreds of young men. We have not looked into the psychological advantages of these processes, and I do not intend to do so now. But there is a moral advantage, and more. A single experience on almost any level is worth thousands of lectures....

The *dervishes* as a whole are more on the occult than the mystical side, but this is no doubt due to the fact that mystical experiences per se come from divine grace. If you don't have some clairvoyant experiences here, you just don't get it. I do not know how far this is so. The books on Sufism are all wrong. Sufism did not develop in Persia. Yes, you had mystical poets there. But the atmosphere of Egypt is thousands upon thousands of years old and electrified and magnified esoterically.

I condemned a young Christian severely until he was pale, and then said, "Wait. I am only half done. Now I am going to answer every one of my objections." He knew nothing of gnosticism or the early Christian yogis who lived in Egypt or even of the Gospel of Thomas. I sent him back to his church. Fortunately, as the engineers clear land here and dig for water, they also combine archaeological digging and may bring to light much of the Christian gnosticism and hermetism that has been covered by the sands. This is more interesting to me than ancient Egypt, and there is a big gap here. But the atmosphere is the same.

October 26

I am overworked largely because my plans are being taken seriously. There are two definite themes here, and they are in some ways similar.

Egypt, after 2500 years of domination by foreigners, is coming into its own. We do not realize the amount of energy awakened by this. And in my own life, every plan I ever had thwarted by selfish persons has been accepted. If there is a single thing of my earlier life not accepted here, I do not know what it is. It keeps me busy, as all business must be done in the morning, and then I have to write, do research, run errands and what not the rest of the day, and this is limited by the warm weather.

I have written some strong letters to the State Department on account of our ignoring the Sufis. Damn it, Bill, There must be at least 50 million people under Sufi training and we pay no attention. Instead, a lot of professors who get their education God knows where deny their existence and give out as Islamic philosophy whatever they choose to.

My plans for introducing American poetry are being completed, to accompany talks on American philosophy. Behind it all we have nothing to fear if we can love people. This is the spirit of Sufism, too. But those who were interested in lnayat Khan became involved in personality.

Not many accept this world as it is, and so we have international misunderstandings. The President makes wonderful speeches and the talks dead-end. Whom is he kidding?

October 30

Yesterday I had the first day off since I have been here. It is easy to get a bus to the pyramids as the terminus is at the square nearby. I used a guide who knows many languages and says he reads hieroglyphics. It does not matter. I visited Mina (which we call Giza), Memphis and Sakkara in one day. What I am reporting is not exactly in line with what I have read. There is no change regarding the esoteric transmission, but the places are different.

Somehow or other I was not interested in the Great Pyramids. I may climb the big one later, and I have been inside. I did not get the impression conveyed by the books; it was psychic, a la Paul Brunton, and not deeply esoteric. I was more interested in the Sphinx, and I came away feeling that Marjory Hansen and Edgar Cayce were right, that there is a lot of excavation to be done.

I get no sense of finality. As the Sakkara pyramids are much older, there could easily be old buildings in the region of the Great Pyramids. I saw nothing like bottom ground, such as I saw at Taxila (in Pakistan), where only after at least six levels of digging were completed was there any conclusion that there were no cultures below. Even where there are 200- and 400-foot shafts here, there is no indication that rock bottom has been reached.

It is about Sakkara I wish to write. When I studied Shure[93] I felt very sure I had at one time been an initiate in ancient Egypt. I have psychically repeated the process, and at certain times this was repeated in my own life. I see nothing to support the Rosicrucian theory that any Amen Hotep IV or Akhenaton developed the ancient mysteries. I have seen no evidence that the ancient mysteries were not very ancient, just as H.P. Blavatsky said. And it was at Sakkara that I got it right in the face - and beautifully.

To begin with, despite all books, there is one pyramid we entered that showed rooms. I understand there is at least one more that was also used. Thirty-three pyramids have been uncovered and 20 more in a state of ruin. The very number is much larger than was taught at an earlier date.

There is no question in my mind that I have been in this pyramid before. It is exactly what I have seen in vision during my Shure days, down to small details. It also validates the saying of Jesus, "Straight is the gate and narrow is the way and few there be that find it." As in Shure you have to climb on your hands and knees; as in Shure, there are the decorations, which I did not see in the Great Pyramid. These decorations were hieroglyphic, esoteric and initiatory. The whole time I was at Sakkara, I was in such an ecstatic mood, I

---

93 Edouard Shure (1841-1929), French philosopher, novelist, author of a number of works on esoteric literature, including *The Great Initiates: A Study of the Secret History of Religions* (1889).

could neither take notes nor follow my guide, because things were constantly attracting my attention. I am quite willing, even anxious, to spend a full day at Sakkara with no Memphis or Mina. To me this was it and is it.

Blanche [Baker] loaned me some books written by a person who seems to have memories of former lives in Egypt, which also indicates a high degree of spirituality and esotericism at an early period. I feel sure of it. Sydney Corrine used to say that the Dendera Circle showed a civilization covering two complete cycles of the equinox, that is, going back 50,000 years or more. I have not been to Dendera, and I am not going to Luxor until the weather calms down, which will be in December. I may or may not have the Paul Brunton experience with adepts down there.

Here I am meeting the *dervishes* whom, as I have said before, are the esotericists. When I told my close brother here of my experience with the pyramids, he said it was the same with him and that he is sure that Sakkara was the center of initiatory rites. I am not so much slapping the Great Pyramid as elevating earlier ones in the point of occult history. The Great Pyramids seem to have been for the dead and some at Sakkara for the living.

November 12

The news from South Viet Nam does not surprise me. A number of years ago, my dear friend Robert Clifton was in San Francisco and gave me a lengthy, objective report on South Viet Nam. I placed this before Alan Watts and the State Department, and they both brushed it aside. I later visited that part of the world, saw Clifton again and had my own direct experience. He visited me in S.F. in 1959.

The establishment of a Christian government on Buddhist people does not go well with those people, and then when that government is corrupt as well, the USA gets the blame. I am not surprised at the revolt, but we cannot predict the denouement. It is certain that we have not regarded the Vietnamese as equals in anything, and they don't like it.

On another plane, something like that is going on here. The masses in Tunisia stormed the U.S. Embassy, and now the Algerians are doing the same. We give them food, culture, morality, kindliness but we do not give them reciprocity. We do not take old civilizations and cultures seriously, and we ought to take them very seriously.

The other evening I was with Professor M. Kemal Hussein, and he gave it to me strongly about the Americans who are permitted to offer their culture here, but the opposite is not true. He considers his nation as an intellectual equal and literary superior, but scientifically and technologically much inferior. He wants reciprocity, but reciprocity is about the last thing that seems to be offered.

The next day I visited the Egyptian Library and picked up a book on the Sudan. What the writer said about the Sufis and *dervishes* in every way contradicts the "textbook" the American Information Service here uses on the subject. This writer had the audacity to go and visit the Sufis instead of writing his pipe-dream about them. He found them, of course. Because of the multiple memberships in Sufi orders, one can deduce that there are more Sufis in Sudan than inhabitants.

November 26

I learned that it is very difficult to get rooms in Luxor after December 1st, so I went down and spent two days there. It was delightful that I found Californians all over the place, including family friends who are on guided tours covering the whole world. There seems to be a lot of that sort of thing. The Luxor-Karnak area seems to be highly "civilized" and advanced, and I did not get much spiritual feeling. But I got even less that the fine art work was done by slaves.

Upon entering the hotel there, I was met by a registering clerk who would accept no tip, nothing, except when he saw my *tasbih* (prayer beads), he said, "I want those."

"Nothing doing," I replied, as they were very expensive. The clerk kept insisting. When we got to my room, I explained that I could not let him have the beads, because not only was I already a teacher and was using the *tasbih*, but I could only give them to a sheikh.

"I am the Sheikh," the clerk said. He was, too. Naturally, I gave him the *tasbih*.

The east (Luxor) side of the river has been called the "living side," which had temples and apparently homes. The west side (Thebes-Valley of the Kings) had the tombs and funeral temples. This includes the celebrated Tut-ankh-amen and the now being excavated tombs of Seti I and Seti II. On the Luxor side, I stayed at the Winter Palace Hotel, which has excellent meals, and I may come again for two reasons not connected with gardening: a) I met *dervishes*, and b) the headquarters of the American Oriental Institute is nearby with an excellent library.

The garden at the Winter Palace is full of the same kind of annuals and perennials which you have around you. The chief difference is the use of phoenix and ficus as foundation plants. The lay out is geometrical and formal, but one is surprised to find even here, where the summer temperature runs to 100 degrees and more, that roses thrive. Evidently some strains must be able to take the heat.

More important is the Queen's Temple [Temple of Queen Hatshepsut, near the Valley of the Kings] itself. It seems she was quite a horticulturist herself, and sent to Punt (which is perhaps Eritrea) for all kinds of shrubs. Chief among these is henna, which grows in that region both as an ornamental and commercial plant. The police came up when they saw I was taking notes. I did not know that jotting down the names of flowers was a subversive activity, but you never can tell....

"Science is Stirring in the Mid-East"

Newspaper Article

(from the *San Rafael Independent Journal*, January 21, 1961)

T he last time wandering Marinite Sam Lewis of Mill Valley made head-lines in the *Independent Journal,* he was just back from a tour of the Orient where he became a member of the mystical *dervish* orders of Chishti and Naqshibandi.

Today, he is in another distant country—Gamal Abdel Nasser's United Arab Republic.

Based in Cairo, he is carrying on a campaign with two general aims:

- To assist the country in increasing its food supply.
- And in so doing, to boost American prestige and reduce communistic subversion.

More specifically, Lewis is dedicated to the bringing of helpful American agricultural and scientific bulletins and magazines to the Egyptians to aid them in enticing more food from their soil.

The project, he says, is the result of his visit to Asian countries in 1956 and a talk that followed with the U.S. Department of Agriculture in Washington, D.C.

The idea explored there was to promote the introduction of suitable trees and crops to help countries deficient in food and timber. Lewis has paid several visits to the UAR's National Research Center where the leading scientists of the Near East coordinate their research efforts.

"I should say that their methods and effectiveness are in general on the level with the best that I have seen in the U.S. and Japan," he reports. "Whenever and wherever possible, they have the best equipment. And personnel is highly trained. Most of this personnel is Egyptian, but large numbers are graduates of American universities, and half of these come from the University of California."

Lewis says the UAR Information Bureau has furnished him with considerable literature on the progress of that country under Nasser.

"In contrast to what appears in the newspapers or even in the magazines, this information is calm, sedate, factual and actually more optimistic than the emotional propaganda. With all the faults here, I find progress has been much more rapid and secure than in many other lands."

Lewis also says that the stress which has been placed on the UAR's position in world politics has tended to obscure its growth and importance in such fields as science, technology and commerce.

Of Nasser's influence in his own continent, Lewis says:

"The new African nations and some others are watching Nasser, and they have been favourably impressed by him. So when the time comes, they will vote with him or for him or both. They probably don't like China and may abhor Russian communism, but they can't understand us."

Lewis has praise for one facet of the U.S. effort to solve this dilemma.

"We are now sending musicians and singers to these countries who can meet people at their own level," he declares. "We are changing the policy of wasting millions of dollars on symphony orchestras and ballet troupes, which reach very limited audiences, and are soon forgotten."

He says the most successful touring orchestra he has seen and heard was a group from the Philippines.

"They played almost entirely American and Latin American music, along with a few tunes from their own country," Lewis says. "There was nothing European on the program."

Goodwill ambassador-observer Lewis, at home or abroad, does not confine his activities to the scientific and horticultural fields.

One interest is the writing of epic poetry. Egyptian scholar Dr. Kemal Hussein, Lewis reports, has written a favourable review after an advance look at his newest piece of poetry entitled "Saladin," which is dedicated to that great warrior and his country.

"I write epic poems to prove that Americans can understand the peoples of distant lands," Lewis says.

In his special field of horticulture, his next project will be research on edible common flowers, he says.

"This looks like a good lot for one man," he admits. "But," he continues, "I take the Cold War seriously, because all the information I have obtained here is that population is going up and agricultural production down in many lands. I think we can help to correct this situation."

Lewis says his efforts are not so much based upon anticommunism or "anti-anything" as they are pro-American.

Egypt, Winter 1961

Excerpts from Letter-Diaries

December 13 Cairo

This afternoon I visited at least six mosques. We went to Bab-i-Zuela, which has two mighty minarets and a wonderful gate. I was struck by the colored glass work, different from that of the Christian churches. The one I cared for least was the grand Muhammad Ali Mosque—very huge, ornate with all grand ornaments, lighting and art work, but no fine feeling. This is built on the top of the citadel near the gates and wall of Saladin, which interested me. But today was Mosque Day, and I did not bother too much about the other remains.

The two mosques that interested me most were those of Sultan Hasan and the Rufai, which are opposite each other, just below the Citadel and are both Sufi mosques. It is certain that the Rufai Mosque gave me the grandest of spiritual uplifts I have had since reaching this land. In general these mosques preserved fine wood carving also, and the Sultan Hasan Mosque is a grand example of Islamic architecture. Nevertheless, if I go to the Sultan Hasan and Rufai Mosques in the future it will be to meditate and pray, rather than to examine art and architecture.

December 19

Last week I went to three *dervish* groups. I visited Sheikh Abu Salem Amria twice. They meet in a very new and clean mosque that is said to have been the property of the late unlamented Farouk.[94] Now it is kept exceedingly clean and bright. There were about 400 people—or rather, men—last night. How many women meet upstairs I don't know.

Each authority on Sufism gives his bosh about it being "derived" from Brahmanism, Buddhism, Christianity, Neo-Platonism, Zoroastrianism, Shiism and what not. None offer evidence, and none consult the Sufis themselves. The Sufis say, and I believe them, that some of the methods are of ancient lineage and the chief difference is the substitution of Arabic and Qur'anic materials for those in existence prior to the time of Muhammed.

---

94 1920-1965, last king of Egypt, overthrown in the Egyptian Revolution of 1952.

But there is a scientific way to test that nobody has looked into at all, and I have never seen in any books excepting those of my own Pir-o-Murshid Inayat Khan. His works are available in English, but with the exception of the World Congress of Faiths in England, not a single "authority" refers to them. He was especially trained in music and his original intention had been to make a voluminous work called "The Mysticism of Sound." This was never done, and instead he wrote a short book on the subject.

The use of music by *dervishes* is far, far greater than even I had dreamed. I had thought, and I found quite different, that only the Mevlevis made much use of music. That order is weak here and has become decadent. The Rufais at the Sidi Sharani had responses and antiphonies, and they even sat in a way that makes me feel there might be Christian predecessors (certainly the gnostics, who have long since disappeared). It is certain that the two kinds of singing that I heard at the Shadhili and Rufai gatherings are not at all like the usual Arabic and far different from the Qur'anic chants.

December 31

I am closing a most edifying year. Everything has turned around and I think every upset of almost every earlier part of my life has been reversed.... I again went to mosques Thursday and Friday and expect to tomorrow also, *in-shallah*. The atmosphere alone is feeding. The loving and lovable people here are far more numerous than one meets in many parts of the world.... Had a wonderful Christmas dinner, taking two young Americans as guests and go out with another one tonight.

It is morning, and the year has greeted me with a great inspiration.

January 4

Yesterday I visited a mosque and dargah that very few Americans see and saw more *dervishes*. The teacher in one place was giving a lesson somewhere between the teachings in esotericism on *wazifa* and *amaliat* (psychology). In the mosque where the *dervishes* met, there was a sign: "God is love," or as we should say, "*mahebudlillah*." You can see the difference in these people in their eyes.

I go as often as possible to Sheikh Abu Salem Amria of the Rufai school. I had experiences in accordance with this school before I met the Sheikh, so I was quite ready when they appointed me as their representative for America.

The main difficulty here is not language so much as their efforts to convince me of what now appear as elementary teachings. There is nothing wrong in this, excepting the wasting of time. The meetings regarding Islamic teachings in the U.S. are very complicated. Some groups here, under the guise of religion, seem more concerned about politics. What is wrong here is that in religion, we are supposed to calm the *nafs* or ego, and the spirit of agitation is the very thing that stands in the way of God-realization. I am trying to avoid any form of correction, but when one sees vibrations rise and fall, and agitation and disturbance, that cannot be the right path.

A paper I gave to Dr. Hussein concerns "surrender consciousness" and "identity consciousness." This may be long and involved, but it is an important teaching. My purpose, *inshallah*, is to draw heavily on the books at the Library when I return and try to "push" those who can be pushed and guide the others at a suitable rate. However, I am still cautious about any sort of division.

I do know that the *karma* that befalls those who essay the position of teachers and do not fulfil their functions is pretty awful. Many of Pir-o-Murshid's early works on this are just bypassed, for instance, "The Confessions of a Sufi Teacher." There he lays down the pattern of the true and false teacher. We must come to evaluate the words, one by one and altogether. Not that the words are any more than shadows-of-truth, as he taught, but they are at least shadows-of-truth, not shadows of imagination and falsehood.

January 4

Yesterday I went on a different errand in the Muski district, which is just on this side of the Khan-i-Khalili bazaars near Al-Azhar. The purpose was to visit the Franciscan Fathers.

I suppose I have two prejudices here. One is that I was not only born in San Francisco very close to the Mission, but socially I have been on the "side of the poor" and consider this order very noble. The other is Puck's protest against the clerical collar, which he considers the worst atrocity—or like the Pushtus, a masochistic device.

The Franciscan monastery is for study and research only. Students come from various countries and are supposed to know Latin, French and English; Greek is presumed but not so compulsory. Arabic and Coptic are the main language courses, and no one can leave until he has a working knowledge of them. Studies are made in early Christianity, not only the church fathers, but all aspects. There is still a big gap between the very early Christianity and the literary periods which developed before the time of the Islamic conquest. I am not interested in theological differences and schismatic quarrels. I am interested in liturgies, music, ceremonies, monastic disciplines

And spiritual experiences—I consider these Fathers clear and clean. While I do not wish to use the term *saint* in the earlier Hebrew sense of "holy ones" or pure ones (as in Hassidism), it would fit very well.

My trip so far has been successful far beyond hopes and dreams. It is easy to bring East and West together. Only nobody does it. Everybody is trying to remake the other like himself. It is true that I think they need dancing and some gymnastics and sports here to release tensions and energies. Outside of that, I see no basic need for alterations that are not taking place.

There is some departure of morality with the loosening of religious ties. They do not see that if there is anything wrong with the US, it comes from just those bad habits they are beginning to adopt. I don't think a person is a fanatic if he prays five times a day or gets up before dawn for God .

I am told there is a place where the Holy Family rested. I am not interested in testing the historicity of it. I am interested in the feeling behind it.

January 8
Sheikh Abu Salem Amria has in part accepted this person. Many of the *ulema* from Al-Azhar were there last night also to hear him. He gave lessons, mostly moral and spiritual—not the humbug words of lecturers. This was the real stuff. The mosque was packed to the doors. There was also present Sheikh Muhammad of Sidi Sharani. I cannot explain this man. There is such tremendous love between us that is real and the manifestation of it astounded even the *ulema*, and many of the devotees. It is Sheikh Muhammad who is taking me out today.

January 13
My visit to En-Shams University was something. Sa'ad Kemal used to be Professor of Horticulture, but now handles Genetics and Statistics. He took me around the grounds and later to his place. He also took me to a farm where he does cotton research as well as work with grasses and ground covers to ascertain their value and usefulness.

He says that the goat has been the enemy of Egypt and that it destroyed all the ground covers but *C.Dactylon* and even much of that. He says that economists, historians and others have overlooked this and tend to blame dynasties and political groups. He says that the goat eats so close that it does not permit plants to revive, especially the Egyptian ground covers, and that this is the prime factor in the centuries-long downhill slide of the soil.

I told Sa'ad that what the U.A.R. needs from the U.S. is neither money nor advanced technology, but the tourism of farmers who have grown cotton, cane and rice. I once wrote Senator Ellender on this subject: ignored.

January 18
My plan for Palestine has never been refuted. Everyone accepted it before, and I am resurrecting it step by step.

Sunday we visited a Sufi *khankah*. I got kicked out of a school in California for using the term *khankah;* the professor didn't believe there were such things. I was urged to make this a *cause celebre*, as it is called, and I probably shall. I went and greeted everybody there.

This week I also met Sheikh Sharabasi of the Rufai *dervishes*. I had already been to the Rufai Mosque and had the most wonderful experience there. The sheikh had me stand up in a public meeting and get an ovation—this is becoming commonplace . In fact, I am supposed today to have lots of *baraka* and some people call me "sheikh."

I have been going to "The Garden of Allah" in the Khan-i-Khalili bazaar for purchases. I was introduced to a shoemaker downstairs who fitted me out. Somehow or other, the story got round that I am a *dervish*. Yesterday, when I was in this shop, the shoemaker came up breathlessly and took me by the hand downstairs. This was surprising, since my shoes were not to be fitted until next week.

There was an old blind man there, a sheikh. We sat silently, and I gave him my beads: "Naqshibandi!" He gleamed all over. He is the Naqshibandi teacher here. We embraced, and then one experienced *baraka*—not just blessing but the warm fire of love and magnetism and joy penetrating all through one's personality. It was a tender moment of happiness. There are things beyond words and language.

Roughly speaking, the people here are Conservative Muslims, Progressive Muslims, Islamic Sufis and Universal Sufis. It is hard to draw the lines. There are no fixed rules and most are Muslims, but the top men are universal as I have written before and underneath a lot of other people are universal, too....

January 24
To Pir-o-Murshid Maulana Abdul Ghafoor,
Dacca, East Pakistan
Beloved Teacher:
Alhamdulillahi rabbil-alamin, ar-rahman ar-rahim.

In pursuance of the duties set before me first by Pir-o-Murshid Sufi Inayat Khan and then by your gracious person in the capacity of Qalandar,[95] I have come to this land with many purposes but little external assistance. Nevertheless, Allah is Great and though a person walk alone, whether through strife or ease, it is possible that heavy burdens or light may come to successful fulfilments.

This week two reports are to be submitted, one to the State Department of the United States Government and one to Sheikh Abu Salem Amria of the Rufai Order of *dervishes*, each in its way marking the culmination, *inshallah*, of my external reasons for being in this land.

On the external side, the purposes were to bring horticultural information first to the U.A.R. and then to Pakistan to assist in the opening and cul-

---

95 An "unorthodox," wandering, ascetic *dervish*. A number of sects operated under this title, but were not connected to any specific *tariqat*. Accurately or not, the term commonly refers to any *dervish* that rejects religious legalism and who exhibits this protest through gambling, games and/or using intoxicants.

tivation of desert and salt-encrusted lands. Also to open things up for an international exchange of agricultural information. No one seems to have been doing this, although vast sums have been collected for such purposes.

One day, in pursuance of these tasks, I was introduced to a brother in *tariq,* one Murtaz Billah of the Shadhili Order of *dervishes.* Like myself, he was engaged in horticultural research, and our private interests are very, very similar. But our grand purposes in life are similar also. Through him many doors have opened, of which I sketch here a few:

1. Yusuf Wali is also a horticulturalist and claims to be a disciple of the living *Qutb* [a secret guardian of the world, according to Sufi traditions]. I have heard from others that this honored person now lives and functions in this region. Yusuf has given me reports on *operative Sufism* that are entirely in harmony with what I have been taught or believe or have experienced. I hope to see him further, *inshallah,* before I leave the country.

2. I have attended many *zikrs,* chiefly of the Shadhilis and Rufais and have seen some of the other orders. I am hoping soon to go to Tantah, which is a large city inhabited chiefly by Sufis and *dervishes* and is the headquarters of the Bedawi order.

3. I have been blessed with visitations of saints and *Rassulillah,* and this week am to make a complete report to Sheikh Amria. I have also met and love deeply one Sheikh Muhammad Dessougi, and one Dr. Sharabasi of the Rufai Order.

I must record one incident. I entered the Sidi Sharani Shrine one night on the occasion of this saint's birthday celebration. There were thousands of people present. As soon as I took off my shoes and crossed the threshold, two arms seized me. I thought, "Now your presumption has caught up with you; you have dared too many times to enter holy places without permission." Instead, I was immediately conducted to the microphone and found myself the guest speaker of the evening! One does not know how these things occur.

Much more could be written, all of a cheerful and hopeful nature. I have lived under many conditions, and now at a later era in my life Allah has removed many of the burdens and brought either the fruit of effort or the grace that is needed to follow the pathway of a Qalandar in life.

In Egypt, 1961

January 29, 1961

I have been going to Al-Azhar for some special training in Qur'an and also to mosques, especially those of the Rufai *dervishes*. Tomorrow I am going again to the tombs of the Mamluks to meet the Sufis there. I want to get as much material as possible.

They celebrate saints' days here even more than in India and Pakistan. It is partly an inheritance from Christianity, partly from older religions and no doubt came to fruition in the Fatimid Period when Shia Islam was in control.

They have *moulads,* which means festivals, like the Mardi Gras and include everything. Last night I attended a circus, which is largely in the form of side-shows, but one side-show proved to include the main events, beginning with liontaming and having a combination of a vaudeville and animal show. I saw the native dancing, perhaps as good or better than at the casinos and much less coarse. I had to buy the candy, which is supposed to contain the *baraka.*

Later I may go to Tantah, *inshallah*, where the Bedawi *dervishes* hold forth, whose candy is particularly sacred. Evidently just as monks made wines or liquors, *dervishes* make candy. It is quite different from most forms at home, although they do have some like peanut brittle and New Orleans types.

At the moment, with my interest in *dervishes*, I may seem over enthusiastic. Religions are like trees and when we try to describe them in seed-form, we are projecting and differentiating and not describing.

Islam, even more than the Catholic Church, includes all sorts of phases and institutions. To regard them as "wrong" is like regarding the oak as a "wrong" rosebush or "wrong" pine tree. There is no "right" or "wrong" about the so-called accretions. They are there, they are part of life. We can study and even come to understand them, but to give them moral or personal judgments is totally nonsensical. It prevents communication and lack of real communication prevents understanding and peace.

January 30

In Pir-O-Murshid's original teaching, there were two paths distinctly marked out:

a) The path of progression in *zikr*;

b) The path of progression in *fana,* which comes in three stages, *fana- fi-sheikh* [effacement in the teacher], *fana-fi-rassul* [effacement in the Messenger], *fana-fi-lillah* [effacement in the Only Being].

In practice, there has not been too much understanding of these ways of progression and I can only refer to them here as part of one man's biography, regardless.

In Hazrat Inayat Khan's teachings on "Moral Culture," we have reference to the Law of Reciprocity, Law of Beneficence and Law of Renunciation. Reciprocity is the moral law for ordinary persons. Call it *karma* or not, it operates, and in the teachings one should take advantage of all the suggestions. Beneficence comes from the spiritual path or *tariqat,* and in Holy Qur'an we find *Bismillah er-rahman er-rahim,* which indicates the identity of surrender (*fana*) with beneficence.

But people identify these qualities with God and do not usually try to live *akhlak Allah,* that is, in the manner of God or in the presence of God.

I find myself at a distance from orthodox Muslims who place all the virtues in a deity and do not try to develop these in themselves. No doubt, it is a first step to see them in God, but it is not a last step, and it is not a path or progression. Whatever way you place religion, it universally teaches: "Guide us on the Right Path," But it is not the prayer, nor the words, it is the adaptation of the life within oneself. This is the "greater *jihad*" that Muhammad spoke of.

Paul had to correct the people of his time who paid too much attention to *fana-fi-sheikh*; he tried to universalize *fana-fi-rassul,* whether people were ready for it or not.

In bringing the Message to the West, people became enamored with *fana-fi-sheikh* and they do not rise to *fana-fi-rassul.* The words of the prayer Salat [English prayer of Hazrat Inayat Khan] become empty. They remain just words. If people wish to change these words into truths, they will likely be misunderstood, but they may also gain understanding and perhaps wisdom.

Here there is a great deal of difference between any invocation of "United with All the Illuminated Souls Who form the Embodiment of the Master" and the direct understanding thereof. It has been insisted by many that there is a living *Qutb* in this area. I cannot argue, though I have not met him yet. But I have met many sheikhs and from them received so much love and *baraka* that I can never thank Allah enough.

Years ago, I wrote "The Bestowal of Blessing." Most of the copies were lost or destroyed except for one which a friend may have in Santa Barbara. I wish to get ahold of it again, for it would be much easier to explain the whole science and art of *baraka.* Jesus started with the Beatitudes, but there is a dichotomy between bliss and happiness, that we do not see "blessings" as "bliss" or "bliss" as happiness.

Actually, there is a living function here. I have received *baraka* both from human beings, usually sheikhs and khalifs, but also in the mosques, especially the Rufai mosques. But there is another form of *baraka* which comes in *fana-fi-rassul.*

Pir-o-Murshid gave us a long list of Messengers ending with Muhammad. I have experienced the *fana-fi-rassul* in and with Muhammad, but immediately after that with Jesus; and in the course of time with Buddha and Shiva and then under the guidance of Muhammad with all the prophets of God of all religions.

In theory, this completed the path of *fana-fi-rassul*. But when one regards God as the Only Being, one does not, maybe cannot, of himself distinguish between *fana-fi-sheikh, fana-fi-rassul* and *fana-fi-lillah*, nor does one care to because, as Pir-o-Murshid said, "Thy light is in all forms, Thy love in all beings ... in an inspiring teacher."

Following the literary method of the Zoroastrian religion, I must paraphrase for my own record the teachings in *fana-fi-rassul* received today wherein Muhammad seemed to play the part with me that the Angel Gabriel did with him:

Sage: What is the difference between prayers in no direction, as Kabir and others taught and prayers in a direction, say, as inherited from Judaism?

The Spirit of Wisdom: In effect there may be none. If one accepts the parenthood of Allah, there, God is everywhere, in everything. But if one also accepts the community of humanity, there should be *qibla* [the direction towards which one directs oneself in prayer]. The effect of the apparent universality of Kabir, in breaking down certain Islamic institutions, has been the dissolution of the spirit of human community. The Sikhs carried the "logical" argument to the extreme and analytically were right but instead of community, nothing but strife followed. So *qibla* is advised.

Sage: What is the difference between Jerusalem and Mecca as *qibla?*

The Spirit of Wisdom: Jesus spoke of Jerusalem as being the city which stoned its prophets. Despite the Hebrew claim that only Jeremiah was persecuted, we have no record of any prophet of God actually being welcomed in Jerusalem. Indeed, the historical career of Jesus ended in failure there.

On the other hand, Mecca has been the *qibla* of success, both with Abraham, the Friend of God, and Muhammad, the Messenger of God. One does not like to put forth the argument that Jerusalem has been the *qibla* of failure, and Mecca of success, but you can still see the Christians fighting each other and the Zionists are all divided as to religion.

Sage: The Muslims always mention your name with a special praise.

The Spirit of Wisdom: That is all right, but it is not my way. Qur'an distinctly says that there are no distinctions between the Messengers of God. And although it is said that prayers are not made to me, there is psychological intercession. The psychological intercession falters if it becomes merely theological, which it usually does; and benefits when people learn to pray *with* the seal of the prophets, and not mention his name at all.

This is very difficult, but the errors in religion usually come from too much zeal. Zeal alone is not bad, but it becomes a substitute for morality and selflessness. There is too much praise for literature called Holy Qur'an and

Hadith and too little concern with the contents thereof. The same is true with most scriptures.

Sage: What, then, is the right path?

The Spirit of Wisdom: Allah has already shown you that Path, and therefore it is not for me to add. Many will reject you, but that is of no importance; what is important is what you accept and do, not what others say or think about it.

Now the initial stage in *fana-fi-lillah* follows the same pattern as took place with Pir-o-Murshid in his 1911 career. Then he was using mostly music and concentration. He often broke into ecstasy and sang loudly in praise of Muhammad. This probably did not go over big. But I have found there are three sorts of praise of Muhammad, and they all look the same, but are different:

The initial stage is that people praise Muhammad, and it may even be that they have inherited this phase of religion. They are using it as a crutch, and it may be a crutch; they are using it as a ladder, and it may be a ladder. Actually, it is no better or worse than the praise of Jesus, Buddha, Krishna or anybody, but neither is there any gain by dispensing with it.

The second stage is that people praise Muhammad, because that is the experience. They are really talking about themselves, and they are not talking about themselves. The change from *fana-fi-sheikh* to *fana-fi-rassul* in one's life is revolutionary. One is no longer restricted in vision or in faculties, and one finds a tremendous universe before oneself. Time and place and stage and condition become small things. One cannot prove this, nor is one doing this by oneself.

In his first sessions on Sufism, Pir-o-Murshid placed Muhammad as the "Perfect Man of All Times." I shall explain this a little below. I think the Sufi in Islam generally works from this position.

The third stage seems impossible, that while one is being immersed in God, the praises of Muhammad become grander. Dante had it of Jesus, but I don't think Dante reached the highest stages. He held onto selfhood. Even the mystics of Christianity, except a few like John Tauler, never got above the selfhood or to the unitarian realization.

Nor does it seem that God praises God. This seems a contradiction. There are two aspects of Allah, the silent and the creative, although neither of these words is exact. The silent praise is discussed in "The Mysticism of Sound" both in the chapter called "The Silent Life" and in the final chapter, which is partially a dissertation on *zikr*. [These writings by Hazrat Inayat Khan are found in volume two of *The Sufi Message*.]

The Bible says that God created Adam in God's image, but Adam is usually associated with "sin." There had to be a "perfect man" for redemption. Now, there are all kinds of differences between them. But the Buddhist does not live like Buddha, nor the Christian like Christ nor the Hindu like Ram or Krishna. We wish to live in an operative world: to raise families and go into business and study and do all those things that we consider human. It is on this point that Muhammad excels. He does not excel in being nearer to God, the Creator, but he does excel in being nearer to humanity, the created.

Anybody has a perfect right to differ from me here, but the point is not argument, but demonstration. One does not see people demonstrate what Jesus did, or Buddha did. We do see people demonstrate what Muhammad did.

Therefore comes the idea that God created the world through light, and this was a living light, which also had to become the essence in and of humanity. The idea of *Adam*, derived from *dam*, earth, is that the light of Allah had to come through the earthly forms. But how did it come? In *Masnavi* [by Mevlana Jelaluddin Rumi], the cosmic evolution is taught ending in human beings. And the cosmic evolution continues until the perfect human being, or as I see it, the perfect perfect human being.

Buddha was a perfect man who showed the way to *nirvana*, and in the Southern Buddhism, this teaching is kept. But it is a limited *nirvana*, not the true, if you have to become a monk to reach it. This assumes that the layman cannot reach perfection. But the layman has reached perfection, and so the later Buddhists said that creation and *nirvana* were identical. Only this means that the common person could attain perfection. But what common man has attained to perfection? One cannot call Rama common, because he was a king. Krishna also had a special place in society, and Jesus and Buddha became monks. There was only one ordinary man who represented both Adam and perfection. So with Muhammad the revelation was "sealed," which does not take away from any scripture or teaching.

I do not wish here to go into stories about Muhammad that substantiate this point. What I am really telling you is my experience. As Al-Ghazali said: "Sufism consists in experiences and not premises." Only previously, I told my experiences, and there is a personality reaction. So I have clothed what I am experiencing in philosophy, which is a veil over it and is not it.

I have written before that I came here with three missions and have accomplished a dozen. Pir-o-Murshid Hazrat Inayat Khan and Pir-o-Murshid Maulana Abdul Ghafoor have given me the whole world to work in and with the intellectual people. So I transfer my experiences into philosophy. But some day when people want truth and will accept it from the simple man, he will give the simplicity. As the simplicity is rejected, he gives the philosophy.

Jesus taught that one must be like a little child to receive the kingdom of heaven. One can always be open to blessings. One can always listen to the "voice which constantly cometh from within." But if we keep on using the mouthpiece, we can't hear what is coming over the receiver.

My destiny sometimes seems to follow the career of the dog in one of Pir-o-Murshid's stories. This dog took two days to go from Basra to Baghdad, instead of the usual 12. "I owe it all to the kindness of my fellow dogs," it said. "Whenever I stopped to rest, they came and barked at me." So the more humanity barks, the faster the progression. Every time a rejection or seeming failure appears, Allah comes and brings me blessings and success. This will probably be my career until I am called hence. I, Samuel, have nothing to do with it.

There has been a school of Sufis called Malamatiyya, which sought out public blame as part of its practice. I do not seek and am not checking on reactions. Every rebuff is followed by meditation and/or prayer, and in turn, something pleasant follows, usually much more pleasant than conjectured. So one comes back to the first lesson: *Subhan Allah, Alhamdulillah, Allaho Akbar.*

February 6

On January 30, I was to submit a full report to the embassy on my experiences including many of the past, and my proposals. I no sooner filed this report when a group of Qadiri Sufis came to my hotel. At that time, I could not see them for without any notice I was asked to go to Alexandria, which I did.

I spent January 31 at Abis, which is the joint undertaking of the Egyptian American Rural Improvement Society (EARIS). In a sense, I found myself in a new world, brave or unbrave. In another sense, I saw exactly the society forming that had been previously revealed to me and recorded, though never taken seriously. It is here, now, and will have to be taken seriously.

My works on social reconstruction and brotherhood were much more prophetic than logical, psychic than physical, but they are here now. The dispossessed are being placed on reclaimed land, given small homes, private barns (which can also be used as storage), farms, animals, seed and a small space for a home garden of any kind. At present, people are not settling as fast as necessary; perhaps this is because the Egyptians have in all ages been good builders and not nearly so good in some other aspects of life.

The next day it poured terrifically and I went to the tourist bureau in Alexandria. There I met Nadya, one of the most beautiful women I have ever seen. This attracted many men there who were not interested in tourism, but in Nadya, and that meant I met a lot of notable persons and had really a wonderful time.

I did not have much time to get acquainted with Nadya when her supervisor, Fuad Leithi, walked in: "Ah," he said, "there you are. I have been waiting for you. How much do you remember of your previous incarnations?" Shades of Paul Brunton, that was it. I did not get it at the Valley of the Kings, but at the Tourist Information Office, Alexandria.

He told me I was travelling to escape, that there was a woman in my life, and I could not think who it could be. When I got back to the hotel, I did remember one such woman with whom I have had a sort of aeonic romance, but she has long gone out of my memory. I had forgotten all about her; but whether it is she or not, I don't know. However, I have had my fortune told five times, all the same and all stressed romances—Sufi sheikhs, card readers, everybody—so we shall see.

Fuad claimed to be telepathic and clairvoyant, and you can put it in my book: he is. He read many things that I have told nobody, almost secret experiences I have had at holy places and which, in a certain way, affect my international peregrinations. I told him that his eyes and forehead look very much like those of an adept mentioned by Paul Brunton in the final pages of *A Search in Secret Egypt*. He told me that all adepts here are Sufis.

Among Fuad's many visitors (or Nadya's, rather) was the district attorney of Alexandria. He began by challenging me right and left and ended with cordiality. We had a delightful time. The result was that the conversations reached a higher and higher pitch during the day. I stayed until 7 p.m. when we went to the studio of Alexandria's greatest modern painter, named Wanli.

Yesterday was a theoretical Sufi celebration being the anniversary of the death of Pir-o-Murshid Inayat Khan. I had one of the dreams of my life fulfilled—riding an Arab horse. Went from the Pyramids to Sahara city and back. I originally took up horseback riding, because I said that someday I would go to Arabia and I might as well learn. I had forgotten all about the incident. But the reason I went was quite different.

I had gone to Mina village (near the Pyramids) at the invitation of two close friends, and they introduced me to a Sufi sheikh. He earns his living by renting horses. So on account of this I hired him. On our way back we had a crazy time chanting sacred phrases. I don't think any Egyptian ever before had such a client. He then took me to lunch, but while waiting I danced for his children. I also left a good gift for them.

Came home, took a real hot bath, then hot chocolate and off to the Rufai *dervishes* where I stayed two and a half hours and then went home, only to meet a delegation of Qadiris from Iraq. They wanted me to visit their country for spiritual reasons. I have neither the time nor money but will visit them and then take it up with the U.S. Embassy. I think one of these days some foundation or somebody should come to my rescue. I am working all alone in a terrific vineyard with an unlimited harvest and nobody else there.

February 20 S.S. Cilicia
I am glad to have a chance to sail on a different kind of ship. I feel quite happy to be on board, although just now it is more like river or steamboating on a lake. At least, I shall be "house-broken" by the time we reach the Indian Ocean.

230

We are now on the Arabian Sea south of Hadramaut. We landed at Aden, and although I did not want to spend money, my friend Abdul Rahman wanted a camera. We were taken to a shop (*taken* is the word), and none of us bought. In the next shop, I noticed a man with prayer beads, and the next thing I mentioned was that I was a *dervish*, and then I found the store owner was the Rufai Sheikh there. We almost fell over each other, and the next thing I knew he was dropping prices like crazy. So I spent more than I had expected and can only hope Abdul Rahman will be satisfied. I know I got a bargain, but I can't tell what the Pakistanis will charge for customs duty....

I have been playing around as "Puck of Pukhtunistan." I have been writing at length about this real-imaginary country. Yet the fact is that on this ship, the Pathans have sought me out and taken to me like a duck to water, acting as friends and protectors. It is seemingly fantastic, but might be explained by reincarnation or otherwise.

Pakistan, Spring 1961
Excerpts from Letter-Diaries

March 4 Karachi

I have now been in Pakistan four days and have had a very rapid start. I went to the US Embassy, where I had three long and successful interviews. In the UAR, I had to take certain rebuffs from Americans on intercultural exchange, and though I lost the discussions, regretfully my prediction of the mobbing of the USIA library came true. At the Embassy, there was also a letter from my close friend Robert Clifton. Between us, in a sense, we cover the whole Asian continent, and have been uniformly successful with Asians, and unusually unsuccessful with the press.

March 16 Lahore

I cannot escape it. It is inevitable. I follow the old E. Phillips Oppenheim dictum: "Fools for Luck." I could not get accommodations when I arrived at Lahore, and I was shunted to the Imperial Hotel, which is an old group of buildings made into a new hotel. I wander around alleys—they are not dark in this section of the city—and the first thing I see is a building: "Agricultural Department." So I nosed in and sent my card.

In about two minutes I meet Mahmood Ali Bokhari. I tell him about deserts and desert reclamation, and that is what he is interested in. I tell him about salt-water from the ocean, and that is what he is interested in. I even tell him my private ventures, and that is what he is interested in.

At the moment, Lahore is very beautiful, and I am not far from the Zoological Gardens. The whole city is in flower: dahlias in full bloom and hollyhocks seeking salvation in heaven and cosmos all over the place. This is springtime, n'est-ce pas?

So far I have met only one lady. I hope she is still married. She is head of the Fine Arts Department, wealthy and mature, of Jewish birth and now a Muslim. I don't know if this means anything, but I am a confirmed bachelor, to which applies the saying: "A man is old when he stops looking" and I have not stopped. Besides, my friend the fortune teller was here, waiting for me, and he told me I am going to live a long, long time yet, so might as well be resigned to it. Which I am. For if life began at 40 for me, it got bigger at 60 and is still growing.

March 23

My immediate host is Abdul Rahman who has long been an American citizen and lived in San Francisco. Tomorrow is Pakistani Day, and I am on the program. The morning and afternoon will be devoted to parades and sports, the evening to intellectual matters. I shall read from "Saladin" and also perhaps one short Islamic poem. Some of "Saladin" may be translated into Urdu, and it is possible that all of it will before I leave the country, *inshallah*.

I have signed many papers which grant me the right of residence for one year, but I expect to leave this region in September, *inshallah*.

March 27

The other day a Mr. Qureyshi came to my rooms. He is descended from an Arab family that became custodian of the Moghul court jewels. They are supposed to have disappeared. I have seen them. He has been negotiating with a Los Angeles firm to sell them. I saw by far the largest and purest rubies in my life and some very ancient specimens, too, from this region. Through Qureyshi I met Chishti Sahib. This man is a real Sufi. He was being mobbed recently, because he denied the efficacy of political prayers. I was told he is very poor. I called on him with Qureyshi and one look in his eye was enough—full of love. He speaks only Urdu and Persian, but Qureyshi knows both and English, so we had a very fine session.

Most of the time he explained Moineddin Chishti and Jelaluddin Rumi, both of whom used music in their spiritual training. He went on at some length, and I gave him the flute chant to show him I understood Rumi. Afterward, he said, "Yes, the real flute is in ourselves." From the occult point of view, the Chishti stories were the most interesting.

Khwajah Sahib [Selim Chishti, spiritual teacher of the Emperor Akbar] had many powers, and he was able to control the water supply at Ajmir. I told him I had been at the very place, and it is mysterious to find a lake high up in the mountains above a desert. I often wondered about it.

The essence of Sufism comes in the *Auliya*-saint or hierarchal development, and a master learns to have control over the elements. This is not nonsense. I am pretty sure that Chishti Sahib has both power and wisdom. He also told part of my future, which corroborated in every detail what my fortune teller friend the *munshi* said, but added more. He gave me his blessing, and I hope to see him often. Both he and another man here are really disguised saints, operating as very poor men.

March 30

I have been the guest of my friend Judge Muhammad Rabbani Khan, whom I visited before and who has been in San Francisco. In our first conference this time we talked about 1.) Agriculture and reforestation in this region. 2.) Establishment of the World Congress of Faiths in California. 3.) A serious program of actual cultural exchange between this region and the U.S. without any more intervention of European and sometimes Hindu obscurantists. 4.) Semitic Archeology: there is evidence that the "Lost Tribes of Israel" came to this region. I have the green light from Harvard (Professor Cross of the Dead Sea Scrolls research) to ask for a permit for the Department of Semitic Archeology to work here.

I am at the moment writing to both the *Pakistan Times* and the *Civil and Military Gazette* of Lahore. I am now ready to disgorge my scientific and horticultural notes and papers, which will lighten my burdens. I shall just keep the bibliography that Harry Nelson got for me and will work on that later on.

The other night I was the guest of a doctor. He told me that most of his patients suffer from malnutrition. The chief crops here are grains: wheat, rice and oats. But the "lawns" are filled with dandelions and the fields with wild mustards. And the people suffer from lack of vitamins. I think I'll tell them how to use the outside cabbage leaves, if they can't afford more. There are oodles of cabbages on the market, as well as turnips, spinach, oranges, carrots and things that look like cresses. They are not too popular here.

April 16

It is morning, and I hope to meet a Pir-o-Murshid and other Sufis today. In some books, Sufism has been identified with *bhakti*. In the *bhakti* I have witnessed, outside of Swami Ramdas, there is an ecstatical relation with what one calls "God" in some form, which is nothing but transcendental infatuation. It brings ecstasy but not breadth of outlook or being.

Real love is a universal communication that runs in all directions. In the spider-web, each ring is connected not only with the center but with each other. Thus the love and community go together.

The other teaching comes from effacement before the teacher. The teacher is real and living. I have read a lot of books about spiritual teachers. The books, as such, are generally true, but the writers often have no capacity for surrender. This is not abolition of self.

In the prayers, one puts one's head to the ground and raises it up. In discipleship, there is something of the same thing. In the mystical side of breath there is the same thing, but none of the professors who ever taught at the Academy knew this. Some of the swamis know it, and therefore I am still compelled to place Ramakrishna and even the Vedanta Society way beyond the empty intellectualism of most professors.

Last night, after finishing what I had written to you, two young men came in. The father of one of them works for Radio Pakistan and is also a Sufi. The young men have been troubled at the seeming dichotomy between traditional religious instruction and modern scientific instruction. I had no trouble in answering their dilemmas.

Actually, there is not much difference between the scientific outlook and the spiritual outlook. But in the West, the metaphysician has gotten in between the scientist and mystic and sent up clouds of effluvia and fog. In Egypt it was not so, and here even less.

April 22

International Art as a Conveyor of World Peace: You know, I was mixed up in the Roerich complexities, and wrote a minority report saying that art would never become a means to world peace and understanding unless the artists themselves were the leaders. Roerich accepted the goodwill of every politician and international gangster, and in the end lost everything. His personal losses may or may not have been important, but he started something that has continued: people as the nexus of world peace through the arts.

So it becomes individual persons, rather than movements, which become the center of the stage.

Ansar Nasri introduced me to Q.U. Shahab who is not only a top intellectual, but Secretary to President Ayub. Shahab accepted every single one of my projects and then, with General Ayub's approval, added one more. The most personal of these was my poetry, and that was demanded on the spot, in his home. I had to copy one section immediately for translation into Urdu.

April 26

It may be hard for one at a distance to understand what is happening in my life, because I, who am in the midst of continual adventures, do not always understand things myself. Part of it is no doubt due to what the Hindus call "*karma,*" which is now "good." But from the Buddhist and Sufi point of view, it is the harvesting of life and some of this harvesting has been favourable.

The Buddhist explanation is better, because while it also teaches that we reap according as we sow, it is not always through the same persons.

I started out early to be a sort of foster-uncle. When my first boy, who was the nephew of a young companion, reached the age of 16, his father suddenly appeared in San Francisco and took him away. This has been my history, that the boys and girls whom I have looked after were often suddenly "discovered" by their parents. But those to whom I was especially attached sometimes died, and in a few cases jealous relatives poisoned them against me. Now here I am called "Mama," which means "maternal uncle," and my pal, Abdul Rahman is called "Chacha," which means "paternal uncle." My belonging to the Chishti order of Sufis has been of great social and material assistance to me, although that was not in mind. The strange and immediate acceptance of my poetry plus the ok given on all my projects at the highest level has undoubtedly somewhat unnerved me.

If you struggle and struggle and get a sudden release, it is not always easy to adjust.

April 27 Abbottabad

Young Arif Khan came in after lunch and asked me if I wanted to go mountain climbing. My hiking shoes were in the middle of the room, and before I could answer the shoes were on. We climbed a mountain on the west side, and the country looked like the hills between Fairfax and Woodacre [in Marin County, California]. There was a lovely gorge which had fresh spring water. Below that was a lovely presidio where the soldiers live, a park-like section with pines, cypress and eucalyptus.

I have been most fortunate with my *dervish* connections. The hostel here is run by one, and also the hotel in Rawalpindi. Now I had a wire from my friend Major Sadiq. We swore "eternal friendship" in 1956, but then lost sight of each other. In fact, my old address book was stolen. As soon as I located him, he wired me that he is living in Lahore, which has been the most expensive place for me. At the moment, this cooperation of friends makes it appear I will be well in the black.

It seems fairly certain that the "Lost Tribes of Israel" came this way, and also the Greek armies. There is plenty of evidence for both, but they have never been properly studied. Most of the students here are Pathan speaking. While my friend Mr. Qureyshi was describing the Swatis to me, and showing me on the map where the "purest" Greeks are, I began showing them sections of Greek dances. All the college boys around applauded and said that these were very much like the dances in their country.

The last time I spoke to Ansar Nasri, a whole hour was taken talking over folk music and folk dancing. The current campaign seems to be to instil people with patriotism. I am running a companion campaign trying to instil people with pride in their cultures, past and present. This is much more attractive, because it implements the raw words *patriotism, loyalty,* and so forth with content. In fact, it reached such a peak that I shall likely have full cooperation in regard to securing folk records and introductions. I already have to go into many of the areas where the traditions are strong and there is a likelihood of picking up dance steps.

The Hebrew and Greek traditions here excite me; the Indian elements leave me cold. The popular Indian dance elements have no depth to them. By depth, I mean, something physiological and physical that causes the whole body to resound or thrill; then a psychic element is added, which I cannot verbalize but which everybody knows—it gives the impetus to dance.

I am not concerned with morals here. There is little hip swaying or but-tocks movement. I think this is due to an ancient "snake" tradition. I mean, just try a "rooster-chicken" dance, an elephant dance, a horse dance or a bird courtship dance and the body becomes different. With the snake, the outside of the body seems to move, there is gliding. The Indian dancers not only seem to move their bodies externally, but they move their "space" that way, and it extends into choreography. Compare the Greek dances or even the slow-er Kolas where the whole body is involved. I think when the whole body is involved, there is something deeper not only physically, physiologically and psychically, but even spiritually.

May 4 Lahore
It is now over 100 degrees in Lahore, and I have braved the weather to come here. It is not easy for me to write.

Tomorrow I understand I shall be speaking in a large mosque. Thursday night I was taken to the tomb of Data Hujwiri,[96] a great Sufi saint whose works I studied first long ago. I was met by a guard of honor and escorted through the place as if I were a very important dignitary.

I was first a guest of a sheikh and then of a Naqshibandi murshid who has 500,000 followers. Garlands upon garlands were thrown over my head and a special turban given me for the evening. I spoke briefly before the sheikh, and the murshid has asked that I come again Sunday night.

From the American point of view, this was fantastic and impossible. From the Asian point of view, we—the Americans—live in a land of dreams and fantasies. Someday, *inshallah*, we shall look at Asia as it really is.

May 7
I am at the moment living in the house of Major Muhammad Sadiq, a brother Sufi with the same spiritual teacher. We are in the strange position of seeing in each other a person who has advanced much in the last five years.

Major Sadiq has been blessed with a healing gift, which is both spiritual and occult. He prefers to hold to the former, but will apply the latter when necessary. He has the gift of healing by touch and of magnetizing water and food with super-physical vibrations, which seem to have remarkable effects on the health. He has even cured people who have been to Lourdes. His legend has spread far and wide, and every day we have a strange sight here—long lines of people, usually peasants, to meet him, and scholars to meet me.

---

96 Shaykh Ali b. Uthman al-Jullabi al-Hujwiri, c. 1009-1072/77, patron saint of Lahore, author of the *Kashf al-Mahjub* ("unveiling of the unseen"), considered the earliest treatise on Sufism in Persian.

The general basis of his faculty, which we both hold is a grace and not a possession, coincides with the theories of Pir-o-Murshid Inayat Khan and some of the details of the applications are the same.

If we begin with the theory of Jesus Christ that the body is the temple of the holy spirit and continue on to include some of the teachings of a Pir who recently died here, we can apply a complete method of "cure" and sanctification. This is entirely in line with the original idea of *savior*, which has little to do with divinity or theology, but meant, in a sense, a metaphysical or super-physical healer.

Lecturing in Pakistan, 1961 (photo from Daily Kohistan, Lahore)

"Misplaced Marin County Found in West Pakistan"

Newspaper article

(From the *San Rafael Independent Journal,* April 13, 1961)

A misplaced Marin County has been found in West Pakistan by a philosophical dervish from Mill Valley.

Samuel L. Lewis, member of a mystical Moslem fraternity and self styled ambassador to various foreign parts, thus identifies the region of Abbottabad, Hazara, in a letter dated April 5:

''Abbottabad is like a misplaced Marin. I have visited Begum Selim Khan here, widow of the first consul-general from Pakistan to San Francisco. Her garden is much like those around Ross [Marin County, California], and she has made it deliberately so:'

Being a dervish paid off for Lewis, he reports: "This country is full of dervishes. They are coming to my aid."

"They are leaders in politics, education and community development despite all the misinformation we swallow."

Of pictures showing Lewis with the *wali*, or guardian saint, of the tomb of the mystic Shamsi-Tabriz, Lewis writes: "I was welcomed and am the first foreigner to have given them a talk on their own philosophy and teachings. Penalty: they all embraced me."

Lewis says U.S. Army engineers are doing a good job of sanitation and pest control in a place where "the fly, not starvation, spaceconquest or communism, has been the bane." He believes "there is a movement toward a real Asian type of democracy."

Shrines and Saints

Book Excerpt From
The Lotus and the Universe (1963)

On my return visit to Pakistan, I was unable to find any of the Naqshibandi Sufis whom I met on my previous visit. Death, illness and change of address took them from my life. But as Allah has willed, many of my movements have been associated with Haji Sarfraz, whose *khankah* is on the Mall in Lahore, across the street from the offices of the Asia Foundation.

In the Naqshibandi School, there is more stress on sobriety, and in the Chishti meetings one finds more people going into "spiritual intoxication." This state called *sukr* (corresponding perhaps to the Hebraic *shikkor*) is fine for the young for it helps them to dominate "lower" forces. But when it becomes an end in itself, it may lead away from the goal, not towards it. At times it would appear to have the same psychological significance as drug-taking, but at other times it can be most elevating.

The Naqshibandi methods certainly keep one away from every sort of drug and artificial stimulant. In Sufism, *hal* indicates a state of consciousness and is often used interchangeably with *sukr* or *wujud*, but it does not imply the intoxication that the latter two terms do. An extreme, but perhaps unfair parallel comes in the story of the Hare (the Chishtis) and the Tortoise (the Naqshibandis), but the Bedawis and others seem to be more "hare-ish" still.

When I was living with Major Sadiq in the Cantonment in Lahore, I was approached one Sunday by two delegations. One was of Qadiris, whose murshid has been most kind to me on many occasions, the other was of Naqshibandis. I do not know how they found out where I was, but it was the continuum of the same group who had hosted me in 1956. The murshid and *khalif* had both departed, and they had moved to a suburb called Sufiabad.

The great center for all the Sufi orders in Pakistan is the tomb of Ali b. Uthman al-Jullabi al-Hujwiri, known as Data Gang Baksh, where thousands gather constantly. It is even more disconcerting that the shrine is almost within walking distance of our consulate in Lahore, and still less distant from the various universities where Americans teach. Yet I have met no American who visited the place, and many go right on acting as if there are no *dervishes* and no Sufi orders.

On every occasion when visiting the shrine, the saint appeared. The first time there were rival ceremonies of the different orders, dominated by two Chishti groups who were singing loudly and simultaneously. Yet such is the nature of a holy place that communion can be much more powerful. There, and at all subsequent visits to other shrines, there manifested something like an oracular power, or evidence of *shahud* [seeing-experiencing].

Muslims all say and repeat throughout their lives: *Ashaduan la ilaha il Allah, Ashaduanna Muhammadar-rassullillah.*[97] Yet do they see, do they experience? It is still mostly an act of faith, not yet of knowledge.

After t his s ort o f initiation, t he tomb o f a nother S ufi, Mian Mi r,[98] wa s visited many times. There is a close personal attunement with this saint who taught the children of Shah Jehan. They learned to "love" Allah, but not one another. The great lesson learned from Saint Mian Mir is that *A llaho A kbar* (ordinarily translated "God is greater") may be interpreted as "peace is power," in such a way to explain the whole of physics and metaphysics alike.

On another occasion I visited Kasur to go to the tomb of Bhullah Shah. The methods of this saint have made such an impression that I hope some-day, God willing, to give instruction on those very simple principles which at the same time become most profound. Bhullah Shah became an adept, because he found all the mysteries of the universe in the Arabic letter *alif*: the straight line and the Divine Unity.

The world is very much divided on the value of visiting holy places. In the West there has been a reluctance to accept the "miracles" of Asia on an equal basis with those of Europe. And even a greater reluctance to accepting reports from Western persons on the unusual in the Orient.

Gates to the tomb of Hazrat Data Gang Baksh in Lahore (news photo clipping from Samuel Lewis' scrapbook).

---

97 I see/experience that there is no reality but God, I see/experience that Muhammad is the Messenger of God

98 1550-1635, spiritual teacher of Dara Shikoh, eldest son of Mughal emperor Shah Jehan, brother of Bibi Jamal Khatun, also a notable Sufi saint. After he succeeded Shah Jehan, Dara Shikoh was overthrown by his brother Aurangzeb.

Pakistan, Spring 1961, Part II

Excerpts from Letter-Diaries

May 9

My dear Wesley:

I have just heard from Leonora that you are in the hospital as a cancer patient, and I am writing to you because this is strangely in line with some "coincidences" going on here.

All my affairs at the moment seem prospering, especially on the higher levels in ways which may be appreciated but not understood in the United States. There seems little hope for the world, for it has divided, not into "haves" and "have-nots," but into potters and clays. Certain nations insist they are potters, and at the moment are having "cold wars." They cannot see that humanity is not divided into potters and clays.

The first thing we have to do if we are going to have peace is to stop this nonsense. Clemenceau was a very wise man who said that war and peace were too serious to entrust to generals and diplomats. We do not need a "peace movement" so much as a Clemenceau movement to entrust peace to others than diplomats and generals. But the "international protocol protective association" of generals and diplomats want to be left alone to carry on their Cold War and consume the wealth of the earth in so doing. It is not Russia that is to blame, it is not America that is to blame, it is protocol. Both Russians and Americans worship that common god.

There can be no peace without friendship. Otherwise, it is just status quo or armistice. Getting rid of arms without getting rid of hatreds is wasteful and useless. We talk about "education," but half the time we mean propaganda. We do not know what is going on in the hearts and minds of exotic peoples.

I am in Pakistan, in the Punjab, which has been the site of innumerable cultures and wars. We do not know much about these cultures or wars, and we know even less about the hearts of peoples.

Wesley, there are sciences of the heart as well as of the mind and body. We live in a body that we do not study. Every time the heart beats it sends a flood of fluid through the organization. This flood of fluid feeds the cells and takes away the wastes. If we do not feed the blood rightly, it cannot feed the cells, and if we do not feed the nervous system rightly, it cannot help take away the wastes.

I am living in the home of Major Muhammad Sadiq, who has the gift of healing. We have studied sciences of which the West is not aware. We have both had the same teacher, a marvellous man whose name is Maulana Abdul Ghafoor. From him I have learned to treat the world as a whole single body and to learn to appreciate the hearts and minds of other people; so I do not travel as a stranger.

May 18 Abbottabad

My dear Harry:

When I left working for the Army in 1945, they refused my resignation until I signed the heroes' war book. "I am no hero," I said. "We know more about you, Mr. Lewis, than you know about yourself. No false modesty." I had been turned down more times by the Intelligence and the F.B.I. than one has fingers on their hands, but I realize today that the rooms were bugged, and perhaps I, too.

I have recently written a cousin a letter entitled "Four, Just Men." I have a personal underground that grapevines the whole of Asia. After Pearl Harbor, of which I had been forewarned, I resolved it would never happen again. But it did no good. I may still have my letters concerning Viet Nam and Laos, but I recently received an invitation from one of these men (Robert Clifton) to come as the guest of the Prime Minister of Malaya, which will probably be accepted.

Another of these men invited me first to go to Asia because it "needed me" [Paul Reps]. The fourth is Bryn Beorse, who is one of the grandest men on earth, a cloak-and-dagger hero, friend of Dag Hammarskjöld, cousin of at least one prime minister of Norway, the clearest thinking man I ever met in economics and long engaged in research to produce fresh water from the ocean at low cost. He has also been in the recesses of the Himalayas, met real yogis in caves and had a long string of experiences.

This is written in a mixture of laughter and tears. Someday some thick-headed editor in the U.S. will recognize that the people of the world are not concerned with "foreign aid," "dialectics," "Cold War" or "space conquest."

Here there are two problems that dominate everything, and to me it shows that the people are far more sensible than most. Their primary concerns are God and soil salinity problems. Anybody coming here not acquainted with these is going to have a hard time. True, the problems of the desert and eroded lands are also immense, but it is impossible to take up all these things at once.

I am not an expert on saline soils, but I am an expert in finding out what bothers others and then trying to do something about it. The imbalance of this report is the imbalance of the facts of life.

May 18

While I was with Major Sadiq in Lahore, there was a feast every night. This was hard because it was very warm in the day time, some times getting up to 105 degrees. I could not walk in the heat; besides, everyone treated me like a great person. It was like living in a dream. You see, this is my home and these are my people. In this life, I had to be born in a Western body, so I could bring oriental teachings to America. I feel at home with both the Punjabis and the Pathans.

Pakistan 1961, with guardian of one of the supposed tombs of the legendary Sufi mystic Shems-i-Tabriz.

Abbottabad

Book Excerpt from
The Lotus and the Universe (1963)

My original home in Pakistan was Abbottabad, in Hazara district in the northwest. It is very much like California there in so many respects. One of my neighbors was Pir Aslam Shah, one of the most childlike persons ever encountered. He used to tell us constantly of his wonderful pir-o-murshid. Indeed, he could not talk of much else.

One day he received a cable asking that I remain in that section until the pir, Haji Baba Abdul Aziz, returned. The Pir lives at Havelian, the train terminus, which is down the gorge from Abbottabad. It was from him that I was to receive the Zemzem water, blessed and from the spring of Abraham at Mecca.

The exchange evoked the divine love that permeates the universe. We live and move and have our being in and with this love, though we may not recognize it and often are unable to maintain it. This is the least that one can say of Pir-o-Murshid Haji Baba Abdul Aziz. He was not to become my spiritual mentor, and I cannot say that my own pirs were "greater," because in the infinitude this word has no meaning.

Pir Aslam Shah also took me to many holy men and pirs in that region . One man decried the fact that I did not have a beard (neither did Pir Aslam Shah), and this has made some of the more conservative brethren hold back. But when I asked Allah, the Compassionate, the Merciful, about it, he told me that his munificence also extended to Chinese and Burmese and Amerindians.

Aslam Shah also brought me to strange holy men who were beyond classification. They might regard Muhammad in highest repute and dress and behave otherwise like Hindus. They might be *munis*, in at least semi-permanent silence. They were always in "states" of *remembrance*.

Pakistan, Summer 1961

Excerpts from Letter-Diaries

June 14 Abbottabad

My Blessed Pir-o-Murshid [Maulana Abdul Ghafoor]:

There are times when one has unusual experiences, and these are tests, no doubt, of one's spiritual and personal ability.

Jesus said, "Let[99] us not into temptation," and I do not know whether what I am facing is temptation or not. I have met a Qalandar whom I see almost every day. He claims to have many followers, including the Chief Justice of the Supreme Court. He is planning to go to America. He wishes, or is guided, to bring the message of spiritualism to my country and to other countries.

He has given me many evidences of his powers and what he calls "*kashf* "[insight, intuition, direct transmission from the divine], but it is not the same as what I call *kashf*. That does not mean that I am right and he is wrong. Only his *kashf* seems to be concerned with seer-ship and the ability to escape from the body, to function in the "heavens," to meet saints and to have grand faculties.

All this is excellent, but to me it is not *tawhid* [Divine Unity]. On the last day I was in Japan, I had tea with the Ambassador of Pakistan. He told me the story of Farid. Farid practiced austerities and one day even made a flock of birds die and become reborn to fly away. Later, he came to the house of a lady and demanded food. She was very slow. Finally, he grew impatient and seemed to threaten her. She said to him, "Do not treat me as a flock of birds that you can cause to die and be reborn." This amazed him and he asked her for the details of the story, which she gave him.

Now I am receiving instruction from the Qalandar, who believes he is one of the most powerful men in the world. Maybe he is. He says he has 38,000 followers who will help him to travel. I have no followers. I am going over the globe a second time, I have crossed the United States many times, sometimes without having 50 rupees at any time, yet lived in both fine homes and poor places. I had nobody but Allah, and Allah showed me. This was a different kind of *kashf*.

---

99 Samuel Lewis translating from his preliminary understanding of the underlying Aramaic word here.

The Qalandar asked me to ask Muhammad where he belonged in the assemblage of saints. I am only in the rear rank of the assemblage. But I told him I could not ask Muhammad, because I had already asked Allah. He did not seem to realize that if I could ask Allah, this might be greater than asking Muhammad.

I told him he was greater than I in all but one thing: I could be a greater pupil than he. I could learn from him, I could listen to him, but he could not listen and learn from me. Although in breath-mastery and insight and teaching he was far above me, I was a greater student. This rather surprised him.

I cannot believe that the higher stages—*haqiqat* and *marifat*[100]—can be fathomed by the human mind. I have not often been in assemblages under Muhammad. I have been in one assemblage under Muhammad as *abdullah*—servant of God. Muhammad said in his lifetime that he was over everybody as Messenger (*rasulillah*) and also slave of everybody (*abdullah*).

I have seen him many times clearing and cleaning a great mosque. He does not use any magic nor any power. He uses love and humility—and such love and humility that I cannot compare it with anyone else's. It is as if everybody were a baby, and he had to look after everybody with love and sweetness.

He is not exactly assisted by Jesus. Jesus washes the feet and looks after the shoes of the devotees that come to this mosque and does other very simple things. I have seen this many times. Muhammad says this is his work as *abdullah*, not as *rassulillah*.

I have seen him in two other assemblages. In one were all prophets mentioned in Qur'an. In the other were also those not mentioned in Qur'an [e.g., Ram-Sita, Krishna, Buddha]. These are described in my poem "Saladin." In it, I was shown a *miraj* (journey through the heavens), not exactly as it appears in the record, but he told me he wished to reconcile Qur'an with Bible, and I had to write it that way. Also, in the highest assemblages, he made me write what I have not believed and I do not think many Muslims believe.

Now I am receiving another poem called "Rassul Gita." It is to be, *inshallah*, the Islamic answer to the Bhagavad Gita. It is very deep and requires me to be in states and stages of receptivity. I have to listen, not see, and to feel and feel more in the heart. There are many things given to me that I have either not believed or not known.

The poem is divided into two parts:

A. *La Ellaha* (There is No Reality), which deals with *fana* (effacement), the "kingdom of the cipher" and the conquest of India—meaning every sort of "other" worship.

B. *El Il Allah* (Except for God), which deals with *baqa* (expression of the real), the "kingdom of the One" (*tawhid*), the conquest of Pakistan and the resurrection of Pakistan.

---

100 See glossary for definitions of these terms.

It is based on *nimaz* [the ritual Islamic prayers] and then further. Anybody who has studied the sciences, inner and outer, knows that certain principles are found there, not certain personalities. The whole poem is based on principles. It is also based on *fana-fi-rassul* (effacement in the Messenger).

People are unhappy, uncertain and do not have enough food. I have been sent here as a servant of Muhammad Abdullah, and he wants me to follow him as servant. People call him "Messenger" or "Prophet" and go contrary to his words in Hadith[101] where he says he does not want a lot of titles like the Christians gave Jesus.

If one says that Muhammad has all power, is the greatest of the great and then is concerned with Pakistan acquiring Kashmir, he is a liar. People here are concerned with Kashmir, and Muhammad is concerned with Islam. People use the word *Islam* and they know nothing about its meaning—submission. They only know insistence, and insistence is the enemy of submission.

"Rassul Gita" is being written in the hopes that it will help spread the messages of Muhammad through the world. The divines can take care of *"rassulillah,"* and they will succeed or not insofar as they follow the will of Allah and not their own.

I have met three Chishti murshids. One does not seem to have any power at all. But all of them had love, plenty of love. You should see the way they cherish their mureeds. They belong to each other. It was the Pir-o-Murshid of Ansar Nasri who gave me the push to begin "Rassul Gita," and you who have given me the push to continue it.

The great questions here outside my ego are those of starvation and unhappiness and the need of having the real teachings of Muhammad broadcast.

There are those places in this universe above assemblages, even above faculties, which are the well-springs of all blessings. I may just be sipping through one little straw, but if I sip truly then I may be fulfilling the purpose of my life.

Those who proclaim *Muhammadar-rassulillah* (Muhammad is Messenger of Allah), let them prove it by radiating love, peace, justice, tranquillity and every sort of healing.

I knew the private secretary of Prime Minister Mosadegh. He is now home in his native village, drawing water and taking it to the people in the hills. This is *ryazat* [spiritual practice], this is *abdullah*. This does solve some problems.

Faithfully,
Ahmed Murad Chisti

---

101   The sayings of Muhammad, sometimes called the "traditions," each of which supposedly has an accurate chain of transmission or *isnad*.

July 1 Abbottabad

My dear Leonora [Ponti, see end of Section V, now married],

I am very, very relieved. As a student of religions I have been most struck with the problem that Buddha faced of human suffering. I am even now writing another epic in which a love-theme arises: there are certain forms of expressed love that are devoid of sympathy. On the one hand, we have the love of passions and on the other a divine love. The former seems to me uselessly hot and the latter uselessly cold. Still, to be *sympatico* is not easily expressed.

It may be odd for me to say that the greatest favour you ever conferred on me was the experience of being able to share your pains and burdens. It was only that I was tied down, perhaps with a dream. This dream was and is now so much like the theme of "Lost Horizons" that I am becoming bolder and bolder in relating my "Lost Horizons" experiences in letters. Sometimes an endless urge drives one on, which one cannot explain.

I was engaged to marry, and a former lover crossed the lady's path. The temptation was too great. The results have been ironical as have the results of all my broken romances. They always end in irony. But even without the lady, and perhaps because there was no lady, I met the very top people in Pakistan whom it seemed to be in the cards to meet through her. In turn, she has through her marriage accepted a much lower strata in society.

On my previous visit, the seers insisted I would be married. Now they are insisting even more—men in different places who do not know each other. They all see the same picture. One man went so far as to give her first initial, and I don't know any woman with that first initial. However, they agree that she will be a rich widow. I am not putting any stock in it, and I am not ignoring it, for the man who wrote "I Led Three Lives" was a simple person compared to us—Sam Lewis, P. Puck, Ahmed Murad, Ameer lean, "Ah Yaint, A Saint," etc. We were much closer than many knew, and there were many secrets that we felt even more than knew. I am told on one hand that I shall live a long, long time and on the other I see all my best associates in the West go. If so, it means one of two things—recognition or residence in Asia. Either is possible.

There is one thing you have to learn—all religions to the contrary—and that is that God and the Devil are often on the same side. At least, they have both joined me in a conspiracy several times.

July 3

My last dancing partner Leonora had a most dramatic month. She lost her two best men friends through death, and in the middle of it received three proposals of marriage from a business associate and finally accepted. I am relieved, because in the last few years, she has had a hard life. Deafness incapacitated her for most employment, despite her efficiency and made her become a laundress manager. She has had nothing but troubles and worries. But me with my faraway determination could not be mixed in these things any more, and if I do marry, which is always possible, it should be to a woman who has a faraway attitude.

I now have two extremely contrary yearnings: to settle down in one place either to study or work with plants, or to travel to certain parts of Europe: Sweden, U.K. and Spain, and to the West Indies. Maybe I may live long enough, but again I do not care; it is always possible I shall have some sort of recognition. I am getting it here, and it looks as if I shall in India, Malaya and East Pakistan. Now it looks like the cards are all loaded for me, and then some.

July 13 Abbottabad

When E.G. Browne visited the tomb of Shah Nimatullah, Persia's most important mystic, he learned that "among the gnostics there is no difference in sects."

So also Professor Durrani is not only a Sufi, he is one of the most complete Yogis I have ever met. I offered one morning that there is a teaching derived from Abdul Qadir Gilani that even his followers, the Qadiri Sufis, do not know. "That is absolutely correct," he responded.

This teaching is that Rama, Krishna, Shiva, Buddha, Jesus and Muhammad all lead to the same Universal Oneself. The Qalandar came by at that moment and never said a word. He had met the professor before and had acknowledged his superiority, and was a little taken aback to be seeing the professor listen to me.

Then I met another Qalandar—a sober type who gave me his blessing. This was not verbal, but a communication in heartenergizing and magnetization. I may meet this man again, but do not know. Then last night, the paymaster (Aslam Shah) took me to a Sadhu Baba who is both a Sadhu and Sufi. He lives a few miles out of the next town from here. He had heard about me and so I went. It was not hard to find him. We sat in attunement and it "took."

I was able to renounce the ego and get into both his breath- and heart-vibrations. I had previously gotten into Paul Brunton's breath-vibrations, but not heart; and into the second Qalandar's heart-vibrations, but not breath. Sadhu Baba is quite an old man and very much respected. One of his disciples gave me a thorough massaging, and I see this is done in some places. I am hoping to go to Azad Kashmir soon and may look into such matters.

August 10

Jacob's ladder was no doubt a symbol, but there is an intercession available in tombs and shrines, and even holy men. There are definite "telephone lines," so to speak, between this world and the vast vistas unseen.

There is a complete guidance of love, beneficence, wisdom, compassion and even mercy. There are no problems excepting those that are made by human beings. There is a wisdom in having these human-made problems so that we, as individuals and societies, can grope and grow.

"Therefore fight, O Arjuna" [Bhagavad Gita] must mean something more than poetry, and in a sense, each of us is Arjuna.

August 15

To: Professor Alfred Cantwell Smith, Institute of Islamic Studies McGill University, Montreal, Canada

My dear Professor:

When I was in the UA.R, I was approached by a group of scientists, who said:

"We are Sufis, and we wish the American government would take more cognizance of us. The Russians are 100% materialist, we are 0% materialist and you Americans stand just between us. The Russians are 100% dialectic, we are 0% dialectic and you stand halfway between. The Russians do not believe in a god, we firmly believe in God and you stand between us. So we are far more anticommunistic than you are or can be, but you will have nothing to do with us. Why?"

The scientists then went on to describe to me their method of counter-espionage and counter-intelligence which is almost impossible for a non-Sufi to understand. I have met other scientists who are Sufis also engaged in counter-intelligence, and I mention this in part because you have placed in your book, *Islam in Modem History,* a number of "cosmic philosophies" in juxtaposition or opposition to each other.

I opposed Hitlerism in full. I did not believe a person or group could evaluate whole cultures and civilizations by any moral or immoral standard. I cannot and do not believe in "scapegoatism," and I am afraid that your book has made the "Sufi," who is not a Sufi at all but a figment of imagination, into the scapegoat.

Indeed, I have not found anybody who has refuted Professor Titus Burkhardt's claim that European writers do not understand the Sufis, because they have not faced Sufi disciplines nor learned from Sufi teachers.

251

Sufi Barkat Ali

Book Excerpt From
The Lotus and the Universe (1963)

If the meetings with sages in the Near East were like comic operas, those in Pakistan became like grand dramas.

Leaving Abbottabad, my friend Pir Aslam Shah said to me: "Murad, I do not think any foreigner coming to this land has met so many holy men as you have," Yet, in the sense of one of our noted cartoonists, "then the fun began."

My friend, Ansar Nasri of Radio Pakistan, introduced me to his pir-o-murshid and by the process of *tawajjeh* [attunement through the breath and eyes] there was an inner awakening that has resulted in much poetic creativity. *Tawajjeh*, in theory, corresponds to the *darshan* practiced in India and is mentioned in *In Quest of the Oversoul* by Paul Brunton. Jesus pointed toward it when he said, "The light of the body is the eye." Few have experienced it to the depth. A similar experience came when I met the pir-o-murshid of my friend Huq who operates the Dawn Hotel in Rawalpindi.

But the greatest drama came when life centered around my friend and spiritual brother Major Muhammad Sadiq. In epic fashion, in the year 1961, we were led or pushed from one holy person to another, from one place to another until we met Sufi Barkat Ali, who lives in Salarwala, Lyallpur District.

All the occult and mystical experiences in books or told through folklore seem to have paled in the separate or common experiences of the Major and myself. In many respects a very childlike man, the Major had been told he had healing powers, and during the years multitudes have come to him for help.

The Pir, formerly an aide to Field Marshal Auchlinchek, retired from military and political affairs at the end of World War II to devote himself to the spiritual life. From the Sufi point of view, his state seems very high, his stations the most advanced yet encountered. He has a vast amount of inner and outer knowledge but devotes himself entirely to recognition of the All-Pervading Omnipresent Deity, and to help humanity to rise from unhappiness, disease and frustration.

252

He has a simple abode in the jungle, the compound terminating in a mosque and courtyard used for study, prayer and ceremonies. But sometimes the crowd is so large that meetings are held in an adjacent field. The women meet separately, and one can easily distinguish the Pir's wife with her remarkably brilliant, loving, living eyes—magnetic and electrifying and more. Children are also encouraged in devotions and present indications are that there will be a large Sufi center in that region as time goes on.

Pir Barkat Ali combines the *tasawwuf* of the Chishti, Qadri and Sabri Schools. The Chishtis use music mainly, and there have been some excellent *qawwals* (songs of devotion) presented there. The Qadri teaching takes into consideration the use of repetition of spiritual phrases, mostly from Holy Qur'an and all in Arabic. The Sabri school has a moral training, not too different from that offered in the Indian Bhagavad Gita. That is, so that one can practice a sort of "indifference" under all circumstances, feeling the presence of Allah, whomsoever, howsoever, wheresoever. Thus to Sufis, God is both being and The Being.

Sufi Barkat Ali in 1979 (photo: Susan Bluestein)

Pakistan, Fall-Winter 1961

Excerpts from Letter-Diaries

September 22

Takht Bhai[102] is Persian for "mountain spring." It has ruins of old Buddhist monasteries and cities. Most of the land nearby is owned and operated by Sattar and Jamshyd Khan. Months ago I informed you that I had hoped to visit the best farm run on modern methods, and this is it.

Sugar is their main crop. They plant only on rows and hills and never broadcast. Both rain and irrigation water is used. But we ran into a difficulty: their harvest was much greater than expected per acre and there are not enough mills to handle the cane.

I had come from the U.A.R. hoping to find some solutions for some problems. Here there was no problem, except on the economic side. There may still be some trial-and-error in obtaining the maximum of sucrose, but the whole thing at Takht Bhai was combined with the proper handling of labor and utilization of soil.

I also found myself in one of the most beautiful orchard gardens I ever visited. If it had been more Persian, it would have been a "paradise," but there were no fountains and few ditches.

The tendency here is to use small modern machines. The operators are happy and proud of their work, but the tradition in this "casteless" society—boy! It is bad enough to have dirty finger nails, but even the kind of dirt is classified!

October 13 *Lahore*

I visited the tomb of the saint Mian Mir. I got stopped several times by people who knew me in Abbottabad or heard of me here. Every body wants my blessing except for the bakshish-wallahs, who want bakshish. At the tomb, I was accosted by some commies [communists] who wanted to know why the tomb guardians should permit a foreigner to trespass on holy grounds. But between my bakshish and my prayers and explanations, the tomb guardians have been on my side.

---

102 Indo-Parthian archeological site of an ancient Buddhist monastery in Mardan, Khyber-Paktunkhwa, northern Pakistan.

Then I went to another saint's tomb. This one has been written off, because the saint did not reveal himself to the commies. It is unfair for saints to take sides in the Cold War or any war—except, of course, when they are on "our side." Saints are supposed to serve Allah, and who gives the orders to Allah? When I went to the saint, known as Data Gang Baksh (or Al-Hujwiri), I got in another grand game of hand-shaking, embracing and blessing. I now have the unamalgamated union of saints, seers, sages, Sufis, *sadhus* and psychometrists working for me. They say that on my birthday I will have more luck.

October 18
This is my birthday, and under other circumstances I should be the "happiest man in the world." Actually, it is a comedy of errors with comedy beating the errors all over. The Indian officials have held up my visa, and I am sitting without a passport.

While I did not meet President Ayub, over the phone he expressed his wish that I assist in introducing the culture of this country into the U.S. I am throwing the ball back to his Excellency and according to his personal or official decision, my future may go up and up.

I have seen enough sages and mystics to know that we have not studied the "rare earth" types or the radioactive types among human beings. We talk about anti-Aristotelianism but are bound by the same time and space psychologically. There may be many kinds of fourth dimensional consciousness.

The possibility and probability of unusual types coming to America may set off some commotion. We shall, of course, try to "normalize" them. We cannot have world understanding as long as we wish to remain ourselves the measuring sticks, the calipers, the micrometers.

November 15
The consulate has become more concerned. Even the experimental letters sent out have not brought answers. The saints and seers all say I shall be going to India, a matter made more difficult because I have been receiving invitations from that end. Pakistanis have no trouble in going to India, provided they have not been mixed in politics.

I met one Hashimi, a saint who lives in a town called Sheikhapura, which is about 25 miles from here. He has been going around making wonderful predictions about me. He has a strange way of working. He does not tell you about yourself, he tells you about your friends. So I have heard through others. He has confirmed what the other saints and seers say, which is still in the stage of prediction.

I also have a plan for my host, Major Sadiq, to start an herb and medicinal garden. They do not have one here, and as there are so many schools of medicine, it should be not only an experimental station but a valuable commercial venture.

I am also beseeched to function as a Sufi teacher. I had so much trouble in America that I hesitate. But I took four disciples—dogs. The result has been that the crows and birds all join in, anybody but the chipmunks. So far they have not come, but you can never tell. I was at the celebrated Faletti's hotel yesterday, and the cat came and joined, right off. I may not have sex appeal, but between you and me, we have it with the birds. Psychologists, please explain.

The university wants me to speak again tomorrow. The schools want me. The kids want me. I could be set up for life here, but "I wanna go home."

December 12

A woman has come into my life. She is absolutely against protocol, and that's how she got there. She mingles with Asians and is against even my own protocol—she is a member of the Fourth Estate. You see, in my endless war against protocol, I have my own protocol of always being against the press. And so it is that the best friends I have here among Americans are Ye Olde Presse, so help me Allah and Mammon!

On top of that she is a Paul Brunton-type, that is, a *news-wallah* who wants Yoga. She spent one and a half years in India getting Yoga. However, shortly after our first meeting I gave her more Yoga than she got in India, no European professors of oriental philosophy being present. She did not believe it until I brought around two Sufis who confirmed what I said....

There is a rumor going around that I am mad and I answer, "Of course I am mad, but my madness is the same yesterday, today and tomorrow. Other people have Sanity No. 1 on Monday, Sanity No. 2 on Tuesday, Sanity No. 3 on Wednesday and another Sanity next week. Of course, I cannot accept that kind of sanity." Inasmuch as I proved to be informed, my position is not easily overthrown.

The other night, Julie [Medlock, the journalist mentioned above] went with me to the Forman Christian College, where an American choir sang carols, and the next day to church, but the Americans who attend church are mostly teachers; the officials are "high" Episcopal.

Anyhow, last night it was a combination of the birthdays of Jesus Christ, Ali (son-in-law of Muhammad) and Jinnah, founder of Pakistan. So there was a big celebration in the Cantonment. The music was all spiritual.

The saint of Sheikhapura was here, and he spent some time with Julie, the first time another American has ever bothered, and she a newspaperwoman to boot. They told me she was more interested in spiritualism than religion and more in phenomena (occultism) than spiritualism, so they gave her the "mageek" formula.

India, Winter-Spring 1962

Excerpts from Letters-Diaries

January 23 New Delhi

My dear Leonora!

New Year's started off with a bang with everything happening right. But the stories of my meeting Sufis and saints are so fantastic, I wonder if and how they can be written.

My trip to Karachi was totally successful at every level. One of the most important events was the meeting with Khawar Khan, whom I shall be calling Saadia. She is a beautiful teacher at the College of Domestic Art and Science. We collaborated on a paper presented at an international gathering of philosophers. It won first prize, she was acclaimed, the paper was sent to President Ayub and is being published.

When I return, I am also going to dedicate a "Garden of Allah" for the growing of medicinal and scented herbs. This may be started in the winter of '64-'65 if my program works out right. I plan to return home and start another war, now that all my former wars are won:

- Against Arthur Koestler and his *The Lotus and the Robot* in which I shall insist that Dr. Radhakrishnan and others are real people.
- Against Captain Lederer[103] on how to beautify ugly Americans. As I told the foreign service, if you write fiction, everybody will read, but if you bring facts, nobody cares.

February 20 Anandashram

I have had to take some ironies and tragedies in my love life. Now the augurs and soothsayers are unanimous that despite my superannuated torso, I may still go to the altar. Only this time the romance is promised for America, not the Orient. The only thing is that now I have three careers in front of me and have made progress on all.

There is another side of Yoga, and this can be associated with the word "Shangri-La." Whatever has happened to me, and plenty has, this *corpus* does not seem anywhere near *delicti*. I am, if anything, more sprightly and have

---

103 Willian Lederer and Eugene Burdick authored the political novel *The Ugly American* in 1958 about the failures of US diplomacy in Southeast Asia.

danced before thousands of children. I bet I have embraced and been embraced by more people than any other *genus homo*!

I am hoping to return in May, but am not sure—terrible conflict within myself between northern and southern California.

I carry my castanets with me and subscribed to *Let's Dance* for the American-Pakistani League. As usual, every folk dance festival I have expected to attend here has been called off by rain. And it is now raining around my next destination: Bangalore.

February Anandashram

[An extract from Lewis's later paper "Genuine Mystical Experience Versus Pseudo-Mystical Experience."]

In 1962, at my revisit to Anandashram, home of Swami Ramdas in South India, I woke up three mornings to find myself not Sam Lewis but Ramdas.

"It is time to go," I said.

"Yes, it is time to go," he replied.

But who comes and who goes? Anandashram was a veritable Shangri-La. Because our metaphysical friends always want to place Shangri-La elsewhere, we often don't realize that the Kingdom of God not only can be on earth, but is on earth.

It is our eyes and senses that are blind. There is no unsolvable problem.

March 21 Agra

Dear Leonora,

"Ah Yaint, A Saint" went to Fathepur Sikri. Rushed to the tomb of Saint Selim Chishti and did the usual bowing and everything including *baksheesh* [Hindi term denoting a cross between a tip and an alm]. Then I had the guide take me to the local saint.

No Americans call on local saints, but Ah Yaint, A Saint did. We greeted and embraced and I gained in holiness—boy! When we returned to the shrine, my friends the Sufi qawwalis came and sang, and I danced and danced—real *dervish* stuff.

A crowd gathered, and when I got tired, I sang and the qawwalis answered. Then the leader got up and asked the crowd for *baksheesh* to watch the American saint! I later made a courtesy visit to the Hotel Imperial where I had stayed before. I was recognized: "Oh, the saint!" So now you are not the only one who knows. Please interpret!

Pir Dewal Shereef

Book Excerpt from
The Lotus and the Universe (1963)

At the beginning of 1962, one felt entirely satisfied, and yet in a strange position with a spiritual teacher of each of the great faiths of Asia. Sufi Barkat Ali seemed to dominate everything in my "occult" life. The practice of *tasawwuri*, which is to keep in tune with the Murshid in thought, breath and vision, manifested in some delightful episodes.

The departure from Pakistan, the welcome to India and the departure from India were all marked by incidents that do not fall within our accepted modes of "realism" or diplomacy.

At the tomb of Amir Khusrau within the compound of Nizam-uddin Auliya in Delhi, I saw myself invested with a robe. I described it to the sons of Hasan Nizami at the time. Upon my return to Pakistan, I found Sufi Barkat Ali and my Sufi brethren ready with that very robe at a public gathering and henceforth I became known as "Sufi Ahmed Murad Chisti."

But self-satisfaction has nothing to do with the spiritual life. *Rida* means "satisfaction" with the Deity Who is Compassionate, Compassionator and Compassionated.

When I had been with Major Sadiq in Dacca in 1956, we had been invited to dinner by his chief, Brigadier Ghulam Muhammad Khan. The general was very careful not to throw rank at us in spiritual matters, but told us anyway that sooner or later we would both come to recognize his spiritual teacher. Having then entered into bonds with Maulana Abdul Ghaffoor and later with Pir Barkat Ali, we believed we had come to the place where we could and would progress without any further aid. But it was not to be.

Pir Abdul Majid Khidri, common-ly known as Pir Dewal Shereef, had his

Pir Abdul Majid Khidri

khankah or headquarters at Islamabad, just north of Rawalpindi. The Brigadier, now retired, had his home nearby. The Pir appeared to be cold both to the Major and myself, but this proved to be a façade.

Pir Dewal Shereef claimed to have received his spiritual illumination through Khidr, that semi-legendary figure who, together with Elijah, remains as one of the two "guardian spirits" of this world and the next. Those to whom Khidr appears are supposed to be specially blessed.

From the moment I had reached Pakistan in 1961, wherever I settled a young emissary of the Pir appeared. It did not matter where. First it was in Abbottabad, my original home in Pakistan. A few devotees in *tasawwuf* would gather at the home of Chief of Police Ghani, and he came and "tapped" me for his Pir. This happened over and over again at Lahore, Rawalpindi and other places. And when I doubled in my tracks, so did the Pir, over and over.

So Major Sadiq and I determined independently to place our cards on the table. It was a case with each of us of absolute, unconditional surrender. The strong, the self-willed, the adamant became like babes. And later I was to see other persons go through even more dramatic performances. There was *bayat* (pledge of initiation) on sight, regardless of earlier commitments.

Later I spent some days with the Pir at Murree, his Himalayan retreat. As with Paul Brunton, it was not necessary to use words or the ordinary means of communication. As the heart becomes more alive, this method becomes easy and effective. Our bodies may occupy different portions of material space; but in the heart-world, there is a totally different sort of arrangement. Attunement is of prime importance.

Pir Dewal Shereef is now superintending the construction of Islamabad University on the site of the new capital of Pakistan. He has been successful in obtaining funds for this new institution, even beyond his own original scheme. The university plans to coordinate the ancient and the modern, to preserve religious and spiritual traditions, to incorporate all aspects of modern knowledge and methodologies, but in particular those arts and crafts which require some use of the hands.

Pir Sahib realizes the weaknesses of Pakistanis: their unconscious Indian heritages of caste and class, their low regard for certain types of labor and their complete ignorance of the personal habits of Muhammad and his immediate successors.

Pir Sahib may even, in a certain sense, be regarded as the spiritual teacher of President Ayub Khan. The President cooperated in several of his ventures and is open to guidance in ways we of the Western world either do not understand or do not accept.

The Grand Sheikh of the Qalandars visited him while I was at Murree. It was a strange sight. The old man, then 115 years of age, acted more like a youth in love. Excepting for his wrinkled skin, he showed no sign of age. It was even more remarkable to find the spiritual leader of one school paying such obeisance to the pir of another order.

Even more amazing, to me, was the absolute surrender of Sheikh [Abdul A'la] Mahdudi, who had been regarded as the leader of those Muslims who wish to be conservative in their religion but "march with the times." The two men had held profoundly different opinions and each seemed rather adamant. Each had a large following and there seemed some uneasiness in Pakistan as to the exact nature of "Islam." They debated for two hours. At the end of that time Sheikh Mahdudi came from the classroom and sat down on a bench with me (we had not met before).

He said: "My whole life is ruined. I have been wrong in everything. All my writings are wrong. All my teachings and contentions are wrong. I have been mistaken in everything. I am ruined." He burst into tears – this from a once proud and self-reliant man.

"Nothing is wrong, nobody has been ruined." I replied. "Allah is the Most Merciful and Compassionate, the All-Wise and All-Loving. You have been calling yourself a Muslim; but you did not know how to surrender in anything. You demanded, you did not concede, you did not surrender. You have until this moment not had the slightest idea what peace is or means. Now you have surrendered for the first time and yourself become a submissive one; you have become a Muslim. *Alhamdulillah*! (Praise to God!)"[104]

---

104 Sheikh Abul A'la Mahdudi, 1903-1979, founded the *Jamaat-e-Islami*, the largest Islamic organization in Asia. His followers were pioneers in politicizing Islam, especially a conservative interpretation of Islamic law or *sharia*. Despite the "surrender" that Lewis reports here, Mahdudi later supported General Zia-ul in his overthrow of Prime Minister Ali Bhutto in 1977 and supported the latter's program of "Sharization" in Pakistan.

Pakistan, Spring-Summer 1962

Excerpts from Letter-Diaries

May 14 Lahore

My horticultural and soil reports have been accepted by top officials, but they have not given me a letter that I am asking for. Neither did I contact the President [Ayub] or Secretary Shahab. I got the run-around and then a "no," but I was told the "no" did not mean "no," because Shaokat (Ayub's son) said "yes." This is what happened. Quit reading fiction, please.

I then met again with Pir Dewal Shereef. I am to be his representative and of Islamabad University in America. He wants me to introduce Sufism with spiritual philosophy and healing. He has been most successful in collecting funds for Islamabad University. I have already written Berkeley for reciprocal relations. He is also the pir of none other than Ayub Khan and visited him twice last week. He refuses the refusal I received, sent me back to Lahore and told me to arrange another visit both to him and the President. He will take care of things, *inshallah*. What we are concerned with is the official recognition of either Major Sadiq or myself or both.

Meanwhile, the Major has extended leave and we are moving. I hope to see him tomorrow and will inquire about my mail. But without word about his business venture in Texas or confirmation at Rawalpindi, we are both stuck. The appointment of me grapevined around and now the whole host of Sufis is pulling for me. Besides, I have seen both Dewal Shereef and the Major perform some miracles: the Pir causing the dumb to speak and the Major the blind to see.

The question is: when shall we get the money and recognition promised us? To make things more opaque, the Qalandar crossed my path twice recently. Unfortunately, he is now immersed in politics and I could get nothing out of him.

I am living near Shalimar Gardens where we had to move and have few comforts or privacy. All these pressures counterbalance with the best inspirations of my life, and in the heat. "I wanna go home" and can't.

May 29

My dear Norman [McGee]:

Guaranteed to keep you in suspense, and in 110 degree weather. I saw Barkat Ali again and told him one does not mind good news, one does not mind bad news, one does not mind in the least having bad things foretold and having bad things happen, but the constant series of good "fortunes" accompanied either by an impasse or by bad events was over-trying.

On the brighter side, I spent yesterday with Khawar Khan, who is slated to be my chief disciple, and with her beautiful and brilliant chum. She now has ownership of the property that was Gandhi's here, and we are planning a big celebration to open it for my spiritual work.

While this is a minor facet of my work, it will establish the seed for my future ventures here—the spiritual half—when I return. The scientific half is already established. And the poetry gets its final review next week.

Now I am going to ask you a favor. My last dancing partner Leonora and I were and still are good friends. I would like the Major to come and help clear the slight deafness she suffers from. She lost all her men friends in a short period by death, excepting me who was far away, and on account of my Asian propinquities, there was no romance.

She then married a multiracial man and has since been involved in some social melees. Now being far away and otherwise involved, I may seem to be apathetic. So I wish you would go sometime to her laundry on Webster St. If you introduce yourself, this will do me a world of good. It is all right to write endearing letters, but a few hard facts would serve better.

Actually, I may even join Martin Luther King's movement when I return. I see no reason why not, and you can tell them this, too. Only my work ostensibly is in Asia.

July 23

My dear Leonora:

Dear Sir or Madam, We have an assortment of Pukhtunistan cloaks (we've taken care of the daggers) that need cleaning. They are all Afghan bordered and have Kashmiri trimmings. We keep them in India Rubber to keep the Indians from rubbering. Please give them careful attention.

My ticket ends in San Diego. I can fly there cheap buying it here. I don't know who is meeting me or where I shall go, but my "son" Norman says he will take care of that. I am glad he called on you. He is as anxious to help you as I am to help him.

Two and a half years—the zest of my life! I'll be glad to get back after 80-105 degree weather and sometimes hotter interminably....

July 23

[To Norman McGee:] The financial prospects with Major Sadiq, Malik Hamid and the Qalandar seem to have left us holding the bag. I doubt now whether I can get back before August 4. This has become a universal "do it yourself."

I have the complete goodwill of the staffs of both the American and Pakistani foreign offices in Peshawar. The monsoons have come and the heat has abated. But I still have to face oodles of red tape.

There is one thing omitted here, and it is stronger and more important than anything and everything else: UNIVERSAL LOVE AND BROTHER-HOOD.

God bless you,
-SAM, Sufi Ahmed Murad, Samuel L. Lewis

VII.
HOMECOMING

April 1968: In front of home in San Francisco with Moineddin Jablonski.

Listening to Insight, Seeking Home

Editor's Note

I n his *The Hero With a Thousand Faces*, the American scholar of comparative mythology Joseph Campbell proposes that all hero stories have basic
elements in common: a call to adventure, finding helpers, crossing the
threshold to the unknown, tests and trials, some form of sacred marriage, an
apotheosis or "elixir" theft, then a return across the threshold with the fruits
of the journey.

In Samuel Lewis's life, his two journeys to the East saw him pass spiritual
tests, meet like-hearted friends and teachers and find a potential new home.
When he returned to California in 1962, he began to integrate all of his past
history and trials, finding a new realization. He felt that his spiritual work
had been recognized and validated. He had yet to find fulfillment in his personal relationships or a family with which to share the elixir of his hard-won
realization.

Where would that fulfillment and family take place? As noted in his letters in Section VI, Lewis faced the choice of moving back to Pakistan to live
permanently or establishing two residences—one in the San Francisco Bay
area and one in Pakistan.

From his return to California in 1962 through to his passing in 1971,
Samuel Lewis carried on an extensive correspondence with his god daughter
and first Sufi *khalifa*,[105] Saadia Khawar Khan. The correspondence runs to
nearly 300 typed pages, far more than to any other person during the last
decade of his life. Published here is barely one-tenth of the total.

Lewis sometimes writes to her several times a week and reports that he
is constantly listening for the divine insight (in Sufi terms, *kashf*) that would
lead him in the right direction.

At the time, Saadia was a teacher at the College of Domestic Arts and
Sciences in Lahore, and Lewis hoped to collaborate with her upon his return there. These letters represent the most complete chronicle of this climactic phase of Lewis's life, from 1962-65. In 1965, he began to meet young
people in San Francisco who were willing to receive what he had to give.

---

105 Senior disciple and representative.

Ultimately this led to the creation the Dances of Universal Peace.

In the early letters to Saadia we see Samuel Lewis offering spiritual direction to her as a Sufi guide as well as contemplating his return to Pakistan, where he would use spiritual walking practice to help children learn "how to breathe." He also planned to pursue his "Garden of Allah" medicinal plant project, mentioned in Section VI.

The discussion gradually turns to Saadia moving to the USA, although always with Lewis's contemplated return to Pakistan. In preparation, and at the direction of his Pakistani Sufi pir, Barkat Ali, Lewis attempts to establish relationships with various Pakistani and other Muslim communities in the San Francisco area. The response is mixed, to say the least.

Letters from a Sufi Teacher

Excerpts from Letters, 1962-66

27 September 1962

My dear Khalifa:

I am busy writing two books and this takes nearly all my time. In this I have been most fortunate or rather Allah has blessed me. So I now have a fairly complete program for salinity and will soon be writing to the *Civil & Military Gazette* and to "Food and Agriculture" at Karachi. But people expect more from one than he can give.

I meet very few happy people, and many of my friends are unwell too. On top of that, the Islamic Center here is in a terrible mess. The leaders never would permit a lecture or report from me, and now they are busy fighting each other. I wrote them saying that a Muslim was one who was either (a) peaceful or (b) capable of surrendering. I have further advised I was interested in (a) religion, (b) informing the American public about Muhammad (on whom be peace) and his mission. They are interested in entertainment, social affairs and praising not Allah, but their ancestors.

My next attention is to those who are in difficulties. As my dancing partner married a multiracial man and was socially ostracized, I have cut myself off from all companions who favored such ostracism. But the time spent at this typewriter seems endless. Allah restricts me to ten letters a day, though I may do creative writing and have interviews. The interviews are almost uniformly excellent, but when they lead to the settling of such a big problem as salinity, you can imagine how deep they must be and they are.

Please give my salaams to your family. I have been well but have not heard from Major Sadiq. On the other hand, Pir Sufi Barkat Ali and his mureeds write regularly. Only they expect me to be back soon. I expect it will take four years to accomplish what was laid before me but then again, Allah knows best.

God bless you.

Faithfully, Sufi Ahmed Murad

May Allah's love be with you forever, Saadia.

PS. These are from the Asma-ul cards [Samuel Lewis uses here a classic Tarot card spread—the Celtic Cross—with cards that represent some of the

"99 Beautiful Names of Allah," the *asma-ul-husna* –editor]:

Al-Ghaffar (The Forgiver); Supreme Crown, covers your soul.
Al-Muhsi (The Accountant); Wisdom crosses your influence.
Al-Quddus (The Holy One); Understanding, crowns your obstacles.
Al-Ghani (The All-Sufficing); Love, beneath rising from your feet.
Al-Shakir (The Thankful); Power, behind you.
Al-Wajid (The All-Perceiving); Beauty, before you.
Al-Hadil (The Equitable); Endurance, you.
Al-Qabiz (The Closer); Majesty, your house.
Allah, Foundation, hopes and fear.
Al-Haqq (The Truth); Kingdom, outcome.

Allah is within you; you are Allah's instrument and through you Allah expresses to the external world.

"The one filled with the knowledge of names and forms has no capacity for the knowledge of Truth." [Hazrat Inayat Khan]

September 1962

Most of my work has been collecting materials for "How California Can Help Asia." But some has been for the Islamabad University, and in general this has been most successful and the people contacted are most interested.

So far I have not met the Consuls General of India, Pakistan and Egypt and have avoided Iran on account of the catastrophes there of a totally different nature.

The other day I went to Sacramento to the State Fair and everything there was so lovely; I shall have to make several tours while collecting materials.

Then I telephoned the woman who had been my *mureed*, who had betrayed me at every opportunity and has been false in everything and to everybody. I simply called her up and said: "This is your Murshid." The reaction was so loving and lovely. I may see her as soon as possible and this is the sign I was waiting for, the beginning of my spiritual work in this country. The astonishing thing was it was exactly as the pirs foretold. But while I felt reassured in other things, this was a test and *alhamdulillah*, successful.

18 October 1962

The next step was to meet with the official Muslims, and this is so horrible I shall not report.

The next meditation suggested I call on what are known as "Black Muslims." I received a most cordial letter from them and met the Imam. I have offered them books I bought at Ashraf (duplicates),[106] which the official Mus-

---

106 Ashraf Publications in Pakistan.

lims either ignore or pigeonhole. Their library is unused, and they make fun of it too. They accepted these with friendship and gratitude. So while this may sound prosaic, it is necessary.

Your suggestion about coming here is most wonderful. I would think it over carefully and pray for guidance, because here I might be wishing. The spiritual love is not the divine love. In the divine love we see Allah and only Allah, and in the spiritual love we see Allah's Attributes rather than Essence. The most important attribute is *Rahmat*, which is the root of *Rahman* and *Rahim*, which is in everybody's prayers and only in the hearts of *dervishes*, not ordinary Muslims. And the reason they are ordinary is that they don't accept *Rahman* and *Rahim* any more than *Allaho Akbar*. They say these things a million times, and yet it does not mean much.

The spiritual love is beyond all religions—everything. So I tell first of the Buddhist I have loved very much. I will skip all stories now but someday, if my biography is written, the details will be given. Our last conversation was this: "Samuel, We Ain't Got It." And I answered, "Robert, We Have Got It!"

10 January 1963
My dear Khalifa:

Between the sad period ending the year and an exciting celebration, I had a spiritual experience about which I have also written to Major Sadiq. In addition, I was given for Christmas *The Whirling Ecstasy*[107] concerning the relations between Rumi and Shams-i-Tabriz. It is the first time anybody here ever saw my true guise, but this has been done and in a sense I would be "exposed," excepting this is a priority. I shall try to find where one can get copies of it as it is published in Mexico. But I must warn you, it will surely lead to ecstasy and blessing. It is a marvelous healing in itself to have it. I would like to get a few of them and in a few days will find out where this can be done.

The politics of the day presume a new course for Pakistan, but I am so disgusted with my own country in many matters that this will hardly involve me. The average American would love to help your country but wishes to do it without loving your country.

7 April 1963
My Dear Khalifa:

As-salaam aleikhum. I have not heard from you directly for a long time, and the next is that you have been unwell. It is not enough to wish you health, but to try to see what is the cause of the trouble and do something about it. Now, I do not remember exactly what I have written in regard to practices to

---

107 By Aflaki, an extract from his "Lives of the Gnostics," 14th century.

maintain health. Disease may be caused by a number of factors. For instance, if one does not know, one may try at your different prayer intervals, one only each:

Allaho Akbar or *Ya Shafi* (inhalation,) *Ya Kafi* (exhalation) or *Ishk Allah* (inhalation), *Mahebud Lillah* (exhalation), these on thought 33 times. See which is most effective in making you feel better. This need be done only one day, and then you select the one that helps most. Suppose it is *Ya Shafi Ya Kafi*, then you may do either of these:

Standing up, 101 times, breathing in and out the nostrils and feel the breath go through the whole body; or seated on what I call a chaise lounge (long seat) with feet off the ground. Feel the breath go out the feet.

When I receive an answer from you, I shall be glad to send detailed instructions on self-healing. Or, if I can get a copy of Hazrat Inayat Khan's instructions on "Health," I shall send you details adding what I have learned from other sources. And I must apologize but I did not have a chance to get the proper ointment from the drug stores.

The most difficult, here in life, in practice, is to radiate the Universal Love that is called *Ishk*. It has little to do with personalities and yet it has everything to do with personalities.

When my first Pir-o-Murshid came to the West he was in the divine love. And when he was not in the divine love, he was rapt in Muhammad in *fana-fi-rassul*. The latter was not understood in the West, and he dropped his music and most ecstatic practices and went into *fana-fi-lillah*. This made him appear the most wonderful of men, and yet he got so far from others that they only could see his person, and very few have ever tried to follow his teachings.

These teachings must be given to the world along with the other Sufi teachings. Hazrat Inayat Khan had the "Four-School Sufism," which is accepted in general practice in Asia.

The Arab Sufism is somewhat different. There, each school is apart, but one may take training in all of them. But in the Indian subcontinent, I found the Suhrawardis, Chishtis and Qadiris so mixed-up that this does not matter, and although the Naqshibandis are separate, there seems to be universal concord.

In Indonesia it is different. Islam was revealed to very ignorant Arabs who were idolaters. It came to India to people who were Buddhists and Hindus. It came to Indonesia, which evidently saw many prophets, cultures and religions. It became the cornerstone of the arch, but not the arch itself. Therefore, in Indonesia, Islam is a universal religion, not a particular religion. If we are going to unite the Muslims, it is not by imposing one system called "Islam" upon another, and the poor Pakistanis find themselves apart from both Arabs and Indonesians, who outnumber them. The question is here, which is the divine way? When people ask me questions, I give them the proper practice—*fikrs*, as above.

Surrender to God is a process, not a religion. It is a way of life, adding to the life. It is not opinions; these wear people out.

Concentration (*murakkabah*): once, 15 minutes, feeling you are before *rassul-lillah* and being instructed by him. If this cannot be done effectively, then try on occasions to go to Dargah Mian Mir for peacefulness. Though they do not allow you inside, that does not matter.

My salaams and blessings to your aunt, the Mustafa and friends.

Faithfully, Sufi Ahmed Murad

20th April, 1963

Beloved One of Allah:

For a long time I have not heard and yet letters come to me concerning you. This is a very difficult thing and yet it is not difficult. The *bayat* is not a pledge between person and person. It is a union between person and person in the journey toward Allah and also with Allah. For we may pray incessantly, "Guide us on the right Path," yet there is neither guidance nor right nor Path. For life is movement, and it is in the change and movement we come away from the *nafs* and into the divinity.

One of the most pressing difficulties in the world is pain and sorrow. All the prophets of God without exception came to deal with pain and sorrow, and all the followers of the prophets praise the prophets and do not concern themselves with pain and sorrow. They concern themselves with saying that their prophet was superior to other prophets.

The other day I wrote a long letter to my friend Shemseddin Ahmed, whom you have met. It is a criticism of an article in *Pakistan Review*. The writer was concerned with the superiority of Muhammad and the Qur'an and to prove his point he contradicted Qur'an and Hadith over and over again. What is this? This is done by so many people. And this shows *kafir* [non-believing], because it suggests not praise to Allah but praise to "my view." And "my view" is not the view of the Supreme.

Once I was travelling in India, and a holy man came and said: "Why are you here?" I said, "The pain of 10,000,000 starving Hindus." "You are crazy, how can you feel the pain of 10,000,000 starving Hindus?" Just then a great swami came and said to the holy man, "No, you are crazy, because this man knows what he is talking about and you do not." All over India you find holy people and spiritual people and they are not much concerned with the pains of others.

Then later I was in Karachi and saw 600,000 displaced, homeless people with nothing. This was my second pledge to Allah. And the first took place years ago when all the great prophets of Allah came to me in the broad daylight, and I vowed willingness to take on pain.

Now you have the pain, and I feel the pain, and sometime it is like a man with arthritis. He is in pain, and yet he has the great duties and responsibilities and in pursuit thereof, he does not try to get rid of the arthritis. For I am in the midst of millions and millions of people, and they know nothing of Islam and very little of God or Allah. Every person sees his own religion of lack.

In one sense there is nothing wrong in it, for Allah, not a human being, is the "Master of the Day of Judgment." At the same time we are in a scientific age, and in this age we rely upon experience.

Hazrat Inayat Khan came and said, yes, it is right to rely on experience but why not the whole experience of life and not just part of it? So one tries to have the whole experience of life and not part. Then he is misunderstood, but this does not matter so long as he understands.

For there is the way of wisdom and the way of love. And they are different and not different, like the two sides of a coin. Today I have two pir-o-murshids and the people of the West say, "How can you have two pirs? And you already had Hazrat Inayat Khan. You have no loyalty." But when *rassul-lillah* died, Siddiq said, "Those who believe in Muhammad let them know that Muhammad is dead, but those who believe in Allah, let them know that he is living, the true (*Ya Hayy, Ya Haqq*)."

If you practice the *"Ya Shafi, Ya Kafi,"* and I think I gave you the instructions, it will remove pain. Or it will give an understanding of pain until you arrive at a great state where pain and bliss become one.

Next is the instruction on *wazifas,* and for these at first only a repetition of 33 is needed and not more than one after prayers, or between the prayers. But if you feel you need more repetitions, then 101 times between the prayers, not at prayer time. These are of two types, also, the oral and the thought, though for both a *tasbih* may be used:

For Health: *Ya Shafi* on the inhalation, *Ya Kafi* on the exhalation; or just repeat *Ya Shafi Ya Kafi* audibly.

For Strength: *Allaho Akbar.* Also for protection against enemies or evil forces of any kind whatsoever.

For Uncertainty: *Subhan Allah.*

For Problems Connected With Love: *Ishk Allah, Mahebud Lillah* as *wazifa;* or *Ishk Allah* on the inhalation and *Mahebud Lillah* on the exhalation.

During illness or nervousness if prayers are impossible, repeat a sacred phrase as above, or do *kalama.* Then there is one more practice, and this should be done best at night before sleeping, but in stress it can also be done more often. For this, one should sit in posture, on the prayer rug or bed and inhale thinking *La Illaha El Il Allah* and exhale blowing the sound *Hu* on the heart.

Even three to five times is sufficient but it must be very concentrated with all feeling, feeling also that Allah is Divine Love and Divine Graciousness and the Heart is Allah's throne (*arsh*). I hope this will help and encourage you.

May Allah give you blessings.

As-salaam aleikhum

Sufi Ahmed Murad Chisti

5 May 1963

Now the nature of people is that they take Allah for granted. Allah is neither thought nor imagined, and when we feel Allah, it is just a little iota of the reality but this is infinitely better than the thought. The thought confuses people and produces *kafr*. It is even worse when the *kafr* is called *Islam*.

Every Sura of Holy Qur'an begins *Bismillah Er-Rahman Er-Rahim*. This is the stage and backdrop for everything. We live in a universe that is replete with mercy and forgiveness; that is its very nature. Yet human beings are not merciful and human beings do not forgive. The result is that they do not know the nature of Allah's deity.

The other day I copied *The Whirling Ecstasy*, and one of the big problems discussed in it was the position of Bistami and Muhammad. When I return to Pakistan, *inshallah*, there will be lectures on it. But during this copying I read Hadith always, because otherwise there is a tendency to magnify Rumi (which is done in the West) and lose sight of Muhammad (which is always done in the West). Yet *rassul-lillah* was the inspiration of both Rumi and Shams-i-Tabriz.

The teachings given in Hadith are extremely different from the loose use of the term Hadith that you find all around you. Muhammad never condemned anybody personally. True there are condemnations in Qur'an but not in Hadith. These condemnations are based on principles, natural laws and universal morals. In Hadith one reads about the "greater *jihad*," which is always against *nafs*. In your country few think of it.

I am having a friendly controversy with a spiritual brother over the use of Arabic terms. The first teachings of Hazrat Inayat Khan agree with Data Sahib (Al Hujwiri); one wonders why even the *dervishes* sometimes went in other directions. The condemnation of ecstasy by Aurangzeb was the interference into religion by a political leader and led to the downfall of the Mughal Empire. But most of humanity does not learn any lessons from mistakes. The spiritual music was taught to me by Pir-o-Murshid Inayat Khan, and in all these years I have not found a single person to give it to.

16 May, 1963

Beloved One of Allah:

Alhamdulillah for the wonderful news! But before going into this, I report the purchase of some allergy pills, which are being packaged forward. There is also a variant called "antihistamine," which I did not get assuming the same was available. But if not, will take it later.

Now as for your future, I am in a strange position for I see three possible paths and myself the beneficiary of none of them. Therefore, it is more necessary than ever to follow the *ryazat*.

Fikr is to concentrate: exhalation on *La Allah*, say 101 times and then a meditation to catch the rhythm of the breath. Then swing any thought and if the breath remains, it is in accordance with the "right path," and if the breath changes that is not in accordance with divine will. The number is a suggestion and can be any from 21 to 1001. Practice enables one to feel what is right with Allah.

I do not wish the visit to Iran to interfere with marriage but even if you "plight your troth," there is a certain gain. For instance, my work is to revive Data Sahib and if you knew Persian, you could go over his work as well as the great poets in the original. But as I benefit personally by this, and your folks felt I might not wish you to marry soon, it is not pressed.

This brings up another matter, what I call the "Three Body Psychology." Freud and his great successor Reich were not theoretically wrong, only their methods of integration often fail, for the whole person is not taken into account. It is very important that the whole person is studied, and the spiritual Islam provides material for thought and consideration.

11 July 1963

The meditation in my life is concerning the difference between *fana-fi-lillah* and *fana-fi-rassul*. Now this word "difference" is usually taken in an analytical sense and thus establishes actual differences. For from a purely logical point of view, to say "Allah and His Messenger" and also, "He hath no partner" causes a difference between the philosophical and psychological outlooks. This has meant that in Saudi Arabia the attitude toward Muhammad is different. They begin by insisting he is not a partner of Allah and end by ignoring his noble character and career.

In the papers on "Moral Culture" [of Hazrat Inayat Khan], which go next, one is concerned with the "Law of Renunciation." This is "Life in God," while the "Law of Beneficence" is the life of the heart and the "Law of Retribution" is natural justice. Each has its place in the world. In the absolute sense, in the "Life in God" there is no Muhammad. But before one reacts on this point, and most people will react instantly and violently, we are missing most of the career of Muhammad (1) as a man on earth (2) in a cosmic career.

The *Miraj*[108] is the experience of a personality but not necessarily of a human being. In this experience, Muhammad came to the heaven of Adam but did not stop there. This shows that he had on the one side something beyond *rassul* and *nabi*. Qur'an says, "We make no distinction between them [the various prophets of humanity]" but Muslims usually do. This is often based on ego ignorance. There is no way to belittle Muhammad more than by saying he was "the last and greatest of the prophets." What is meant by "greatest?" Why do we say, "*Allaho Akbar.*"[109]

But from another point of view, when one examines the purpose of creation, the purpose of creation was for the manifestation of *insaan-i-kemal,*[110] so that Muhammad, in a sense, *is* the creation. And yet there is beyond creation. In "Rassoul Gita" there is a vast distinction made between "La Illaha" in which we must deny and "El Il Allah" in which we must affirm, and it is easy to fall into a trap.

The *fana-fi-sheikh* today is Sufi Barkat Ali and Pir Dewwal-Shereef, who are on earth. It is not that there is more love between your Murshid and them than other spiritual sheikhs he has met, but that the divine will ordains it. And *fana-fi-pir* means contact with one who is gone, chiefly Hazrat Inayat Khan, Hazrat Mian Mir and Hazrat Data Sahib and in India, Nizam-ud-din Auliya. And *fana-fi-rassul* is 90% Muhammad and 10% Jesus. But when one prays for the guidance, it is any one of these means that may occur. Holy Qur'an says we always have the guidance, but it does not say that the guidance is restricted to any form, and guidance is not necessarily *kashf* alone.

In the meanwhile, your Murshid has been going to a Yoga teacher who is a gymnast. And they were giving lessons on the use of Hindu *mantras*. So one day he said: "You teach *mantras* and you teach weight lifting. Did you ever try to see whether the *mantras* operate in the weight lifting?" So your Murshid lifted a heavy bar, concentrating on OM and did pretty well and then he tried without the OM and had difficulties and said to the Yogi: "See the *mantra* works, try it. The Yogi was impressed. Then your Murshid picked up the heavy bar and lifted it most easily. "What did you do?" "I had another *mantra.*" "What was it?" "*Allaho Akbar.*"

Your Murshid did not try to impress the Yogi more but in the next meditation he was given a tremendous, let us call it, "revelation" for the proper training of children in gymnastics, dancing and all kinds of things. He went to the Yogi and the Yogi was astonished.

We do not begin at the beginning. However your Murshid was told it will be two years before this can be written and when it is written, it will be

---

108   Prophet Muhammad's visionary journey through heavens, called the *Miraj.*
109   Literally, "God is greater," meaning larger.
110   A complete, perfected human being.

dedicated to Khalifa Saadia K. Khan so that within the world of Islam again there can be proper spiritual training from the beginning. For this it may be necessary to copy his Murshid's teachings, for there have been difficulties in getting books. But you might try Ashraf and see if you can obtain more literature of Hazrat Inayat Khan, including what is now being sent.

What he has written in theory on education can be made operative and one can join the spiritual and physical sides of education.

24 July 1963

Beloved One of Allah:

Hazrat Inayat Khan was born in 1882 and died in 1927. He began his work in the West in 1911 when he gave *bayat* and *khalif*-ship to Rabia Ada Martin, who was my first teacher, but who did not give me the formal *bayat*. I received both the *bayat* and what may be called "initiation" from the pir-o-murshid. He also gave me some special training, which is helping me very much now.

I have amply found perfection (*kemal*) in Holy Qur'an, and when I read in Data Sahib (Al-Hujwiri), it sets the soul on fire. The way he interprets it, you know, it is all revelation. Some Muslims think it is merit to praise the Prophet, and I think it is merit to find out what the Qur'an means inside oneself (as well as outside). Therefore, if one can get others to understand the *Rahman* and *Rahim,* the "right Path," the *Allaho Akbar,* and the *Rabb Alamin*—this is a big job.[111]

This was Bhullah Shah's way of studying, and I think it is very good for all times. Now I have three big works in Sufism. The first is to get literature to people. The second is to get the *ryazat* for practices. The third is to simplify for the next generation a Sufism more in line with devotion and less with metaphysics so everybody can learn.

The third step will take some time and *inshallah*, it will be worked out with my Khalifa, Saadia Khawar Khan, who shows so much promise and is also interested in education. Now I know some very simple ways to teach the young, so simple that the whole world has skipped them.

And the next thing is that while Hazrat Inayat Khan wrote that an artist subscribes his creations to Allah, in humility but not modesty, one must here relate the personal history. Hazrat Inayat Khan asked your Murshid to write commentaries on his writing, and your Murshid could not. Then exactly three years after his death he manifested and began dictating these commentaries, according to the capacity of your Murshid. And neither the language nor the wisdom belong to your Murshid but are products of *fana-fi-sheikh* and *tasawwuri Murshid.*

---

111 "Right path"—*sirat-al mustaqim,* and *rabb il-alamin,* usually translated "lord of the worlds," are both phrases from the first Sura of the Qur'an, Al Fatiha.

29 July 1963

My very close friend Saladin [Paul Reps] has been here for one day. He has sent me all his books written by Hazrat Inayat Khan and on arrival, I expect to copy these materials. Much of this writing will need commentaries.

Praise be to Allah who is giving me the most complete teachings in *ryazat*, which can be incorporated in any system of Islamic education, at any age. It is too tremendous at the moment for me to write it and, with some other doors opening through my brother Saladin, there is a new big world.

30 August 1963

Now as to *fana*. This means self-effacement. To explain it mathematically, people think effacement means becoming zero, becoming nothing. Actually it is the removal of *nafs*. Therefore for *nafs*, it is negative. As one moves negatively toward the negative infinity, one learns in the end that the negative infinity and the positive infinity become the same. In other words, *fana* implies that the more one removes the self, the more the divine infinite life (*baqa*) manifests.

Those who move positively can only move at a certain rate, and those who move in effacement increase the divine accommodation. So instead of being a "nothing" or "no thing," it is as Hazrat Ali has said, "Say Allah and Allah you will become."

31 August 1963

Muhammad, not the people, declared by the grace of Allah that Jesus, Issa, was a Muslim. Yet Issa never married, and Issa prayed, "Give us this day our daily bread." He was also concerned with the stomachs and bodies of people.

The Universal Islam therefore includes all teachings not abrogated in Qur'an, and if these teachings are contrary to Hadith, it was the Prophet, not the Muslims of later date who said, "My word can never abrogate the words of Allah but the words of Allah can abrogate my words." Actually your Murshid has been saying, "spiritual food for the West, material food for the East."

The other day he received a confidential soil report covering many nations, but Pakistan in particular, corroborating everything he has said, done and tried. But this came after having received from his spiritual brother, Saladin Reps, some of the latest and most revolutionary advances in the sciences. There are no problems, just tests from Allah, the Compassionate, to humankind to work out salvation and wisdom. The answer is really always available. The question is whether the *nafs* can accept them.

6 September 1963

As-salaam aleikhum. Yesterday I moved into the new address, 58 Harriet St, which is in a poor part of San Francisco, but which has ample room to house one other person. I felt by *kashf* that this would mean a change in outlook and felt the presence of Allah almost immediately.

I have taken up one by one the grievances that Pakistan might have or does have and protested against your country being treated like a poor relation, always taken into consideration but never consulted. It is not even a question of right and wrong.

Among the things mentioned were the parts the *dervishes* play in world affairs, something to which America, as a nation, wishes to close its eyes. Between my history in the UAR and that in Peshawar, covering several persons, some of whom you know, even without any *kashf* one gets a pretty good picture of world affairs as they are.

This nation [the USA], verbally dedicated as being "under God," is under hypocrisy to say the least. That is why I am hesitating to work too hard to propose reforms for Pakistan, because we spend billions on "foreign aid" to keep corrupt governments in office and harass our own Negroes who now for the first time are offering human protests.

My brother Saladin was here, and the first steps were taken to show somebody the spirituality of how to walk, how to breathe and how to use the name (or attributes) of Allah. This is really the gist of *tasawwuf*, with or without books, and lectures and sermons.

My love and blessings to you both and also Major Ikram because the new methods of instruction in *tasawwuf* would benefit all his children, down to the smallest; and they also could become integrated into national instruction from the low grades to the highest.

September 27, 1963

Now before me is the Qur'an translated by Dawood and, while this may not be the best translation, it serves a purpose. There are the Suras that have the name of "Dua" and these can be repeated for self-protection. Or again, when the problem was put before the Prophet he said: "Say Allah and leave them to their devices."

When one is concerned with spiritual duties, he is too busy for anything else but the nearly perpetual *zikr* or the concern with the affairs of humanity. Nevertheless, the critics have rendered a signal service for Sura 95 begins, "By the fig, and by the olive!" And while your Murshid did not realize this, this is at the very basis of his planned book and articles on "How California Can Help Asia."

In 1926 Hazrat Inayat Khan gave his last will and testimonial to your Murshid, and nobody believed it or accepted it. So the Sufi organization has split into many parts and they all talk about "Sufism" like the people in Pakistan talk about "Islam." But there is no consideration of Allah. Yet now, after all these years, for the first time the elder son of Hazrat Inayat Khan has agreed, just a bit, that his father just might have confided in your Murshid. And the truth is that Hazrat Inayat Khan gave him the sobriquet of *Sufi*, but that he never used it until it was publicly announced by Pir Sahib Salarwala [Sufi Barkat Ali].

Inasmuch as I have been criticized, let me explain something. I did not meet any imam until 50 years of age. As each Sura was studied, the parallel passages in the Bible were searched, and commentaries were written (destroyed in a fire long ago), which showed the connection between the Bible and its prophets and Muhammad as *khatim al-nabi*.[112]

In "Saladin," where Muhammad appeared to me as *khatim al-nabi* he not only showed the unity of religions, but himself taught me Yoga systems that are practically unknown today in India.

To me, all discoveries, inventions, ideas which have benefited humanity some are because of Allah, and without Allah's permission nothing would ever have been to humanity's welfare. And it is quite obvious that all these things did not come to and through Muslims, although this was once the case many centuries back.

29 September 1963
[To Pir Barkat Ali]

Now Hazrat Inayat Khan taught that peace in the world depended on the acceptance of the hierarchy (*Qutb, Ghaus, Auliya*, etc.). He left a whole ceremony for this purpose, but the meaning was not accepted and the practices (*mujahida, mushahida*) are hardly known at all. So instead of having peace, we have turmoil.

Last week this one performed for the first time the *tawajjeh* of Khalif Usman, and gave the feeling of peace to all. No doubt, superficially or otherwise, it is like some forms of *darshan* in India. The way this person has been given *darshan*, it has often been a ceremony but when this person had the *tawajjeh* of Hazrat Inayat Khan (he had it in two ways) it was transforming. This also is in harmony with the *darood* practices.

You will appreciate, dear Murshid, that one is always busy and now, for the first time, *alhamdulillah*, there may be some help of a nature badly needed, for a spiritual brother is moving here who can be entrusted with typing and so help prepare lessons. And the amount of lesson material that has come, come from all nations, is very great and unorganized, and if published, the meanings remain unknown.

---

112 The "seal" or guarantee of the prophets.

So one is satisfied, and Allah has given the strength and courage to continue at an age when my companions have become feeble and worn out and here again is the testimony that one's spiritual practices, *wazifa* and *darood*, are effective. They operate through the person and preserve, increase and encourage his vitality.

With love and blessings to all,
Sufi Ahmed Murad Chisti

November 3, 1963
[To Shemseddin Ahmed]

There is a spiritual hierarchy which is recognized by all the Sufis, east and west, and they have at least this in common. And there is the idea of the *Ghaus* or *Qutb* at the head of the living hierarchy, and under that person a number of nearly perfect souls who have functions. The lower of these is called *Abdal*, who can change their natures; and below them the *Ansars* or helpers, of whom there are supposed to be 360.

Now your Murshid was not sent on the path of the *murshid* but on the path of hierarchy, first due to Khidr, and then to the whole chain of prophets, whomsoever, wheresoever. And this involves the responsibility for very big problems. Some of these appear in my poetic verses, but my diaries were destroyed in a fire. And if one, say, is a *Buzurg*[113], he is not concerned with *bayat*.

At the home of Major Sadiq and also at the home of our friend Hamidin in the cantonment, I was challenged by one Abdul Latif, an old wanderer, "Why aren't you a Murshid." So I broke from the path of *Buzurg*, which one does not proclaim, and gave the *bayat* and sent him to Mian Mir. There he experienced the *hal* and *shahud* and proclaimed Ahmed Murad to be a true Murshid.

Now your Murshid has a whole compendium of *tasawwuf* inside, as well as the writings, to show even little children how to walk with the *zikr* and *kalama* from earliest childhood. Only this must be illustrated. And when it is taught and done, there will be no boundary to either Islam or *tasawwuf* or anything, and even children will have direct wisdom from their own capacity.

For in the pursuit of Allah, one does not trouble about religious differences. There was a Christian mystic named Rufus Moseley, and he was supposed to be the greatest Christian mystic in the country. He taught a lot of famous people. So when your Murshid was travelling within a hundred miles of this mystic, he went to the city of Wilmington in the state of North Carolina to meet him. It was something like the meetings with Sufi Sahib at Salarwala.

We had never met and we accidently turned a corner and immediately embraced each other—no introduction was necessary. We spent time togeth-

---

113   See Glossary.

er and on the Sunday I went to a crowded church to hear the sermon. There was a vast audience, because there are not many Protestant Christians who stand out as being particularly spiritual. But I never heard the sermon. After a long introduction he said: "Ladies and Gentlemen, my beloved brothers and sisters, I must beg God's pardon for even coming to this pulpit, for I am unworthy to address you. There is in the audience a man. I summon him to the altar to continue this discourse." And he got down and left the altar and everybody looked around and as a few people knew me, I had to continue the discourse.

So sometimes one goes and works under guises, which is the course of *Abdal*, which means chameleon-like, or changeling. Yet with time the inner guidance is different. So you can understand and even explain the different religions.

December 29, 1963
Meditation is the English word used to describe sitting quietly, keeping the breath in rhythm and not having any particular thought. However, it is a Buddhist rather than an Islamic practice. So I learned to use the Invocation [of Hazrat Inayat Khan], which is at the head of all the papers as a Darood, though in another sense it is two complete Daroods. And sitting down or posturing, for say fifteen minutes, or longer, just watch the breath and hold the Invocation before the mind. This has a multitude of advantages and it also prepares for *murakkabah*.

January 1964
In the practice of *fikr* every breath gives renewed life, and in the prayers each Fateha should be as in and of itself. Consequently, tradition must not carry weight.

It is one thing to quote Holy Qur'an and another to accept it without the interposition of any tradition. If Allah is wherever one turns one's face, one's inspiration need not be measured by tradition, *fiqh*[114] or something called *shariat*. The *shariat* is the derivative but not the measuring stick.

New discoveries in science, art, human wisdom may harmonize with *shariat* but need not be measured by it. Anything not forbidden may be valid, although if one were to ask me as a Murshid, there is quite a different way. That is to consult either Holy Qur'an or Hadith, or as I do, certain sayings of Hazrat Inayat Khan and draw inspiration and measurement from that.

If Islam means surrender to Allah, this surrender may come any time, any place, anywhere. One does not agree with the critics of Ibn Khaldun or Moineddin Ibn Arabi. They set the precedent, they added to the human

---

114   Traditional rules of Islamic jurisprudence.

wisdom and knowledge. Your president has had it published that Islam is a progressive religion. How can it be progressive if anything is measured by the habits of one's predecessors?

Now the reorientation of Islamic philosophy means on one hand going back to Qur'an and Hadith but without ever using the phrase "Back to Qur'an and Hadith." But this is one half of it.

The other half is to re-evaluate the human knowledge of the time as well as human problems and failings. The knowledge of the time in science, art, technology, accords with Islam. Allah gives to whomsoever Allah wills, regardless of the person's religion or character. Without the divine consent, humanity could learn nothing.

And therefore orthodox Muslims are stuck when they try to evaluate the contributions of what they call "non-Muslims" to human welfare. The result is that they do not even recognize the real contributions of Muslims to human welfare. And they are substituting themselves for Allah as *maliki yaum ad-din*.[115]

If we study modern physics, we can see it acceded to the unity of Allah (*wahdat, tawhid*) without confirming any theology. If we study modern biology, we can see how the *kemal, jemal,* and *jelal* operate in the living forms. If we study the characteristics of chemical elements and then we study the *sifat-i-Allah*, we find in each case a sort of unifying essence behind each while manifesting through differentiations. Ibn Khaldun discovered this, and it is in *Muqadimmah*, but since his time, Islamic philosophy went down because it was necessary to please the *ulema*[116] rather than Allah.

March 9, 1964

Beloved One of Allah:

As-salaam aleikhum. These words have a different meaning with a Murshid, for the Murshid must strive at all expense to preserve the peacefulness of the *mureed.* And yet, the Murshid sometimes has three different careers all at the same time: (a) with the world; (b) with the self; (c) in cooperation with the spiritual hierarchy, which is most real.

You will find enclosed the last of the preliminary portion of "The Way of Illumination," which is needed by all seeking *bayat* according to the system of Hazrat Inayat Khan, which may be called "Four School Sufism." But according to the *bayat*, one must regard himself as the brother or sister of all persons in all branches of *tariqat*, whether Sufi Inayat Khan had the *bayat* of those schools or not. In any event, this person is a multiple "school" disciple.

---

115   Another phrase from Sura Fateha, usually translated "master of the day of judgment."

116   Transmitters or guardians of Islamic law and doctrine, usually educated in *madrasas*, religious institutions.

20th March, 1964

Beloved One of Allah:

As-salaam aleikhum. It is always a test, beginning with the *Bismillah* to maintain the spirit of peacefulness. Or as Saint Mian Mir taught: *Allaho Akbar,* which means *Peace-Power.* One does not to wish to go into a long explanation here, and the availability of this aerogramme gives a rapid, but incomplete, reply. However, under all circumstances your Murshid wishes to maintain the Peace, both of *Bismillah* and *takbir* [the phrase *Allaho Akbar*]. All other things are vain, whether of this world or the next, which interfere therewith.

There has been financial pressure eased by a few small jobs, but each of these consumes time. Sunday, *inshallah,* for the first time, a group of young men are calling here to consider *bayat.* There is not only no Islamic teaching here (exception: see below), but there is very little spiritual teaching of any kind outside of Zen Buddhism.

California, especially, is the home of cults, and there are three cult movements derived from *tasawwuf*: (a) A Russian named Gurdjieff, who was undoubtedly a *mureed*, but mixed Islam with some Caucasian folklore; (b) Subud, which has done the same with Malayan folklore and magic; (c) Meher Baba, an Indian Parsi who claims to be a leading Sufi. None of these conform to the book called *The Sufis* written recently by one Sheikh Idries Shah of England and which is getting much favor.

Your Murshid is trying to write for Murshids from the writings of Hazrat Inayat Khan. The notes on *kalama* are relatively simple, but those on *nimaz* give importance to every little item of the prayers. It is here where your Murshid was in constant turmoil with the *mullahs.* They thought he has come to reform Islam, and he found them formalists, who knew the movements, but not the wisdom.

There is a relation between words, movements and wisdom, and even this is an incomplete statement. However, in the *ryazat*, there are many veils to be uncovered, and even since the last correspondence, Allah has placed more material in your Murshid's hands.

Pir Barkat Ali has given your Murshid certain wazifas. And along with your Murshid's shortcomings, at the same time, there is constant rejuvenation. At least, a friend who sees me often said this last night. He knows nothing about the *ryazat* and undoubtedly thinks Sufism is just Islam. But even in Islam, few know the relationship between the *asma ul lahita'ala* ["highest names of Allah"] and living energies. And as one goes over prayers, one finds that in rituals there is often teaching given word for word, without full appreciation of each of those words. This is a common failing of all religions, which lose vitality and spirituality in their rituals. The rituals themselves are not wrong if we regain their component parts.

June 21, 1964

My dear Saadia:

Nafs salima is not only at rest, but pouring forth magnetism, *baraka*, without stint. The training being received from Sufi Sahib, and perhaps also from Madzub Sahib at Salarwala is in this field. For it is one thing to be at rest, even be happy, and another thing to communicate to others.

This brings up the point that ultimately, to me, the true Muslim is one wherein the stage of *nafs salima* is active, and one through whom the *baraka* flows, reaching others and also drawing them to—as written previously "Grace, Glory, Wisdom, Joy and Peace."

Now we put it another way. *Nabi* Issa said that the kingdom of heaven is found in little children, and this teaching is even emphasized more in the recently uncovered Gospel of Thomas. There the words of Issa are entirely in accord with the Hadith that every child is born a *muslim*, and it is his parents which take him away and lead him astray. In other words *nafs salima* is active in little children and it is clouded later. You can see this yourself that it has been recovered soberly in Sufi Sahib and with intoxication in Madzub Sahib.

The *nafs salima* follows the explanation *Allaho Akbar*—that Peace is Power; that kinetic energy proceeds from potential energy, and the same truth that is in *tasawwuf* is also the truth behind all the modern knowledges and sciences.

The finality here comes in the practices of *mushahida* and *mujahida*. In the "greater *jihad*" one finds one's enemy is *nafs* and nothing but *nafs*. In combating *nafs* one finds, in the words of *Nabi* Issa, the kingdom of heaven. Or to quote the Christian Scriptures, "Blessed are the pure in heart for they shall see God." The "seeing" is *shahud*, and the purification is *mushahida*, and the blessings, of course, are *baraka*.

July 11, 1964

There has always been a question in your Murshid's mind on the place of marriage for very spiritual persons, and although he is not married, he has not ceased to look. The lady who seems from an analytical point of view most suited for him is now in West Africa. The heart-friendship ladies have not accepted *rassul-lillah*, which must be done either intellectually or spiritually before he can make a bond, but the problem or question here is yourself.

There can be no dogma here. Many people in Cairo visit the tomb of Saint Zainab. In Basra, Rabia has been venerated. In Dargah Nizam-ud-din Auliya, one finds the tomb of Jahanara, and the life of Emperor Humayun was recorded by this sister. No Muslim has ever decried these and other ladies, and there is even hypocrisy over marriage. Certainly Issa was, in his time, a Messenger of God.

The other day I explained to Hashim and his friend Muhammad, the relation between these terms—*alamin, ilm, ulema, alim*, etc.[117] Fortunately, they understood. These words coming from the same Arabic root have a great relationship in the cosmos, but in the narrow, analytical sense they may seem far apart.

When Allah is Lord of All Worlds, Allah is Lord of Thought, Feeling, Form, Love, everything, and not just of unseen materialist "heavens." Without the wisdom, we are very confused about such matters.

September 7, 1964

Beloved One of Allah:

Your Murshid does not perform *dua* without permission. He says we perform *sijda*.[118] But we start it by putting hands to our ears in prayer; only, we don't listen. Your Murshid interprets this as meaning, "Allah, I am about to pray. My ears are open for an answer." Then we put our heads to the ground and ask Allah if Allah is listening or not. But prayers have become in all religions God-bribes and formalism, but do not bring the communication between the devotee and the Devotion.

Your Murshid might explain all kinds of hand-holding, but your problem was put to him also by a lady who is a very good friend and had the same problem in Egypt. It was always the married man. It is not the hand-holding that is wrong; it is the offer from a married man. And even this is not wrong if he would hold your hand in the presence of his wife or in society. But when it is done when you are alone, that is very wrong, even if he loved you. For if he loved you he would observe convention, even low convention, and would consider you and not himself.

As the *baraka* increases in and through your personality, there will be more and more of this. You will have to learn to live with it. But you will have to treat such people, and especially the males, like we treat the dogs and cats here. They are given the petting, but the magnetism is never the same. Only for you in the practical, or rather the esoteric, sense you must protect yourself, and not just to follow the traditions, many of which have to be broken. In all cases, the married man must learn.

Your Murshid also has had this experience, but there may be only one or two women on earth that could stand before the power needed to uphold the projects mentioned in the other letter. The pirs know this and yet they have admonished him to look.

---

117 All come from Semitic roots that mean a "gathering" of something—time, levels, worlds or individual pieces of human knowledge.

118 Meaning here a prayer for a personal request. *Sijda* means the prostration that occurs several times in the ritual prayer of *salat*.

The most difficult of all *tasawwurs* is that of *tasawwur Muhammad*. This is said by one who has had a multitude of *tasawwurs*, not only with the saints of Islam, but with the ideals of other faiths. Your Murshid has followed Buddha to Hell, Christ to the cross and Muhammad through the Heavens ("Saladin").

This was the real sealing after he had all the basic experiences of all faiths; and it is not written just to confirm the orthodox or heterodox Islam. He can offer you the *tasawwur* of Pir Barkat Ali or Sufi Hazrat Inayat Khan or Mian Mir, one of these, but not more.

October 16, 1964

About two weeks ago, when a lady who has been most friendly and is of wonderful character, broke an engagement for a number of weeks standing, always with an excuse, your Murshid said, "This is the end." He hung up the phone and heard the divine voice saying, "Samuel, I need you." And then as he turned to his rooms, the telephone rang, an emergency call.

This was the first of several such emergencies—people in dire trouble, seeking spiritual or psychological solutions and trusting your Murshid. This is one of his real functions, and it seems only great pain or difficulties cause people to turn to that way. This Sunday he is having a meeting, the first meeting in response to the cry of those who are in deep pain or difficulties, caused always by so-called "spiritual colleagues" who are mostly so concerned with their own spiritual development that they have lost all humanity. And this means a new direction, one in answer to problems of pain, suffering, illness, for which your Murshid was especially trained.

You will remember a few weeks ago, your Murshid said he would not stop working on the Gathas of Hazrat Inayat Khan, because there were others now preparing and ready for them. At that time there was one young man, now there are four. This faculty, known as *kashf* in Islam and *prajna* in Hinduism and Buddhism, is the divine voice that always speaks to us, though sometimes it is hard to hear. And at this writing, with two distinct paths pointed out at the moment, both leading to spiritual functioning on the part of your Murshid, there is this important response.

Even praise or blame do not affect your Murshid, but when the proper questions are asked, then he is either transformed or transforms himself. And here again, there is large sector of your Murshid's history in Cairo that looks as if it came out of something more bizarre than even "The Arabian Nights." For behind Sufism and the Sufi orders, there is that hierarchy that controls the destinies of the world. Yet this hierarchy is not only manifesting through Islam, it manifests above and beyond all religions. You have read this in Part II, "Saladin," which came from *rassul-lillah* himself. All wisdoms of the world come through him, and not just what we call "Islam" alone, separating it from

288

anything. Indeed, your Murshid has had initiations into six great religions, even from the Chinese.

December 15, 1964

This person has two faithful young mureeds and has been teaching from "The Unity of Religious Ideals" [by Hazrat Inayat Khan]. And as he taught, there would be some external experience to support the teachings. But now each has partaken of an outside experience. One saw the leader of the Congress Party greet this person, to the dismay of the audience. The other saw the complete surrender of a heretofore resistant audience and their acceptance of "Peace is Power," which is the interpretation of *Allaho Akbar*, taught over and over again by the blessed Mian Mir at the dargah. When they cannot but see the manifestation of teachings, and the change in people, their faith is increased.

December 30, 1964

Then the Bible teaches that, "In Allah we live and move and have our being," and it is mostly by *kashf*, but it is "clear evidence" that comes and then one knows. One does not stop to analyze whether it falls under the type of phenomena discussed in "Cosmic Language" of Hazrat Inayat Khan, or whether it is direct from Allah. It is as Abu Said Abul Khayr explained the "eighth seventh" of Holy Qur'an. The seven-sevenths are the Book; the eighth-seventh is the continual guidance from the Supreme (*Ya Azim*).

My prayers are also always for you and your aunt. The obstacle is not to be in a hurry to return to Pakistan, or even now for the coming of Major Sadiq. Only, now he must be my younger brother and not a partner any more, unless there is word from the pirs to that effect

March 1, 1965

Beloved Pir-o-Murshid [Barkat Ali]:

As salaam aleikhum. One writes not knowing whether one is reporting or seeking advice. One writes because there is a sort of "psychic climax," which may or not be important. One writes knowing the extreme difference between actual surrender to *Al-Hayy* and something private called "Islam," which may or may not have meaning.

When a *mureed* is put on spiritual practices, especially the *daroods* that you so graciously presented, there are bound to be effects without one knowing whether effects are the direct results of one's devotion or the effects of grace, which do not necessarily depend upon fervor or ardor. Contrariwise, if the repetition of *wazifas* or *daroods* does not change the personality, the circumstances, the inner and outer life of a person, then there is either something wrong with either the *ryazat* or the devotee.

It is now some time since my return from Pakistan, and the total fruit of effort in relations between that country and the personal self have not been very much. True, money and time have been spent even to the limits of one's capacity. But the major persons in your country, for whom apparently these efforts were put forth, have either failed to appreciate what was being attempted, or have failed in their own private lives.

This person has been entrusted with two general duties in life, one concerned with the sciences and food production, the other with the awakening of hearts. Both of these will come to a climax this year in California, especially in southern California.

There will be a scientific gathering in July and this will bring to a head all the materials for "Project: The Garden of Allah." But now the original geographical application of the project may change. And in September, one will be on the panel at another gathering in which the audience will be scientists, but the speakers will be those versed in the great religions. It is then one must come forward as a champion of *tasawwuf*.

The coming into my life of Hassan Hashim from Sudan has totally changed the feeling of being a sort of exile. True, almost every group that "logically" should have welcomed me has done everything but listen. But now one does not care, and as one does not care, there is growing attention from truth seekers of various kinds.

Hashim has discovered that this person is not only versed in many more sciences and branches of culture than the average man, but also in many branches of Islamics. This is the first person he has met who knows these things; also, who is acquainted with the Swahili Islamic culture of Africa, which your countrymen largely ignore. This has led to very serious consideration of northern and central Africa.

Today I receive little from Pakistan other than from Shemseddin Ahmed of Lahore. How can one help persons, or a country, without receiving literary courtesy. This is very difficult. My personal will has been to visit Thailand, India and Pakistan, and possibly Ceylon but the personal will should not determine one's future.

June 8, 1965

Fikr: Think *La Illaha* with the exhalation, *El Il Allah* with inhalation. The breath should be purified and in rhythm either with *wazifa* or short meditation and with the Invocation, either *Bismillah* or Hazrat Inayat Khan's "Toward the One, The Perfection of Love, Harmony and Beauty, the Only Being. United with All the Illuminated Souls, Who form the Embodiment of the Master, the Spirit of Guidance" (or translated into Urdu language, unimportant whichever you choose).

Fikr may be done first after prayer or almost in place of prayer (prayers five times a day do not mean rituals five times a day, but remembrance). But *fikr* can also be done walking, especially if you do not exercise much and your courtyard would be excellent for this. The norm might be 301 times but if you cannot do that, then 101 (one hundred and one) times; or if more, 701. But if you do not do all the 701 at one time and split it up during the day, there may be a total of 301, 501 or 701 for each day.

Pay attention to the count and do not worry about impeding thoughts. The swing may take some time; that does not matter. This also should be done in *khilvat*[119] and for the time being, in place of *khilvat*.

This answers for the time all your questions about the word *Allah* and *ism-i-azam* [the "highest" name of Allah]. But the word *Allah* may be repeated at any time with or without counting. The difference is that here one does not use the inhalation and exhalation as above. One repeats constantly without regard to the breath. This is a separate exercise and can be done quite independent of prayers and rituals and is definitely not a substitute for prayers (*nimaz*) as *fikr* above.

June 27, 1965

Your Murshid goes to the prayers of all religions now, being able to pray with all people but finding finality in *Fateha*. Problems are not solved by self-assertions but by direct surrender to the Unfathomable (*Ya Latif*). He therefore leaves this house in love, humility and gratitude.

July 31, 1965

Until this month there was no cooperation from the foreign service of your country. They want help and do not want to help. The divine guidance is to get the help. And who is concerned? Pir Dewwal Shereef. He is anxious for a prosperous Pakistan so people can be fed and comfortable. He also wants to see them develop aptitudes. Everybody knows answers in their minds; in the field of actions, things are different.

Or again, the difference between the *Wali* and the angelic person: The angelic person pleases everybody, and it is a question whether that one pleases Allah or not. The Wali pleases Allah, and it is a question whether that one pleases people or not. Our duty is to the "inner *jihad*" and to cooperate. There has been enough inner guidance in your Murshid to carry him through, and if he is at fault; he does not ask Allah for forgiveness, he asks Allah for the just punishment.

The other matter is the family lawsuit. A letter was received from an uncle indicating that all the materials for testimony are now available and that

---

119 Spiritual retreat.

we shall make every effort for some sort of just settlement. My brother, who has always been a wrong doer, is very much in a hurry. And this brings what is almost a dilemma. The longer your Murshid holds out, the stronger his position will be. And yet the longer he holds out, the longer before he can return to Pakistan.

September 9, 1965

To my Daughter and Khalifa, Saadia Khawar Khan:

As-salaam aleikhum. This letter is written under both pressure and pain, with the great assurance it will reach your hand. A copy is being sent to our Beloved Pir-o-Murshid, Sufi Sahib [Barkat Ali]. And besides the contents, there are some very legendary or true factors and facts that the heart says you will respect.

Know, my daughter, that the divine light has been given to all people. All people have had their prophets. At Karnak, your Murshid astonished his guide by explaining the Egyptian religion in terms of the Sufi *sifat*. He was a Muslim and did not know it though he knows the hieroglyphics. But it is of the Greeks one would speak.

There was an article recently that Pakistani husbands are poor lovers, and in the western sense, which is largely non-sense, they no doubt make poor lovers. Three times in life your Murshid went through the Majnun experience, but the other could not conceive the role of Layla. Here in the West, the women who are pampered and egocentric believe women can love men much more than men can love women, but in the divine love, there is no such thing as man or woman, there is no identity.

In the Greek myths, when Zeus showed his love to Semele, that destroyed her. But there is another Greek myth and symbol, which is Zeus carrying Pallas Athena in the palm of his hand, or Jupiter carrying Minerva, which is the same thing. And this is the soul carrying the mind, or the heart carrying the person. And sometimes your Murshid symbolizes himself as carrying the Daughter Mureed as Jupiter carrying Minerva. This has not been so expressed before, but is now in the time of turmoil and dismay.

The Greeks also have a story of Damon and Pythias, two friends who were so close they lived and died as one. Your Murshid had such a friendship and the man became a great leader in Buddhism. He died of a broken heart, for he tried to preserve peace in Vietnam and nobody believed him, not even many close to him. Now he is being called a "saint" and will be written up in the Buddhist encyclopedia.

There was an American lady named Edna St. Vincent Millay who wrote a poem called "Renascence" to express her experience that all love and all suffering were hers, by which she meant all love and all suffering and not some symbol. But it was not understood. This is the Christ experience, which has almost nothing to do so with Christianity.

In the higher reaches of the soul's deep expression, the I-ness and thou-ness disappear. We may have to choose between the "truths" of the deep Sufi poets and the "truths" that most people accept as true.

In this life your Murshid has had to function as a Shams-i-Tabriz, not as a Rumi. It does not bring friends. It brings insight and power and a form of love and tenderness, which it is hoped is conveyed here. Your Murshid is this inner being and carries you like a Jupiter carries a Minerva, which is the correspondence on the masculine side, to mother and child.

My first Zen teacher, who also became a disciple in *tasawwuf*, used to repeat often, "I Never Think of You Because I Always Think of You." This body is safe here; the heart has no time or place.

September 25, 1965

A number of months ago, this person sent a peace proposal for S.E. Asia. It was accepted at once by her serene highness, Princess Poon Diskul Pismai of Thailand, now President of the World Buddhist Federation. She came to this city and there were lines of dignitaries to greet her. Perceiving this person in the background, she gave a cry of joy, rushed forward with two hands extended and did not look at anybody else. The Princess herself is the most unprepossessing looking person, woman, I have known, less than five feet high. She is also the most powerful woman I have ever met and the most spiritual lay disciple of all the Buddhist world, which has been recognized.

Now the peace plan that she accepted depends on the practice that Sufis call *mushahida*, and this has been performed. It was also performed during the war [World War II] under grace. One had the tutelage of Ghaus-i-Azam,[120] and if you wish the mythical life of your Murshid, perhaps this should be done. Only it is most honorable and most revealed that whatever anybody says, be assured that Allah is *Ar-Rahman, Ar-Rahim*. This is most certainly not piety, it is direct experience revealed in a soft way in "Saladin," but in a hard way in one's own life.

In being given choice, this person asked for increased capacity for pain rather than for what we call "love." And when the fighting took place, he was willing to dispense with sleep again. But having once passed through the trials of sleeplessness, Allah, the Gracious, the Merciful, has given the Wisdom that this trial is not necessary, that it is important to keep calm, benign and active. So one continues to concentrate and at present, it is on problems of drainage for your country.

---

120   Abdul Qadir Jilani.

January 18, 1966

From your remarks there is some confusion between the Islamic way of life and the exact *fana-fi-rassul* method, which you regard as only properly Islamic. There is the tradition about Ibrahim and 50 prayers a day, brought down to five.

Now you must be fair-minded and not increase over the five for the generality. I believe in five prayers a day, but not necessarily the generally understood ritual. If one keeps on adding other prayers it can be weakening not a strengthening of faith, for ritual would be more important than heart. Is there not a Hadith that the Beloved of Allah said that even *kalama* would save a soul from Hell?

January 18, 1966

[Later the same day]

Beloved one of Allah,

As-salaam-aleikhum. Your letter of 10 January has been received and filled me with tremendous joy. It would appear we drink from the same foundation of wisdom, and time and place do not separate us. But I am compelled now to answer only in part and will write further soon. The end of the university semester is close, and one has to appear for examinations.

Hazrat Inayat Khan has given us a number of volumes of books, now being published. And the young, perceiving these books, want the material explained. Now one has a small group of mureeds and a larger group of people coming to lectures and several of them also have asked for *bayat*. And the teaching given so far is that the *mureed* must fulfill the meanings of the *ryazat* and study materials, but the Murshid is responsible for the meanings of anything in the literature.

For the mureeds one has begun with "The Mysticism of Sound," and for this one must explain the elements (*nour, baad, atesh, sab, khak*), although we use here either English or Sanskrit equivalents. And this involves knowledges of breathing and sound. And for this we have *zikr* with some stress on the use of the "neck-vein," to make them realize that "Allah is nearer than the neck-vein." For the others the main thing is the training of the ego.

One found some material in Hazrat Inayat Khan, the subject of which this person has been speaking for years—*prajna*. Previously it was rejected, and now when one reads from Inayat Khan, the same people who previously rejected it, accept it coming from Hazrat Inayat Khan. This is another proof of the strength of *nafsaniat* and requires much patience.

March 10, 1966

The greatest books I know—and this is one man's opinion—are the recent issues of Rumi. One does not like Professor Arberry's translation of Holy Qur'an. There are several points on which exception is taken to most translations. *Bismillah* is of little value if it be translated "In the Name of Allah." It makes Allah a name like other names and this goes contrary to "He begetteth not, neither is He begotten, and there is none like Him."[121]

When we use Allah as Name, and *SM*[122] means much more, we overlook "Allah is the Light of the Heavens and Earth." Although Holy Qur'an was revealed in its time, the real revelation is *umm al-kitab,*[123] and it was unrolled as well as revealed. Excepting for *Fateha*, there is no valid reason for arranging the Suras either in the historical order or in the orthodox arrangement. What one has to bear in mind is that the revelation must be used to explain the Revelation.

The *Bismillah* suggests that to understand it one must feel in the presence of the everlasting light. The *wazifas* and *daroods* presented by Pir-o-Murshid take one out of time into eternity but do not destroy the time. And in looking at Holy Qur'an, whereas we do have words and explanations, they are on the background of infinite light with all its mercies, symbolized by *Ar-Rahman, Ar-Rahim.*

May 1966

Your Murshid is today successful, *alhamdulillah*, with and in a type of teaching that is not in books.

Before leaving, one showed some children the positive and negative ways of walking, that these could be used in ritual and even lead to spiritual dances. A number of circumstances have led to more windows in this field.

A spiritual teacher died here in California and left his final lesson, which was on "how to breathe with the feet." Hazrat Inayat Khan said that he learned this through the Naqshibandi School. Also one demonstrated certain forms of it at the Dargah Mian Mir. When one combines this "breathe with the feet" with *kalama* or *zikr* or *fikr*, it leads either to a type of attunement or surrender, or even spiritual realization.

Next month, *inshallah*, there will be a conference on this LSD, and this will give one an opportunity for praise to Allah. The conference is in the hands of men who have much respect for this person. One of them in particular is a top leader of the young who seek new outlets. We parted some time ago with him asking instruction in *zikr*. And the problem is: how to get humanity to recognize that there are other ways to joy and enlightenment than drugs. Religion has failed but the heart of humanity, feeling that there are ways, is resorting to drugs.

---

121 A verse from Sura 112, *al-Iklas*.
122 One could translate the Semitic root *SM* as either "name" or "light." Lewis harkens back to the work of Fabre D'Olivet here.
123 Usually translated as "the Mother of the Book," the source of all written revelations in "heaven."

No doubt all the experiences of drugs are also found in the Mevlevi dancing. Your Murshid agrees entirely with Data Sahib (last chapters of *Kashf-al-Mahjub*), but differs from Muslims in that they will praise the book and the saint without putting these things into practice.

As one goes from explanation to practice, there is both more joy and more response. This is an entirely new direction.

May 13, 1966

As-salaam aleikhum. Today one has to write in a different capacity and this is partly an inquiry, partly a communication.

It has pleased Allah that you have had some recognition in psychology, a science that this person has not studied. But while waiting for the settlement of legal disputes, the *kashf* was clear that one should study anthropology and in these studies learn about the religions and consciousness of humanity at all sorts of levels. While this studying began in response to what one considered divine guidance, it has reached at this point a degree of understanding that was not present when one began such studies. And in arriving at this point there has been effort, grace and insight altogether so one does not know where each of these begins and ends.

There is an immediate problem here that a great many young are resorting to what we call drugs, and they obtain experiences that are labeled LSD, the meaning of which is not clear but the types of experiences are clear. All religions tend to limit humanity to certain methods of self-realization. Quotations, say beginning with Hazrat Ali, have been crystallized and hardened so the soul of humanity is not free. Your Murshid believes that religious phrases are keys and may be doors but are not the palaces. One has to enter the palace, and veneration of the key or door does not mean being in the palace.

Then there is the matter of touch and sex relations, which are so different in all parts of the world. Your Murshid did not take kindly to touch from either man or woman for a long, long time. He could not explain this. Then he had to go through processes wherein he practiced the habits of this part of the world where men and women are supposed to touch, but men are not supposed to touch men.

After he became used to that, he had to live with the Arabs where men are supposed to touch men. Gradually he was able to sustain all kinds and conditions of touch and non-touch, and none of these affected any portion of his psyche or anatomy that has to do with sex. He learned also how to evaluate people through the touch but by far prefers evaluation through the breath. Indeed it is this subject that is more interesting to him than anything else.

So if he uses the breath and not the touch, it is because he finds something both scientifically and spiritually far more interesting. It becomes as if all touch relations were for the children of Allah and the breath relations for the wise in Allah.

One would be glad to go into that further. It is not easy to find that Allah has created all sorts of people who behave very differently. All are Allah's children and all in different grades of evolution. Thus there is accumulation of knowledge, and joy-knowledge and wisdom-knowledge and all sorts of knowledge.

The verse of the Sura [112], "He begetteth not, neither is He begotten," is fine, but "There Is None Like Unto Him" is fundamental. The nearer one seems to approach the divinity, the further Allah seems to recede in magnitude and magnificence. At the same time, while one walks toward Allah, Allah rushes toward one.

This shows that humanity and its reason will never really understand Allah. This of itself is a wisdom and blessing.

June 24, 1966

Now as for walking. Till this time I have walked as devotee, to feel the presence or the *sifat* of murshids and saints and Allah (*akhlak Allah*). And now your Murshid must walk as a murshid to attune to and help the mureeds in so far as Allah permits and blesses. This has never been tried, but now his Blessed Majesty of Mecca Shereef [Prophet Muhammad] gives this as instruction. It shall be tried either after this letter is completed or, if it be long, then during the writing.

Return to Family

As Samuel Lewis became more engaged with his young San Francisco disciples, he felt the spiritual wisdom from a lifetime of practice being drawn through him to help them—wisdom of the Sufi, Buddhist, Hindu, Jewish and Christian mystical traditions. As we saw in the letters to Saadia Khawar Khan, he begins to address their needs for joy and vision and to offer alternatives to the ways they currently sought it through hallucinogenic drugs and casual sex.

Not coincidentally, during that same period his own family issues were taking a dramatic turn. The reconciliation with his father had provided the funds for him to visit spiritual teachers and pursue his ecological work in two trips abroad. As Lewis mentions at the end of Section IV, he was also estranged from his mother. When she died, she disinherited both him and his brother, who had previously been a lifelong enemy. Now he and his brother reconciled in order to fight their mother's will.

On the Pakistani front, the hopes that Samuel Lewis placed in his connections with President Ayub Khan took a severe downturn. Khan narrowly won the presidential election of 1965 against Fatima Jinnah, the sister of Ali Jinnah, one of the founders of Pakistan. However, critics reported widespread vote-rigging and intervention in the election by the Pakistani intelligence services. After years of protests in the street over governmental corruption, nepotism and the suppression of free speech, Ayub Khan finally resigned in March 1969 and invited the military to take control of the country. Although Samuel Lewis was still writing to Saadia Khan about returning to Pakistan, he pushes that prospect progressively into the future.

As we see in the following chapter, it becomes more and more clear to Lewis, who is now functioning as a Sufi murshid, that through divine guidance he is addressing and healing his own lifelong issues with intimacy, touch, love and joy through his work with his young California disciples.

The following excerpts come from recordings of five classes that Samuel Lewis offered to these young students in February and March 1968. They are based on the Sufi lessons on "Rasa Shastra" (love and sex relationships) written by Hazrat Inayat Khan. A longer selection of these classes was first published in 1981.[124] As we saw in his letters to Saadia Khawar Khan, Lewis's own relationship to touch and gender had changed many times, perhaps in response to what he called his function as an *abdal*, a spiritual changeling.

---

124 Lewis, Samuel (1981). Neil Douglas-Klotz, editor. *Talks of an American Sufi*. San Francisco: Sufi Islamia/Prophecy.

"We're in Love!"

Excerpts Edited from Recorded Talks

February 18, 1968

This book is called "Rasa Shastra" and it's by my Sufi teacher Hazrat Inayat Khan. It deals with what might be called sex and love and other such questions. This is from the chapter on "Celibacy."

Now, I'm not laying down any rules. We'll see there are all kinds of people, and I don't know what the relations in the New Age are going to be. I am so out of tune with our customs and traditions I'm liable to accept anything— even things I used to despise—because it may bring about a re-generation of the human race. This is not particularly my field, but one sees that the term *love* is used so lightly.

The English word *love* represents three distinct modern Greek terms and five distinct ancient Greek terms. When you come to the word *love* in the scriptures, it has nothing to do with any of the meanings of the word we have today. Not a one. This makes communication very difficult.

Reads: *At every moment of life and with every breath, the human being gives out and takes in energy; and whenever he gives out more than he takes in, he draws death nearer.*

Now this is the whole secret here. We can draw in energy, or we can give it out. And when we have sex energy, we give out what we call the etheric current, and we have no means of replenishing it. Don't think that I am therefore going to suggest that we give up sex in order to live long. That is not the idea at all, because when you do that you've fallen in love with yourself. This is far worse than any form of love that has someone else under consideration. Of course, this is done, and I've known men who have lived very long because they have lived celibate lives. But I don't think this is good to do for a particular purpose.

Question: The energy goes out, but does it go out from both partners, male and female?

A: Oh yes.

Q: So it goes out, but it doesn't go into the opposite partner?

A: Not the etheric. Other energies go, but not the etheric, which carries the life itself.

Q: So it is just dissipated?

A: It is dissipated. But I'm saying this is the ordinary thing. I'm not—now don't get any moral ideas. This is occult knowledge not moral knowledge.

Q: Can't you replace the etheric energy through meditation?

A: Partly, but not entirely. It takes more than just meditation. You can do it by meditation in certain ways. Even the meditation I gave you earlier would help the etheric element, definitely. It would do that, but it isn't ordinary. I'm not telling you to be celibate. I'm just explaining something, not advising you.

Q: Is what you read a warning against indiscriminate sex?

A: Definitely. But it's a warning on occult grounds, that you lose energy rather than that you are "bad."

Q: Well, what difference does it make? What grounds, as long as it's a warning?

A: It's a warning. I'd take it as a warning. The object is to make people strong and united in themselves. It's the integration we're working for whether you use one thing or the other.

I never said anything at all about abstaining. People are going to be curious. All the warning in the world isn't going to stop them.

There's a story of a Sufi student who was put in seclusion. He couldn't see anybody. He had to spend all his time reading Qur'an and doing Sufi practices. And his meals were brought to him by a beautiful young girl who was the *murshid's* daughter.

Finally at about the end of two weeks, he wrote a note, "I want to leave seclusion. I can't take it. The spiritual life wasn't meant for me. I can't take it, I can't take it, I can't take it."

The murshid sent for him. "What's the matter?" "I'm in love. That's all I can think about. I can't think of God. All I can think of is this beautiful young girl who comes to me." The murshid said, "So what's wrong with that?" "You mean to say it isn't wrong?" "Who's suggesting it *ever* was?" "But I'm in love with her, I want her." "Oh, you *want* her. Do you know who she is?" "No, who is she?" "She's my daughter, and did you ever stop to think I have no objection to your being my son-in-law at all?"

So the student got married, and after that his spiritual progress was so fast he became a murshid. This is one of those things in semantics that goes like I was saying before: "Don't let the facts becloud the issues."

February 25, 1968

I'm not reading tonight from "Rasa Shastra" by Inayat Khan. I want to go into another aspect of the same subject, which is love. And I'm going to divide it into five different planes: animal, human, genius or gandharva, angel and divine. Now, none of these must be taken too dualistically.

If you believe in God and you look at nature, you will see God even in the animal kingdom. Deer are beautiful animals, aren't they? Do you know anything about their sex life? Foxes are not such nice animals, are they? Do you know anything about their sex life? Anybody here know which of these two animals is nearer to God? Nobody knows? Well, which is nearer to God?

Q: I think that with the foxes both of them take care of the young.

A: Exactly. They take care of the young and they take care of each other. Just like birds. So when I use this term "animal love," it's not necessarily in any dualistic sense.

Only I don't think that human beings that indulge in animal love indulge in fox-love at all. Or in eagle-love. Or even in dove-love. So if I speak against animal love, I am not speaking against animal love. I am speaking against human beings who indulge in animal love without having the wisdom of the animal. I've not told any of you not to indulge, but only to respect the other person with whom you have relations. And if you can't be as respectful to your mate as the fox or the eagle or maybe even the crow, then we have something to learn.

Now we come to human love. In presenting human love to you I have to be very, very careful not to get into any entanglements. But don't stop here because you'll miss the whole story. There are two spiritual teachers I know who make it their business to pick out the young ladies among their disciples and keep the fellows away from them. This is exactly what I will never, never do or permit myself.

From the lesson we had in college the other day in modern psychological philosophy, you would think the lecturer was preparing a philosophy for the world of what we call hippies. And perhaps he was. He was sizing up the earth as he saw it, not as he thought about it. Now the whole relation of the sexes has to be taken in a larger context. We're going into that in a minute, and then we're going out of it, because we can get out beyond.

When we come to the love of geniuses, it's based on more than just love and companionship. It's based on common ideals, common purposes in life. When you have these common purposes, a good deal of what Freud would have called transmutation takes place. But it's not a discipline here, it's a natural evolution.

I tell you—who are hippies and ex-hippies—that I was amazed, not at the amount of sex among you, but the lack of it. What do you think of that? Have any of you here seen "Moulin Rouge"—that French picture? The life of Toulouse-Lautrec. That had sex in it. You don't find anything like that here. Oh yes, you have a little, but when it comes really down to it.... I can show you a lot of novels—not the loose novels either—regular, ordinary novels of the school of realism that have a lot more sex than hippie life. That's because indulging in the life of the genius doesn't mean the abandoning of the body, but it takes on a wholly different significance. Sex doesn't become the aim. It becomes part of the game.

Now we come to the angelic love. And there people love because they love. Or if you want to add, they love because they love because they love. And you either love or you don't love, but that's all there is. Nothing else but that. That's the higher heaven called *deva-loka*. It's made up of love. It's hard to explain what this is because when you make an explanation, that's something intellectual.

Beyond that is the divine love, which I won't go into much unless you ask me questions. In the divine love there is no other self. There isn't you and me and God—and there is you and me and God. Only which is which? Which is which? That's the divine love.

I'm not telling anybody what to do or not to do. As I said before, the essence of Zen is to look into your own nature and understand yourselves. When you understand yourselves, you establish your own codes. And as you may or may not be of different ranges of evolution, you may not all have the same codes.

I myself think a lot of you are of the same range of evolution. I think you have influences of the planet Neptune which cause you to act differently and yet understand each other. You have one strong thing in your favor: you understand each other, and your critics don't understand each other and don't understand you.

I'm not laying down any rules. I'm not a social psychologist. I'm trying to make people believe and see their lives on the inner planes. There are, as I said, the genius plane, the angelic plane, and the divine, which is above planes. This is my field, not the human love.

But I am teaching this, or reading from a book on the subject, which I'll resume next Sunday again. Tonight I wanted to go into these other planes, because unless you know facets of yourself, you won't even be able to put up a good case for yourself. If you know the facets of yourself, you will be. You don't need anybody to accuse anybody of anything. Can you understand that?

When I was younger I was a staunch believer in right against wrong. Now I don't know what is right and what is wrong. In the first place, as I sometimes tell you, I'm not a police. So I'm not sure what is right.

But I will tell you what is right and wrong from another standpoint: when your eyes glow it is right, and when they are dull it is wrong. Now this gives you a chance to find out something. And I think there's a lot behind it. When your eyes glow it is right, and when they are dull it is wrong. You find this out by yourself, and learn this by yourself.

I've got two or three other ways of doing this too, ways in which you can measure yourself. That is, measure the plane of your activities according to you, not according to another person telling you something. If you feel dull you've done wrong. If you feel glorious, you've done right. And if you're neither dull nor glorious then the thing was neither right nor wrong.

You know I've had romances, but I never got married in this life. I think God didn't want me to, but it doesn't make any difference—can't say I didn't help by trying. I'm satisfied now that I'm just papa or grandpapa or something.

I'm going to confess one of my sins. Every now and then I fall in love. Now I've stopped because I'm in love with everybody, I think.

March 3, 1968

We're going into a new age with new moral standards, and I'm not trying to lay down the future norm, because I don't claim to know it.

My friend Father Blighton[125] does claim to know it, and probably does, but I don't. I want to bring you self-understanding. When you have self-understanding, you are able to make out your own courses in life.

The fact that I lived a certain type of life, perhaps successfully, doesn't mean that others should do that. It's been at least 50 years since I started my spiritual studies, and at least I can say I have vitality and vigor, which comes out of types of self-discipline. But one wonders whether that is necessary. I don't know.

I want each one to learn something so they can gain control of their own selves. And as types are different and paths are different, I can't say that a *bhakti* couldn't have self-realization very quickly. At least I've had the impudence to have self-realization in the presence of many masters, contrary to what is written in books by people who have never had any discipline.

[Reads from Hazrat Inayat Khan:]

Passion is the desire of love. Passion is the expression of love and it is the satisfaction of love. It is no exaggeration to say that passion is the end of love; for the purpose of love is fulfilled by passion.

A person's life is composed of many lives, and the circle of each is completed when the passion that inspires each is satisfied. All things in life have a purpose; the purpose of some is known and of others unknown. And beyond life and beneath life exists that activity, which the limited mind cannot comprehend. But so far as human understanding can probe, it can discover nothing of greater purpose and value to the world than passion. Under that covering is hidden the hand of the creator.

This is my point of view. I've never said to any of you either to have or not have sex, but to regard the relation as a sacred one. I don't mean that means you have to have sex to produce children. Actually, if I went through the Kama Sutra, there's all kinds of ways of using sex without bringing about children. And some day I don't see any reason why this couldn't be

---

125 Co-founder with Samuel Lewis of the esoteric Christian order called The Holy Order of M.A.N.S.

a part of our general education. But the Western world refuses to accept devotion. Refuses.

The Sufi teaching is not "don't do this" or "don't do that," but do everything as if God were present, which is quite a different thing. God is not the fuzz [police], and God is not the chief justice of the Supreme Court, and God is not the super-international banker or any of this nonsense, which we're getting rid of. These are dualistic attitudes.

God has put faculties into us for us to try or not to try. And when you get through, and God asks, "Did you have a good time?" you better answer honestly. Because you'll know the answer. You say "yes," good, and if you say "no," let's see what we can do about it. Maybe this is anarchistic, maybe it's radical, maybe it's conservative—I haven't the slightest idea. Not the slightest.

Well, last night I was out with a woman I've known a long time, and she was wearing daphne [a type of laurel fragrance]. It was just marvelous. And I told her, "Well, I have to be very careful of daphne, I don't care about you." It was all right. We're old friends. I call her my niece. Her mother and I were dancing partners for 15 years, and then her mother got paralyzed. Just at that time I was about to propose to her. I guess God didn't want me to be married. Anyhow, I remained a friend until she died.

Now when I first met Hazrat Inayat Khan he was a tremendous creature that overwhelmed me. At the same time, later on he fell in love, and I read his letters. They were almost like the letters of a little boy or a young man falling in love: oh, this new experience, oh that new experience. He'd had the God-experience, but he hadn't had the other experience. He brought into the world four children, and died before they were very old.

In my own poetry I have *kama* yoga, which is the yoga of sex-passion, but it's a yoga. You treat the opposite person as if they were divine. You go through the same physical movements, but you treat them not only with respect, but with reverence. Utter reverence. Your passion is to a divinity. The other person is a divinity, you are a divinity, when you do that.

I don't know how this is going to affect things physiologically, and I don't even care. But this attitude is what I hope to instill in human beings. Whatever comes is going to come. And you can let the rest of the world go by.

March 11, 1968

What I'm trying to present is the attitude of respect and consideration. And even of a holy ritual. You know, this is also in the Talmud, if you know much about the Talmud. When your heart opens, and the intuition is open and your insight is open, you will do what is right without consulting memories. They will be in front of you: it will be your life, and you will add to your life.

Despite the fact that I'm reading and teaching this, I have no views any more on what we call *marriage*. I'm not going to teach the people of today some holdover from the people of a previous generation, which is again based on some other generation, which is based on some other generation, and nobody knows the origin of such things.

Now I did have an experience, which is slightly dramatized. I'm going to only tell you one little incident. It was a dream or vision: A mature woman came into a room, and there was a couch about three times as long as this. At one end was one of my mureeds, and at the other end I was sitting.

The lady asked, "Why do you sit that way?"

"We're in love."

"In love!"

"Yes, we're in love."

"I never saw anything ... People who are in love, they sit next to each other and fondle."

"We're not at all infatuated—we're in love!"

"But don't you show your affection?"

"Certainly we express. What do I want to be fondled by an old goat like this for. We're in love. Do you know anything about the aura?"

"What do you mean?"

"When auras touch there's such a joy, a feeling of love and such delight. But we had a hard time, because the touch of the hand is one thing, the touch of the auras is another, but the light of the eye ... To get the light of the eye, you have to stand 30 feet away, and that wouldn't do. We had to work out a system where the magnetism of the eye-love and the magnetism of the aura-love would be in balance. So we have this long couch where we sit, and our auras touch and we're in divine ecstasy." Well, the girl involved had the same experience the same night. Just like Marie Corelli's *The Romance of Two Worlds*.

So I'm telling you, I have the greatest respect for the Beatles, and I'm not telling you not to hold hands. For God's sake, no. If you can't tell the auras don't try, but when you can feel them that's a different thing. Then you will know what this meant. And when you can look and get the flash of eye to eye, this is still a greater thing. This is the angelic love. But I'm not presenting one of these to abolish the other.

I'm reading something to you with which you may or may not agree. There are two types of agreement—the agreement of philosophy and the agreement of your own lives. What I'm trying to do is build you up into experiencing love more, without defining it. Joy more, without defining it. Hope more, without defining it. And a purpose in life without telling you exactly what that should be, because each one has to form their own purpose.

The Walks and Dances Begin

Editor's Note

I n March 1968, just after Samuel Lewis offered the five classes on "love, sex and relationships," he began the first classes in spiritual dancing for a small group of his initiated Sufi students. As we saw in his letters to Saadia Khan and Shemseddin Ahmed, quoted above, he had already begun work with spiritual walking practices, integrating his Sufi, Zen and yoga training. Eventually the "Walks" would come to embrace work with the elements, centers (*chakras*), astrological planets and *tasawwuri*, that is, walking in attunement to teachers, prophets, Avatars and Messengers in the unseen world.

The early catalyst for this outpouring was a visit that Samuel Lewis made to Ruth St. Denis in Hollywood in April or May 1964. The chapter that follows features excerpts from his letters during this time, which describe his meeting with St. Denis as well as the development of the early Walks and then the Dances of Universal Peace themselves.

"I'm Going to Start a Revolution"

Excerpts from Letters and Recordings

January 14, 1964

[Addressed to "Dear Heart"[126]]

Now I have learned the Walks, and there are the Walks under *karma*, and there are the walks under salvation. These two stand distinct. The Walks under *karma* can be analyzed and learned and mastered, or they can master us. The Walks under salvation can be learned and mastered but not analyzed. When you were in love, could you analyze the walks you took to your beloved, or the walks your child took to you?

But there are these Walks, and they will be taught in the orient and to a few here. And for these Walks either there must be an understanding of the breath or the breath will bring the understanding of the Walks.

April 21, 1964

Saturday I had one hour with my "fairy god-mother" Ruth St. Denis. It was she who hosted Pir-o-Murshid on his first trip to the United States, and she still looks to him with grand admiration. Without contacting her I have done exactly what she wants—words and communications are not necessary between spiritual persons. Indeed I have worked out a complete system of education beginning with early childhood based on "Alif," a story that is found in some of Pir-o-Murshid's early records.[127]

September 1, 1967

Actually I only have room for twenty here, and if the groups get large I will break them up. Saturday morning is based on walking. We have the "walking yoga," and it has been effective not only in awakening the inner consciousness but in helping the devotees to walk a long time without fatigue and also to climb hills.

---

126 Samuel Lewis writes a number of letters to this person, but it is unknown who it is.

127 This is the story of Bullah Shah that Lewis alludes to earlier in his correspondence and which Hazrat Inayat Khan tells several times in his writings: Bullah Shah was a saint who attained enlightenment in childhood by focusing solely on the letter *alif*, drawn as a straight line—one— symbolizing divine unity or oneness, until he sees this oneness in every tree and plant.

Ruth St. Denis. Inscription reads: "To Samuel L. Lewis with the blessings of Kwan Yin July 7, 66" (photo: Marcus Blechman).

March 13, 1968

[From recorded class]

Saturday afternoon [March 16, 1968], my work is going to be slightly more complicated, because I am adding to the work on the Walk, for a select few only, the others can sit and watch perhaps, the elements of spiritual dancing. I don't want to teach this to more than four people.... It is necessary to get this beginning in.

The Sufi dance will not be on different principles from the walk so far as the inner practice is concerned, but instead of space taking us in, we will take space in. And that is the difference between the dance and the pilgrimage.

April 18, 1968
[From a recorded class]
[Hazrat Inayat Khan] came here to America at the call of the lady whose picture is on the wall there, Ruth St. Denis. And his son [Vilayat Khan], at least, remembered that and went to call on her. Inayat Khan toured this country and came to San Francisco. He played musical instruments and she danced. And so therefore I've always regarded her as a sort of divine mother, or sometimes I speak of her as my fairy godmother.

And I learned something from her, which I hope to teach to a few of you here—I don't know if it's easy or not! Pick out the dances out of the cosmos. Pick the dances right out of the cosmos, without any intellectual interposition at all. You do it by concentration and by attunement. And the person picking them out will start dancing, and always correct.... As soon as one person has it, it's in the ether, what they call in Buddhism *alayavignana.* Nothing belongs to anybody, a discovery is a discovery.

Then I saw this was what Ruth St. Denis was showing her pupils. She'd get up and give a lecture, I'd go out and dance. She didn't tell me what to dance, how to dance—it was always right. This is the essence of spiritual dancing as opposed to intellectual dancing.

If we want to restore the ancient wisdom, we can restore the ancient wisdom. But I'm more interested in our expressing our own wisdom, not necessarily going back to the ancients.

May 8, 1968
[To Julie Medlock:]
Several years ago I said to Miss Ruth St. Denis, "Mother I am going to revolutionize the world." "How are you going to do it?" "By teaching children how to walk." Ruth taught me how to draw dances from the *akasha*, and later I told her of having performed the "Dance of Universal Peace" at Fathepur Sikri.[128] It was the same dance that she and Ted Shawn had performed in the same place 30 years before. It is based on the rituals of the four major religions. And I am now training a few young people in it, showing them what our "superior more equal people" *a priori* reject, God bless them.

May 25, 1968
[To Gavin Arthur:]
Sam Lewis was initiated into real occultism by a master many years ago. He dropped it but, finding so much nonsense being paraded as "occultism,"

---

128   March 21, 1962. See letter in Section VI: "When we returned to the shrine, my friends the Sufi qawwalis came and sang, and I danced and danced—real *dervish* stuff."

is now using it to build up his "Dance of Universal Peace." This "Dance of Universal Peace" came out of the ethers. It was done once at Fathepur Sikri in India, and one learned later it was placed there in the ethers by Ruth St. Denis and Ted Shawn. Friday one is preparing for "Dance of Universal Peace," first by giving instructions in Occult Dancing. This class is small and select, but will increase on the return of several students who are away at the moment. After the Occult Dancing, we shall go into Mystical Dancing and then into Ceremonial Dancing, and then Dance of Universal Peace. It is demonstrable.

October 2, 1968

[From a recording]

Last year, for the first time in my life, I landed in the hospital. When I was flat on my back, unable to move, God came to me and said, "I make you spiritual teacher for the hippies."

At that time, I had six disciples. At the end of the year, I had 30. A spiritual brother came, and the 30 became 60. And I think I'm ready for the next step, which I don't know....

I'm involved in two revolutions. One of them was when I told Ruth St. Denis:

"Mother, I'm going to start a revolution."

"What is it?"

"I'm going to teach little children how to walk."

"You have it! You have it! You have it!"

The second revolution is to say the Lord's Prayer in Aramaic....

December 1, 1968

The book of bitterness is closed. A new cycle has definitely begun. It is obvious that there is a huge integrative movement going on. This may be indicative of the "Aquarian Age," for something like this is certainly happening. The group has displaced the individual, but it is a dynamic, organic group, demonstrating "I am the vine and ye are the branches thereof."

December 5, 1968

[To Paul Reps:]

Esoteric sciences are very difficult to impart. The behavior of electricity through rubber, steel, nylon, silk, copper, etc. is very different. The blockades in the breath-functions of people may be in any part of the anatomy from the pituitary to the feet.

We gave six sessions in *dervish* dancing, three in yoga dancing, and two on walks last night. The murshid-guru has to act as a *condenser-transformer*. This is very important and functional.

Channeling, Spiritual Attunement and the "New Age"

Excerpt from Paper for Students, "On Channeling, Tasawwuri and Telepathy"

(Editor's note: The paper was found in the archives of Murshida Vera Corda in 2008, sent to her by Samuel Lewis. References to both the Dances of Universal Peace and Walks would indicate a date late in Lewis's life.)

Guidelines for the New Age

At this time, humanity is going over old ground but with a renewed perspective that offers incredible scope for further development. The *zikr* has been spoken aloud by many and realized by some—and those who have realized have been people of the generality. This is the most significant single factor in the qualities of this "New Age." This realization of un-separateness with God, to whatever varied degree, is the keynote in this time.

"Channeling" will soon become so common as to appear normal, at least to the generality, and more slowly to many "experts." Yet the attributes that apply for mental health—balance; coherence; unity with one's whole self; acknowledgment of shadows (both "bright" and "dark"); a capacity for love, for compassion, and control of ego—all these still apply, perhaps even more so in this time.

Illness may unbalance one into the appearance of intuitive, psychic, or spiritual awareness. Rather than demonstrate the unreality of such states, it argues for the basic prevalence of them.

Intuition and inspiration both come from God, hence they are spiritual. Channeling entities, as mentioned before, is a psychic process. And yet it is raised towards the spiritual when it has a real effect for the growth of humanity. But all must recall that the human will must be kept paramount when dealing with the psychic, and completely attuned when dealing with the spiritual. This is especially true for those who surrender themselves to psychic phantasms or apparent entities in order that these may do the channel's inner or outer work for them.

There is some confusion between "will" and *nafs*. "Let Thy will be mine," all too often means, "Let your ego be mine, and my ego be yours." But *will* in the sense that we use it here means the divine center of a human being, the Intelligent Force that acts upon all universes, both inner and outer.

So one may better say, "As Thy will *is* mine, so my will is Thine." And yet the surrender of responsibility and the surrender—or tuning—of will are not at all the same. In the first, one is spineless; that is, one has stepped aside from one's natural power, the harmony of the *chakras*. But when tuned to the divine note, one realizes and acts from unity.

Peace is power. Phenomena is not power. Perfect attunement is desirable, not a babble of spirits. Psychic channeling will become of greater and greater reality in this time. We cannot escape it, nor should we wish to. But in time it will lead beyond itself into a kind of unconcerned, everyday realization, which will have at its base an acknowledgment of the profound limitlessness of the human reality.

It may well be that when everyone starts channeling Moses, for instance, then the phenomena of Moses will be set aside for the sake of the actual being. This is to be hoped and will come about only through the grace of God. And yet there is much jubilation here on the inner planes, because so much has been accomplished and now so much more may be accomplished.

The renewal of humanity becomes more and more imminent with each newly perfected breath.

On the Practice of Tasawwuri

If one takes the practice of *tasawwuri* into one's daily life as a conscious practice, one should consider various factors. Primarily an accommodation should be made, not only in the heart and breath of the student, but into the situation of life in which the student finds him/herself placed. The physical being must be tuned through breath and the Walks. The mental *akasha* must be cleared of all save the purpose at hand. And there must be enough physical scope to ensure that the practice may be carried out in an enhanced manner.

What is *tasawwuri*? It is the union in harmony of soul to soul, vibration to vibration. It is not simply practicing the presence of the teacher (alive or dead), even though it be to the point of being that teacher's amanuensis if that teacher has passed. Rather it is the utter attunement of will to will through heartfelt intention, the mingling of breath to breath until one color—one transparency—is achieved.

That this may be done with a teacher who has passed is not surprising, because the divine all-pervading Breath is the foundation of all that has been created, and remains so.

Now I'm going to let you in on a little secret. In time the practice of *tasawwuri* will become commonplace and necessary to even the ordinary person, because the expansion of the *akasha* of the human race will have become great enough to permit these easy harmonies between loving soul and loving soul.

In other words, seeing from the point of view of another will not only become likely and beneficial, it will become vitally necessary and fully natural. This is the day of *Qayamat*[129] of which many have spoken, and only by this and in aspects of this attunement will humanity survive.

The mistaken delusion of an entropic universe will give way to the understanding that energy is, for our purposes, infinite in substantive reality and extent. This new understanding will ease fears and break down barriers to divine realization. Humanity will be able to take the next step into a higher *makam* (spiritual station). The unity of wills—not ever uniformity, but unity —represented and actualized in the practice of consciously embarked-upon *tasawwuri* is the first step in this change of *makam*.

The links in the chain of the *silsila* should not be viewed as straight and rigid lines but as the linked hands of dancers in spiral, of hearts that attune to any breath, whatever be their time/space. For it is true, and must never be forgotten, that for two hearts that are linked, time and space mean nothing, and death itself is but a filmy veil. Indeed the intention of the practices of *tasawwuri* is unity with the Divine Being, who is Omnipresent, All-Pervading, Eternal.

Sufi Ahmed Murad Chisti
One who has been given Grace by God.

---

129 Usually translated as the day of resurrection in the Islamic tradition; from the same root as the "Beautiful Name" *al-Qayyum*.

Bestowing Blessing

Editor's Note

In the following snapshots from letters of Samuel Lewis's last two years, we find more young people gathered around him. As might be expected, there was pressure to name the community and legally formalize it. Understandably, due to Lewis's past misadventures with organizations—Sufi, Buddhist, academic and political—he resisted this pressure. As he said in a recording from April 18, 1968:

> Divine truth does not belong to any organization. If I organize here, it will be organized under the title of "Islamia Ruhaniat Society," that is, the complete teachings of spiritual sciences which lead to realization of peace. As I'm working with my colleagues in other faiths, this will demonstrate this. We're not going to be called "Sufis" to distinguish ourselves from somebody else.

The name *Islamia Ruhaniat Society* had been given to him to use by Pir Dewal Shereef of the University of Islamabad. Notwithstanding Lewis's initial objections, a legal organization entitled the "Sufi Islamia Ruhaniat Society" was incorporated five months after his death. It kept this name until 2001.[130]

The fruits of Samuel Lewis's hard-won realization had finally found a reception in the hearts of young people who were open enough to accept him. Many of them, like Lewis, had been rejected by their families and were willing to receive the *baraka* or blessing-magnetism that Murshid Samuel Lewis offered. This expression of a grateful family is witnessed in the remembrances of him by early students published in the 1975 book *In the Garden*.

Yet even in the hippie community, Lewis found too much talk and too little actual work. He said that, for most of his young students, "the name of the commune was Santa Claus. And Santa Claus (or God) is supposed to provide while others sit back." As he expresses in the 1970 film *Sunseed*, he came to peace with this situation, once again through a vision:

---

130   At that point it was changed to "Sufi Ruhaniat International."

I feel like a gardener who planted a bunch of seeds and nothing came up; and again the next year he planted a bunch more seeds and nothing came up; and again the next year more seeds with the same result; and so on and on and on.

And then this year, he planted a bunch of seeds: not only did they all come up, but all the seeds from the previous year came up and all the seeds from the year before, and so on.

So I've just been frantically running around trying to harvest all the plants until Allah came to me and said,

"Don't worry. Harvest what you can and leave the rest to Me."

In subsequent years, the work Samuel Lewis had begun in promoting peace through the arts, especially music and dance, prospered, although at times through the efforts of only a very few people.

In addition, in a more subtle way, the lives that Murshid S.A.M. touched (or were touched by those he touched) carried some of his elixir of divine love into whatever their occupation or situation might be. It didn't matter whether they stayed involved with a Sufi or spiritual organization or not. They were, as he put it in his *The Book of Peace*, "bringing Allah without religion." In the same vein, Lewis wrote in an early unpublished book entitled *The Bestowal of Blessing*:

The great work of the initiates henceforth will be to spread *baraka*. By so doing, they will purify the general atmosphere, and by that the Message, which belongs to the sphere itself, will gradually touch the hearts and minds of all who pass through it, who breathe the air or go to the places where the seeds of *baraka* have been sown. This is the selfless propagation of the Message.

Giving darshan at Lama Foundation, 1970 (photo: Saul Barodofsky)

"An Age of Warm Delight"

Excerpts from Letters and Recordings, 1968-71

April 18, 1968
[from a recorded class]
(Reads from a biography of Hazrat Inayat Khan)
"Although his own murshid had initiated him into the Chishti order, Hazrat Inayat Khan cannot, strictly speaking, be considered the link between the Chishti teaching and the West, for neither his origin, culture or esoteric training should obscure the fact the essence of Sufism he taught is the product of his own individual achievement and originality."

This statement is bunch of nonsense put out by people who want to set up their own separative organization! Inwardly there is a chain of Sufis, and it is upon this that we depend. We have the saying "Toward the One, the perfection of love, harmony and beauty, the Only Being. United with all the illuminated souls who form the embodiment of the master, the Spirit of Guidance."

And this means being connected… the spiritual hierarchy is very real. And it is not affected by any kind of organization whatsoever, no matter who calls it what.

[Hazrat Inayat Khan] never wished this [the things written about him]. He was a great Sufi teacher. He was one of a great many souls who appeared in the world at this time, including Sri Aurobindo, and in another sense [Papa] Ramdas. He was against establishing a cult, and he was all for establishing the brotherhood of humanity.

The Sufi order [referred to by Hazrat Inayat Khan] is not an organization. The Sufi Movement is the organization. The Sufi order is a chain of spiritually developed persons who have had some form of realization. I was not accepted by Hazrat Inayat Khan as a disciple until I proved I had God realization. What do you think of that? It wasn't just a ceremony like I put on now. And yet, when he came, we were all so happy we never thought of such things.

But that is why he entrusted me with things that he did not entrust to the people who have all these powers and possessions. Except for the one secret thing: the divine transmission, which is in the heart. The transmission of love, of joy, of peace, of tranquility, of magnetism. The awakening of the intuitive side in humanity. Becoming one with yourself, becoming one with

God and finding these two things are one. Why should we say that this belongs to us—it doesn't. It belongs to the universe.

I am only a Sufi in one sense, that Sufis have recognized the spiritual existence of other schools, and these other schools don't always recognize each other. That's the only point on which I differ....

Muhammad taught the acceptance of all prophets and teachers, and he definitely said "we make no distinctions and differences among them." And all his followers do. And if I prove to you that Muhammad was the greatest person that ever lived and you accept it, you must never demonstrate it. Never! Because this would disprove it. As soon as you proclaim him greater than somebody else, he has that weakness. That's a weakness—to make separations from humanity. It's a weakness, not a strength....

Divine truth does not belong to any organization. If I organize here, it will be organized here under the title of "Islamia Ruhaniat Society." That is, the complete teachings of spiritual sciences that lead to realization of peace. And as I'm working with my colleagues in other faiths, this will demonstrate this. We're not going to be called "Sufis" to distinguish us from somebody else. At this point, I differ from the several organizations that have persons with titles who think they are "Sufis," a name that would horrify people in the orient.

January 27, 1969

I am addressing about a hundred young people every week, but the signs are of breaking out. My colleague, the Rev. Earl Blighton, who went through the "valley of the shadow of death" with me (or I with him), has also jumped from three to a hundred disciples in a very short time and has three centers and cannot handle it.

As the psychotherapists said, the young seek love and peace and all their elders give them is "excitement." The quest for "excitement" is the only quest today. Or is it?

The giving out of moral instruction by dancing and psychic sciences is in some ways a departure. That is why I have to give so much time to Hazrat Inayat Khan's teachings. In this, and in a few other mostly unpublished Sufi manuscripts, seem to be the keys to everything.

Today it is necessary to start many new ventures. Advice is easy, suggestions are easy, but I am not the universe. I have a little secretarial help, far less than is needed to attend to the wants of a growing number of disciples.

February 12, 1969

So many go around claiming God-experience, and when they ask Sam, he always says, "Never mind their claims. Show me their disciples." And we hear stories of the rise and fall of this great personality and that, but never a sign of any great disciple. So many churches and so many cults, but only the young experience God. So we shall have a "New Age" in which the God-people may be separate, in a sense, from the church-people.

February 16, 1969

While a Murshid does not like to point out the errors and sins unless they are big and important, you have been more concerned with your possible shortcomings than with the glories of Allah. My own work especially with *wazifas* and their repetition in the dance is on the glories of Allah, not the shortcomings of humanity.

March 7, 1969

I am at the moment in an awkward position. There has been a constant increment of both attendance and financial income, and yet I am in debt. It may require a complete house-cleaning. I have refused to accept the tragic deaths of Hazrat Inayat Khan, Robert Clifton and Dwight Goddard as an example and either will avoid a tragic death (some success here), or it will be of a different kind.

March 20, 1969

I am to take a day off next week. This is a rarity. It is not yet 6 a.m.

I am like the director of a gigantic psychiatric hospital. You may not be able to understand it, but a Sufi is one who sees from the viewpoint of another as well as of himself.

It was necessary to call one group after another to account, and I boldly insisted that there were to be no more requests for questions and interviews after meetings. This has been the bane, and yet when Fudo came out I think it worked. True, there were more interviews and questions than ever before.

March 31, 1969

Dear Sufi Sahib [Sufi Barkat Ali]:

As-salaam-aleikhum. There has been no particular time to stop to write. One does not know what the supreme practices of a devotee should be. There is an almost constant *zikr*, the practice of *Ahklak Allah*, and the conscious realization of the noble *daroods*, which by the grace of Allah you assigned to me.

The shortest report would be to say one is in much better financial circumstances, one has a large and growing following, and the health is remarkable due entirely to the grace of Allah, to whom be all praise. This is not empty devotion. It is almost two years since one was on his back in a hospital. The voice of Allah manifested with grace and direction and what was communicated at that time has come into manifestation....

Our blessed daughter, Miss Saadia Khawar Khan, is now in this country. She hopes, *inshallah*, to be here in the late spring.

When Daughter Khalifa is here we shall discuss both a further visit there by this person or the possibility *inshallah* of taking a small group. You must understand that Americans have not had Islamic traditions; there is no operative Imam here. We have no relation to politics of any kind, and God-seeking is becoming an order of the day in an ever-growing number of young people.

There is always a question as to how far what one is doing pleases Allah or otherwise. The Messenger himself said that those who die repeating *kalama* will surely not go to hell. I am satisfied in view of the multiple confusions of the day that we are both being guided and being guided on a Right Path.

May 10, 1969

Every time a group comes, Allah bestows a blessing. The other night one had the disciples get up and do another dance—these dances are always coming. It is based on nothing but *Bismillah Ar-Rahman Ar- Rahim*. It is real, it is effective. It is based on the knowledge of psychic and mystical law, which pretenders and proclaimers do not know. These dances are pouring out of one.

May 27, 1969

Pir Vilayat wishes to organize, and I am at my wit's end now, because one cannot hold more than a hundred individuals close to one, look after their spiritual, psychological and social needs, etc.

And so one has to "institutionalize." And my now scattered disciples also want the dance, and so far I have failed to obtain a proper secretary, but must start all over. My senior friends have plenty of suggestions, but direct help is a rare thing to get, and I am not demanding it.

June 4, 1969

With all the love and apparent harmony around, there are some fierce obstacles to face. We came here to establish a spiritual cooperative and then made an entity of the place. It is called the "Garden of Inayat." But the name does not matter.

To too many of the so-called "New Age" people, the name of the commune is "Santa Claus," no matter what they call it. And Santa Claus (or God) is supposed to provide while others sit back. It is not only that others sit back, but there is a certain degree of *baksheesh* [Hindi slang for begging] on top of it.

September 2, 1969

The first lesson taught here is *Allah* and also the last. The sins of Americans are not the sins of the Arabs "in times of ignorance"[131] and have to be approached differently.

There is more and more a tendency toward universality. The Dance of Universal Peace, first presented before the tomb of Selim Chishti at Fathepur Sikri [near Agra, India] was fully blessed by my late Fairy Godmother Miss Ruth St. Denis. It has expanded into all sorts of dances, beginning with Dervish Dances. Of course, the "good Muslims" object to anything that their grandfathers did not know. And the first step was merely to integrate the efforts of the Rufais, Bedawis, Chishtis, Mevlevis, etc. Then it expanded.

I have returned from New Mexico where a summer school is being provided. There are more and more young Americans who seek spiritual perfection. The demise of the Parsi Meher Baba left a vacuum and people see a need for a universal approach to universals.

Why, I even had to give a "mountain climbing yoga" practice, which enabled people half or less than half my age to climb high in the Rocky Mountains along with me. But I assure you it was a Sufi and not an Indian practice. And it worked. Some day we shall accept that *Akhlak Allah* works.

September 23, 1969

[To Sufi Barkat Ali:]

Now on the matter of Khawar's marriage, this person has no views. He is trying to keep his mind clear realizing that he might even benefit materially and otherwise from such an event. The only belief one has is that Saadia Khawar be permitted to complete her schooling, and, *inshallah*, obtain the degree a of Doctor of Philosophy (or some variant), for which she has been working so hard.

On our last night together Khawar had a display of Pakistani costumes, and this person led about 150 young people in reciting "ALLAH," something that has perhaps never been done in this land before. And the program of Dervish dances is making considerable headway.

Khawar gave lessons on Hadith and one is amazed to find, with all the books on *tasawwuf*, the lack of recognition that the inner sciences are all derived from Hadith. This was the original teaching of Hazrat Inayat Khan also, but his original teachings have been suppressed, and there have been some changes in the reissuing of his earlier works. And with all this material available, neither Muslims nor non-Muslims have made proper use of it.

---

131 A reference to the Arabic term *jahiliyah* or "ignorance," used to name the period in Arabia before the advent of Islam.

My own belief is that every Messenger of Allah is a Universal Human Being and an *insaan-i-kemal,* but the evidence is internal based on the Hadith themselves and not on any personality reaction to them. Here we utter all our praise to Allah, which does not stop us from mentioning Muhammad in our dances and chants. Only never on an equal footing with Allah.

There are now a number of movements in the West calling themselves "Sufi." Three are mere corporations building up personalities with hints of secret esoteric practices—very, very secret—although not one of them that I have heard cannot be found in books—such as the one on Persian Literature alluded to and *Awarif-ul-Maarif* [132] and others. But without the *baraka* all the practices were of little avail.

We also practice *tasawwuri,* which reaches its highest aspect (so far discovered) in *tasawwuri Muhammad.* This is the Perfect Walk and leads also to Perfect Behavior.

October 21, 1969
An old friend has shown up, and it is possible, *inshallah,* that he will take over. One now has, praise to Allah, sufficient funds to handle such emergencies.

There are a growing number of young disciples, and they say they love Murshid and would like to work for him, but they are so unsettled as to where they live and how they live. There has been both necessary and unnecessary moving about, and in this so much concern with the ego-self. It is a touchy problem, but there could be worse ones.

November 9, 1969
I do not believe you have to become a Sufi devotee to become perfect. I find perfection in devotees of many paths. I am not talking junk-theory or emotions. My friends include many realized souls of many faiths, and I can substantiate this with facts, not emotions.

November 11, 1969
We have gone through the phases of simple art and concentration practices. But a higher dimension has intervened in the form of dance, ritual and pageant. One could hardly imagine the effects of three- and four-dimensional application of the Gatha studies [the esoteric study papers of Hazrat Inayat Khan]. This is what is being taken up today.

This will mean the reproduction of the eternal Mysteries to the human race. These dances first come in visions at night with no explanations. It

---

132 "The Knowledge of the Spiritually Learned" by Shihab al-Din Suhrawardi, 1154-1191. Translated into English in the version that Samuel Lewis knew by H. Wilberforce-Clarke as *A Dervish Handbook.*

generally takes three nights before they are clear mentally. The vision comes with no explanations. It proves later to be totally rational.

November 19, 1969
It was during the War that when it was said that Hitler was going to call in psychic powers, I asked God what to do and God said, "Go upstairs!"

December 24, 1969
There is a great resonance that takes place in singing *Ramnam*,[133] using the head as a dome. Now the resonance has become complete, using and vibrating the whole body, demonstrating what is taught but not studied in the Christian Bible: "The human body is the temple of the Holy Spirit."

January 1970
I am teaching "Dances of Universal Peace." I led one thousand young people in a version of this in Golden Gate Park just before leaving San Francisco. The idea of "Peace through the Arts" came to me years ago when the old Roerich Museum was functioning during the lifetime of that once celebrated, but now forgotten artist. Unlike Nicholas Roerich, I am appealing to the young and not to the "*les fameuses*" [the famous].

January 18, 1970
Sam has just been reading the Sufi saint, Shah Latif Ibn Sind, and gave the following short talk: "Allah is not your jailer, Allah is your lover."

March 6, 1970
I shall be leaving here toward the end of this month for Geneva to attend a conference of The Temple of Understanding with the ambitious program of peace through religion. I have been in this field for many, many, many years without any reports ever being accepted by persons or bodies *verbally* interested.

But now action of some sort is necessary. The failure of important persons to study history, or to be aware of what their fellows are doing is as much an obstacle to peace and understanding as are all the connivances and machinations of the presumably powerful. Besides, it is so easy to blame others.

A few years ago, when the Jewish peoples, however defined, were in many respects the unfortunate victims of intolerance and persecution, a great deal was heard of Boccaccio's story of the three rings and the sequel of "Nathan the Wise," written by the German philosopher Gotthold Lessing. But now no more. Why?

---

133 The mantra *Om Sri Ram Jai Ram Jai Jai Ram.*

I hope to present a "three-ring" approach to the complex of Palestine, but I shall not favor any "resolutions" whatsoever. Resolutions are invariably followed by wars and conflicts even worse than those of a previous era. If religion will not accept its own living God, if religions do not accept the promises of their own scriptures, we must look for something new or something destructive.

For the first time youth—and not apologists for youth—is going to be given every opportunity to express itself, and this alone will help toward peace and understanding. It is the acceptance of God, not the acceptance of words that will bring peace.

March 11, 1970

Sam was influenced to maintain a diary after reading the words of Thomas Jefferson, Ralph Waldo Emerson and Papa Ramdas.

But, in retrospect, it must be said that the more one considers it, there is no diary. There is only the fulfillment of the divine life in and through what would appear to be an ego-personality, which is nothing but a mode of God Itself expressing Itself outwardly.

And daily Sam seems to find that there is really nothing else but this divine life.

March 11, 1970

No doubt there is a time for all things. And now, instead of lapsing into the presumable securities of old age, Sam's life is becoming more and more public. No doubt it requires considerable patience when one's theme, so to speak, is "The stone that is rejected is become the cornerstone."

March 22, 1970

The day has gone when audiences are impressed by lofty emotions apart from direct experience. The young want direct experience; they are getting the direct experience; they love the direct experience. They mount the ladder of *Ananda* [bliss], which in a certain sense is the same as "Jacob's Ladder" in the Hebrew Bible.

My friends, it is a New Age. It is an age of warm delight in the divine presence. There is hope for the world when it accepts the evidence of spirituality not only as presented by, let us say, a guru, but when it is reflected in the awakening of hearts, in the brilliance of faces, in the manifest joy and delight.

The second lesson Sam has learned is that of and from pain. To him, this means the wiping out of *samskaras* [impressions on the reactive mind]. It is in no sense an evil. The wiping out of *samskaras* helps free the spirit, helps one to appreciate joy.

A series of reports have shown that the harm done by alcohol is 40 times as great as all problems—moral, legal and otherwise—due to partaking of psychedelics. Sam never used psychedelics, because he felt the superiority of the *mantra* to begin with—not the philosophy of the *mantra*, but its recitation.

April 1970

[At the conference in Geneva] it was the top intellectuals themselves who labored to see that love and devotion, not exhortation and emotion dominated. And it was so.

The dominant figure was our very good friend, Swami Ranganathananda of the Ramakrishna Mission. Sam has always called him the Vivekananda of the age. He has immersed his whole life in Vivekananda, but now he has functioned as Vivekananda. He was probably without peer. He was so recognized chiefly by Dr. Seyyed Hussein Nasr of Tehran, Iran, who represented spiritual Islam (and so Sufism). When the supreme personalities of different religions meet in amity and devotion, a certain goal has been reached.

I put on a little show that I was an incarnation of Lessing's "Nathan the Wise." Nathan the Wise was a grand hero during the rise of Hitlerism. But today nobody refers to him.

I have written three epic poems, the themes of which are respectively the Jewish, Christian and Islamic divine aspects of Palestine. They were shunned by the different religionists, but recently have evoked such wonderful response that I can see that today there are persons and forces who are really concerned with peace.[134]

June 2, 1970

Then we came to Lama [Foundation, near Taos, New Mexico], which may well become the center of a sort of American Lama-ism. While I am here to present Sufism, it becomes obvious that something more is in the wind.

Both Sufism and Mahayana Buddhism teach the transcendental intuition (*kashf* or *prajna*) and no nonsense. It is operational and it has made me bang down hard on rump-ritualism called "Zen," which ignores the fact that Zen is *prajna* (insight or wisdom) and not *dhyana* (meditation).

The Qur'an teaches that the divine light is neither of the East nor West, and I presented that therefore the Rockies were as holy as the Himalayas, and that this was the place to present the *mahamudra* meditation.

---

134 The names of these poems are respectively "The Day of the Lord Cometh," "What Christ, What Peace?" and "Saladin." They are contained in *The Jerusalem Trilogy*, published in 1975.

June 17, 1970
To: Pir Dewwal Shereef, University of Islamabad, Pakistan
Beloved Pir:

As-salaam Aleikum! It is a long time since one has attempted to write. The experiences, favorable and unfavorable, which have occurred in the last nearly seven years are now resolving themselves into a grand symphony.

No doubt everything has happened, is happening as Allah wishes. One finds oneself in a rather strange universe in which neither orthodoxy nor heterodoxy seem to matter very much, but there is a more and more constant *akhlak Allah*, and this *akhlak Allah* becomes even more natural than necessary.

About five years ago, one reversed one's habit of peacefulness and non-violence and brought suit against a member of one's family. The suit was never terminated. Not only was it settled out of court, but it has resulted at the lowest level in a much larger income, which keeps on increasing, until at this day it is about four times as great as it was when one was in Pakistan, *alhamdulillah!*

Just before this change, one suffered from an infection, ptomaine poisoning to be exact, and when one was flat on his back in the hospital, the voice of Allah appeared and said, "I make you spiritual teacher of the hippies." One may surrender to Allah willingly or unwillingly, or one may refuse to surrender to Allah. But when one is flat on one's back, one has not even a choice.

This was followed immediately by a series of visions; every one of those visions has now come into outward manifestation, down to tiny details. Now this is in harmony with the predictions or commissions of several pirs and holy men that one was to get 50,000 Americans to say and repeat "Allah" and believe in Allah. This of itself looked immense, and when one considers in the past that this person was a recluse and an outcast, it looks even more ridiculous. But so did the outlook, no doubt, of As-Siddiq[135] when he was in The Cave with the Blessed Messenger.

One began teaching spirituality through the Walk. This was a grand adventure during which three of the original six disciples deserted this Murshid. But it was remarkable that one has not had three desertions since. This method was blessed by the late Miss Ruth St. Denis, a very spiritual dancing teacher who knew how to receive inspiration from the very space itself.

The Walk developed in two directions: extensionally and intentionally. In the extensional walk, disciples learned to climb hills and mountains and walk long distances. The sacred phrases needed for these are comparatively few. But then the question arose: if the *sifati-Allah* and Hadiths can be used to help one walk long distances, climb mountains and work without fatigue,

---

135   Abu Bakr As-Siddiq (573-634 CE), a companion and father-in-law of Prophet Muhammad and the first of the four "rightly guided" *khalifs* following him.

couldn't they and other *wazifas* be used to help humanity in its greater education, purification and development? So now we use many of the sacred phrases in psychic and moral procedures. These take on two entirely different aspects:

Moral Development. By applying the divine qualities to humanity one helps to remove the evils, the shortcomings, the impediments and all the grosser aspects of being. A sacred phrase is better than a chastisement. A chastisement is a reliance on a human being. A prayer or devotion is a reliance on Allah. All theories, doctrines and orthodoxies aside, the simple fact is that these methods work.

The next phase seems to be coming—that these methods can be extended to deal with psychological problems. Without going into details, there were two such instances just before I left San Francisco about a month ago and both turned out successfully, a*lhamdulillah!*

Psychic Purification. The great pseudo-problem—it is a pseudo problem and not a real problem—is that the young people in this part of the world and others are resorting to the use of products of the vegetable world to open themselves up or to be opened up to what might be called the subtle world (following an Indian term) or possibly to *Malakut.*[136]

The simple fact is that this is so. The soul of humanity knows very well that the material world (*Nasut*) is only one of several planes of existence. All the common or uncommon sense cannot change this. In the last days of his life, Aldous Huxley concluded that this hidden world was real. It was also known as *faerie* by the Celtic people. It was considered variously immoral, illegal, insane and perverse to have any dealings with it.

People diatribe against materialism but keep themselves bound in it just the same. There have been many predictions supporting the principles of psychic and spiritual evolution. One began with the theme "Joy Without Drugs." It is so easy to have a formula, words. Then the question came: how to implement these words with actualities?

It is one thing to say "*La illaha el il Allah.*" It is beautiful to say, "As one takes one step toward Allah, Allah takes ten steps toward one," but how about the actualities? This is exactly what has happened.

Now one is daring two tremendous things: the first is based on a Hadith: "In that day will the sun rise in the West and all people seeing will believe."[137] It is true that the Blessed Messenger said, "Seek wisdom even unto China." But try it. You will have down on you almost all the Islamic world except the most advanced sages and seers.

---

136 Sufi term for one of the "heavens," the realm of ideas and ideals, the mental plane.
137 This is traditionally viewed as referring to the *yaum al-qiyamah* or day of resurrection in the Islamic theology.

Well, the voice of Allah came to me and presented more visions of Dervish Dances. These dances are based only slightly on the methods of the Mevlevi School. They also have in them elements of the Rufai and Bedawi Schools. And along with them, the operative aspects of *kashf*.

So we began Dervish Dances and everything has followed exactly to details of what Allah showed in vision: the growth from 6 to 30 disciples, from 30 to 60, from 60 to 100 and then the aureole burst into another dimension. I have not yet organized to that dimension.

One felt his participation was entirely satisfactory in a conference of the world's religions where Sufism, so to speak, was represented by our good friend Dr. Seyyed Hussein Nasr. After that, one was entirely successful in communicating the Sufi dances to the young in London, Boston and now in the Southwest.

Then the question arose of this body and other bodies being overworked, whereupon the wise Allah intervened and gave the commission that Sufi Ahmed Murad Chisti would be called upon, *inshallah*, to play a role in the United States similar to that of Saint Moineddin Chishti in India.[138] Although the vision was clear, it was so daring that one could not face it, but instead surrendered himself entirely to Allah. From that moment a new type of *qawwal* [sacred song] was born.

So during the dancing classes we intersperse the rest periods with chanting. The next thing is the revolution going on in the Western music, and the inspirations from Allah seem to blend in these modes with the chanting of sacred phrases.

One has, so to speak, several missions and commissions from Allah about which one does not wish to speak here. One sees the need of a return to Pakistan, *inshallah*, in 1972 or '73, unless Allah directs sooner and money is forthcoming, and of bringing a group there, especially to the Universities of Islamabad and Punjab and presenting this material.

This would not only improve American-Asian relations, but would do much to raise the consciousness of the young so that they would realize that whatever experiences are derived from so-called drugs, these are very little when contrasted to the experiences of *kashf* and *shahud*.

Upon my return to San Francisco, I am commissioned to write on the coalescence of the moral teachings of my first Pir-o-Murshid, Hazrat Inayat Khan, with the Hadiths. This will be in part a labor of love and joy, and in another a directive to the very questionable situations in the world today.

Fortunately, I have three wonderful secretaries who are very devoted. I also have two remarkable young men serving as Khalifs, and at least one

---

138   1142-1236, who brought the Chishti Sufi tradition from Persia to India in the early 13th century.

young man and young woman almost as advanced. Their dreams, their visions, their outlooks, their high standards almost cause one to weep.

This is written high in the Rocky Mountains in a place more comparable to Natha Galli than Murree [where Pir Dewwal Shereef lived], some 9,000 feet up.

Although well on in years from the worldly standpoint, the mind is such that this letter was dictated without pause and the body also is remarkably active, *alhamdulillah!*

Love, Blessings and Respects,
Sufi Ahmed Murad Chisti

June 24, 1970
The difference between the emotionalist and the mystic is vast. The emotionalist meets somebody and has what, for him, is a transcending experience, and it usually is. But when it is all over, he has *hal*[139] and not *makam*. He does not grow and thinks others are his inferiors and that he has a "world message" for them.

July 19, 1970
I am very optimistic, because I believe the young will live longer than the old. That is all. The young have the ability to *think through* the problems of pollution, soil preservation and reclamation, even slum clearance, because they have simple capacities, simple natural capacities totally outside the "realisms" current in America and the Communist countries.

July 28, 1970
My fairy godmother, so to speak, Ruth St. Denis, approved of all my plans, and before she left the world I had begun my "Dances of Universal Peace." These dances are dedicated to The Temple of Understanding of Washington, D.C., which is endeavoring to take to heart the psalmist's words, "My house shall be a house of prayer for all peoples."

July 28, 1970
Some time ago, a young man thought he would see a battle royal by introducing me to the Hassidic Rabbi Shlomo Carlebach. We took one look at each other and there was a love-embrace. I have had such love-embraces from a Greek Metropolitan, Franciscan Fathers, a Vietnamese Thien,[140] some Chinese Buddhist masters and innumerable Muslims and Hindus.

---

139 *Hal*: A temporary state of consciousness, not a station embodied in human life. *Makam* (or *maqam*): One's reliable, relatively enduring, "station" of consciousness.
140 The Vietnamese name for Chan Buddhism, called Zen in Japan.

July 31, 1970

This is really my diary entry. Qualitatively, things were never so good. Quantitatively, I am in a quandary, and perhaps this is for the good of my soul.

Today, I must telephone my attorney about organizing legally. I understand this is what Vilayat wants, but I have not seen the official report of the meeting. Vilayat and I have a tacit agreement that if we are separate, we can both be reaching new audiences. I am thoroughly satisfied with his plans, programs and endeavors.

Yet I am not so concerned about planning as in putting the plans into action. I was given the same instructions in Pakistan, and within a short while, we may be *doing*. But today I am trying to get a few hours off. I have had no leisure whatsoever since returning from New Mexico. Nearly everything is proceeding favorably, but nearly too much.

August 31, 1970

My disciples and friends have already successfully programmed joint Israeli-Arab dinners. We have even been successful in getting young Jewish people to recite the *kalama* and Arabs to recite the *shema*. As I do not believe in any ethnocentric religion, and as I absolutely believe in theocentrism (and I think Moses did, too), I see no reason why we cannot put into practice, "Love thy neighbor as thyself."

September 6, 1970

In 1928, Dr. Henry Atkinson of the World Church Peace Union came to this city and was so satisfied with our interview that he asked me to continue my studies of the religions of the world.

In fact, my program for the Near East was part of a larger program of "How California Can Help Asia." As part of this program, I know what the graduates of the "Multi-versity" of California have done, and can do, toward the solution of water, desert and soil problems in the Near East. In 1930, I proposed that all religious holy places be de-nationalized and de-politicized. After the UN was established, I felt that it, or some co-coordinative or subsidiary group, should in some way be given jurisdiction over the holy places of all religions. The peace plan that I proposed was accepted as wonderful by Mr. Gunnar Jarring[141] and separately by at least three other UN officials. It included at least mutual recognition of all religions by each other and even the establishment of a Papal residency in Palestine.

---

141   1907-2002, Swedish diplomat and Special Representative of the Secretary General of the United Nations for the Mideast peace process between 1967-1991.

The welcomes finally received at Geneva from the real leaders of the real world's religions and later receptions from the youth make me feel certain that something will be done.

I am optimistic enough to believe we can have peace in this world on two simple bases:

A. Facts should be considered as more important than subjectivities about them by important persons.

B. Facts should be evaluated, not reactions to the personalities presenting them.

I am very much for one world. I have lived in many lands. I have had no trouble with strangers anywhere, no matter how exotic we may claim them to be.

October 4, 1970

We have eaten in a Syrian restaurant, owned and operated by Jews. Although it is impossible to convince "realists" about hard facts, this very institution shows that some human beings would rather make money off of others than kill them. This, as you know, is a feature of our peace plan.

December 23, 1970

Beloved Pir-O-Murshid [Sufi Barkat Ali]:

As-salaam-aleikhum! It is very necessary to make some reports. One did not write sooner because one has been overworked and had problems on the material plane, nearly all of which were given as tests for the personality. Arising out of these problems has been a nervous disorder which put one under the doctor's care, but if people are foolish to react about this? If one were to summarize everything it would be the pursuit and, *inshallah,* the fulfilment of the Chishti-Qadiri-Sabri Order[142].

One does not know where to begin. Some very wise disciples have secured the best works available in English of the founders of the Chishti, Qadiri, and Suhrawardi Orders. At least two disciples and this person were reading *Futuh al-Ghaib*[143] when the disaster struck East Pakistan. We all felt independently that an attitude that could be called Qadiri-Sabri was the best. But that has not stopped us from sewing longyis[144], which may soon be sent to East Pakistan, *inshallah.*

In their Murshid's absence, a number of disciples planned a "Dervish Bazaar." This was originally to help promote peace in the Near East, but

---

142 The branch of the Chishti Sufi transmission with which Sufi Barkat Ali was connected.

143 "Secrets of the Unseen" by Abdul Qadir Jilani, 1077-1166, Persian founder of the Qadiri lineage.

144 A simple piece of cylindrical cloth used as clothing in South Asia.

has changed in order to raise funds and get other assistance for the unfortunate humanity of East Pakistan. Evidently Allah was with us, for the first time the newspapers and radio stations took some interest in our work.

We are now getting hundreds and hundreds of Americans to say Allah, and when you get 300 "unbelievers" to join in singing "*La ilaha el Allah, Muhammad ar-rassulillah*," this is something no *tablighi* [Islamic preaching] group has ever accomplished. Muslims have said to me, "Muslims will not approve." I said to them, and I say again, "It is not whether Muslims approve, it is whether Allah approves."

Other than the disturbance alluded to in the first paragraph, the health and strength are now being recognized. We are also working on "Six Interviews With Hazrat Inayat Khan," which grew out of the original Khidr experience, which Hazrat Inayat Khan accepted and his followers almost unanimously rejected (excepting Mr. Paul Reps, a fairly well-known writer).

Regardless of what so-called Muslims think, Holy Qur'an teaches that the divine light is neither of the East or the West. Allah has made all people, and there is even the possibility of our reaching some of the top Zionists.

The number of disciples is growing. The attendance at meetings is growing. The Christian year, coming to a close, has brought love, blessing and work. Maybe this is as Allah wishes. All our activities are expanding.

With family, 1970, leading Dances of Universal Peace.
Photo: copyright Mansur Johnson 2020.

A Journey Further

Editor's Note

Tragically, Samuel Lewis's vision of bringing his Asian and Western families together by taking some of his young American students to Pakistan in 1972 or 1973[145] did not happen. On December 28, 1970, at about 4:30 a.m., Murshid Samuel Lewis fell down the stairs of his home on Precita Avenue in San Francisco.

He suffered a concussion and was taken to the hospital with an initial diagnosis of a fracture of the left arm and possible subdural hematoma. He died eighteen days later, on January 15, a day after being moved to a second hospital at his request. His nearest living relative at the time, the aforementioned Mary Lou Foster, felt strongly that his death was due to mistreatment in the first hospital he was taken to, and that Lewis had died of uremic poisoning due to dehydration.

Because the death was the result of an accident, an autopsy was required and performed ten days later. After obtaining a copy of the official coroner's report, I consulted a doctor skilled in conducting autopsies and reading such reports. The coroner's report concluded that death was due to concussion of the brain. There was no subdural hematoma (blood on the brain) but there was edema (swelling and fluid retention) in the brain itself due to the fall. There was no evidence of any other external trauma. No operation would have helped in this case, and there was no evidence of uremic poisoning or dehydration.

During the eighteen days that Samuel Lewis was in the hospital, he returned to consciousness at various times. On 2 January, he dictated the letter below to Pir Barkat Ali. At the time, it was unclear that this was his last letter, since he did not die until thirteen days later.

Murshid's closing chapter of *The Lotus and the Universe*, entitled "Peace," is both a coda to that book and to the story of his life, a journey of meeting remarkable beings and ultimately becoming one himself.

---

145   See June 17, 1970 letter above.

Last Letter

January 2, 1971
Pir-o-Murshid Sufi Barkat Ali
Lyallpur District,
West Pakistan
Praise be to Allah!

This has been a glorious exit, and one which will go down in history, a sign of all the beauty, truth and goodness in the universe.

One has been truly saved from the jaws of death and adversity, and may live on indefinitely as God wills. It is the sign and symbol of all goodness, and the establishment of God's Message in the Western world forever, praise be to Allah.

For I am the first one born in the West to have received the Divine Message, and believe to have representatives in all the purity and goodness of which Allah is capable and which will now be presumed done forever.

Peace

Book Excerpt from The Lotus and the Universe

Every ten years a Nobel Peace Prize, Every five years another war.

"Peace, peace, when there is no peace."—Jeremiah 6:14

"War and peace are two things too serious to entrust to diplomats and generals."—Clemenceau

E very soul longs for peace, and every mind—by its nature—brings a disturbance.

The snake offered the fruit of knowledge to Adam and Eve, and with it agitation and excitement. So humanity has sought the excitement. It is still seeking the excitement and crying because there is no peace. Everybody blames somebody or something else.

According to the Sufi view, and perhaps this covers all mystics, one must find the peace within and by the *power* gained thereby, radiate one's atmosphere. Thus there is an explanation of *Allaho Akbar* that not only is there "no power or might save in Allah," but that *in peace there is power.*

This age, bent on excitement, no longer recognizes the small print of Newton, that "every body remains in a *state of rest* or...." Nor can it be compelled to accept the words of Jesus Christ in the *Gospel of Thomas:* "The sign of the Father is an activity and a rest."

The saga of Noah and the Flood, not being studied from the fourfold Hebraic PARDES point of view, gives us at best but symbols.[146] What is valuable is hidden. *Noah* means either "Mr. Peace" or "Mr. Rest."

The theme here is universal. There is a world of agitation and beneath it a world of rest. Or perhaps they are so intermingled that the universe is a "razor's edge." Indeed, we find this in and under all religions. Yet it is also true, as one oriental sage put it, "I have come to abolish religion—and bring God." Until we find the depths, we are concerned only with words or thoughts. These proceed from peace. Peace is their origin; it is not affected by them.

---

146 The fourfold consideration of any passage or story—literal, poetic, symbolic, experiential—were said to lead to an experience of PARDES, root of our word *paradise.*

The scientist, the artist, the adventurer, and the mystic are alike in that they tend to confine themselves to experience. Therefore, they are often regarded as queer or egocentric by those who rely on analysis and dialectics. Jesus has declared that by taking thought we cannot add to the hairs on our head.

The founders of religions have presented similar programs. Moses went so far as to present a complete political system which could, in a sense, bring peace, equilibrium and prosperity.[147] In historical times, the one effort to establish such an order, by Jesuits in South America, came to an end because it interfered with selfish politicians.

Jesus offered the communion, in which each and all would share in the universal life, and so in the lives of each other. This theme is presented again and again in the Christian scriptures, but unfortunately communion has remained either symbolic or formal. This is not enough.

Peace is not concerned with mere negations. Life only ebbs in the cemetery. The Indian *"neti, neti"*[148] may bring a form of satisfaction. It does not bring life. For peace is not mere euphoria.

Our LSD experiments make us discover that there is an ocean of consciousness beyond our immediate ken. But we only dip our little toes into it. The practice of meditation in one of its many forms can bring us to the experiences of peace at many levels, until we find we are one with the Grand Consciousness that embraces us all. But so long as dualism persists, we cannot have the peace.

St. Paul has said (my own translation): "To each is given the manifestation of the spirit to universal benefit" (I Corinthians 12:7). The Greek prefix *sym* corresponding to universal comes from the same origin as the *samma* used by the Buddha in his proclamation of the "Eightfold Path" [usually translated *right* as in "right views"]. It is the universality, the collectivity as against the each, the individual.

We again come back to the need to cultivate peace within ourselves, howsoever it be done.

Peace cannot come from a pact. We must alter "foreign aid" into "foreign understanding" without changing policies. Changing policies may bring satisfaction, but not peace. Changing attitudes might be tried.

Without any of the credentials of the scholar, the writer has communed with the trees in the Imperial Gardens in Tokyo as a guest of honor. Without any of the credentials of the diplomat, the writer has communed with the

---

147 One feature of this included a year of *rest* every 50 years during which all slaves were to be freed, alienated property returned and the land left untilled (Leviticus 25:8-17).

148 "Not this, not that."

President of India. All this besides meeting the sages and saints and holy men of many faiths. In each case, one became aware of the grand ocean of stillness in which we live and move and have our being.

Not only do we fail to find the kingdom of God by "Lo here! Lo there!" We do not find any peace by ascribing its absence to some particular "devil" here or there.

Hazrat Inayat Khan taught:

O Thou, Who art the Perfection of Love, Harmony and Beauty,
Lord of Heaven and of Earth,
Open our hearts that we may hear Thy Voice
which constantly cometh from within.

In other words: God is here. This can be practiced, this can be realized, this can be known.

My love and blessings to you all.
OM MANI PADME HUM!
Hail, the Jewel in the Lotus!
Samuel L. Lewis
Sufi Ahmed Murad Chisti

In the garden at Lama Foundation, 1969.
Photo copyright 2020 Mansur Johnson.

Afterword
Tracking A Wild Life

In 1976, when I came to the Sufi community founded by Samuel Lewis in San Francisco, my teachers recognized an unregenerate intellectual, albeit with professional editing and writing skills. Rather than tell me to stop all that, they put me to work.

One of the first projects I faced was to compare a pre-press version of Samuel Lewis's unpublished book *The Lotus and the Universe* with the original manuscript, written in 1963. The goal was to check whether the editing done by the prospective publisher was accurate and faithful to the author's original. This task involved two jobs: first, comparing, word for word, the original and the galley. In the pre-computer era, this experience was almost the equivalent of Zen master Marpa asking Milarepa to build and then take apart a stone tower three times. Second, I needed to look up all of Murshid's references to people, places and events to see whether the changes the publisher had made were accurate. Again, no internet. The "search engine" was me in a public library using research skills learned previously as a young investigative journalist.

Samuel Lewis had written the book in response to Arthur Koestler's *The Lotus and the Robot* (1960) and made many references to it. So I read that book as well. After many months' work, I reached several conclusions:

- The publisher's editing of Lewis's *The Lotus and the Universe* was very inaccurate. Many of Lewis's words and references had been changed, seemingly out of ignorance. To publish the book as written, it would be better to start the editing from scratch.
- Koestler's book was already long out of print, and no one seemed interested in it, or his approach to debunking mysticism. On the contrary, The Tao of Physics (1975) had just been published, and interest in the connection between science and mysticism was very high.
- The polemical parts of Samuel Lewis's book were not very strong, and since Koestler was not really "on the radar," there seemed little reason to publish the book in its original form. On the other hand, the book contained many wonderful stories about Lewis meeting and studying with his spiritual teachers, including Hazrat Inayat Khan, Nyogen Senzaki, Sokei-an Sasaki, Mother Krishnabai, Papa Ramdas and others.

I set out to discover whether Lewis had told these stories elsewhere in his writings and to find the best examples. This took me into his letters, of which he kept carbon copies to serve as his diary. At the time I did that research, the letters were housed in multiple file cabinets in the basement of the Mentorgarten, Murshid Samuel Lewis's home in the Mission district of San Francisco.

It was a long project that involved sorting through and deciphering the second and sometimes third generation carbon copies. I came to recognize Murshid's various typewriters, which made it possible to infer the approximate time period for manuscripts that lacked dates. I also became familiar with his typing and punctuation eccentricities.

Many times, I found references in Murshid Samuel Lewis's writing to letters or documents that were missing from the file. I began to use what I called "editorial dowsing." This involved breathing "Use us for the purpose that Thy wisdom chooses" (a phrase from one of the prayers of Sufi Hazrat Inayat Khan) and then letting my heart and hands search through the file cabinets, trying to think as little as possible. Amazingly, I was invariably led to a missing document that had been misfiled, or in one case was printed on the reverse of an entirely different document (probably to save paper).

Again, in an era when computer scanning was only an expensive dream, compiling all of the texts involved typing them slowly into an early laptop computer with a screen five lines deep, which saved files onto cassette tapes, about ten pages at a time.

Then there was the question of editing Murshid Samuel Lewis's grammar or syntax. As those who have read him know, he had his own way of punctuating sentences and using words like "Now" at the beginning of some of them. As a journalist, I had transcribed many interviews from tapes and adhered to the theory that the printed text should try to re-create the subject's speech pattern and rhythms as much as possible. I began listening to tape recordings of Lewis, then reading all of the texts aloud, getting into his speech rhythm, and letting him direct me. The work gradually became much easier, and I began to receive a very deep inner connection with him.

The whole project lasted nearly ten years, from start to finish. Two days still stand out for me.

First, in 1978, I had become disheartened by how long the whole process was taking. Late that year, along with 12 other Sufi students, I went on a pilgrimage to Turkey, Pakistan and India to find the Sufi and Hindu teachers of Samuel Lewis who were still alive. My teacher Murshid Moineddin Jablonski, Samuel Lewis's spiritual successor, had asked us to make this journey. He expected to die shortly of kidney failure and wanted Murshida Fatima Lassar, who was then his successor, to receive the blessing of Murshid S.A.M.'s teachers. (Murshid Moineddin did not, in fact, die at the time, as reported in his own autobiographical collection, published as *Illuminating the Shadow,* 2016).

Toward the end of the trip, in February 1979, we met Sufi Pir Barkat Ali of Pakistan. From Samuel Lewis's correspondence with him, as well as from what people had told us, the Pir was very conservative, so we had learned the *salat* prayers in order to be able to pray with him. He lived in the jungle outside Lahore in a little village near Salarwala, where he had established an eye hospital for the benefit of the community.

Later, I learned from Barkat Ali's archives that for fifteen years he had been an officer in the Royal Indian Engineers. He was discharged in 1945 for perhaps being too devotional, that is, having visions. After the partition of India and Pakistan he moved to the jungle near Salarwala. By the time we met him, a small community called *Dar-ul-Ehsan* (the house of blessing), had grown up around him. Four years after our visit, so many people had gathered there that he decided one night to leave. He moved to a different area, on the bank of a canal near Faisalabad, living with only his small portable camp bed. Of course, a village began to form around him there, too. By the time he died in 1997, he had authored 400 books on different aspects of Islam, particularly the study of *hadith*, the sayings of Prophet Muhammad.

When Barkat Ali met with us in 1979, as Murshida Fatima later described, he *became* Murshid Samuel Lewis. Not "acted like" him, but actually became him, in a process that can only be described by the word *fana*. You can see a photo of Barkat Ali giving the *darshan* of Murshid S.A.M. in this book. He was also on a vow of silence during our visit.

Over the next several hours, he laughed and played with us, herding us around his mosque complex and generally baffling his followers. At one point, he took our group into the mosque itself and began to throw pieces of bread to us. Then he brought out a typewriter and put it in front of me. He mimed dictating a letter and motioned to me to type. Of course, there was no paper in the typewriter, but I got the message.

Later he took us into his office, which was part of what one might call his "Qur'an refuge." He had put out the word for people to send him old, disused Qur'ans, which he lovingly rebound and then gave away to anyone who needed one. Since he wasn't speaking during our visit, he wrote a message saying that if we prayed for something in the presence of all these Qur'ans, it would surely come true. I had already learned that praying for things was a mixed blessing, because you might get them. So I just prayed again, "Use us for the purpose that Thy wisdom chooses." Really, at that point, I had no idea what was best for me or where my life was going.

One afternoon a year or so after we returned, I was looking through the drawers of a bureau in the Mentorgarten and found, tucked away behind some folders, several cassette tapes. One was dated "October 2, 1968" and was a talk by Samuel Lewis that had never been transcribed. In that talk, he says:

> I'm involved in two revolutions. One of them was when I told Ruth St. Denis:
> "Mother, I'm going to start a revolution."
> "What is it?"
> "I'm going to teach little children how to walk."
> "You have it! You have it! You have it!"
> The second is to say the Lord's Prayer in Aramaic.

Murshid had started the Dances of Universal Peace and Walks. No one could remember him doing anything with the Lord's Prayer in Aramaic. This idea became a seed that I couldn't remove from my head or heart. It set me on a path of discovery that continues today and features in many of my other books.

After reading this book, you might wonder if the types of experiences Murshid Samuel Lewis describes are still possible today. Are there really such remarkable beings to meet and remarkable experiences to have? Having travelled around the world over the past 40 years, I can tell you that there are. However, the spiritual path—if one wishes to bring it into an embodied life— is not for the faint-hearted. It is not a Disneyland amusement park offering escape from everyday problems and challenges.

If you are willing, as Samuel Lewis was, to take on seemingly impossible projects in the name of service, to learn from both love and pain, all doors are open to you.

Ya Hayyo Ya Qayyum! May Allah preserve the secret of Murshid Samuel L. Lewis!

—Neil Douglas-Klotz

1970, walking with children

Dates from the Life of Samuel L. Lewis

1896   Born on October 18, at 2:20 a.m. in San Francisco. His father was a Vice President of the Levi Strauss Company and his mother was Harriet Rosenthal. As a child, Samuel reports that he recited from the Bible and other scriptures unknown to his family.

1898   Reading before the age of 3 (see "Intimations of Immortality").

1902   Completes reading of Old Testament (see "Intimations of Immortality").

1905   Rinzai Zen abbot Soyen Shaku returns to the USA and arrives in San Francisco. He had previously participated in the 1893 World Parliament of Religions in Chicago. On his second trip, he is joined by his student Nyogen Senzaki.

1914   Involved in one of the socialist movements (see "Intimations of Immortality"). Begins spiritual studies in comparative theology, Theosophy and Scottish Masonry.

1915   Contacts the Theosophical Society for the first time at its booth at the International Exposition in San Francisco.

1915   Begins reading the Upanishads. Begins studying non-Euclidean geometry and mathematical philosophy under Professor Cassius Keyser of Columbia. Keyser later introduces him to the work of Count Alfred Korzybski, who developed the philosophy/psychology called General Semantics, best known for its axiom "the map is not the territory."

1919   Meets Murshida Rabia Martin, a student of Sufi Pir-o-Murshid Hazrat Inayat Khan, and begins work with her Sufi group based in San Francisco and Fairfax. Meets and begins studying with the Rev. M. T. Kirby (Sogaku Shaku), a disciple of Soyen Shaku.

1920.　　Meets Beatrice Lane (later to marry Daisetz Suzuki) and Nyogen Senzaki, both also through Kirby. When Kirby is assigned to Hawaii, his teaching work is continued by Senzaki.

1922　　First zendo in US opened by Nyogen Senzaki in San Francisco, aided by Samuel. This "floating zendo" moved from place to place in the city for a number of years.

1923　　At age 27, following a vision of Hazrat Inayat Khan, is initiated by the Pir-o-Murshid in San Francisco, the first person to "touch his heart." Introduces Senzaki and Hazrat Inayat Khan; they "go into samadhi together."

1924　　March. Retreat at Kaaba Allah. Reports great visions and blessings received from Khidr and the prophetic Messengers, culminating in the blessing of Prophet Muhammad.

1926　　Six interviews with Hazrat Inayat Khan in Hollywood. Given the title of "Sufi," appointed "Protector of the Message" and assigned commentary work on esoteric writings as well as "brotherhood" work to bring world of the intellectual and mystic closer together. Introduces Senzaki and Paul Reps. Meets Rev. Gido Ishida at the San Francisco zendo of Senzaki.

1927　　Pir-o-Murshid Hazrat Inayat Khan dies in New Delhi on February 5. Samuel alternating living between San Francisco, Fairfax, San Luis Obispo (the "Dunes") and Los Angeles from 1927-1949. Serves as chief representative (khalif) of Murshida Rabia Martin as well as gardener and director, in Rabia Martin's absence, of Kaaba Allah Sufi khankah in Fairfax, California.

1928　　Meets Dr. Henry Atkinson of the World Church Peace Union, asked to study lesser-known religions. Around this time meets Robert Stuart Clifton (Phra Sumangalo) in San Francisco. Rabia Martin travels to Europe, is rejected as Hazrat Inayat Khan's successor by European meeting of the Sufi Movement. After many years of argument, Inayat Khan's brother Maboob Khan is chosen to lead the Movement, precipitating a three-way split among two European branches and one American one.

1929　　Concerned with reconciliation program for Middle East in religion and desert agriculture, continues work for World Church Peace Union.

1930	February: vision of Hazrat Inayat Khan, begins receiving commentaries and other writings from him in a state of *fana* (effacement). September: visit to New York, meets Zen Roshi Sokei-an Sasaki and receives "dharma transmission," says his eyes opened to the future for the period 1930-1945, which resulted in predictions contained in Samuel's *Book of Cosmic Prophecy*.
1930s	Meets Ruth St. Denis and Ted Shawn in Los Angeles, where they have established the Denishawn School of dance, whose students included Martha Graham and Charles Weidman. Samuel is influenced by her vision of dance as a way of spiritual and cultural change. Many of his writings on spiritual activism and cultural change during this decade, including "The Social Directions," "The Spiritual Attitude and Class War," "The Book of Peace," "Spiritual Dancing," and the first half of "Introduction to Spiritual Brotherhood."
1934-35	Works for the Townsend Plan in San Francisco, one of several forerunners to the US Social Security system. See "Dark Nights and Dancing Lights." Acts as a whistle-blower against Townsend when he discovers the founders of the plan embezzling from contributions.
1935-38	Collaborates with Luther Whiteman, with whom he co-authors *Glory Roads: The Psychological State of California*, published in 1936 by Thomas Y. Crowell, New York.
1937	Meets Vera Van Voris at Sufi center on Franklin Street in San Francisco. Studies yoga of Ramana Maharshi with Paul Brunton. From 1937-38, also works as a researcher and writer for the Works Progress Administration, one of President Roosevelt's "New Deal" programs.
1939	Through Whiteman is introduced to Bryn Beorse (Shamcher), engineer, economist and Norwegian mureed of Hazrat Inayat Khan.
1940	September: During meditation at Sufi Rock (Pir Dahan) in Fairfax, told by God if he could sleep through the night London wouldn't be bombed.
1941	Following the attack on Pearl Harbor, Nyogen Senzaki and Sokei-an Sasaki, along with tens of thousands of Japanese-Americans are relocated to internment camps. Senzaki spends the duration of

World War II in Heart Mountain, Wyoming. Sasaki spends from 1942-1943 in camps on the East coast, including Fort Meade, Maryland and Ellis Island, New York. He was released early due to the legal pleas of his students in New York City.

1942   Works for US Ordnance Office in Oakland, California.

1945   Awarded citation for work with Army Intelligence (G2) during World War II, probably as a researcher and historian. The exact work was never revealed, but may have included reporting troop movements in North Africa, seen clairvoyantly.
        Rabia Martin, after being convinced that Meher Baba is the "Avatar of the age," turns over her Sufi organization and khankah in Fairfax to him. This organization later becomes known as Sufism Reoriented. After visiting Baba's Myrtle Beach, South Carolina center, Samuel Lewis travels to New York to see Sokei-an Sasaki, who died the day he arrived, May 17.

1946   In the inner world, reports that Hazrat Inayat Khan has turned him over to Prophets Muhammad and Jesus for guidance. Receipt of name "A. Murad" from Muhammad.

1947   Rabia Martin dies, after appointing Ivy Duce as her successor. Samuel attempts to continue work within her Sufi organization, but withdraws two years later.

1949   Fire at Kaaba Allah in Fairfax destroys upper house of the khankah and most of his writings and library. Samuel is blamed. Attends City College of San Francisco, studies horticulture/agriculture and receives an Associate of Arts degree in 1951.

1952   Meets Gavin Arthur, astrologer, long-time friend and author of *The Circle of Sex* and other books. Arthur introduces him to the therapist Dr. Blanche Baker, a practitioner of the "person-centered" therapy of Dr. Carl Rogers.

1953   Recommended by Paul Reps to meet Swami Papa Ramdas. Ramdas appears to him in vision and predicts meeting in the flesh one year later.

1954   Upon the death of his father, receives a legacy that allows him to travel abroad. Corresponds with Dr. Sarvepalli Radhakrishnan.

Living on Harriet St. in San Francisco. Meets Swami Ramdas in October 1954.

1956   First journey to the East: Japan, Hong Kong, Thailand, Burma, East Pakistan, India, Pakistan.

1957   Upon return from travels, living in Mill Valley. Reports his mother is dying. Last conversation with Nyogen Senzaki. Death of his friend at World Church Peace Union, Dr. Henry Atkinson.

1958   Continuing correspondence with Bryn Beorse on the latter's plans for salt water conversion and energy generation using ocean thermal difference, particularly in the waters near Egypt and Tunisia. Nyogen Senzaki dies on May 7. Begins therapy sessions with Blanche Baker. During his therapy with Dr. Baker, Samuel attends various folk dance clubs in the San Francisco Bay area. During this decade, long-term correspondence and relationships begun with various dancing partners, including Ramona Carillo and Leonora Ponti. Writings on gender in "Intimate Relationships."

1959   Attends Rudolph Schaeffer School of Design in San Francisco. March or April: Meetings with Robert Clifton (Phra Sumangalo).

1960-62 Second trip to the Middle East and Asia, including Egypt, Pakistan, and India.

1961   Travel and residence in Pakistan. Meeting scientists on land reform and agriculture, meeting saints and Sufis, lecturing on international cultural exchange.

1962   India: Meets with President Radhakrishnan, Swami Maharaj Ranganathananda, and Hussein Nizami. In New Delhi, visit to dargahs of Amir Khusrau, Nizam-ud-din Auliya, Hasan Nizami, and Hazrat Inayat Khan. At dargah of Amir Khusrau, initiated in vision as successor to Muhammad Iqbal in the poetic school of Rumi. Visits Anandashram of Swami Ramdas and Mother Krishnabai near Kanhangad in southwest India.
          Returns to Pakistan. Meets Pir Dewwal Shereef, who appoints him representative of Islamabad University. Invested with robe by Pir Barkat Ali, receiving the name "Sufi Ahmed Murad Chisti." Reports he is to return to the USA and begin a mission patterned on the

life and career of Moineddin Chishti. Meets Saadi Khawar Khan, whom he initiates and who becomes his *khalifa*.

1963   Upon return to San Francisco, begins writing *The Lotus and the Universe*. Speaks at Rudolph Schaeffer School with wonderful response (calls this the "turning point in my S.F. story"). Appointed to work on material for the *Encyclopedia of Buddhism*. Gathering material for "How California Can Help Asia" project for his planned return to Pakistan. Death of Swami Papa Ramdas, 25 July.

1964   Reports his brother wishes reconciliation. In response to Rachel Carson's book *Silent Spring*, working on water problems and developing nonpoisonous sprays while studying at City College of San Francisco. Visits Ruth St. Denis; out of this meeting comes "The Dance of Universal Peace." Begins teaching spiritual walking practice. Asked to represent World Buddhist Federation. Attends Zen Master Kyung-Bo Seo from Korea.

1965   Attempting connections with various Muslim groups, on behalf of Pir Dewal Shereef and Pir Barkat Ali. Ongoing extensive correspondence with Saadi Khawar Khan as well as Pir Barkat Ali from 1962-1971, mentioning a planned return to Pakistan.

1966   Dispute with his brother Elliot settled, each receiving money from their father's trust. Sidi Abusalem Al-Alawi visits San Francisco, confirms him as a Sufi with baraka. Initiates his first young American disciples of a new wave. Mentions writing of "Dharma Transmission" in progress. Assists in founding The Holy Order of MANS, a Christian mystical school in San Francisco together with Father Paul (Earl) Blighton.

1967   April: hospitalized for "ptomaine poisoning" or possible heart attack. God tells him in vision, "I make you spiritual teacher of the hippies." England trip cancelled. June: moves into a house near Precita Park in San Francisco Mission District with Ed Hunt, which he names the Mentorgarten. August: grand opening house party at Mentorgarten. Reports 11 male disciples, 3 women. Conducting Saturday morning walks class. Receives Senzaki's papers from Lottie Fernandez. Ordained "Zen-shi" by Master Kyung-Bo Seo of Korea.

1968   Begins first classes in spiritual dancing (March 16).

1969   Visits with Vietnamese Buddhist Rev. Thich Thien-An, who was living in Los Angeles while teaching at the University of California. Meets with English Soto Zen Roshi Jiyu Kennett, who founds Shasta Zen Abbey in northern California the following year. Conducting classes on Christian mysticism and biblical interpretation at the Holy Order of MANS in San Francisco.

1970   In the spring, visits London and the Congress of The Temple of Understanding in Geneva with his esoteric secretary Mansur Johnson. His brother Elliot dies. Visits Lama Foundation near Taos, New Mexico. June: writes to Pir Dewal Shereef about bringing a group of his young American disciples to Pakistan in 1972 or 1973. July: meets Rabbi Shlomo Carlebach. Also working on a peace plan for the Middle East involving de-nationalizing all sacred sites in Israel and Palestine.
        On December 28, shortly before sunrise, falls down the hall steps of his home and suffers a severe concussion. For two and a half weeks is in and out of coma.

1971   January 2: dictates last letter to Sufi Barkat Ali in Pakistan. January 15, dies at age 75. Buried at Lama Foundation, near Taos, NM.

Acknowledgments

Interviews with people who knew Samuel Lewis were conducted by Wali Ali Melvin Meyer and his staff for the initial efforts toward a biography of Samuel L. Lewis that began in the mid-1970s. The transcripts of these interviews proved invaluable for preparing both *Sufi Vision and Initiation* as well as for this new book. At some point soon, Meyer's own extensive biography of Samuel Lewis will see the light of day, and I wish him and his present staff all the best for its completion.

For this new edition, I was especially helped by Wali Ali's erstwhile main researcher in recent years, Tawwaba Samia Bloch, who found the US federal job application Samuel Lewis submitted in October 1942. Referenced in Section IV, this document proved to be a "skeleton key" that unlocked the door to what had been a missing part in Lewis's life story. This one document made it possible to correlate papers he wrote during this period with events from his life.

One of Samuel Lewis's earliest students, Mansur Johnson, recorded most of the audio of Samuel Lewis on reel-to-reel tape. I cleaned up and re-engineered four of these into cassette tapes in the late 1970s with the help of Ali DiAmico, using the relatively primitive means then available. As I mentioned earlier, Mansur's own book *Murshid* provides a very engaging and personal "fly on the wall" record of what life was like for the early students of Lewis in the late 1960s San Francisco. Mansur also kindly reviewed the manuscript of *Gardens of Vision*, gave feedback and served as a crack line editor and proofreader. Ya Shakur!

As technology improved, another team took on the task of converting all of the original tapes of Samuel Lewis into digital form and cataloging them: Abraham Sussman, Zahir Roman Orest and Hallaj Jim Steele. My deep gratitude to all of them for their service!

Professional editor Devi Mathieu went over the entire manuscript with a fine-tooth comb, smoothing out the rough patches that I could no longer see. Her husband, another original student of Samuel Lewis, the multi-talented composer and writer Allaudin Mathieu, also reviewed the manuscript and offered his loving appraisal and assessment.

Final proofreading of the galleys of the manuscript was done in her usual detailed and loving way by Subhana Elizabeth Ferrio, who has served as

351

"proofer of final resort" for a number of my Sufi books.

My thanks also to Dr. Aslan Scott Sattler, a longtime friend who examined Samuel Lewis's autopsy report and was able to explain the nuances of it to me.

From 2015 to 2016, a group of Sufi students translated into German the collection of Murshid Moineddin Jablonski's autobiographical writings (*Illuminating the Shadow*). The same group, led by Sophia Onnen and Hans-Peter Baum, began in 2017 to translate the original version of *Sufi Vision and Initiation*. Their efforts prompted me to finally tackle the long-delayed project of updating the book, which I began in 2018. My great thanks to them all, especially for their patience when I had to ask them to pause midway through their work for all of the new selections.

The design and layout for both the book and its cover were done by professional designer Jelaluddin Hauke Sturm in Berlin, with whom I have collaborated on many projects over the past two decades. I am proud to call him a friend.

Finally, boundless thanks to my friend, partner and wife Natalia Lapteva, who offers patient, loving support for all of my seemingly endless projects as well as my many wild goose chases.

A royalty from this book will go to the project to continue to refine, proofread and make accessible the online archives of Samuel L. Lewis through the website of the Sufi Ruhaniat International, Inc.

Glossary

This glossary emphasizes terms that Samuel Lewis uses repeatedly and are not defined in the text itself. In the book's text, I use the following approach to the use of italics and capitalization for esoteric terms.

Where a term, like *zikr*, is used in the same sense as it generally is used in classical Sufism, Vedanta or Buddhism, it is italicized in lower case.

Where a term appears as the title of a paper or lesson, such as Hazrat Inayat Khan's Githas on Sadhana, it is capitalized without italics. In these cases, use of the term is not necessarily identical with its usage in classical Sufism or another tradition.

A good example of the distinction would be *salat* (italics), the form of Muslim prayer, and Salat (capitalized without italics), a particular English language prayer given by Hazrat Inayat Khan.

Capitalization in Samuel Lewis's poetry is as he wrote it. My general editing theory is that slavish consistency seldom increases readability and may inhibit understanding.

Arabic (Ar) Hebrew (Heb) Sanskrit (Skr) Greek (Gr) Japanese (Jap) Persian (Per).

Abdal (Ar): "substitute." A rank of saints in the Sufi spiritual hierarchy, which involves being a "changeling"(*badal*)—transforming oneself by the will of Allah to be whatever the situation requires. Murshid Samuel Lewis said that he was an *Abdal*, and a number of references to this are made in the book. Other grades in this spiritual hierarchy include *Ansar* (helper) and *Wali* (friend).

ahadiat (Ar): From Al-Ahad, one of the "beautiful names of Allah," the process of the divine in one that recognizes that only Reality exists, that the One includes everything, or figuratively, that while we can feel Allah in our hearts (*wahid*) in reality we are in Allah's heart (*ahad*). See also *tawhid*.

akhlak Allah (Ar): the "manner" of God, a practice or grace associated with experiences of *baqa*, subsisting in the divine. See also *baqa*.

Alhamdulillah (Ar): "all praise to the One," every praiseworthy essence returns to or moves toward Allah.

Allaho Akbar (Ar): Sometimes transliterated *Allahu Akbar*. "Allah is larger," the essence of which Murshid Samuel Lewis translated as "peace is power."

apsara (Skr): In Indian cosmology, one of a number of female supernatural beings, perfected in the art of dancing, often the consorts of *gandharvas*, musicians in the palaces of the gods.

auliya (Ar): plural of *wali*, one of "friends" of Allah, referring to a saint.

baqa (Ar): resurrection, salvation, "subsistence" occurring after *fana* (effacement). See also *fana*

baraka (Ar): blessing-magnetism.

bayat (Ar): pledge of loyalty to a Sufi teacher, used to mean the "first initiation" in the Inayati Sufi schools descended from Hazrat Inayat Khan.

Bismillah (Ar): "With or within the name/light of Allah/Unity." Invocation that begins all but one of the suras of the Qur'an, and traditionally used by the Sufis to begin any undertaking. The full formula adds the "beautiful names" of compassion and mercy: *bismillahir rahmanir rahim*.

Bodhisattva (Skr): in Mahayana Buddhism, one who vows to attain enlightenment for the benefit of all sentient beings.

bhakti (Skr): spiritual path of love.

Buzurg (Per, Urdu): Elder or noble saint. One of the levels of the traditional Sufi spiritual hierarchy in the unseen world. Samuel Lewis commented: "Buzurg is one who can kindle the hearts of others even without speech; his personality alone may be able to accomplish this. Everyone is a potential Buzurg, which is to say, Bodhisattva – the essential nature of the Sufi Buzurg being the same as that of the Buddhist Bodhisattva. Such a one is an instrument of the Spirit of Guidance, the incarnate spirit of the Divine Master. Buzurg can affect most everybody, but in two ways. Some are like the wax candle, that once the heart is kindled it is always kindled. It may require some effort to light it, but once the flame appears the rest is sure. In these there is the fire of love. But others are like the piece of iron or steel which is magnetized in the presence of some force but does not retain its magnetism.

Often these souls appear brilliant, even highly inspired in the presence of Buzurg, but elsewhere and otherwise they are no different from ordinary people".(Commentary on Hazrat Inayat Khan's Bowl of Saki, October 4).

chakra (Skr): "wheel," an energy point or node in the subtle body.

chela (Skr): disciple in the Hindu path.

cherag(a) (Per): "lamp" or "light." As used here, a minister of the Universal Worship inspired by Hazrat Inayat Khan.

darood (Per): literally, "health," "well-being," "thanksgiving." Traditionally, any invocation made to invoke the presence of and blessing to and through the Prophet Muhammad. Also called in Arabic a *salawat*. Here the word Darood (capitalized) also means a rhythmical breath meditation or *fikr* using the first words of the invocation originally used by Hazrat Inayat Khan to begin his talks and lectures: "Toward the One." (See also *fikr*)

darshan (Skr): the giving of a blessing through the glance.

dharma (Skr): literally "that which supports or holds together," the "way" or "path," righteous duty. Dharma (capitalized without italics) is used for the title of Samuel Lewis's long paper in Section III, and also has informal uses like "Dharma Bums."

dharmakaya (Skr): divine "form."

Dharmashastras (Skr): genre of Sanskrit theological texts dating to around the 1st millennium BCE with different commentaries on duties and ethics relating to family and community life.

dhyana (Skr): meditation, or the process of entering into it.

Djabrut (Ar): sometimes spelled *jabrut*; from one of the Arabic words for "bridge". In Sufi cosmology, relates to the realm of power or angelic realm that connects or bridges the various realms of unmanifested creation with those of manifestation. According to Murshid Samuel Lewis, "Divine breath is at the basis of personality. The soul has attuned itself to a certain keynote in *Djabrut* and gathered certain experiences and characteristics in *Malakut*. These remain as seeds until the body is big and strong enough to express them." See also *Malakut*.

dervish (Per): or *darvish*, a word with a number of variations in Persian and Urdu, with indistinct origins, meaning a wandering saint or mendicant. Most often linked to the word "door," as "one who goes from door to door" or "one who sits in the doorway" between this world and the next. Also used here in the name of Samuel Lewis's "Dervish Dances."

dhikr (Ar): see *zikr*.

fana (Ar): effacement.

fana-fi-sheikh (Ar): effacement in the being of one's living teacher or sheikh.

fana-fi-pir (Ar): effacement in the being of a teacher who has passed.

fana-fi-rassul (Ar): effacement in the being of one of the messengers or prophets.

fana-fi-lillah (Ar): effacement in the being of Unity itself. See also *samadhi*.

fikr (Ar): from an Arabic word meaning to "think," here used to mean keeping a sacred phrase on the breath in the heart and so in consciousness. From Hazrat Inayat Khan: "The breath is like a swing which has a constant motion, and whatever is put in the swing, swings also with the movement of the breath. *Fikr*, therefore, is not a breathing practice. In *fikr* it is not necessary that one should breathe in a certain way, different from one's usual breathing. *Fikr* is to become conscious of the natural movement of the breath, and picturing breath as a swing, to put in that swing a certain thought, as a babe in the cradle, to rock it. Only the difference in rocking is an intentional activity on the part of the person who rocks the cradle."

gandharva (Skr): one of the court musicians in the palaces of the Gods in Hindu cosmology. See also *apsara*.

gatha (Avestan): usually meaning one of the hymns of Zarathustra in Avestan, the ancient Persian language. In Sanskrit, the word means "song" or "verse." Gatha (capitalized) in this book usually means one of the original written lessons for mureeds from the writings and talks of Hazrat Inayat Khan, which included the following series: Takua Taharat (Everyday Life), Etekad Rasm u Ravaj (Superstitions, Customs and Beliefs), Pasi Anfas (Breath), Saluk (Morals), Kashf (Insight), Nakshi Bandi (Symbology) and Tasawwuf (Metaphysics).

Al Haqq (Ar): the "truth" of being, "what is," one of the 99 "Beautiful Names" of Allah.

haqiqat (Ar): "fact," "truth," or "reality." (Ar) The stage of mystical knowing or experience after *tariqat*. From Hazrat Inayat Khan: "Haqiqat is to know the truth of our being and the inner law of Nature. This knowledge widens the heart of a person. When he has realized the truth of being, he has realized the One Being; he is different from nobody, distant from no one: he is one with all. That is the grade where religion ends and Sufism begins." See also *tariqat*.

hal (Ar): a spiritual state of consciousness, something that passes with "time."

Al Hayy (Ar): life energy, one of the 99 "Beautiful Names" of Allah.

hikmat (Ar): wisdom or truth. Arabic word originally based on the Hebrew and Aramaic words for wisdom, *hokhmah* and *hakima* respectively.

ilm (Ar): divine knowledge, as the understanding of levels, worlds, differences and distinctions.

insaan-i-kemal (Ar): "complete or perfect human being," one of the attributes of the *rasul* or messenger of Allah. The Arabic word *insaan* most likely derives from the Aramaic (*nesyuna*) and Arabic (*nasiyan*), words for "forgetting."

inshallah (Ar): by the will of the One.

ishk (Ar): divine love as passion, what brings or holds things or beings together. According to some Sufis, *ishk* in its most profound sense is what created the universes and is identical with the only Being.

Ishk Allah Mahebud Lillah (Ar): variation of a traditional sacred phrase frequently used by Murshid Samuel Lewis. Explained by him in the following manner, consistent with the literal meaning of Arabic: God is love (*ishk Allah*, love as passion); loving, being loved and love itself—the whole process (*mahebud*)—is *for* or *toward* (the meaning of the preposition *li-*) the One (*lillah*).

jelal (Ar): condition of expressiveness.

jemal (Ar): condition of responsiveness.

jihad (Ar): struggle, exertion.

jnana (Skr): spiritual path of knowledge, including self-knowledge.

Kabbalah (Heb) the various strands of Jewish mysticism.

Al Kafi (Ar): that which suffices, the "most necessary" remedy.

kalama (Ar): Islamic affirmation of divine unity: *La ilaha illa 'llah Muhammad-ar-Rasulillah.*

kashf (Ar): direct mystical insight without an intermediary.

kemal (Ar): periods of the breath being in a state of stagnation or stasis, which is similar to the outer situation where two atmospheric pressures collide.

khalif (Ar): "steward" or "deputy." Traditionally, the representative of the head of a Sufi esoteric lineage. Used here, usually capitalized, to mean one of those permitted to give *bayat* and teach in various of the Hazrat Inayat Khan (Inayati) lineages.

khankah (Per): sometimes also spelled *khanqah*, a building or group of buildings that house a Sufi community or provides a place for group gatherings or spiritual retreat. The equivalent term in Arabic is *zawiyah*. Murshid Samuel Lewis had a khankah at the Mentorgarten in San Francisco and at the Garden of Inayat in Novato, California.

khatim al mursaleen (Ar): "seal" in the sense of "guarantee" of the embodiment of the messengers or *rasuls*, the chain of guidance.

khilvat (Per): also *khalwat*. Seclusion, solitude, spiritual retreat.

koan (Jap): in Japanese Zen Buddhism, a story, question or statement meant to test a student's progress.

madzub (Per): from the Persian *majzub*, "possessed," a God-intoxicated being. From Hazrat Inayat Khan: "The fifth form in which a person who lives the inner life appears is a strange form, a form which very few people can understand. He puts on the mask of innocence outwardly to such an extent that those who do not understand may easily consider him unbalanced, peculiar, or strange. He does not mind about it, for the reason that it is only his shield. If he were to admit before humanity the power that he

358

has, thousands of people would go after him, and he would not have one moment to live his inner life. The enormous power that he possesses governs inwardly lands and countries, controlling them and keeping them safe from disasters such as floods and plagues, and also wars; keeping harmony in the country or in the place in which he lives; and all this is done by his silence, by his constant realization of the inner life. To a person who lacks deep insight he will seem a strange being. In the language of the East he is called *Madzub.*"

makam (Ar): sometimes also spelled *maqam* in Sufi literature, the "stage" of consciousness that one maintains in everyday life.

Malakut (Ar): in Sufi cosmology, the realm of intelligence, the world of symbolic forms, the "mental plane." From Murshid Samuel Lewis: "Mental attitudes and opinions find their source in *Malakut*, the mental region or mind-world, which is compounded of various grades of light, shadow and darkness. *Djabrut*, the spiritual sphere, from which the spiritual attitudes arise is the heart plane and is compounded only of various grades of light—there is no darkness there." See also *Djabrut.*

marifat (Ar): from the Arabic verb *arafa*, to know. The stage of mystical knowing or experience that arises after *haqiqat*. Hazrat Inayat Khan: "Marifat is the actual realization of God, the One Being, when there is no doubt anywhere. When these four classes [*shariat, tariqat, haqiqat, marifat*] are accomplished, then the full play of Sufism comes. Sufi means *safa*, pure— not only pure from differences and distinctions, but even pure from all that is learnt and known. That is the state of Allah, the pure and perfect One."

mujahida (Ar): literally, "greater struggle." Used here to mean the process of clearing the heart from impressions that prevent one from accessing *kashf* or direct insight from Oneness.

murakkabah (Ar): concentration, focusing the mind on one theme.

mureed (Ar): spelling used in the Inayati Sufi lineages, also spelled *murid* in some Sufi literature. An initiated student in a Sufi order or lineage, one who has made the pledge of *bayat*. See also *bayat.*

murshid (Ar): "guide" or "teacher," a term used in some but not all Sufi *tariqas*, particularly those in South Asia. Based on the same root as *Ar-Rashid*, illuminated guidance toward a goal, one of the 99 "Beautiful Names" of Allah.

mushahida (Ar): Sufi practice of inner witnessing, seeing through the heart as through the eyes of Unity. See also *shahud*.

nabi (Ar): a divine prophet, from the Hebrew *nebi*; also (capitalized) the name of a prayer of Hazrat Inayat Khan.

nafs (Ar): the "personal" breath or "self." Samuel Lewis describes various refinements of the personal self that are used in classical Sufism, such as *nafs salima*.

nafsaniat (Ar): the realm of personal name and form.

nafs alima (Ar): a state of "self" that knows or understands from the divine viewpoint.

nafs salima (Ar): the "peaceful" self, which gives blessing freely.

nimaz (Per): also transliterated *namaz*. Adoration, worship, usually referring specifically to the five times a day prayer ritual in Islam, *salat* in Arabic.

nirvana (Skr): from the Sanskrit verb meaning to "blow out" a candle. A state in which all desires and aversions have been extinguished. From Murshid Samuel Lewis: "It is easy to imagine Nirvana far away from turmoil; it is marvelous to imagine and attain Nirvana in the midst of trouble. Therefore if the sage once finds the Universal Peace in the midst of strife, it will be natural for him to find it anywhere and everywhere. The descent of Jesus into Hell is nothing but the willingness of the awakened soul to face all and fear nothing for the sake of God."

Pir-o-Murshid (Per): "elder." Also (as a title) Pir, which is usually the way Samuel Lewis uses it. Used in Sufi lineages where an elder murshid guides the *tariqa*. See also *murshid*.

prajna (Skr): insight, wisdom.

prakriti (Skr): nature, the original primal matter with three qualities, modes of action or *gunas*: *sattva* (creation), *rajas* (preservation) and *tamas* (destruction).

purusha (Skr): cosmic being or consciousness, the universal, unchanging, uncaused, connecting everything, cf., *prakriti*.

Al Quddus (Ar): holiness, sacred spaciousness; one of the 99 "Beautiful Names" of Allah.

Qutb (Ar): axis, pivot or pole. The head of the spiritual hierarchy according to various Sufi lineages. Other "grades" of this hierarchy include *Ghaus, Buzurg* and *Abdal.*

Ramnam (Skr): The mantra "Om Sri Ram Jai Ram Jai Jai Ram"—Homage to the One who is both personal and impersonal, both truth and power, victory!

rassul (Ar): divine messenger; also Rassoul (capitalized), in the name of a prayer of Hazrat Inayat Khan and the name of an epic poem by Samuel Lewis, "Rassoul Gita."

ryazat (Ar): body of spiritual practices used in a particular Sufi school or *tariqat.*

samadhi (Skr): "together" or "integrated." A state of meditation in which subject and object become one. From Murshid Samuel Lewis: "It may be asked if there is perfection in meditation, and the answer to this depends largely on what one means. Yes, there is a state called '*samadhi*' wherein one continues to live, when one lives and moves and has his being in God, or at least one has a realization which is not limited by the ego outlook. The attunement to God which comes through meditation and heart-awakening is such that openly and consciously as well as conscientiously one finds himself beyond the distinctions and differences which divide men."

samsara (Skr): the cycle of life and death, of material existence.

sangha (Skr): assembly, association, spiritual community.

satori (Jap): Zen Buddhist term for an experience of initial awakening or enlightenment, often used interchangeably with *kensho*, "seeing into one's true nature."

Ash Shafi (Ar): that which cures or quenches, source of divine healing.

shahud (Ar): direct sight, from the Arabic *shahid*, to witness or experience. Murshid Samuel Lewis: "Contemplation or Mushahida is an advanced practice among adepts. Lessons about *shahud* appear in 'The Sufi Message of Spiritual Liberty' [by Hazrat Inayat Khan] and also in studies on *azan*, the call to prayer. No doubt these are proper introductions, but the real practice of *mushahida* comes when one delves deeply into one's whole heart, sees the universe as within one's own heart and identifies oneself with the Divine Mother, so to speak, feeling the whole creation as if within oneself."

shariat (Ar): traditional religious law. From Hazrat Inayat Khan: "Shariat means the law that it is necessary for the collectivity to observe, to harmonize with one's surroundings and with one's self within. Although the religious authorities of Islam have limited it to restrictions, yet a thousand places in the Qur'an and Hadith one can trace where the law of Shariat is meant to be subject to change to suit the time and place."

Shema (Heb): Jewish affirmation of the only Being: *shema yisrael Adonai (or Yah) eloheynu Adonai (Yah) echad.*

sheikh (Ar): also seen as shaykh. Used here, a spiritual teacher in one of the sufi traditions. Lineages often define this differently. For instance, in most Middle Eastern traditions, the shaykh (ital) is the most senior teacher. South Asian lineages tend to use the term pir (ital) for this function or office.

sifat (Ar): a sacred quality or activity of the One.

sijda (Ar): position of placing the forehead in surrender upon the earth.

silsila (Ar): "chain," "link" or "connection." From Murshid Samuel Lewis: "The Hierarchical Chain, known as the *silsila sufian*, is a linkage of realized personalities whose teachings reflect the age in which they have lived and functioned. There are many such Chains, each associated with a particular Sufi order."

Subhan Allah (Ar): "glory be to Allah," the purity of original Essence.

tanasukh (Ar): "transformation," or mantle of transmission. From Murshid Samuel Lewis: "We give names to various angels thereby making distinctions which may not exist in reality. For it is discovered by the sages that all the illuminated ones form the embodiment of a single Master. This has led to the promulgation of *tanasukh*, or return, a doctrine which has been confused with reincarnation. According to *tanasukh* there is One Divine Spirit which constantly ascends and descends, although Jacob saw it in symbolic form in dream." For more on this idea of Sufi cosmology, see Hazrat Inayat Khan's book "The Soul Whence and Whither."

tariqat (Ar): "way" or "path." A dervish order, and also the Sufi methods of discipline and meditation. From Hazrat Inayat Khan: "*Tariqat* is the understanding of law besides following it, that we must understand the cause of all things that we must do and must not do, instead of obeying the law without understanding."

362

tasbih (Ar, Per): a form of zikr or remembrance. Often used as a term for the prayer beads used in the Sufi path.

tasawwuri (Ar): literally, "imagining," as in imagining oneself to be acting with or in the presence of one's teacher, a type of spiritual "gestalt" used in Sufism.

tattva (Skr): literally 'thatness,' an element or aspect of reality, recognized by many Eastern cosmological systems, including Jainism, Buddhism, Samkhya, Tantra and Kashmir Shaivism.

tawajjeh (Ar): also *tawajjuh*; attention, regard, turning toward. A practice used by Sufi teachers of giving blessing through the glance. From Murshid Samuel Lewis: "Sufis also have two practices which help increase *baraka* by the use of the eyes. When the power is concentrated upon a person, place, affair, incident or thing—that which tends to a point, to contraction or *qabz*—it is called *sulp*. When the same power is radiated over a larger area, covering many persons, things, affairs, incidents, it is called *tawajjeh*."

tawhid (Ar): unity with Reality, Oneness itself, and any philosophy or statement taking as its first assumption that Reality is all that exists. See also *wahdat*.

urouj (Ar): "rising," "ascending." As evidenced in the breath, the desire or activity of acquiring or gathering towards a "self," an "initiating" energy. From Murshid Samuel Lewis: "One of the main reasons for the *nafs* was to bring about the existence of many forms. To create means to form discrete things out of a universal substance. This comes from the *urouj* activity of Allah by which the Supreme Spirit is converted into matter. This is the primordial matter called *hule* (*huyyal*) which means primal stuff, and was termed *aretz* by Moses and *arek* by the Chaldeans and which means nothing but 'hardened spirit.'"

wahdat (Ar): from the "beautiful name" Al-Wahid, the divine essence of singularity, or unique "oneness." Hazrat Inayat Khan combines the names Al-Ahad and Al-Wahid in his invocation as "the Only Being." This emulates Ibn Arabi's idea of the "unity of being," (*wahdat al wujud*) that absolutely nothing exists outside alongside of Reality. See also *tawhid*.

wazifa (Ar): "assignment," "lesson," work to do. Sometimes transliterated *wasifa*. Here used to mean the repetition of sacred phrases, usually including one or more of the 99 "Beautiful Names" of Allah.

wujud (Ar): "being found," in the Sufi tradition, the state of annihilation (*fana*) in the essence of Allah, or sometimes meaning (as used here by Samuel Lewis), the state of ecstasy that results.

zat (Ar): also transliterated *dhat*, the sacred essence of the One. Both *sifat* (quality) and *zat* (essence) are grammatically feminine, to balance the grammatically masculine form of the word "allah."

Zen (Jap): Japanese school of Mahayana Buddhism, emphasizing direct insight into the nature of reality. From Murshid Samuel Lewis: "Kashf or Prajna is an operation or an immediate function of the insight of the entire personality. It is independent causally of time and space. It may or may not justify itself logically, but it certainly fulfills what Jesus has said: 'By their fruits ye shall know them.' One may also read of the benefits of meditation. Dr. Daisetz Suzuki has proclaimed that Zen in truth is not just meditative practice, it is operative Prajna function. Sufis would agree on this point." See also *prajna* and *kashf*.

Zikr (Ar): also sometimes transliterated *dhikr*. Literally "remembrance," a practice performed by Sufis in various ways to "remember" the prevalence of Reality in every being and process that one perceives. Often accompanied by the verbal or silent repetition of a form of the phrase *La ilaha illa 'llah*. Samuel Lewis tended to use the variation he had learned from Hazrat Inayat Khan, which emphasized the sound EL in the solar plexus, as in *La ellaha el Allah*.

Index

T

Printed in Great Britain
by Amazon